AN INTRODUCTION TO THE STUDY
OF INDUSTRIAL RELATIONS

An Introduction to
the Study of
Industrial Relations

J. HENRY RICHARDSON

M.A., PH.D.,
*Montague Burton Professor of Industrial Relations
in the University of Leeds*

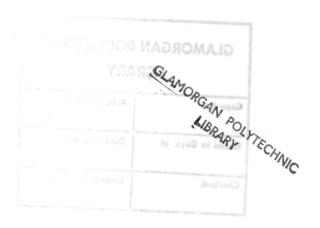

LONDON
GEORGE ALLEN & UNWIN LTD
RUSKIN HOUSE · MUSEUM STREET

331
331.1

FIRST PUBLISHED IN 1954
SECOND IMPRESSION 1956
THIRD IMPRESSION 1959
FOURTH IMPRESSION 1961
FIFTH IMPRESSION 1965
SIXTH IMPRESSION 1970

ISBN 0 04 331025 7

PRINTED IN GREAT BRITAIN
BY PHOTOLITHOGRAPHY
UNWIN BROTHERS LIMITED
WOKING AND LONDON

(30/8/94)

Preface

THE PROBLEMS of industrial relations are among the basic elements in the economic and social life of any country, and in recent years they have commanded growing attention not only among industrialists and workpeople, but by Governments and the public. Co-operation between all sections in industry and fair conditions of work are essential for productive efficiency and industrial progress.

Some aspects of industrial relations, especially wage questions, have long been studied in the universities of this and other countries. In the inter-war years more comprehensive attention was given to the subject in the universities, and professorships and departments of industrial relations were established. In the early 1930's Chairs in Industrial Relations were established in the Universities of Leeds, Cambridge, and Cardiff, this development being made possible by endowments generously provided by the late Sir Montague Burton, who, as a leading industrialist, was aware of dangers to the national economy from a continuation of the bitter conflicts which had hitherto disturbed British industry. He believed that such conflicts were frequently based upon misunderstandings, and that the universities could make a contribution to improvements in industrial relations by systematic and impartial studies and investigations, and by the training of students who would later undertake responsibilities for dealing with human problems in industry. Since the Second World War, many other universities have made appointments for specializing in industrial relations and related fields.

The main purpose of this book is to give a comprehensive survey of the field of industrial relations in the hope that it will prove useful to university students and others interested in human aspects of industrial management and in the regulation of working conditions by collective agreements between employers and trade unions or by statutory methods. Also the subject is still fairly new in the academic field, its boundaries are not yet clearly marked, and this book may make a contribution towards its definition.

Throughout the book attention is directed to general principles and problems; though no attempt is made to describe the systems of industrial relations in any country, illustrations are drawn from the practices adopted in many parts of the world. The personal experience upon which this book is based includes that gained during nine years as a member of the permanent diplomatic staff of the International Labour Office in Geneva, as Montague Burton Professor in the University of Leeds since 1930, as a member of Wage Boards, and as adviser to Governments on labour policy and the regulation of working conditions. Contact has been maintained with British Government departments concerned with industrial relations, and with industrialists and trade union leaders. Many visits have been made to undertakings in all the main British industries, in order to obtain first-hand information about conditions of work and the attitudes of management and of workpeople. Investigations have been conducted in European countries, in the United States, Canada, Venezuela, Burma, Australia, and New Zealand (where special attention was given to systems of wage regulation and to compulsory conciliation and arbitration for the settlement of disputes). Several years have also been spent in studying economic, labour, and social conditions in British Colonial Territories especially in West Africa and the West Indies.

J. HENRY RICHARDSON

The University of Leeds.
June, 1953.

Contents

7

CONTENTS

PART IV—STATE INTERVENTION

PART V—INTERNATIONAL ASPECTS

1

Introduction

MAN HAS been described as a social animal and, whether from choice or necessity, individuals spend a large part of their time at work or play in association with their fellows. The hermit prefers to live alone, while force of circumstances compelled Robinson Crusoe to spend several years in the isolation of his desert island, but such are only an infinitesimal part of the world's 2,000 million population, and the rest in varying degrees live among their fellows and must adjust their individual desires to those of others. Some dislike crowds, they prefer to work on their own, they associate with only a few chosen companions, and they enjoy best a vacation in the remoteness of the moors, dales or highlands. Others are more gregarious, as witness Hampstead Heath, Blackpool, and Margate during holidays, and for such people "getting together" seems to be essential for their enjoyment. This range of individual attitudes towards social relations must be kept continually in mind by those who deal with problems of human association.

The most fundamental human organizations are the family and the tribe or State. In origin the tribe is an extension of the family, but in modern times the State is often more than the tribe grown big, being a political organization which may include many tribes or races who find it convenient to live together under one government for security, cultural relations, and productive co-operation.[1]

Political, economic, and social systems extend beyond State boundaries, but big advances in world organization must be made if mankind is to benefit from and not be destroyed by such recent discoveries as jet propulsion and atomic power.

Within the State and also in the wider setting of world affairs, there is an almost infinite variety of relations, domestic, political, economic, religious, social, and cultural. People meet together in societies, clubs, and unions, with their own regulations, customs, and

[1] Nazi Germany on the basis of an untenable doctrine of race and racial superiority tried first to bring all people of German "race" into one State and then to dominate the world. Human relations are, however, much too complex for the application of so crude a system.

traditions. The laws of the State regulate legal relations, voluntary societies make their own rules, while informal relations in the street and market-place are settled by convention.

THE PROBLEM OF INDUSTRIAL RELATIONS

In this complex mosaic, the pattern of which is continually changing as the needs, desires, and moods of men and women evolve, one of the main elements is the association of people together to earn a living. Unlike those of the State, these associations are mostly voluntary in the sense that people usually choose their own job and place of work, though workpeople have little opportunity to select their workmates and necessity compels them to work. This is the field of industrial relations, the term "industry" being used in its widest sense to include agriculture, mining, and other primary production, the heavy industries (e.g. iron and steel), manufacturing, building and other construction, wholesale and retail trade, banking and transportation. It covers manual, clerical, and technical workers. How people get on together at their work, what difficulties arise between them, how their relations, including wages and working conditions, are regulated, and what organizations are set up for the protection of different interests, these are some of the main problems of industrial relations and indicate the wide scope of the subject. It is concerned with relations between the parties in industry, particularly with the determination of working conditions. No advantage would be gained in attempting a more precise definition of the boundaries, as there are considerable areas of "no man's land" with other subjects. The emphasis, however, is upon "relations," human relations in the processes of production. The processes themselves, and the material organization of production, types of machinery and equipment, sales organization, banking and transport systems, are all outside the subject except that improved efficiency yields more production and this provides a basis for better working conditions.

The establishment and maintenance of satisfactory relations in industry is one of the main social and political tasks in a modern community. An industrial worker in the Western world spends in the factory or workshop about eight hours a day for about three hundred days in the year and for forty or fifty years. This represents a large part of his life, and is the part during which he is most active and vigorous. If the lives of workpeople are to be generally agreeable it is essential that working conditions shall be healthy, convenient, and attractive, that the work itself shall be as interesting as possible, and that relations between the workpeople themselves and between workpeople and management shall be friendly and co-operative.

A large proportion of the whole population, at least one-third in Great Britain, spends these long periods at work, but the effects of factory conditions are not limited to the workpeople. They have repercussions upon the lives of the workers' wives and children. The wages received may provide a good or poor standard of living for the families; if factory conditions undermine the worker's health, his family suffers, while irritation and discontent during working hours often lead to strain and tension in the home. Thus for these reasons alone improvements in industrial conditions and relations are of benefit to the great majority of the population

Although this volume is concerned with human relations in industry, these are inseparable from working conditions. The two interact closely and conditions greatly affect the state of relations. Improved relations almost invariably lead to improved conditions, while improved conditions usually react favourably upon relations.

Evolution of Relations

Industrial relations are as old as industry, and, being inherent in industry, will always remain as a feature of industrial life. In medieval times, although industry was on a small and often domestic scale, relations had to be adjusted both in organizing the work and in paying the worker. Included were relations between masters and journeymen, and the organization and methods of guilds of masters and of craftsmen. But conditions in earlier times were both different from and simpler than in the industrial communities of the Western world to-day; relations were more direct, by contrast with the complex problems of modern factories employing thousands of workpeople, many of whom rarely come into personal contact with their employer or with the owners of the capital which they use. Also in earlier times workmen frequently owned the simple instruments which they needed for their work, whereas an outstanding development of the industrial revolution has been the use of great factory buildings and costly machines, and the concentration of their ownership and control in the hands, not of the workers, but of the employer or the capitalist.

Industrial relations to-day are largely determined by the conditions of the industrial revolution with its capitalist system and specialized labour, but in the future they will change in pattern as the economic system evolves. Already industrial relations problems are very different in some countries from those in the middle of the nineteenth century. For example, the autocracy of the employer in dealing with labour has gone, trade unions have full recognition for collective bargaining to regulate working conditions, social security is a twentieth-century phenomenon, and *laissez-faire* policy has been abandoned in favour of partial Government intervention. Again, in the typical nineteenth-century factory the employer owned a large part of the capital and managed the factory, selected the work-people, and regulated their working conditions. The "profits" which he earned were partly a return on capital and partly a payment for his work of management. When, however, the man who had built up a business died, his children frequently lacked the interest or ability to run the undertaking, and while continuing to profit as owners of the capital they put a manager in charge. Ownership was also increasingly divorced from management when undertakings grew so large that the capital could not be held by one family or a few partners but was spread over a large number of shareholders. Firms vary considerably from one another in the extent to which the persons supplying the capital are different from those who manage the business, though there is a tendency for such persons to become increasingly distinct from one another. Legally, the shareholders control policy, though, except sometimes in a crisis, they remain in the background and policy in many companies is shaped by management. Also in all the main direct relations with its workpeople, a company is represented by its management and not by its shareholders as such. Capital and management are therefore distinct and vital elements in industrial relations.

Effects of Nationalization

If the private capitalist is eliminated and an industry is owned and operated or controlled by the State or municipality, the part played by management is usually still greater than in private industry, though the "power of the purse" remains ultimately with the State or municipality as "capitalist." Thus in Russia the overall economic plans approved by the State determine the framework within which industrial relations shall operate, but it must be noted that in the shaping of these plans influence can be exercised by the management of undertakings and the trade unions as representatives of the workers.

Not only did problems of relations in industry exist in earlier times, but they also exist within every economic system. Some people argue that the capitalist system is responsible for industrial unrest and that the adoption of socialism would bring an era of industrial peace. Except, however, through effects upon the attitude of manage-ment and workpeople towards one another and towards their work,

14

the problems of industrial relations are very similar whether industrial capital is privately or publicly owned. Enough evidence is not available to show what these effects would be. No longer would profits go to private capitalists, but an increase in bureaucratic control might result and efficiency decline when the stimulus of competition was withdrawn. Thus, new problems would be created. This is not the place to discuss the relative merits of private versus socialized industry, but to emphasize that though some problems of industrial relations might be solved by socialism, most of them are common to both systems and are inherent in the organization of production. Wages have to be regulated, including the relation between the wages of skilled, semi-skilled, and unskilled workers within an industry, and the relation between wages in different industries. Piece rates, standards of output, and hours of work, including overtime, must be fixed. Changes in methods of work must be adopted when new machines, processes, and products are introduced. Continuous relations between management and workpeople must be maintained to ensure effective co-operation. Trade unions would have important functions, though their bargaining relations in a nationalized industry would be with a State authority instead of with private employers, and this would involve changes of policy and method. That the problems of industrial relations are not automatically solved by nationalization is shown by the fact that nationalized and other publicly owned industries, like privately owned industries, have experienced industrial unrest and have suffered from strikes. These problems, in varying forms, are a permanent feature of human relations irrespective of the economic system.

Some, though only a small part, of the problems would be solved if a classless society could be established. Such a society is conceivable in theory, and it is also both practicable and desirable greatly to diminish the class divisions which are found to-day in every community. But a system in which all sections of the community are united in complete harmony and identity of interests will not be established in our time, if ever.

To adopt a simple doctrinaire basis would make the writing of a book on principles of industrial relations relatively easy. A thorough-going policy of individualism would lead to one system of relations. Other systems and sets of principles would result from a socialistic or other authoritarian approach. Each would enable a logically or intellectually satisfying structure to be built, but the results would be merely façades, which, though architecturally interesting, would conceal confusion in the interior of the building. Neither would be appropriate for practical affairs in the world of industry. Industrial

15

communities cannot be made to conform permanently to logical systems or doctrinaire theories. Individualism may predominate for a time, as it did in Britain during the nineteenth century. Authoritarian and totalitarian systems may sometimes prevail, as in some European countries during the 1930's. Often the swing of the pendulum goes too far now in one direction, now in the other.

Neither system alone can satisfy the complex needs of individuals or of communities. The more difficult task of achieving a suitable blend of the two must be attempted. In this volume emphasis is laid both upon the needs of the individual worker and firm with their desire for freedom and independent initiative, and upon the equally important need for collective organization and regulation to restrain individualism in the general interest.

Attention is directed in this volume mainly to the problems of industrial relations in modern Western communities, though reference is made from time to time, for comparative purposes, to conditions which preceded those of to-day. Also it must not be overlooked that large numbers of workpeople, for example in Africa, India, and China, still work under primitive conditions which have persisted for many centuries. In these countries there has as yet been little development of large-scale mass production with modern machinery in great factories. They are, however, being compelled to adjust themselves to the impact of Western industrial systems, and it is desirable that, by careful study, they may be safeguarded from the evils which arose during the development of industrial technique and methods in the West. In applying these safeguards the experience of Western industry must be utilized. Some countries, whose industries until recently remained domestic in type, or whose economy depended upon production and export of food and raw materials, are already rapidly transforming themselves by the introduction of Western inventions and organization. The Soviet Union, Australia, Japan, and parts of India, and South America are outstanding examples. They can learn much from the countries which first became industrialized, but they also, by their own experiments made under conditions of freedom from industrial tradition and convention, have a contribution to make to the solution of the problems of industrial relations.

The Human Factor

Interest in human relations in industry has greatly increased during recent decades. This is shown by the work of Governments in promoting collective negotiation, joint consultation, and industrial training. It is also shown by the formation and development of such voluntary organizations in Britain and similar bodies in other countries as the Institute of Personnel Management, the Industrial Welfare Society, the National Institute of Industrial Psychology, the Industrial Health Research Board, and organizations to raise the standards of foremanship and to promote better administration of industry. Trade unions also increasingly recognize that in addition to bargaining about the division of the products of industry they must contribute to greater production by promoting efficiency, better training, incentives, and joint consultation if they are to serve the best interests of their members.

One thread which runs through the whole fabric of industrial relations and which is essential for success is that labour must not be regarded "merely as a commodity or article of commerce." This was given a prominent place in the labour provisions of the Treaties of Peace in 1919, and is a warning against the danger of thinking of workers in the mass without making proper allowance for individual variations and human needs. In the days when economics was described as the "dismal science" many people believed that attempts to improve working conditions by collective action or State intervention were doomed to failure. Men were in the grip of economic laws which, it was claimed, worked with the inevitableness of the laws of the physical sciences in the material world. Dismal indeed was the iron law of wages according to which, if wages rose above subsistence level population would grow until standards of living were forced down again to that level by increases in the supply of labour. In its crudest form this depressing doctrine ignored the possibility that rising standards of living, better education, and wider interests would lead to greater efficiency of the workers and to a diminution of excessive birth-rates, and it neglected those dynamic factors which, in recent generations, have resulted in such great increases in the productivity of industry.

It must be admitted, however, that these changes operate relatively slowly, and that immediate or quick general permanent improvements in standards of living are impossible. These standards are largely determined in the short period by the existing efficiency of labour and of productive organization, including the capital equipment and inventions being applied in industry. Improvements in efficiency, organization, and capital equipment, and new inventions and discoveries take time, and although the rate of improvement may be accelerated, the course of progress must inevitably seem slow to people whose working lives are limited to forty or fifty years, and who are impatient to enjoy much better standards in their own time. Except through their children they have little interest in subsequent progress. Also, the rate of advance, in its effects upon standards of living, is seriously retarded by costly wars and defensive armaments.

Progress in industrial efficiency, the laws of demand for and supply of labour, statistics showing the state of the labour market, and the detached, impersonal calculation of labour costs have an important place in economics and business administration, and they are also significant in industrial relations. But they are not its main concern. The centre of the stage is held by men and women. However mechanized some branches of industry may become, and however the methods of mass production may result in monotonous semi-automatic repetition, the worker must never be treated as a cog in a machine if industrial relations are to be satisfactory. The necessity for guarding against this danger is especially great in big undertakings.

OBJECTS AND SCOPE OF STUDY

The study of industrial relations is undertaken partly to gain knowledge of the problems involved, including interplay of motives, methods of collective organization, conflicting interests and ways of reconciling them. In addition to making such a study for its own sake there is usually a practical purpose. For some this is to secure the greatest amount of work at the lowest cost and with the minimum of friction and unrest. The proper purpose, however, of the study and practice of industrial relations is to secure the highest possible level of mutual understanding and goodwill between the several interests which take part in the processes of production, trade, and transportation. This will depend primarily upon fair dealing and establishment of good working conditions, including the highest general standards of living and of amenities at the workplace which industry at the time can provide, but a friendly atmosphere and a spirit of working together for a common purpose must be developed. Progress towards this objective entails obligations both upon the organizers of industry and upon the workpeople. The demand for a fair day's wage implies willingness to perform a fair day's work.

Some may place industrial peace as the first purpose of the study of industrial relations. But if so peace must be recognized to be a consequence of fair dealing, mutual confidence, and satisfactory working conditions. It is a result and not a cause. The foundations of industrial peace can be strengthened by fair dealing, but a "peace at any price" policy cannot, however, be supported. To quote the labour provisions of the Peace Treaties of 1919 again: "Conditions of labour exist involving such injustice, hardship, and privation to large numbers of people as to produce unrest so great that the peace and harmony of the world are imperilled." Only by removing the causes of friction can industrial or international peace be durable.

Usually the economic loss from conflict greatly exceeds the gain which either side could hope to secure, while the bitterness engendered leads to further disputes. If the parties are reasonable, fair settlements can be reached by negotiation and compromise, conciliation or arbitration. Conflict is, however, difficult to avoid if acute differences arise on fundamental principles. Also resistance to a policy of aggression and exploitation is better than submission. In the last resort conflict may be the only effective way of causing workers to abandon unreasonable demands, or employers to remove abuses, give up autocratic methods and establish fair conditions. Here it may be noted that not all the conflicts of industrial relations are between workpeople and employers. Many struggles arise because of rivalry between unions each striving for leadership of the workers, or because policy differences develop within a union, and sections of the rank and file may become dissatisfied with their leaders and revolt against them.

Industrial peace, in the sense merely of freedom from strikes and lockouts, is no reliable index of good relations. It is well known that workpeople employed under bad conditions are often too illorganized to demand improvements. In such circumstances absence of unrest is a measure of misery. Sometimes it marks denial of freedom, as it did, for example, in Nazi Germany, and Fascist Italy. The State fears liberty of action by groups within it, and enforces prohibition of strikes and lockouts by using its over-riding power tyrannically. Superficially a spurious peace is preserved, but the inevitable discontent is driven underground, where it is more harmful than if it were permitted or encouraged to come into the open.

Industrial relations can conveniently be divided into four parts:

(1) Relations within the undertaking.
(2) Collective relations.
(3) The functions of the State.
(4) International aspects.

These divisions are used in the plan of this book, which, however, includes also a separate part on wages and hours of work. They are arbitrary but convenient, and as with many other classifications there is overlapping, and no sharply defined boundary can be drawn between each. For example, wage questions have a place in each division. Wage agreements reached collectively between trade unions and employers' organizations are applied within the factory, while if working conditions in the factories were so fair and satisfactory that grievances never arose there would be no need for a collective action or State intervention in industrial relations. The same individuals whether as workers, managers, employers, or electors participate in industrial relations at each level. Yet, the divisions are appropriate to the practical affairs of industry. Many problems arise and are settled within the undertaking in the course of day-to-day relations between workpeople and management. Often they are peculiar to the undertaking and often concern individual workpeople or small groups. They are reviewed in Part I. Those wider questions which extend beyond the individual undertaking, whether on the side of the workers or of the undertakings, and are dealt with mainly by the parties directly involved, are discussed in Part II on collective relations, including the trade union movement, employers' organizations, and collective bargaining. Wages and hours of work are reviewed in Part III. The objects and methods of State intervention, which are considered in Part IV, are of outstanding interest to-day, when in many countries the scope of State action is among the most vital of political issues.

The relative importance of the divisions of the subject differs from country to country and from period to period. In Britain collective relations have long been of great interest, though in recent years growing attention has been directed to the other divisions of the subject. In the U.S.A. before the New Deal gave an impetus to collective bargaining the central features were personnel management, labour incentives, time studies, and other aspects of relations within the undertaking. Collective relations, as these are usually understood, were terminated in Germany when the Nazi Government abolished trade unions and employers' organizations, leaving only the labour policy of the State and the relations established within individual firms. In the Soviet Union, though a somewhat artificial system of collective agreements has been evolved, and though interesting experiments are being tried in the factories, the policy of the State dominates the scene.

Industrial relations is an art, the art of living together for purposes of production, and it applies principles derived from many other studies. Industrial relations is in part an application of economic principles, and knowledge of economics is, therefore, of value both for students of the subject and for all who have practical responsibilities for human problems in industry. This connection is recognized in each British university which has a Chair of Industrial Relations, the work being closely associated with that in economics. Emphasis is placed on wages, cost of living, employment and unemployment, industrial organization, and division of the product of industry, rather than on economic theory. Economic and social history are necessary, as it is impossible to understand the present and forecast the future without knowledge of the past. They give the background and evolution which are indispensable for a proper knowledge of relations in industry to-day. Other studies are relevant, including individual and mass psychology, with specialization on industrial psychology. There is also sociology, while philosophy and social ethics are of value, for without a philosophy of life practical action is taken without a sense of direction and progress is delayed by confused meanderings. Some of the problems need a physiological or a biological approach.

Law and jurisprudence are useful, as both common law and statutory law apply to working conditions and relations in industry. Some parts of the law of contract apply to contracts of service between workpeople and employers; the law of torts is of interest in connection with the activities of trade unions, while the legal liability of employers is important in the legislation on workmen's compensation for injury resulting from industrial accidents and industrial diseases. Many questions of juridical interest are raised by the law on trade unions and trade disputes, while in practical industrial administration knowledge is necessary of the Factory Acts, legislation on the regulation of minimum wages, social insurance, conciliation, and arbitration systems for the settlement of industrial disputes, and other laws and Government orders regulating working conditions. Political science has a contribution to make, especially in considering the functions of the State and the activities and limitations of trade unions and other voluntary bodies within the State.

Most trade union officials, employers, labour managers, and government officials who take a leading part in industrial relations have acquired their competence by practical experience together with such background as they have been able to obtain in the course of their work. Yet their success is no argument against a broad and systematic study of the subject, including specialization in one part of the field, by those who can undertake it before entering upon, or while engaged in, practical work.

The scope of the subject is so wide that a series of volumes is necessary to give specialists a complete survey of all the problems. This book is introductory and attempts to present a balanced general view of the subject and the interrelation of its different parts as a basis for more advanced specialized work. Attention is focused on essentials, and descriptive details are as far as possible avoided, though the principles and conclusions are based upon extensive detailed first-hand investigations. In an appendix a list of books is given, including a number which are specialized.

PART I

Relations at the Workplace

2

Personnel Management

COMPETENT, EXPERIENCED and fair dealing by management with the workers in each undertaking is essential for the establishment and maintenance of sound industrial relations, and it must permeate the whole heirarchy of management from charge hands and foremen to top level directorate. Each person who gives instructions to others about their work, about what shall be done, how it shall be done, and the conditions under which it is done, bears his share of responsibility for personnel relations, and this responsibility rests upon all ranks of management including those in large and medium-sized undertakings where people are appointed for personnel work as a specialized function. Personnel management, which includes the management of office, technical, and supervisory staff as well as of manual workers, is as old as industry, commerce, and public administration. Organization is necessary wherever people work together, and this implies management. Only in the last three or four decades, however, have the human problems of industrial organization been systematically studied and personnel management developed as a specialized function in many progressive undertakings. Formerly, the head of a works handled staff and labour problems along with his many other responsibilities, and similarly each manager and foreman within their own departments dealt with all aspects of labour organization while also controlling material and technical aspects of production. This is, indeed, the method still in operation in most firms, but the number of firms is increasing in which the chief executive and his departmental managers and foremen are assisted by a personnel officer and staff specialized in human aspects of industry. These specialists give their whole time to personnel problems, they advise the chief executive on personnel policy, and co-ordinate the application of this policy uniformly throughout the undertaking. Often they are also responsible for administering certain activities which primarily concern personnel, for example, employment, welfare, canteens, education. The change in attitude towards the human factor in industry is due partly to insistence by workpeople on better treatment and conditions than those tolerated in the past. Spread of education and democracy have led to the necessity for winning the confidence of the workers and securing their goodwill. Such relations, combined with suitable incentives, continuity of employment, provision of welfare facilities, and safeguards for health are necessary not as expressions of paternalism or merely to satisfy humanitarian standards, but they pay by leading to greater efficiency.

GENERAL PURPOSE

The purpose of personnel management is to promote the productive efficiency of an undertaking by securing the best use of those employed in it. This can be done only by securing sound co-operative relations and cultivating a team spirit between management and workpeople and among the workpeople themselves. It is an essential part of management, the human factor being inseparably linked with other aspects of management. The emphasis is on efficiency, and one of the main roads to efficiency is to secure the interest of the workers in their work and recognition by them that their working conditions are fair. This involves understanding the workers' point of view, paying due regard to them as individual personalities, and willingness to enter into consultation with them. Managers and workpeople are partners mutually dependent upon one another, and upon the consumers of their products, who are in effect their ultimate employers, and managers and workers alike must meet the needs of consumers both in quality and price if they are to ensure their own employment and prosperity.

Efficiency and the well-being of the individual are emphasized by the Institute of Personnel Management in defining personnel management as the maintenance of relationships "upon a basis which, by consideration of the well-being of the individual, enables all those engaged in the undertaking to make their maximum personal contribution to the effective working of that undertaking." The dependence of efficient production on good relations between workers and management is indicated in a war-time report of the House of Commons Committee on National Expenditure which said that "maximum efficiency cannot be attained unless the human factor in production is recognized as being of at least as much importance as the engineering and research sides. Once this principle is accepted, the management, in order to ensure the whole-hearted co-operation from the workers, must adopt a clear policy for all personnel and welfare matters."

26

Specialization

Specialization in production, sales, finance, and technical research has long been recognized in business firms, with a manager or other executive in charge of each of these departments. Until recently, however, the human problems of industry rarely received specialized attention. Yet the attitudes and emotions of workpeople, their capacities, interests, and health, all require special study and understanding if the best results are to be obtained. These involve complexities which require more thought and care than do the machines and materials of industry. Yet managers responsible for the organization of production are often too busy with the material and technical sides of their work to give sufficient time to the human aspects of production. Also, while some departmental and works managers have a flair for understanding their workpeople and are natural leaders of men, others who are technically competent and are efficient in organizing the material aspects of production are unable to get good results from their men. Even those with a natural gift for leadership cannot know all the specialized aspects of personnel relations, as these demand continuous study and attention.

Specialization is essential in big undertakings, as personnel officers can help to bridge the gulf between top management and the rank and file workers. The personnel manager, if he has senior status in the business, can ensure that the human aspects of production are fully considered before executive decisions are taken. He can advise the managing director on personnel policy, and he and his assistants can explain the policy throughout all departments so that it is understood and uniformly applied by all executives and supervisors, similar problems being treated alike in whatever part of the undertaking they arise.

Specialization is desirable in small works as well as in large ones, but whereas in the latter a full-time staff may be needed to deal with personnel matters, in small works members of the staff who have other duties can be given specific personnel responsibilities to which they will devote enough time to ensure that personnel problems receive proper attention. Thus the works manager may deal with grievances and disputes, the chief engineer with safety, and the office manager with personnel records and perhaps with appointments.

TYPES OF ORGANIZATION

Businesses differ from one another so much in size, structure, and processes of production that systems of personnel management similarly show wide variety, being based on the policy and conditions of each business. No single pattern would suit the widely varied circumstances of different firms. Some undertakings are large but compact, with thousands of workers together in one factory, while others have large or small works scattered in different localities. Many undertakings are small with less than a hundred workers, or are of medium size with several hundred workers, all employed in one building. Then some works are in cities or large towns, while others are in small towns or rural places where the firm may have to provide facilities for entertainment and recreation, and perhaps also transport. Each of these kinds of business has its own personnel problems and needs its own form of personnel organization; it is not practicable to devise a standard system to meet these varied needs. Also the system adopted depends largely on the attitude of the board of directors or of the managing director.

In small undertakings the managing director or the works manager will usually deal with personnel policy, though he may delegate some of the work to selected members of his staff. In large undertakings, however, there are advantages in appointing a personnel officer with assistants to formulate personnel policy and take part in its application. For success, the head of the firm and his senior colleagues must have faith in the value of a specialized personnel department, and must convince junior executives, foremen, and supervisors that the department can help them in their work. The head of the firm must ensure that a spirit of co-operation with the personnel department permeates all ranks of management.

The policies of a firm, including its personnel policy, are decided by the board of directors, and authority in the application of policies is transmitted by the "line" system to the head of each division, by them to their departmental managers, and by them to their own foremen and supervisors. Each executive is responsible for seeing that the policies, orders, and instructions given to him by his immediate chief are put into effect within his own "territory." Alongside the line system, however, many firms have a "staff" system, in which "staff" officers are appointed for specified functions affecting the whole undertaking or at least several of its departments. Personnel officers usually have such staff functions, an important part of their work being to advise the chief executive on personnel policy, to initiate and devise personnel plans for consideration by the chief executive and to recommend the development of existing schemes. Thus, the personnel officer may propose incentive systems, workshop rules, improved methods for dealing with grievances, the development of facilities for welfare and recreation, methods of training workpeople, and policies for dealing with trade unions.

Decisions on labour policy are taken by the directors or the chief executive, but a competent and experienced personnel officer giving his whole attention to such problems can save much time by recommending the general lines of policy and working out the details. When a decision to apply a policy has been reached, it must be made clear by the chief executive that this is the policy of the firm, and the personnel officer may then act as his representative for seeing that the policy is understood and effectively applied by managers and supervisors throughout the undertaking. Here the function of the personnel officer is no longer only advisory, it has become one of co-ordination; he does not give orders to the foremen and departmental managers, and he can succeed only by winning their confidence and co-operation and by proving that he is able, with his specialized knowledge, to assist them in their work. He will be greatly helped if it is known throughout the undertaking that the chief executive is keenly interested in the application of the policy and will give all necessary backing to it. In firms where personnel organization is well developed the personnel officer should have direct access to the chief executive and should be responsible to him.

In addition to these advisory, consultative, and co-ordinating functions as a staff officer, many personnel officers have line responsibilities with executive authority. For example, they may be in charge of employment, training, welfare, recreation, sickness benefit schemes, and old age pensions. In administering these schemes the personnel officer gives effect to the policy of the firm in the same way as production and sales managers ensure that the production and sales policies of the head of the firm are applied. If the works is large, he will have specialist officers each responsible to him for one of the subdivisions of the personnel department. For this side of the work the personnel officer is a line manager responsible to the head of the firm for the work of his department.

Much care is necessary to ensure that the functions and responsibilities of the personnel officer and his assistants are well understood by other managers and supervisors, who may resent what seems to them to be interference by the personnel specialists with the work of their departments especially when a personnel officer is first appointed. Before such appointment, each manager had full authority in his own department to give effect to the directions received by him, and he applied the firm's personnel policy in his own way. After the appointment of a personnel officer, however, he is expected to co-operate with the personnel specialist who is responsible for seeing that the firm's personnel policy is applied in all departments. In order to avoid friction and clash of authority, the personnel

29

officer must not give directions, but exercise his influence by persuasion and constructive suggestions based upon his expert knowledge and experience. If his advice is rejected by a departmental manager and the issue is of sufficient importance, they can ask the managing director to decide, but this should rarely be necessary. It is essential for the personnel officer to know what is going on in the departments and he should be consulted before decisions on personnel affairs are taken. In some big firms contact is secured by having a personnel assistant in each of the main departments. They take part in the work of the departments and help the managers or foremen in dealing with personnel problems, such as grievances and discipline which arise in the day to day life of the workshop. They are responsible to the departmental manager, but they represent and apply the firm's personnel policy in the workshop, and are given time for frequent consultations with the personnel manager.

Difficulties have arisen where workpeople are recruited by an employment officer in the personnel department, as foremen may complain that the right kind of worker is not chosen. Such difficulties have been overcome in some works by arranging that the personnel department shall apply the general standards or qualifications required for appointments and make a short list of suitable candidates, but leaving the foreman to make the final selection. Before decisions on discipline or other personnel matters are taken by a production manager he should normally consult with the personnel manager and take his suggestions into account. Also when the personnel manager is preparing new schemes and policies for consideration by the directors he should obtain the opinions and advice of line managers and also the attitude of representatives of the workpeople.

There is wide variety in the status and responsibilities of personnel specialists in different firms, and this variety is due not only to differences in the size and kind of firm, but also to the attitudes of boards of directors and chief executives. In some firms the specialization is limited to welfare work, and the welfare officer has a relatively subordinate place in the managerial heirarchy. In some companies personnel officers are of rather low status, but in others they rank with top level managers. Some firms have a labour director with wide responsibilities including wages, employment, relations with trade unions, safety, health and welfare, and he has a labour officer assisted by an employment officer, a welfare officer, a safety officer, a medical officer, and an officer for education and training. Sometimes the medical officer because of his professional status is independent of the personnel department, or, if associated with it, has direct access to the directors or the chief executive. In some firms there is no personnel officer, and those in charge of employment, safety, welfare, health, and training respectively are each directly responsible to the managing director. Some large firms have a staff officer responsible for the personnel problems of the clerical and technical staff, and a separate labour officer to deal with the problems of manual workers. Differences in the status and scope of chief personnel officers are indicated by the various titles given to them, the following being some of those used in Britain and the United States: personnel director, personnel manager, industrial relations director, industrial relations manager, labour manager, labour superintendent, labour officer.

SCOPE

Some indication was given in the previous section of the scope of the personnel department's work, which will now be reviewed more comprehensively. In general terms the department is interested in everything which affects the relations between the workers and the management of a business, whether individual or collective. This is, indeed, a wide field, the responsibilities for which are distributed in various ways between the specialized personnel department and all other managers and supervisors. As already indicated, in some firms the role of the personnel department is limited to a small part of the field, while in others it extends over the whole field with, however, the distinction that in some parts of the field its work is essentially advisory and consultative but not decisive and executive, while in other parts it also has executive authority as defined by the head of the firm. On matters which are directly linked with production, for example, time and motion studies and incentive methods of wage payment, decisions are usually best left with departmental managers and foremen, after, however, full consideration has been given to the views of the personnel department; they should also decide on appointments and promotion of those workpeople who will be under their authority, though the personnel department should do preliminary sifting to eliminate those who are not of suitable standard and experience, and should assist by advice in the final selection. Often on welfare questions, canteens, social activities, recreation, the operation of sickness, superannuation and other financial schemes, and the maintenance of personnel records and statistics, the personnel department has executive control.

Some of the subjects within the field of interest of personnel departments are considered in later chapters on selection, training, motion studies, time studies, methods of wage payment, and joint

31

consultation. These, together with the subjects now reviewed more briefly, indicate the wide scope of personnel work.

Employment

This comprises the recruiting, selection, induction, placing, transfer, promotion, and dismissal of workers. In large works these jobs are largely undertaken by an employment officer and his assistants who are usually on the staff of the personnel department. Records are kept of each worker, particularly his grade, qualifications, qualities, efficiency, conduct, and regularity of attendance, including time-keeping and absenteeism. By job analysis the type of worker needed for each kind of job will be defined, standards being set and good selection methods devised for use in choosing the most suitable of the candidates. At the induction stage, many firms arrange for newly appointed workers to be shown round the works, when they are told about its main products and processes and the place of their own jobs in the organization. They will be informed about works rules, and will be given copies of the rule book. The employment officer will keep in touch with them to see the progress they make.

Special attention is given to labour turnover and to ways of reducing it. The employment officer receives notices from workpeople leaving, and has a talk with them about their reasons for going; in this way grievances and defects in working conditions may be discovered and remedied. He will also give notice to workpeople who are being dismissed, though the decision to dismiss them has been made by the foreman or departmental manager. This centralization of dismissals prevents arbitrary, ill-considered action by foremen, and it ensures that workmen in one department are not being dismissed because of lack of work when other departments for which they are suitable are short of labour; similarly, it prevents a foreman giving a job in his department to a worker who had previously been dismissed rightly for incompetence or bad time-keeping by the foreman of another department.

Wages and Collective Bargaining

An important task of the personnel officer and his staff is to see that wage rates and conditions fixed in collective agreements are understood and applied by supervisors throughout the undertaking. In particular they will see that the piece rates and other incentive wages are consistent with the terms of agreements, and this involves consultation with those conducting time studies, who are, however, usually responsible to the production manager or his departmental managers. The personnel officer will advise on methods of wage payment, including incentive systems, will co-operate in their application, and should be consulted before changes in standards of output are made. He will advise on job evaluation investigations, the results of which will be a guide in fixing the relative wages for different grades of work; if there is merit or service rating of individual workers, he will see that the system is understood by the workers and is applied fairly. Where wages are unfair to individuals or to grades of workers, the personnel officer will recommend remedies. This will involve study of wage records, including individual earnings. He will take part in discussions with local trade union officials when disagreements of interpretation arise over the application of the general terms of collective agreements to the special conditions of the firm.

In the United States where agreements on new wages and conditions are commonly negotiated between trade unions and single firms, the personnel officer often is the firm's leading representative in the negotiations, even though the head of the firm makes the decisions. In Britain, where agreements are usually negotiated between representatives of employers' organizations and of trade unions, he will take no direct part, except where he is one of the employers' representatives. He will, however, systematically study wage and cost-of-living trends, and prepare data for use by the directors in forming their own policy and influencing that of the employers' organization to which the firm belongs.

Workshop Rules and Discipline

In the framing of workshop rules the personnel officer often takes a leading part, but should work in the closest co-operation and agreement with all the managers concerned. Also, representatives of the workpeople should be given opportunities to make suggestions before decisions are taken on the rules governing them, this being one of the ways in which industrial life can be made more democratic.

In matters of discipline the personnel officer will share in deciding the firm's policy, and in ensuring that this is fairly and consistently applied in all departments. Decisions on discipline should be the responsibility of foremen and other supervisors, as otherwise their authority would be undermined, or confusion arise from divided responsibility, but in all the more serious cases, particularly those involving dismissals, the personnel officer should be consulted before a decision is reached. If the personnel officer and the line manager cannot agree on the decision, they may refer the matter to the head of the firm, but this should rarely be necessary.

33

Grievances and Disputes

Grievances should, wherever possible, be settled "on the spot," directly and without delay between the supervisor and the worker or workers concerned. If a settlement is not reached at this lowest level, the shop steward is likely to be brought in, if he has not already taken part, or the workers may call for the support of an official of their local trade union branch. Unless the shop steward or the trade union official is a "trouble maker," he will discourage workers from raising petty grievances. The personnel department should be consulted about grievances which raise questions of policy or result from differences over interpretations in the application of policy, and should advise on the terms of settlement. It should be brought into the discussion before attitudes have hardened and the dispute has become acute.

In some firms the department keeps a record of each dispute and of the decision, and these data are useful in the development of policy. It will help in the devising of policies which will reduce the risk of grievances, especially by anticipating and removing causes of friction when changes are made in working conditions, standards of output and methods of payment. The department can also ensure that policies and methods approved by the firm are, as far as practicable, applied uniformly throughout the undertaking. Disputes can be substantially reduced by this means and by training supervisors in the best ways of handling grievances.

Health and Safety

Basic standards of health and safety are established by law, and personnel departments must know the provisions of the Factories Acts. These standards are, however, fixed so as to be reasonably attainable by all firms, and are usually much below those of progressive undertakings. Indeed, progressive firms do pioneering work which later leads to the wider adoption of improved methods and to a raising of legislative standards for general application.

A growing practice is for large and medium-sized firms to employ a full-time works' doctor, and for smaller firms to employ one part-time. Because of his professional status and specialist responsibilities, a works' doctor is rarely subordinate to the personnel officer, and has direct access when necessary to the managing director. However, in practice, the works' doctor and the personnel officer usually work in close co-operation and agreement. The doctor studies working conditions in the undertaking, and makes recommendations to safeguard the health of the workpeople, giving consideration to ventilation, temperature, lighting, cleanliness, removal of dust and fumes, and the use of protective clothing, precautions against industrial diseases, the fixing of maximum loads to be lifted by workpeople, introduction of rest pauses, reduction of noise, and other ways of diminishing strain and fatigue. On all these matters, standards are set by the Factories Acts, and the works' doctor should arrange investigations and research to ensure their effective application in the undertaking and to introduce higher standards. He also advises individual workpeople who wish to consult him, gives emergency treatment to any who are taken ill in the works, and, if it is the practice of the firm, conducts the medical examination of new entrants. In conjunction with the personnel department, he examines sickness records and advises on absenteeism due to sickness. In large works, the services of a dentist, optician, and chiropodist may be available, and ultra-violet-ray treatment given.

In small works, the arrangements are much simpler, but a restroom and first-aid room are frequently provided, with an experienced nurse in charge. They are usually under the control of the personnel officer, who will also undertake investigations and make recommendations on working conditions which affect the health of the workpeople. The results of researches by the Industrial Health Research Board and other bodies should be much more widely applied in industry, and the methods adopted in these researches will suggest ways in which investigations can be conducted by doctors and personnel officers in individual undertakings. It must be emphasized that losses from sickness among workpeople are much greater than those from industrial unrest, and improvements in health conditions in factories and workshops, together with a raising of the general health standards of the population, would make a notable contribution to increased production and high standards of living.

The kind of organization needed for promoting industrial safety varies according to the risk of accidents in different undertakings. Where the risks are considerable, for example, in undertakings in heavy industries, a safety officer or safety engineer is appointed to give continuous attention to prevention of accidents. Often he will be in the personnel department, but in some undertakings he is responsible to the production manager. A prevention of accidents or safety-first committee is often set up, while there is usually an ambulance brigade trained to give first-aid treatment to victims of accidents. As carelessness and errors of judgment are responsible for many more accidents than are defects in machinery and equipment, periodic safety campaigns are valuable in emphasizing the dangers involved, but such propaganda drives should not be so frequent that workpeople are little influenced by them. Accident statistics should be studied and used as a basis for prevention measures. High standards should be adopted for the fencing of dangerous machinery and driving belts, for safety arrangements for lifts and hoists, and for precautions against fire. Designers of machinery are of great assistance in devising automatic guards to protect workpeople from dangerous moving parts which would otherwise involve the risk of cutting or crushing operatives' hands when feeding material into the machine. Co-operation with factory inspectors is essential for maintaining safety standards and for assisting in their progressive improvement.

Welfare, Social Activities, Recreation, and Financial Benefit Schemes

Adequate provision for welfare and amenities should be regarded as one of the essentials of industrial employment with a contribution to make to productive efficiency either directly or by better industrial relations resulting from the greater convenience, comfort, and satisfaction enjoyed by workpeople in their work and in the community life of the workplace. Yet many firms have been reluctant to provide welfare facilities because the results are intangible. If the question is asked, "Do they pay?" the answer cannot be given in a statement showing a cash surplus of income over expenditure.[1] Some employers have regarded them as expensive luxuries, while others have introduced them from motives of paternalism or philanthropy, but these are not likely to win the best response from the workpeople. Welfare arrangements are necessary for efficiency in modern industry, and are not to be regarded as a gesture of benevolence.

One of the most widely adopted welfare facilities is the provision of canteens or dining-halls where hot, nutritive meals are provided at prices which usually cover only the cost of the food, cooking and service, cleaning and breakages, and, in many firms, the salary of the manageress; the firm provides and maintains the canteen and its cooking equipment and furniture, and may also pay a subsidy towards running expenses. Good midday meals in the canteen are better for workpeople than the meagre food many of them bring from home, and they avoid the fatigue involved to those who would otherwise rush home and back again, often a considerable distance, hurriedly to swallow a meal there. Tea and snacks during rest pauses

[1] It is "almost impossible for any firm to give a cash value to the results of their welfare work, but practically all are convinced that it is an advantage considered from the purely economic point of view," in ensuring greater efficiency, particularly by diminished sickness, better time-keeping, freshness at work, reduced labour turnover, and a general spirit of contentment. Committee on Industry and Trade, *Survey of Industrial Relations*, 1926, p. 191.

are often prepared in the canteen kitchen and taken round the workshop. A proper supply of drinking water, preferably by jets or fountains, and also washing facilities and sanitary conveniences, are necessary, while if the work is specially dirty, the provision of baths and changing-rooms enable workpeople to go to and from work in clean clothes, which reacts favourably on their self-respect. Cloak-rooms, heated so that overcoats are dried in wet weather, and controlled to prevent pilfering, add to the comfort and are likely somewhat to reduce sickness among workpeople. Many of these welfare arrangements must now be made by firms in accordance with the standards set in the Factories Acts.[1]

Many employers provide transport to and from work for workpeople who live some distance away, or they arrange with the transport authorities to run services at convenient times. Workpeople are assisted in finding housing accommodation, newly appointed workpeople from other parts of the country may be offered lodgings until they are able to find accommodation for themselves, while some firms organize hostels. In addition to specific arrangements for the comfort and convenience of workpeople, a sense of well-being can be promoted by making the outside and inside appearance of factories more pleasant and attractive, as workpeople are subconsciously influenced by their surroundings. It is only reasonable that the places where workpeople spend so much of their time should be made as pleasant as possible. Even old factories in congested areas can be brightened up and some of their depressing drabness removed, but the best results can be obtained with new buildings in suburban and rural areas, and the phrase "The Factory in a Garden" can now be used to describe many modern works.[2]

Outside the working day many firms foster leisure-time activities among their workpeople. These activities vary widely according to the policy and size of the firm, whether it is in an urban, suburban or rural area, and whether it is near to or far from the workers' homes. In order to avoid overlapping and duplication, firms usually survey the facilities for sport and other forms of recreation provided in the neighbourhood by local government authorities and voluntary associations. Also, efforts are made to find out which activities the workpeople are really keen about. This is done by active participation of representatives of the workpeople in the work of organization. It is sometimes argued that it is better for workpeople to arrange

[1] In 1940 a Government order in Britain made canteens compulsory in war factories employing more than 250 persons, and by 1943 there were about 10,500 canteens in use.

[2] It was first used to describe the works of Cadbury Bros., Ltd., at Bournville.

their social life and recreation apart from their workplace, but there is considerable weight in the counter-arguments that many workpeople enjoy taking part in leisure-time activities with those they get to know during their daily work, that these activities are more easily organized because the participants are assembled together during work-time, and that large firms often provide better sports grounds, social club rooms and other facilities than voluntary associations, while in rural and semi-rural areas the facilities provided by the firm may be the only ones within easy reach. The capital expenditure is almost always borne by the firms, many of which regard this as a form of "prosperity sharing."

In the more developed schemes there may be football, hockey, and cricket grounds, tennis courts and bowling greens, with a pavilion, dressing-rooms, and shower-baths, and groundsmen to look after them. Some firms have an open-air swimming-bath, provide facilities for athletics, and organize clubs for cycling, rambling, horticulture, and other interests which attract sufficient participants. Some organize excursions and holiday tours, including visits abroad. Indoor arrangements often include club premises, with a hall suitable for concerts, lectures, dancing, and other social entertainments, and with a refreshment counter, billiard-room, reading-room and library. Hobbies and crafts are catered for, including photography and wood-working, while classes are arranged for dressmaking and cookery. Societies are formed for choral and instrumental music, dramatic art, and folk dancing. Membership is voluntary, those workpeople who take part usually paying a small regular contribution to general expenses, and a small special contribution to each sectional activity in which they join. Responsibility for organization is usually under-taken by joint committees representative of management and work-people, with general supervision by a welfare officer in the personnel department.

Financial schemes for the benefit of workpeople are another form of welfare activity organized at the workplace. Sickness and benevolent schemes have a long history, originating in *ad hoc* collections of money among workpeople to help one of their fellows in distress. Such collections were, however, haphazard and uncertain, and popular workpeople were likely to get more help than others equally deserving. Therefore, to make the relief less precarious, regular funds were established and principles were adopted for their systematic use. Some of these funds have developed into sickness benefit schemes with specified rates of contribution and of benefit, but others provide assistance only in cases of proved need whether due to sickness or other causes.

38

Many firms have savings schemes to encourage and assist thrift among the workpeople. These range from saving for annual holidays or for the purchase of his home by the worker, to saving for a "rainy day," or for old age. In recent years, saving schemes for old age have increasingly been transformed into provident funds or pension funds based on actuarial calculations and with contributions by the firm and the workpeople. In some firms, saving is linked with co-partnership, the workers becoming owners of shares in the company. Most of these financial schemes are administered by joint committees representing management and workpeople.

From time to time workpeople have personal problems, often unconnected with their work, on which they need advice. Sometimes legal or financial questions are involved, and workers who feel able to talk about these private affairs with the personnel officer or a member of his staff, are given opportunities in some firms to do so, and in this way they may obtain information about their rights and responsibilities, and guidance in their difficulties. Many workpeople can benefit greatly from the wise guidance of someone with much wider experience than themselves, and who, by his contacts, can get legal or other advice and information for them from specialists.

All these welfare, social, recreational, and financial schemes indicate that firms and factories are not merely workplaces, but are communities which provide a basis for social relations and organization. Indeed, workpeople spend more of their time in these than in any other community, except the much smaller one of the family. In social activities and on the playing fields, those with similar interests join together in ways which promote better understanding and respect, and the more formal relations of working hours between management and workpeople and between different grades of workpeople tend to be broken down. In the most progressive firms, opportunities are given for the creation of a "community in which the workpeople shall find full scope for their physical, mental, and moral development."[1]

QUALITIES OF PERSONNEL OFFICERS

Enough has been said to show the range and complexities of the work of the personnel officer and of his department. Clearly, the officers responsible must have qualities of a high order if they are to win and retain the confidence of all grades of management and also of the workpeople, and to influence decisions taken by line managers, some of whom may prefer to act without consultation with the

[1] Committee on Industry and Trade, *Survey of Industrial Relations*, 1926 p. 192.

personnel officers. Such difficulties can be overcome only by the exercise of tact and diplomacy, by showing that line management can be helped by a specialized personnel approach, and by a willingness to keep in the background and let line managers take the credit for decisions which are based on suggestions made by personnel officers.

In the early days some firms, especially in the United States, appointed as personnel officers men of the "Hale fellow well met type" who mainly tried to keep the workpeople cheerful, but who rarely had the qualities needed to investigate and cure deep-seated ailments. In other firms, especially where the emphasis is on the welfare side of the work, the personnel officer has been of the "fatherly" or benevolent type who does what he thinks is good for the workpeople, but who often fails to secure their co-operation. Where the main task in the initial stages of a new personnel department is training, a person with good teaching experience may be put in charge, but may not have the qualities needed for a fully developed department. Similarly, a successful organizer of social life and sports in a club or settlement, may suitably be put in charge of a firm's welfare and recreation, but may not be able to deal effectively with employment, selection, and training. Sometimes departmental managers or foremen who have shown a capacity for handling workpeople are appointed as personnel officers, but they often fail from. lack of education and social standing to secure that easy access to the higher management which is valuable for success in personnel work.

Much consideration has been given in Britain and the United States to the qualities needed for top-ranking personnel officers.[1] There is general agreement that the right qualities of personality and character rank before training, knowledge, and experience, and that "bigness" of outlook is needed to prevent niggling pettiness from hampering the growth of goodwill and mutual understanding. The main qualities and qualifications are:

1. Intelligence, clear thinking, and a capacity for dealing with new problems with energy, initiative, and imagination, so as to be able to devise workable solutions. People who prefer routine methods are unsuitable for personnel work, except at a low level.

2. Personality and equable temperament, with a liking for people. an interest in their problems, and ability to win their confidence, Capacity for leadership is essential, including ability to convince and persuade, and courage when faced with ill-founded opposition and

[1] See Dr. Northcott's book, *Personnel Management*, pp. 305–308; also *Problems in Personnel Administration*, by Richard P. Calhoon.

prejudices. A natural dignity of manner and appearance, a sense of humour, and ability to gain the respect of management and work-people alike are necessary. Extrovert temperament should not be so strong as to prevent effective planning, accuracy in detail, and sensitivity to the feelings of others. Preference should be shown for moving about the works so as to know what is going on, and not spending too much time at the desk. Emotional stability, with freedom from moodiness and outbursts of temper, are essential. Patience must be shown, together with ability to persevere and overcome discouragement when things go wrong.

3. Strength of character, integrity, reliability, and a sense of justice and fair play, without which confidence and goodwill between management and workpeople cannot be established.

4. Good education. This increases ability to make systematic research investigations, to devise plans, and to gain the support of management and workpeople for the schemes proposed. Training and experience along the lines indicated below are also necessary.

These qualities and qualifications set a high standard, yet they are needed if the best results are to be gained, and heads of many firms could with advantage give much more thought than hitherto to the selection and training of those who are destined for the top jobs in personnel administration. To many of the lower posts within the personnel department of a big firm, specialists can be appointed who may not have the range of qualities needed for the key jobs. For those suitable for routine work, there is the keeping of records and the compiling and analysing of statistics according to established systems. The staff of the department should include people whose qualities are complementary.

Those who are chosen for training for the more responsible jobs will include some who seem suitable because of the qualities they have shown in the productive departments of the firm. They should spend from six to twelve months in the different divisions of the personnel department so as to gain an all-round view of the work. During this period they should be given a succession of definite practical tasks, and then be allotted to their more permanent job. Others are brought from outside, and in increasing numbers they are recruited direct from universities, where they have usually studied economics, sociology, psychology, or some other Arts subject. They should first work in one or more of the production departments before beginning their specialized personnel training.

41

3

Selection

THE MAIN purpose in devising and using good ways of selecting workpeople and managerial staff is increased efficiency, and this results partly from better industrial relations. If people are in suitable jobs, they are more likely to be contented in their work, and this will react favourably on their output both directly and by promoting co-operative relations. Good selection results in substantial economies by leading to reduced labour turnover, higher output and earnings, and lower labour costs. Heavy costs may result if an unsatisfactory worker is selected, including the cost of training and supervision of a worker who is later dismissed as unsuitable. Although the cost varies greatly according to the kind of work, some firms have estimated the loss to be £20 or more a worker. Dismissal itself may be a painful process, and the worker may become disgruntled and a trouble-maker in other firms. Considerable costs before dismissal may also have been incurred by poor work, perhaps leading to dissatisfaction by customers, and by damage to tools, machinery, materials, and even accidents causing personal injury. The work of training and supervision would have given better results if applied to workpeople more suitable for the job.

It is conventional to say that the object of vocational selection is to find "the right man for the right job," and to avoid putting "square pegs in round holes." But the right men may not always be available and it may be necessary to adjust jobs to the capabilities of the workpeople who can be recruited. Although some jobs cannot easily be altered, others may be readily modified to suit the qualities of the workpeople who can be found for them, and this may be specially necessary when labour is scarce. Again, selectors must consider not only present capacity but also potentialities, particularly when choosing young persons with a view ultimately to highly skilled work or senior managerial responsibilities.

Recruitment comes before selection and the allocation of workpeople to jobs, and selectors should know where to find the kind of labour they need, and how to secure enough applicants from whom to choose. The sources of supply include employment exchanges, youth employment services, private employment agencies, trade unions, professional organizations, and the appointments boards of universities and other educational bodies. Published advertisements play a big part, while workpeople already employed by a firm tell their relatives and friends when there are vacancies. If all persons seeking work and all employers with jobs to fill were registered at government employment exchanges it would be possible for these exchanges to do most if not all the work of supplying labour, but this would be too stereotyped. The employment exchanges in Britain find successful candidates for about 20 to 30 per cent of vacancies filled, except in war-time when Government control over manpower is greatly increased. It is desirable that, in addition to using the official exchanges, employers and workpeople should show independent initiative to meet their own employment needs. In addition to unemployed persons seeking work, many persons who are in jobs want a change, and apply for posts in other firms. Those firms which have a reputation for good working conditions and amenities often have applications from workpeople employed by firms where conditions and prospects are less favourable.

In the past, and indeed in many firms to-day, the selection of workpeople is unsystematic. Far too frequently departmental managers or foremen, who may think they have a flair for judging men's qualities will make their choice after a brief interview, leaving the weeding out of unsuitable workers to a process of "trial and error" on the job. Even with the most careful selection methods, mistakes cannot be entirely avoided, and therefore some weeding out on the job is inevitable, but by good selection this can be much reduced.

Who should do the selection? Manual workers are usually chosen by the foreman or manager of the department for which the workers are needed or by the personnel or employment officer. Perhaps the best way is for the personnel or employment department to pick out from the applicants those who are up to the standard required for the job, and for the final selections to be made by the foreman or manager concerned, or by agreement between him and the employment officer. For women and girls it is desirable that the choice should be made by a woman or that a woman should take part in the selection. In choosing people for posts of high administrative responsibility or to be trained with a view to promotion to such posts several senior members of the firm should take part.

Before selection begins and even before a job is advertised, a clear idea of the job itself is necessary, and this is best obtained by "job analysis" which will indicate the qualities, skill, and experience required. For many skilled crafts these requirements can be defined fairly exactly and will include competence in operating certain machines or in performing specified processes. What the selectors will look for in applicants and the selection methods they adopt will differ for each kind of job. In selecting unskilled workpeople less time will be necessary for casual than for permanent employment. The methods adopted in selecting young persons to be trained for skilled or semi-skilled work will differ in detail from those used in choosing adult skilled manual workers, while different again will be the procedures for selecting foremen and managers. There are, however, common features in all selection procedures.

Information on which to base selection may be obtained from written statements by or about the candidates, from interviews, and from tests. There is almost always an interview, and this is often associated with one or both the other methods. Tests have been increasingly used in recent years by progressive firms.

Written Statements

Candidates for posts may apply by letter in which they state their age, qualifications, and experience; alternatively these may be given in an application form or sent to prospective employers by the employment exchanges. Applications often include testimonials written by responsible people who know the candidate, and these may give useful indications about personal qualities, character, and reliability, but their authors in preparing testimonials for use by applicants will naturally emphasize strong points and will not mention weaknesses. Of greater value are confidential statements by teachers or former employers, especially if they are in reply to specific questions asked by the prospective employer. Many candidates can be eliminated because their qualifications shown by their applications are not good enough, and the selectors can then concentrate on a "short list" of the best candidates.

Interviews

"The employment interview is the most used, misused, and abused tool in the employment process."[1] Yet, with all its difficulties it is almost indispensable for selection.[2] Too often undue weight is given to appearance, mannerisms, and attitudes, which for many jobs may have little bearing on efficiency. Errors of judgment can be reduced if applicants are seen independently by two interviewers, while at least three should take part in selecting supervisors. Interviews

[1] Calhoon, *Problems in Personnel Administration*, p. 101.
[2] Interviews are used also when considering transfers and promotions, and in dealing with grievances.

should be planned to cover all the qualities required by the job. They should be held in a quiet room and be free from interruptions. They should be friendly, and interviewers should encourage candidates to talk, instead of doing most of the talking themselves, but in addition to getting information about the candidate, they should tell him about the job. This will enable applicants to decide whether they want to accept the job if it is offered to them, and it may enable unsuitable candidates to eliminate themselves by realizing that they have not the necessary skill and experience.

For manual work those selected must be physically fit for the job, be intelligent enough to understand instructions, have the required skill and experience or the ability to learn the job, be reliable, and be co-operative in team work. If the job is likely to lead to promotion or if supervisors are being chosen, additional qualities will be sought, including strength of character, capacity for leadership, mental alertness, resourcefulness and initiative, ambition, tact and sense of humour, a suitable standard of education and personal appearance, and ability to command respect. These qualities of character and personality are difficult to assess in an interview, though much can be gained by leading candidates to discuss their attitude to their work, its problems, and their interests and ambitions. The difficulties are less where promotions are made from among workpeople already employed by the firm, as contacts with them and the records of their work will throw much light on their potentialities for supervisory and managerial responsibility.

Interviews will be long or short according to the kind of vacancy to be filled, and most interviews are from ten or fifteen minutes up to half an hour or an hour. In recent years, however, one of the methods of selection for the administrative class of the British Civil Service has included, as a final stage, what is in effect a combination of interview and a series of tests extending over several days. Unsuitable candidates having already been eliminated, a group of candidates with the required academic and other qualifications spend this period together with several experienced selectors who thus have extended opportunities to judge the character, personality, manners, and social qualities of the candidates. Intelligence tests are used, and each candidate is given assignments similar to those he might be given if appointed. He may, for example, be asked to prepare a memorandum, make recommendations for the solution of some governmental problem, or act as chairman of a committee (consisting of the other candidates) which will consider some question of policy or administrative action. By such means the selectors can make estimates of the ability, initiative, and interests of the candidates. Somewhat similar methods are used by several big industrial firms for selecting young people to be trained for senior posts, the candidates spending a day with the selectors.

For most jobs an interview of not more than half an hour is usually enough to give the selectors a general impression of the candidate's qualities, and this, together with the facts about education and experience, are sufficient for making a decision. Many of those chosen for interview on the basis of their written applications would be able to do the job quite well. The interview eliminates those who seem least suitable, and although, owing to the difficulties inherent in selection, it is too much to expect that the persons chosen will always be the best, they will usually prove reasonably qualified for the job. Records are often kept of the information obtained in interviews and of the opinions and decisions of the interviewers.

Selection Tests

Subject to limitations outlined below, tests give an objective measure of the ability of candidates and are free from the prejudices and errors of judgment of the selectors. But the objectiveness of the results is restricted by the need to make allowances for good candidates who, because of nervousness or other reasons, are not at their best in tests or examinations. Three main kinds of tests may be distinguished, natural aptitude tests, trade tests, and medical tests. There may, however, be some overlapping of aptitude and trade tests, while medical tests are made to ensure that candidates considered to be suitable in all other ways are physically fit for the job and are free from infections which would be a danger to the health of their fellow-workers and to consumers, this latter being specially important for food-handling work. Eyesight tests, including tests for colour-blindness, are essential for some jobs, for example, air pilots, road and rail drivers, while for intricate work good eyesight is needed to ensure better output, less fatigue from eyestrain, and fewer accidents. Physical measurements within specified ranges are necessary or desirable in some occupations, e.g. mannequins, chorus girls, the Guards Regiments; certain road transport authorities only accept as bus drivers men who are, for example, not less than 5 feet 7 inches or more than 5 feet 11 inches tall, while in some manual occupations a good length of arm or finger span is an advantage.

Trade tests, like medical tests, but unlike aptitude and intelligence tests, have long been used. A skilled fitter or carpenter, for example, who seems the best of those available, may be asked to do some job, to see how he sets about the work, how he uses tools and machines, and how good is the result. Shorthand typists are often given tests for speed, together with accuracy and quality. Usually, however, where workpeople have gone through a regular apprenticeship or learnership, a trade test is not considered necessary, and instead selectors inquire about the kinds of work done for previous employers. The Civil Service Commission conducts examinations for the selection of administrative and executive officials, and these examinations, though mainly directed to assessing educational standards, intelligence, and initiative, are in some ways akin to trade tests. Many employers, however, accept the results of school and university examinations in judging educational standards, and recognize the qualifications of professional bodies, e.g. of accountants, lawyers, and architects; selection for particular posts is then based on the standards reached in these examinations, together with experience, personality, character, and other personal factors.

While some tests are for general ability and intelligence, others are based on the requirements of particular jobs. They cannot be copied from other firms but must be devised to meet the needs of each undertaking and grade of work. Not only will tests differ greatly for semi-skilled repetition jobs, skilled manual work, shorthand typists, shop assistants, and telephone operators, but within some of these classes the operations and processes vary from industry to industry, from factory to factory, and from job to job, and some special tests are needed for these variations. Even large firms may have no one on their staff who has the training and experience to devise tests, but this can be done for them by specialized industrial consultants who will make a study of the kinds of work for which tests are needed. The consultants will also train a member of the staff in methods of applying the tests and compiling results.[1]

Tests for aptitudes and intelligence should be reviewed periodically. If the abilities of workpeople on the job differ much from their scores in the tests, then the tests are unsuitable and should be changed unless the differences are due to moral qualities not covered by the tests. If workers who gained the highest marks in the tests prove to be less efficient than those with lower marks, then the tests should be systematically reconsidered and may need to be revised to secure closer correlation. A useful check both in devising tests and in revising them is to apply them to a number of workpeople already

[1] The National Institute of Industrial Psychology, for example, devises tests, and also arranges courses on interviewing and testing procedures. The Institute has published a useful pamphlet on *Selection and Placement.* In its work on vocational selection and also on vocational guidance, it directs attention systematically to physique, attainments, previous experience, general intelligence, special aptitudes, interests, disposition and special circumstances.

employed by the firm. The firm knows from its records which of these workpeople are the best and which are less efficient, and if their scores in the tests correspond reasonably well with their known efficiency, then the tests may be used with some confidence in the selection of newcomers.

Natural aptitude and intelligence tests may be grouped into those which measure manual dexterity, those which measure mental alertness, and those which measure such qualities as visual and oral memory, power of concentration, ability to plan the use of materials to obtain a required result, determination, perseverance, and ability to carry out instructions. Series of tests have been devised in large numbers for use by industrial firms, schools, and public authorities in Britain, the United States, and other countries, and a survey of many typical examples would be necessary to give full indications of the variety of tests used in selecting people for different jobs. Here only a few illustrations are given.

For manual dexterity, the natural aptitude tests include rhythm, speed of reaction, and co-ordination of hand and eye. A natural rhythm is an asset for athletes, and this is true also for repetition jobs in industry. Training and practice in the best movements is necessary, but workpeople who have a natural smooth rhythm usually learn quicker and become more efficient than those whose movements are irregular, jerky, and awkward, involving waste of energy and greater fatigue. One test for rhythm is to require candidates to do circular, oval, and figure eight movements, clockwise and anti-clockwise, with each hand in turn, a simple apparatus being used to record electrically, without the candidate being aware, any considerable irregularities of movement.[1]

A test for reaction time is for a small electric light to be shown at irregular intervals, the candidate being told to put it out as quickly as possible by pressing a switch. The time intervals between the showing of the light and its being put out are recorded. For co-ordination of hand and eye together with accuracy, a test used by the General Electric Company in the United States was for candidates to pick small metal pins from a box and fit them in threes in each of a hundred holes; this was based on an assembly job done in the works. Speed and accuracy can be tested by asking

[1] In its simplest form the apparatus may consist of a hollow cylinder, about the size of a large jam jar, lined with copper, and with a copper-covered core fixed vertically in the middle of the cylinder. Into the space between the core and the cylinder, candidates are instructed to hold a copper pencil-like rod and move it round and round at a reasonable speed without touching either the core or the cylinder. All contacts made are recorded electrically by an instrument connected with the rod by a thin, flexible wire.

candidates to sort a mixed pack of coloured cards into separate piles according to colour.

Many tests for mental alertness or "intelligence" have been devised, and they range from simple exercises for primary school children to more advanced tests for youths and girls about to enter industry, and to highly complex tests for adults who have reached mental maturity.[1] A difficulty in devising these tests is to make sure, as far as possible, that they test inherent ability rather than knowledge and experience which result from environment and training. Yet it is impossible in practice entirely to exclude these influences. The theoretical ideal would be a series of tests which would be fair and equal in assessing the relative natural mental qualities of a Cockney from the East End of London, an Irish peasant from Connemara, an Esquimo from his igloo in the frozen north, and an African from his village in the jungle. Few tests, however, reach this standard. There is also the criticism, frequently heard in the educational world in Britain, where tests of mental alertness are used in selecting children for places in grammar schools, that teachers in many primary schools give intensive training in the tests, and that those who have had such training get better results than others of equal or greater ability who have not had this specialized coaching and drill. There is evidence to support this conclusion, especially in borderline cases.

Most series of mental alertness tests demand high speed as well as accuracy. Thirty questions of simple arithmetic may be set with a time limit of twenty minutes; they may include easy additions and

[1] Intelligence tests were compiled as early as 1905 by A. Binet and T. Simon for use in French schools to pick out children whose intelligence was so low that they could not benefit properly from ordinary school teaching, but needed special courses. In 1916 the Stamford tests were devised by L. M. Terman of Stamford University, U.S.A., who also prepared rules for the uniform application of tests so that results obtained in different places would be comparable, and he introduced the now well-known "intelligence quotient" (I.Q.) which is the ratio of the mental age of a person as shown by the results of the tests to his actual age.

During the First World War and still more during the Second, intelligence and aptitude tests were used successfully for sorting recruits for the fighting forces and sending them to those branches of the service for which they seemed most suited, professional psychologists being employed to plan and organize the tests. These successes led to exaggerated claims for the value of tests in industry, where, however, the problems are different. For example, in war-time few recruits for the Services are rejected except for health reasons or because they are in reserved occupations. All were to be fitted quickly into some branch, and if by mistakes in selection some were sent to a branch for which they were unsuited, these errors could soon be corrected, whereas in industry if a mistake is made and a good worker is not chosen he is lost to the firm.

multiplications of money, which may be appropriate in selecting shop assistants. Forty questions to test accuracy in the use of words may be set with a 15-minute limit; these may include the correction of sentences which are inaccurate. A general knowledge paper of twenty or thirty questions about people, places, and things is included in some selection schemes, though this is only in part a test of natural intelligence. Other tests are for accuracy in recognizing series of numbers or letters, and classifications, and in following instructions.[1]

A test for visual memory is to show a dozen or a score of objects (e.g. knife, scissors, apple, cigarette, hammer) to candidates for say half a minute and then, with the objects removed, ask them to write down as many as they can remember, either immediately or after the distraction of going through another test. The difficulty of the test can be increased by using a board divided into squares, putting an object in each square, and asking candidates to memorize and later write down the names of the objects in the order in which they had been shown. Oral memory may be tested by reading a series of five or more numbers or letters (e.g. 2689761) and asking candidates to repeat or write the series. Tests of this kind have been used in selecting telephone operators. Among many tests for ability to do simple planning, fitting, and using materials to obtain a required result, one is to have wooden blocks of many shapes and sizes, which, as with a jig-saw puzzle, can be fitted together. The times taken by candidates to complete this task are noted and their methods observed.

For road transport drivers, aeroplane pilots, and other occupations in which risk of accidents is substantial, special tests have been

---

[1] Such tests are illustrated as follows:

(1) Cross out the word which is most unlike the others in these groups: (a) shout, sing, whisper, walk, talk; (b) pin, needle, wire, string, chain; (c) grass, tree, orange, knife, carrot.

(2) If in the alphabet A is changed to C, E to G, I to K, and so on, what would the word CHAIR become?

(3) In a code letters are used for figures with A = 0, B = 1, C = 2, and so on. Give in code the difference between DHE and 253.

(4) Fill in the missing numbers in this series, 1, 4 ( ), 10, ( ), ( ), 19, 22, 25.

(5) If the word "interesting" has fewer letters than the word "destructive," cross out the last letter of the word "country"; if it has more letters, cross out the middle letter, and in any case cross out the second letter of the word "country."

(6) Draw a square, put a triangle inside it, write a figure 3 inside the triangle, a figure 5 inside the square but not inside the triangle, and a figure 9 outside the square.

(7) Fill in the missing dates: yesterday was May ( ), in six days from to-day it will be June 4th, and seven days ago it was May ( ).

devised for accident proneness. Statistics have been compiled which show for certain groups of drivers that a small number, about one-fifth, of the drivers were responsible for nearly one-half of the accidents. These are known as "high accident rate" men. Among the factors which lead to accidents are carelessness, lack of attention and foresight, slowness of reaction, tendency to take undue risks, recklessness, instability of temperament, failure to adapt quickly to complex rapidly changing situations, and inability to judge speeds and distances properly. People who suffer from such defects should be excluded from dangerous work, and the use of tests which reveal these weaknesses has resulted in remarkable reductions in accidents, with a consequent saving of life, limb, and equipment. Searching tests are applied to air pilots, including tests for ability to take unexpected shocks calmly and for emotional stability and resourcefulness in emergencies.

How are the results of tests to be used? For some kinds of work applicants who get the highest total score in five or more different tests may not necessarily be the most suitable. One job may need a high score for speed of reaction, with reasonably good results in each of the other tests. Some applicants may be too intelligent for simple routine work, and if appointed might soon find the job so monotonous that they would become discontented or might do poor work because it did not interest them and because they did not give it sufficient attention. Sometimes, however, it may be desirable and practicable to give them the job, with the intention of transferring them before long to work calling for greater intelligence. Tests which are related to particular kinds of work do not show whether those who get good results may be better still in other jobs.

The factors which make for success or failure are many, and some are not revealed by objective tests. One candidate may get high marks under the stimulus of tests and yet be lazy or erratic in the daily round of work, while another with a lower result under test conditions is steady, reliable, and co-operative. Interest, keenness, determination, and energy enable people to overcome natural disadvantages and handicaps. Tests are, therefore, no substitutes for interviews and other ways of estimating such qualities of personality and character. While tests are being conducted, skilled selectors can observe the attitudes of candidates and can thus supplement information gained in more formal interviews.

Properly devised aptitude and mental alertness tests used by people who know the limitations of these tests, have proved their value in the selection of semi-skilled manual workers, of persons to be trained for skilled manual work, and of the lower clerical grades. Some firms claim that they have reduced dismissals of workers who proved unsuitable to one-half or even one-quarter of those before tests were applied. A few firms claim good results in the selection of foremen and other junior supervisors and executives. Their value should not be exaggerated. They are no automatic and infallible means of selecting the best. Tests for mental alertness mainly call for nimbleness of mind of the kind often associated with the "quiz," and rarely reveal originality or creative or constructive intelligence. These qualities are not, however, expected in repetitive work for which aptitude and mental alertness tests have had their greatest application. Many selectors use the tests to make a "short list" of applicants with natural aptitudes and intelligence needed for the job, those with the results below a suitable standard being eliminated. The final selection is then made by interviews and other information which enable opinions to be formed about personality, character, reliability, and other moral qualities not covered by the tests.[1]

Reliable tests have not been devised to select people for leadership and the higher grades of management. In such work success depends on character, personality, sound judgment on policy, originality, imagination, and ability to choose good colleagues, win their loyalty and inspire them in their work. No routine "mechanical" tests can measure these qualities. They can be assessed only by experience, and particularly by seeing how people carry progressively increased responsibilities and how they handle problems of ever-wider range and greater magnitude.

[1] Professor P. E. Vernon, in his presidential address to the Psychology Section of the British Association (Belfast, 1952), said he could not honestly claim that he, or other psychologists, had made much progress in the practical task of assessing personality simply and accurately. "We are certainly not in a position to provide the teacher, the youth employment officer, or the personnel official with a straightforward battery of personality tests at all comparable to our tests of aptitudes and attainments. At the same time there have been considerable advances, especially in experimental work, into problems of personality."

4

Training[1]

BEFORE TRAINING begins, new workers should be inducted or "introduced" to the works instead of being sent immediately to the bench or machine where they will work. In more and more undertakings they are taken for a tour of the main departments, are told about the firm's organization, the raw materials used, where they come from, the firm's products and the markets where they are sold. These may be illustrated by a film, especially where the raw materials come from abroad or the products are sold in foreign markets. Someone from the personnel department will tell about the firm's labour policy, the rules of the works and its welfare, sports, and recreation clubs. All this can be done in a few hours and it stimulates the worker's interest in the firm and its work, and also in his own job by showing how the work he will do is an essential part in the making of a great or intricate machine, an article of clothing or furniture, a processed food, or other final product.

All this information is often best given in two or three stages at intervals of a day or two so that it can be absorbed gradually, as otherwise newcomers are bewildered. If an employees' handbook is issued, attention should be directed only to its main features at first, and an opportunity given later for further explanations. Although a representative of the personnel department may begin the induction process, and will subsequently keep in touch, the foreman of the department in which the newcomer will work will be responsible for setting him to work and helping him to find his feet. The foreman should introduce him to the workpeople who will be near his workplace, and should arrange for a reliable established worker to take an interest in him, so that he will not be isolated and be made to feel an outsider by the gangs and cliques which abound in most works.

[1] The training of workpeople is mainly done by employers, but with the help of the Government and of the education authorities. In Britain the Government provides rehabilitation training for disabled persons, and under the Employment and Training Act, 1948, it can provide training for industries of national importance if the industry agrees and cannot itself provide enough training. The work of the Ministry of Labour in the training of supervisors is outlined later in this chapter.

Management should make special efforts during the first few weeks to help newcomers to adjust themselves to their surroundings and workmates, as early impressions will affect their work and relations favourably or unfavourably.

Induction along these lines is specially valuable for young people who have just left school and are making their first entry into industry. This is a big change which they feel very much, involving adjustment to a new kind of life and to a society of workpeople who have established customs and attitudes which are difficult for young entrants to understand. It is a period of strain for many, and the stress is greatest where, as too often happens, youngsters are thrown into this strange world and left to sink or swim.

Training is too often haphazard, the learner being attached to an experienced worker or "old hand" who may be good at his job but either is not able to teach what he knows, or will not take the trouble. If the worker is paid on the basis of output, his earnings will fall if he gives time to teaching the job, and he may even use the learner to fetch and carry for him instead of instructing him in the skilled part of the work. The learner is therefore left to pick up the job as best he can, mainly by watching; he may get little practice and unless he is very keen much time is lost. Also the worker may have faults in his movements and the learner imitates them and acquires inferior ways of working. This method of training by an experienced worker gives good results only if the worker is good at his job, is able to teach it, can stimulate interest in it, and is given time to do so without loss of earnings. In some works suitable experienced workpeople are given training by the personnel department in methods of teaching the job.

Large firms with systematic training schemes appoint education officers or training supervisors often attached to the personnel department, though some heads of firms prefer to keep training, and also promotion, especially of executives, in their own hands, with the training officer directly responsible to them.[1] Training methods differ greatly from firm to firm and from industry to industry, but they may be grouped broadly into those for workers who will do semi-skilled jobs, for apprentices and learners who will become skilled craftsmen, and for persons who are already or are likely to become foremen or managers. Methods suitable for juveniles differ from those for adults.

Young people, especially apprentices and others in training for

[1] In some firms the personnel department helps the foremen and managers to do their own training, but in others the training is undertaken by instructors in the personnel department.

skilled jobs, if they have the ability to benefit from continuing their education should be encouraged and given facilities to do this. It should include both general education and technical education for their job, and will help to make smoother the change from school to industry. The advantages of undertaking systematic training and further education, including the greater interest of skilled work and the possibilities of rising to managerial jobs and even industrial leadership, should be emphasized, as all but a small percentage of youths have a strong feeling that they have finished with schooling when they get a job. This reluctance is difficult to overcome even when firms pay the fees for attendance at technical schools and offer prizes. By such ways some firms encourage their young workers to attend evening classes in general education and technical subjects organized by the education authorities, while others send selected juveniles to classes in such subjects often for one or two half-days a week during working hours. Again, some firms appoint teachers who give courses at the works in English, mathematics, and technical subjects during several half-days a week.

Training in the actual movements of the job, whether skilled or semi-skilled, is often given in the workshop under the normal conditions of production. The learners take part in production, and they are usually paid time wages until they have made considerable progress in jobs for which trained workers are paid piece rates. An alternative is to give basic training in a separate room, but using machines and tools similar to those in the workshop. The teaching is done by specially selected instructors who are themselves competent workmen, and the learners can concentrate without the distractions of the workshop. In such training schools the learners should from the start or soon afterwards be on production similar to that in the workshop. For some jobs, however, preliminary exercises to develop manipulative flexibility have been found useful. Such training schools have proved valuable in big works with many trainees, but in small works with few trainees at any time, employers prefer the workshop method. Also, in undertakings where the machines and equipment are costly and elaborate, it is impracticable to spare some of them for a separate training school, and most if not all the instruction is given in the workshop. Whether training is in the workshop or in a separate school, the best way of doing the job should be taught, this being the result of systematic movement study, the significance of which is outlined in a separate section later in this chapter. After training is completed a "follow-up" from time to time is desirable to see that workers continue to use the best methods.

For semi-skilled repetition work the period of training is a few days, a few weeks, or at most several months, and if changes in industrial demand or in the national economy result in there being too many workers in some unskilled jobs, and too few in others, workers can be transferred and quickly trained for new jobs. For skilled work, however, apprentices and other learners go through a training which extends over several years, and if in any period too few or too many are trained there will subsequently be shortages or surpluses. Yet in times of rapid change in industrial processes and in falling demand for some products and growing demand for others it is difficult to forecast future needs for workers in each of the many specialized skills. In order to try to avoid unemployment among skilled workpeople, many trade unions have demanded for various crafts a limitation of the number of apprentices in any works to a specified proportion of the number of skilled craftsmen, for example, one apprentice to seven craftsmen, and such provisions have been included in collective agreements. The purpose of such limitations can be approved, but in practice the proportions have often been kept too rigid to meet the changing needs of industry.

For many years agreements and custom fixed the period of apprenticeship at seven years, largely to ensure that the apprentice gained the skill and range of experience necessary for his craft.[1] But the training was often unsystematic and much time was wasted. With proper training any apprentice with reasonable ability could have learned the job in half the time. In Britain, where to-day the period of apprenticeship is usually five years, the time could be further reduced without lowering standards of skill if training were made more intensive.[2] Alternatively, apprentices could be taught during the five years the essentials of a second related craft in the same industry, thereby becoming more mobile in meeting changing needs. Another alteration which could with advantage be made in the rules governing apprenticeship would be to allow suitable young adults to have apprenticeship training. This can be done in the United States, but in Britain unless apprenticeship is begun at 16 or 17 years of age it is rarely possible in many industries to enter a skilled occupation. The adoption of the changes suggested would need to be accompanied by safeguards both for standards of skill

[1] A *Report of an Enquiry into Apprenticeship and Training for Skilled Occupations in Great Britain and Northern Ireland*, 1925–26, Volumes 1–7, gives a comprehensive survey of the methods then in use.

[2] The present higher school-leaving age ensures a better education at the start of apprenticeship.

and for avoiding as far as possible the training of more than are likely to be needed for each craft.[1]

MOTION STUDY

The object of motion study is to enable a job of work to be done in the most efficient way by eliminating unnecessary movements. It includes arrangements by which the materials and tools used by the worker are conveniently placed so that he does not waste time in reaching for them. Thus, closely associated with motion study are the provision of trays or moving belts so that raw materials and finished products are suitably controlled instead of hampering the worker by lying around in confusion, and the fitting of tool racks or ledges in order that the tools are immediately at hand when wanted.

Though usually linked with time studies and incentive methods of wage payment, and often regarded by the worker as a device for increasing speed of work, motion study must be clearly distinguished from them. Its sole purpose is to find the best possible way of doing a job, and the discovery of the most efficient sequence of movements has nothing to do with the speed of the movements. Whatever the job may be, for example shovelling sand into a cart or digging a trench, the worker can complete a given task with the minimum of fatigue if he uses the most effective movements and is equipped with the most suitable tools. Of course, he will usually be required to work as many hours a day as before, and may be as tired at the end of the day, though not necessarily so, as if his movements were awkward and ill-suited to the job. His output for the day will be greater, unless he does the efficient movements more slowly than the clumsy ones, and the workers' distrust of motion-study experts arises in part from the possibility that the whole benefit from the increased output will accrue to the firm, the worker being left perhaps as fatigued as before and with no increase in earnings. This would be an unusual and unfair application of the benefits of motion study, and as a rule the increased output leads to increased earnings. Conflict of interest between employer and worker, however, arises over the sharing of the benefits, and if severe cutting of the rate of wage or dismissal of surplus labour results and the workers derive little advantage they will rightly be discontented, suspicious, and unco-operative.

[1] These problems could be appropriately considered by the apprenticeship and training councils set up in most of the main British industries in implementing the recommendations on recruitment and training of juveniles for industry, made in 1945 by a Joint Consultative Committee.

Along with its value as a labour economy by increasing output and reducing fatigue, motion study is useful for the training of workpeople. Once the best way has been found it should be taught to workpeople, especially those on repetition work. Even a small saving of effort in a sequence of movements which is repeated hundreds or perhaps thousands of times a day is a tremendous gain. People doing unfamiliar work fumble and are clumsy in their movements, mislay their tools, and often damage themselves and the materials they use. With practice efficiency increases, but it cannot be assumed that practice makes perfect. Some workpeople may gradually discover the best way for themselves, but many will include unnecessary movements which become habits difficult to overcome. These can be avoided if the best way is taught at the start.

The acquiring of the best movements by a worker finds a close parallel in sport. The straight swing of the bat is not a movement which a cricketer would naturally develop, and yet it has been proved generally the most effective for the combined purpose of defence and attack. The beginner finds the movement restrained and stiff by contrast with the more natural swing of a cross bat. Similarly in golf, tennis, and other sports, unnatural but effective swings, grips, and rhythms are taught and must be practised until they become almost automatic. An exceptionally brilliant player with perfect co-ordination of hand, eye, and footwork may gain by abandoning the constraints of orthodoxy. Similarly there may occasionally be a workman who gets better results by his own way than by conforming to the standard method, but he is the exception who proves the rule. For the great majority of workpeople there is "one best way" of doing a job, as is shown by the investigations undertaken by the Gilbreth organization in the United States and by many other experts as well as by practical experience in thousands of workshops.

It is sometimes argued that motion study increases monotony and boredom, but this criticism has little force. Just as a golfer gets a thrill from a perfect drive, so a worker gets more satisfaction from doing his work by efficient rhythmic movements than by awkward, less appropriate ones. Nevertheless, motion study does sometimes lead to a complex sequence of movements performed by one worker being divided into two or more parts with a worker for each, and this often leads to more efficient production but reduces the variety in the job or involves loss of skilled craftsmanship and may therefore increase monotony. It may, however, enable workpeople to be employed on the simpler, specialized work who would not have been competent to do the more complex original movements, while the more skilled worker whose job has been broken up can be transferred

58

to other suitable work. Also some of the simple movements may be so mechanical that a machine can be invented to do the job. Sometimes the specialization takes the form of providing a skilled worker with an assistant, thus enabling him to concentrate on those parts of the job which require skill, leaving subsidiary work to his assistant.

The work of addressing envelopes and putting circulars in provides a good illustration of motion study methods. If the number of circulars is very large, it will probably be found that the envelopes should be typed by workers who keep to that work, the circulars will be folded to the right size by machinery, while if the envelopes are not supplied with the flaps turned back, some workers may specialize on this, or the filler-in will turn back the flaps of a large number of envelopes before starting to insert circulars. The putting in of the circulars and turning in the flap will be done in a combined movement unless the flap is to be gummed, when the gumming process will be done separately later, the envelopes being spread out in line to overlap one another so that many flaps can be moistened by one movement. Similarly the systematic study of any process involving frequent repetition of movements, whether in manufacturing, construction, assembling, packing, or other kinds of work, is likely to lead to improved ways of performance.

When work is easy going and little is done to eliminate unnecessary movements there are often periods of relaxation interspersed with effective effort. These are greatly reduced if, as a result largely of specialization and mechanization, but in part also of motion study, workers, especially semi-skilled, are required to concentrate on a frequently repeated rapidly performed restricted sequence of movements. Such concentration though efficient involves strain and fatigue if maintained for long periods without a break. In many jobs experiments have shown that the introduction of a five- or ten-minute interval several times in a four-hour period of work relieves the strain and results in increased production, especially if the workers are able to change position and relax. Whenever practicable after several hours on one job workers should change to another one, the variety being beneficial. Hours should also be reduced as work becomes more highly concentrated, this being necessary for the health of the workers.

How can the "one best way" be found? A useful first stage is to watch the job being done by workers with good output records. Their high output though perhaps partly due to quicker movements is probably the result also of better movements, including some deft action which makes the job easier. Intelligent workers are quick to think out ways of saving trouble for themselves, and also increasing output if this affects their earnings. The movements of such workers if studied systematically and analysed into their components often provide a basis for building up the best way, by combining good features from different workers.

This study can be facilitated by taking cinematograph photographs of the movements, which can then be examined in detail on a screen, by slow motion if necessary, to reveal some useful knack which a worker may have acquired but which he does so quickly that it escapes ordinary observation. The path of his movements can sometimes be shown more clearly in the cinematograph if he wears a small electric light on his hand. Another method is to construct a wire model of the line taken by the sequence of movements, this having the advantage over photographs by being in three dimensions and it also enables the course to be seen as a whole.

The study should be directed to securing a smooth-flowing rhythmic movement, and to avoiding jerkiness, sharp angular changes of direction, and other awkward movements which involve waste of time or energy. The advantage of a good rhythm is very evident in athletics, the smooth pace of a successful runner or hurdler, for example, being most noticeable, particularly when examined in a slow-motion picture. With some people a good rhythm is natural, while others are inherently awkward, but most people can with practice acquire a reasonable standard if trained aright. Among a group of untrained men whose job, for example, is to lift and carry heavy sacks or to dig trenches, some will apply their energy in the right way and so avoid unnecessary fatigue, while others will tire and strain themselves by awkward, clumsy movements; yet the latter could be saved much waste of effort by being shown a better way. In addition to acquiring a smooth rhythm, long-reaching movements of the limbs should be avoided as much as possible, as should unnecessary bending and raising of the body, these being relatively slow movements which also, if repeated, involve considerable fatigue because of the use of energy to raise several stones of body weight time after time. For some operations the achieving of balanced rhythmic movements by both hands is essential for efficiency.

Consideration should be given to the size and weight of tools so that workers are "fitted" according to their build and strength. The need for this is well illustrated outside industry by the army practice of providing rifles with long, medium, and short butts or stocks, so that each soldier can be suited according to his build and length of arm. He is thereby able to hold the rifle firmly in his shoulder and to control bolt and trigger action without being cramped or strained. His movements are therefore more efficient and this contributes considerably to his shooting accuracy and speed. Other illustrations can be drawn from sport. Thus, golf clubs and cricket bats are made of different lengths and weights to suit individual requirements. In motor cars the driver's seat can be moved forwards or backwards for the convenience of those with short or long legs.

The same method gives good results in industry and yet it is too often neglected. Spades, shovels, sledge hammers, and other tools should fit the worker. Where a worker is seated at a machine the height and position of the seat should be adjusted to give him the best possible control over levers and pedals. The machines themselves are usually uniform in size and design, and difficulties no doubt prevent the manufacture of different sizes, but whenever operators are hampered because of uniformity an attempt should be made to overcome the difficulties. Even if the machine remains of standard size it may be practicable to vary the position and length of controlling levers so as to suit operators of big, medium, and small build respectively. In connection with this adaption of machines to men, it may be noted that intelligent workers often invent gadgets and devices for themselves to enable them to operate their machines more easily; for example, by fixing a weight or a bit of string, wire, or a rubber band to the end of a lever so that it can be operated with less effort, or even work semi-automatically. Such methods should be carefully examined, as they may suggest useful additions or modifications which can be included in the manufacture of new machines.

In some kinds of work almost the only way of reducing movements is to change the construction or the fittings of the machine. Thus a typist using a standard machine may be so efficient that her movements may be perfectly adapted to the job, and yet a new typewriter with an improved keyboard bringing the letters and symbols into an even more efficient arrangement may enable the movements to be reduced. Again, studies have been made of the best movements and arrangements for bank typists copying amounts from drawn or paid-in cheques on to the account sheets of the individual customers of the bank. Here the greatest improvements were made by fitting racks with easily moved clips to hold the cheques and account sheets in convenient positions for the typist to read them while using the typewriter, and with other racks to receive them with the minimum of movement as soon as used.

To summarize, the purpose of motion study is to find how a worker by eliminating unnecessary movements and effort, can do a job in the best way. It therefore reduces fatigue in doing a specified amount of work, and is of value in training for repetition work. It is labour-saving, it often leads to specialization of labour by splitting into several parts a complex movement hitherto done by one worker, while it frequently leads to the development of machinery to take over a mechanical job, to improvements in the machines used and in the arrangement of the work, and to the provision of more suitable tools.

Usually learners are required to do slowly the whole sequence of movements in a job, and to increase speed as experience is gained. The rate of progress is often rapid in the early stages, but after a time a level of output or "plateau" is reached beyond which little or no advance is made. This is often well below the reasonable capacity of workers, and yet once it becomes habitual there is great difficulty in breaking through to higher levels. For some jobs higher levels of output have been reached by splitting the sequence of movements into several simple parts, each being taught and practised separately until high speeds are reached and then joining them together. This method has given its best results where the whole sequence of movements is rather complex, and for workpeople of ordinary ability. It has no value for simple jobs, or for the more intelligent workers learning a complicated movement as they are stimulated by its intricacy.

In many firms a standard time for learning each job is fixed by experience, and this is useful as a target for learners. If, for example, the output of experienced workpeople is rated as 100 per cent, then on a given fairly easy job the standard for learners may be 40 per cent at the end of the first week, 70 per cent after two weeks, and 90 per cent after three weeks. The progress of each learner can be compared at regular intervals with the standard, and those who are badly below can be dropped out as not likely to be successful. Progress can be checked each day for jobs which can be learned quickly, while for other jobs a check each week or at longer intervals may be suitable.

TRAINING FOR MANAGEMENT

The growing complexity of industry and its problems makes increasing demands on management, and one of the greatest needs of industry is to improve the quality of management at all levels. For this purpose, training has a big part to play. This is primarily the responsibility of employers, and must be done largely within the undertaking, but such training is, and can increasingly be, supplemented usefully by universities, technical colleges, voluntary industrial organizations, and Governments. Training in its widest sense should continue throughout working life, and refresher courses should be arranged at intervals to supplement initial training.

Although they have many similar features, it is convenient to consider separately the training of foremen and others for the lower executive jobs from training for top-level management. The qualities and experience needed differ greatly, and whereas large numbers are required for lower and intermediate grade posts, only relatively few people can rise to the top executive jobs, and their "training" is distinctive.

Usually, training for foremen and other junior executives is given after they have been appointed to these jobs, but some firms give preliminary training before promotion to workpeople who seem to have the right qualities including leadership, and the progress made during the training period influences the final selection. This reduces the risk of transforming a good skilled worker into a mediocre foreman, though it may have the disadvantage of giving training to more people than there are jobs to fill. The training will include testing the ability of individuals by trying them on special jobs, getting them to assist the foreman and to take charge when he is absent. Much training is undertaken by a more senior supervisor who discusses problems with those in training and asks them for suggestions.

In addition to individual training "on the job," many firms arrange group training schemes.[1] These range from talks and discussions once a week or once or twice a month led by senior managers of the company to week-end conferences or residential courses lasting a week or more, which include lectures, discussions, the preparation and presentation of reports by small groups, and visits to other factories. Some firms arrange for a group of supervisors to attend a residential course of one week every two months for a year or more. Small firms which cannot release enough of their own supervisors at any one time to make up a course of their own may arrange for one or two supervisors at a time to join in a course with supervisors from other firms, and this has the advantage of enabling them to share experiences. Some undertakings with factories in different parts of the country arrange courses for supervisors from each factory, while in some industries courses are organized for supervisors from the various firms of the industry.[2] Courses for junior supervisors include such topics as principles of management, the foreman's

[1] Frequently the personnel department is responsible for preparing schemes, and in large firms the department often includes a training officer to plan training for supervisors and workpeople. The department keeps records of the progress of those undergoing training.

[2] Notable as an example are the courses organized as part of the training scheme of the British Iron and Steel Federation.

responsibilities for the organization of production, his status as a manager, his part in the training of new workers, time studies, costing, incentives, the importance of clear speaking and writing, joint consultation and other aspects of human relations. Attention should be given to the special problems of the firm, and the case study method has proved to be of great value. Accounts are also given of the economic, industrial, and manpower problems of the firm and their relation to the problems of the industry and of the country. Experience has shown that courses should consist of members who are of approximately the same grade, as otherwise the more junior members are likely to be passive because of diffidence.

All members should be active in the work of the course, and not passive recipients of information. Directors, works managers, production engineers, costing officers, personnel managers, and welfare officers give talks which provide the basis for discussions. Experience has shown that the best size for discussion groups is 12 to 15. If the group is much larger there is not opportunity for all to take an active part, while a small group may not have enough variety of experience and points of view. Training should be spread over a period long enough for the ideas to be assimilated. Each member of a course should be given opportunities to raise problems arising from his own experience, and to suggest subjects he would like discussed. Long lectures should be avoided, but introductory talks by senior officers of the company should indicate problems for discussion by the group. If such talks are given to a large meeting or conference, small groups each with a leader should be formed for discussion and report. Success largely depends on the leader who should keep a clearly defined practical problem or subject before the group, should try to ensure systematic discussion, rule out irrelevancies, and help the group to reach sound conclusions. The object should be to promote clear thinking, systematic examination of all relevant facts and circumstances, and effective expression of opinions and conclusions, which, as far as possible, should be suitable for practical application. Especially in residential courses some written work should be required from each member.

In addition to training which can be given only by officers of the firm and dealing primarily with the firm's organization, policy, methods, and problems, there is need to broaden the general education of supervisors and for them to study the general principles and theories underlying technical and other aspects of their work. Courses for these purposes may be arranged by firms, but are often provided by local education authorities, and firms give facilities for their supervisors to attend them. These courses include many of the management topics mentioned above, together with economics and other less specialized subjects. Much educational work is done by associations of foremen and of managers, through conferences, discussions and the publication of journals. In some cities, clubs have been established for foremen employed by local firms in an industry, and these clubs provide opportunities for social contacts, exchange of experience, and for the organization of discussions on topics of mutual interest.

The T.W.I. Scheme for Supervisors[1]

Mention must be made of a special scheme of training within industry for supervisors, usually called T.W.I., which was applied successfully in the United States during the Second World War to enable foremen and other supervisors to deal more rapidly with big changes in processes and products and especially to teach their workpeople quickly how to do their war-time jobs.[2] In the autumn of 1944, the British Ministry of Labour and National Service decided to sponsor the scheme, and since the war the Ministry has continued to promote its application. The scheme has also been adopted by firms in other countries.

T.W.I. concentrates on those parts of a supervisor's work which are common to every industry and firm, and makes no attempt to deal with technical processes, machines, policies, forms of organization and other matters which supervisors must know but which are special to each industry and to individual firms. Training in three "skills" essential for supervisors of all ranks in any industry or firm if they are to be effective in their work is the purpose of the scheme. These skills are: ability to instruct new workers and give clear directions to experienced workers, ability as a leader in promoting good relations between all members of the working force and to win willing co-operation of the workers to give of their best, and ability to improve working methods and organization and to cut out unnecessary work and other wastes.

Training in these skills, which are known shortly as (1) Job Instruction, (2) Job Relations, and (3) Job Methods, is given in three programmes, each requiring five two-hour sessions. Supervisors are trained in groups of eight to ten at a time, usually on consecutive days in working hours, and on the premises of the firm

---

[1] The system was made available to all United States firms on war contracts by the T.W.I. Service of the War Manpower Commission.

[2] An article giving an outline of the main features of T.W.I. was published in the *Ministry of Labour Gazette*, February, 1950, and is used as basis for this section.

to which the supervisors belong. The discussion group or conference method is used, lecturing being avoided, and the training is related to the day to day problems with which supervisors are faced, most of the time being devoted to the practical application by each supervisor of basic principles to some of his own jobs or problems.[1] This method is "learning by doing."

In the Job Instruction programme, supervisors are helped to become better leaders of their men. They are shown how to prepare to instruct and gain the worker's interest, how to divide the job into convenient stages, how to pick out and emphasize important or "key" points in the job, how to give directions so that the worker can understand what he has to do, and how to check the worker's performance and correct mistakes. They must show as well as tell how the job should be done. The object of the programme is to develop the supervisor's skill in giving clear directions, and in systematically instructing workers in what they have to do and how they should do it. In the Job Relations programme, supervisors are taught to be methodical in dealing with human relations, especially by first getting all the facts about any problem, considering which is the best of alternative courses of action, applying the selected method, and checking its results to make sure that the desired object has been achieved. Emphasis is laid in this programme on the importance of treating people as individuals, of giving credit when it is due, of telling people in advance about changes that will affect them, with the reasons for these changes, and making the best use of each worker's ability. The Job Methods programme indicates ways by which supervisors may make better use of available manpower, machines, and materials by studying in detail how each job is being done and by questioning whether any part of the job is unnecessary and should be eliminated, or could be done in a better way. They are urged to arrange materials and equipment in the best positions for least effort, and to make use of gravity aids, devices for holding, and to let both hands do useful work. The objects are better output, less fatigue, less waste, and greater safety. Improved and simplified methods should be tested, proposed for adoption, and then applied if approved.

For the purpose of the scheme, supervisors are defined as all those in an organization who direct the work of others, and this therefore means all levels of management from directors to foremen. The scheme is, however, mainly devised to help foremen, but senior and

1 Up to the beginning of 1952, the number of British firms which had adopted T.W.I. was 2,970; the number of supervisors trained in Job Instruction was 193,000, in Job Relations 124,000, and in Job Methods 37,000.

intermediate grade managers are urged to take the courses of training so that they may get a thorough knowledge of the principles and methods, in the belief that they will become convinced of the value of T.W.I. and will be better able to ensure its practical application at workshop level. Success depends on constant personal interest of top management in the scheme. At the introduction of T.W.I. at any firm the Ministry of Labour therefore advise that the first group to take a course should consist of eight to ten members of senior management with whom a trainer from the Ministry will go through one of the programmes.[1] The group may usefully include a supervisor who might be suitable after more comprehensive preparation to become a trainer for the firm. Subsequently courses would be given to other grades of supervisors, working downwards to foremen and charge hands.

At the headquarters of the Ministry of Labour and National Service there are a few T.W.I. leaders who are alert to introduce improvements based on experience and to adapt the programme to industrial changes. They also train those who will become the actual trainers of supervisors. Almost all these trainers are employed by the larger individual firms which have more than fifty supervisors, and they were usually chosen for this purpose by the firms from those selected to become trainers among their supervisors. Experience has shown that each firm employing more than about five hundred workpeople should have someone to act as trainer at least for part-time. Those chosen to become trainers should be intelligent, able to express themselves clearly, and likely to be able to establish good relations with the supervisors they will train, and to stimulate their interest. They should be somewhat higher in rank than the supervisors to be trained. There are also several trainers at each of the Ministry's regional offices mainly to train foremen and other supervisors in the many firms too small to have a trainer of their own. Trainers go through much longer courses than those for supervisors, eight to ten weeks being necessary to train them to be competent instructors in all the three programmes when they go back to their firms. The full training consists of an intensive forty-hour week course in each of the three programmes, followed by practice in training groups of supervisors. Many trainers have, however, been trained in only one programme, the great majority being trained only in job instruction.

The whole scheme is based on common sense, and there is nothing new in it for those who have given much thought to the training of supervisors, but it has the great merit of being methodical and it

[1] Instruction by trainers from the Ministry is free of charge.

ensures that supervisors who use the system will not overlook anything essential. From many firms in a wide range of industries there is evidence of valuable results, including reduction in the time taken to train workers, better output in quantity and quality because of improved methods, better relations between supervisors and workers, and increase in the number of disputes settled directly between workers and their immediate supervisor without having to be taken to the higher management. To the direct results from the initiative of the Ministry of Labour and National Service must be added that of stimulating employers to give more attention to the training of supervisors. T.W.I. provides a basic training in three essential aspects of any supervisor's work, but along with it must go other training both within and outside industry to raise the technical competence and educational standards of supervisors. These tasks are being increasingly undertaken by employers, education authorities, and management organizations.

Top-Level Management

The training systems and methods already outlined are primarily for foremen, departmental managers, and some grades of technicians. Each of these managers must give almost the whole of his time to one part only of the firm's work, and this is true also of specialists and experts such as those in accountancy, advertising, time study, personnel, maintenance engineering, and research. Growth in the size of undertakings and the greater complexity of their work involves division into more departments and increase in specialization. Yet an undertaking must function very much as a living organism with co-ordination between all its parts, and this is done by relatively few people at and near the top, who, while understanding the problems of each department and of the specialists and technicians, can see the undertaking as a whole and are able to integrate the work of all its parts in order effectively to achieve its purposes. These men must have a broad outlook and knowledge of affairs which will enable them to see the interrelation of production, finance, and trade, they must be leaders of men, skilled in human relations, with ability to organize, to take decisions, and to get people to work together, and they must have alertness of mind and initiative to adjust or transform the policy of the undertaking to significant changes in industrial processes, products, and technique, and be shrewd in forecasting trends of market demand. They must also be convincing in putting forward their policies to boards and committees within the undertaking, to trade associations and to Government departments.

Although the number of top-level places to be filled is relatively small, it is often said that there is a shortage of people who have the necessary width of vision, strength of character, initiative, vitality, experience, and willingness to shoulder responsibilities. Indeed, the work of highly qualified and experienced specialists becomes so absorbing that many of them seem to suffer from agoraphobia and are fearful or unwilling to leave their own limited though clearly defined fields for wider-ranging work which, however, appears to them vague and ill-defined. Some show themselves unable to cast aside departmental blinkers.

How then are top-level administrators recruited, and can they be prepared by training for their high responsibilities? They come from no one source, but from a number of different streams. Some were specialists or departmental heads in the firm who have developed "all-round" qualities and interests. Not infrequently responsibility for the financial and accountancy sides of a business gives a broad view of its affairs which opens a road to the top. Where a big financial stake is held in a business or where sons of the heads of a firm enter the business training and experience in top-level responsibilities are arranged. Some rise to controlling positions in small or medium-sized firms where there is less specialization and where in consequence the interrelationship of all departments is more easily seen, and they then become leaders in bigger firms. Others are brought into senior positions in industry because they have been successful in the financial world, in public administration, or in other kinds of work.

It is often said that top-level leaders are "born, not made," and undoubtedly from the start they must have the necessary qualities of personality, energy, ability, and initiative, but training, experience, and opportunity play their part. A potential leader may lose the necessary range of outlook if circumstances keep him too long within the confines of a specialized job or of departmental responsibility. Firms should be alert to find people who seem to have the qualities for top-level management, and make sure that they are given opportunities to broaden their outlook. There are two stages in this search, the first being to recruit enough people of ability and personality with the reasonable expectation that though many of them may not "make" the top grade and may prove suitable only for intermediate level responsibilities, some will merit promotion to the highest level. The second stage is to give to those of outstanding promise opportunities to broaden their experience and carry greater responsibilities under the guidance of senior officers, and this training by doing may be supplemented by attendance at training courses.[1]

[1] Although it is convenient to call this the "second stage," the process is continuous.

These methods are adopted in the British Civil Service and by some big industrial firms.

For the first stage some firms select university graduates with good qualifications and personality, and give them, together with promising people chosen from the firm's employees, courses of training which last up to two years without requiring them to undertake any continous responsibility. Those in training may be given experience for some months in each of several departments, including the head office, workshop production, sales, and personnel management, so that they may gain knowledge of all the main aspects of the undertaking, and also find which kind of work is likely to suit them best. They attend lectures by heads of departments and senior executives, and the training may include experience abroad if the firm has factories in other countries. The recruiting of university graduates to be trained for managerial work is greater in the United States than in Britain, where, however, it is increasing.[1] In some firms in the United States, graduates in training spend several months doing manual work and then go for six to twelve months to three or four departments where they have time to observe, combined as soon as possible with responsibility for specific managerial jobs. It is unsatisfactory for them to go from department to department merely to watch what is being done. Graduates usually have no special privileges, and compete on merit with other employees for promotion. The subsequent broadening of experience and responsibility depends partly on vacancies occurring, and some people are fortunate in having a succession of opportunities to move up after only relatively short periods in any one job, while others may remain for long periods in one or two jobs and become more limited in their outlook. The discovery of those suitable for the leading appointments is not easy. Some people are thoroughly efficient in junior or intermediate grades of management, but do not show the mental growth and other qualities needed in the highest grades. Some people by ability combined with thrusting energy and ambition stake out their claims for promotion, while others who may be even more suitable are more modest and may be overlooked.

Those who have made good in intermediate grades and seem suitable for further advancement may be given special courses of training. For example, in recent years British firms and Government departments have sent selected people to the Administrative Staff College for courses of three months. Those attending the courses are

[1] For scientific and technical work, university graduates are recruited by industry in large numbers in both countries; and training for such work is relatively straightforward.

mostly from 28 to 40 years of age, and have already shown themselves to be competent administrators and are likely to merit further promotion. Being drawn from a wide range of businesses they are able, by working in syndicates, to exchange experiences, broaden their outlook, and gain a better understanding of administrative principles and methods common to all undertakings. Many firms hold frequent meetings of middle grade executives to discuss specific problems affecting all their departments and to submit reports and suggestions to the managing director. A more developed form of this method has been adopted by a few firms which have set up junior boards of specialist managers who consider the wider problems of the business and make recommendations to the top executive authorities on questions needing decision.[1]

[1] This method has been adopted by Crompton Parkinson, Ltd.

5

Time Studies

THE OBJECT of time studies is to establish a reasonable speed of work or standard of output to which workpeople should be able to conform, and it is therefore closely linked with the idea of "a fair day's work." In many occupations the work is too variable for measurement in defined units, and time studies are therefore mainly applied to repetition work where large numbers of similar articles are produced in succession. If a worker makes many units in a short time, the time study will fix the number of units which should be produced in an hour, but if a considerable time is required to produce one unit then the time study will fix the number of hours and minutes which a worker should take to produce the unit. These standards once established become the targets at which the workers must aim, and which a majority of them should be able to reach without undue fatigue.

It is essential that the standard should be reasonable. If it is set too high and if the workers are paid in proportion to their output, then either earnings will be too low or workers will have to work at unduly high speeds in order to earn a satisfactory wage. If the standard is too easy in relation to the wage rate per unit, workers in the occupation will be able to secure high earnings and thus discontent will be caused to other categories of workers who are earning less money for a similar amount of work. Alternatively, the workpeople concerned could secure their ordinary earnings by more leisurely work. Whatever they do, too low a standard implies too high cost of production to the undertaking.

Difference of opinion about speed of work is a frequent cause of friction between management and workpeople. Managements often believe that their workpeople could work harder without strain or injury to health, and also without loss of craftsmanship or quality of work. On the other hand, workpeople suspect that the management is always trying to speed them up to greater output and then, by cutting their wage rates, will pay them no more than before. Here, therefore, is ground for conflict. The suspicions of workpeople have been increased by methods sometimes adopted by time study experts who have made their investigations more or less secretly either by timing themselves under specially favourable conditions on a machine in a separate room, or by observing workpeople in the factory without indicating in any way that a time study was being made. Use has been made of such devices as concealing a stop-watch in a recess cut in a note-book and taking records of output surreptitiously which are then adopted as the basis for standards of production. These methods are entirely unsatisfactory and should never be used. On the other hand, although workpeople are fully justified in insisting that they should not be expected, except to meet a temporary rush, to work at greater speeds than they can maintain without strain month after month and year after year, and must conserve their energies throughout a long working life so that they are not worn out and "too old at forty," there are undertakings where the customary pace of work is too leisurely and where management can reasonably demand higher standards and introduce incentives to increase output.

It must be emphasized that there is not the slightest objection to time studies if the method is properly used. Indeed, for suitable work time studies are of value both to management and workpeople, and if standards of output are fixed by mutual agreement, as they usually can be, they remove a cause of friction and lead to more harmonious relations in the undertaking. This has been recognized by trade unions as well as management. The following quotation taken from a publication of the Congress of Industrial Organizations of the United States, a body which would never subscribe to practices unfair to workpeople, indicates agreement by organized labour that time studies can be fair and useful: "In the past time studies and incentive wage systems were too often made very mysterious and outside of labour's concern. Labour's protests against the stopwatch was natural when we had no voice in its use. But with Union protection and our demand for better production, efficiency and scientific management can be placed at the services of labour. The time study in itself is not injurious if properly handled. It is a technique, an instrument—just like a gauge or a caliper."[1]

In order that both management and workpeople will accept as fair the standards set by time studies, it is essential that representatives of the workers should take part in the studies. The studies themselves and the working out of the results are usually undertaken by time-study experts employed by the management, but representatives of the workpeople should be satisfied that the conditions under which

[1] *Producing for Victory. A Labour Manual for Increasing War Production,* published for the Congress of Industrial Organizations, Washington, D.C.

73

the studies are conducted are reasonable and should be given an opportunity of checking the calculations. The representatives may either be trade unionists or some other workmen recognized for this purpose by their fellows.

Not infrequently in the past, time-study experts have deliberately selected the best workers and arranged exceptionally favourable conditions for the tests and in consequence the resulting standard of output has been higher than would be reasonable for the majority of the workers under the ordinary conditions of the workshop. It is true, as already indicated, that in some workshops the workpeople have got into the habit of working at an unduly slow rate, and are taking things too easily, but this can be remedied only gradually by a variety of incentives, and certainly not by incorrect application of the time-study system.

In order to obtain a fair result, the workers tested should be of average experience and ability. It would obviously be unsatisfactory to fix a general standard upon results obtained from workers who are better or worse than the average, and workpeople are right in objecting if standards are based on the output of workers whose output is above the average. It should not be difficult to decide upon workers who are "average," as there are usually records of output of each worker in the department covering weeks or months for somewhat similar kinds of work. Then the conditions under which the test is conducted should also be "average." An unsatisfactory result would be obtained if the machines were prepared to be in specially good running order and the materials used were easier to work than those in general use. Other conditions, including light, temperature, and ventilation, should be those ordinarily found in the workshop, and, if necessary, the period of the day and week when the test is conducted should be chosen carefully. Records show appreciable fluctuations in output in different parts of the day and on different days of the week, and periods of high or low output should be avoided. Agreement between management and workpeople upon all these points should be reached and detailed notes kept of the conditions under which the test is conducted so that reference can be made to them if difficulties arise later in applying the standard.

Then workpeople vary in their response to test conditions. Some try to "show off" and work faster than their usual speed, while others, knowing that a standard is being set which will affect their earnings, may deliberately go slow but do this so skilfully that it is difficult to detect. However, the time-study expert must try to recognize such variations and warn or stop the workers concerned, and in this, the representative of the workpeople may be useful. When all the results have been obtained the standard must be worked out carefully, any "freak" times being eliminated, and allowance made for breakdowns, rest pauses, and other interruptions of work. If the product for which the standard is being set differs considerably from any hitherto made in the department, there is considerable risk that the results of the time study may not be entirely reliable, and in these circumstances the standard should be applied experimentally for a period and be subject to revision in the light of experience. This may not be necessary if the product differs only slightly from others on which the men have been previously engaged and for which production records covering many workers over a period are available as a check for the new standard.

Once the standard has been recognized as fair and adequate, it should not be changed unless the tools, machinery, or methods are altered so that the work is made easier or more difficult, or if the material subsequently used is easier or harder to work than that used in the test. If any permanent changes in material, tools, methods, machinery, or product are made, a new time study should be taken. Temporary variations in conditions, however, are liable to occur and affect output; for example, machinery not being in good running order or workshop organization not going smoothly. Such defects will be remedied but until this is done an allowance should be made which will compensate the workers for any fall in output for which they are not responsible.

Once a standard has been set it becomes applicable to all the workpeople concerned. Some of these are "average" while others are quicker or slower. Just as athletes differ in their speeds of running or in their capacity for long or high jumping, so workpeople differ in their normal speed of work. This, of course, results in differences of output and of earnings. It is sometimes desirable, however, to avoid a very wide "spread" from the slowest to the quickest workers in the group to which a standard is applied, because of the psychological effects of big differences in earnings. This can be done by grouping the workers into categories or grades within each of which the speed of workers is fairly uniform, and putting each category on a different job with its appropriate standard of output and rate of pay.

If carefully applied, time studies can be of great value. Workpeople are set a reasonable standard or pace of work, and know that they are giving satisfaction so long as their work approximates fairly closely to the standard. The foreman in charge can concentrate on organizing the work instead of driving the men to work at higher speeds, as the workers know the task expected of them and will usually make reasonable efforts to come near to or exceed the standard upon which their earnings depend. Also the management is better able to plan production and calculate costs.

This section may be concluded by two examples which illustrate some of the problems which arise. During the war of 1914–1918 time was lost because workpeople went on strike in protest against piece rates being changed whenever the output standards set by time studies yielded high earnings, and Mr. Lloyd George therefore warned munition factory managements against "cutting the rates." In one of these factories a time study was made for the work of painting pieces of metal of uniform size and shape with the result that a standard of so many units per hour was fixed. After a few days, however, it was noticed that the workpeople were doubling or trebling their earnings, thus raising their wages very much above those of workpeople in other parts of the factory, with consequent discontent among the latter. It did not take long to find the cause of this unexpected increase. When the original test had been conducted, the workers used the usual size of brush issued by the firm for the purpose, but they soon realized that they could do the work equally well and much quicker with brushes two or three times as big. These they bought for themselves and began to earn big money without greater effort. The time study had, no doubt, been quite satisfactorily conducted and the resulting standard was reasonable for the size of brush originally used, but the management were at fault in not considering the most efficient size of brush to use and in supplying these to their workpeople. In the circumstances, a change in the standard was inevitable.

The second example illustrates some of the factors which determine the amount of work a person may reasonably be expected to do, and though a time study is not directly involved the conclusions are relevant to time studies. In the early 1930's there were many disputes in the New England cotton weaving industry over the mill-owners' policy of more looms to a weaver. This became known as the "stretch-out," each weaver being "stretched" to control an increased number of looms, which were automatic, often fairly wide and used for weaving plain cloth. In some mills thirty-six, forty-eight, or even seventy-two looms (twelve rows of six looms each), were operated by one weaver assisted by two or three bobbin boys who, moving about on roller skates which they had provided on their own initiative, kept the drums of the automatic looms supplied with bobbins of yarn. In one mill at least, a weaver was in charge of one hundred and five looms (twenty-one rows of five looms each). When some companies increased the number of looms to a weaver their competitors tried to do the same, arguing that what weavers at other mills could do theirs must also do. After several months it was found that at certain mills the weavers seemed to have no difficulty in controlling a large number of looms, whereas at other mills the weavers in charge of a similar number complained that the work was much too strenuous, and strikes were frequent. An impartial investigation was then conducted which revealed that where the more looms policy worked well the companies had good looms, saw that the maintenance engineers kept them in perfect running order, and the yarn was specially prepared so that breakages would be minimized. In mills where these conditions were provided the weavers, even if in charge of seventy-two or one hundred and five looms were not overworked. They had general responsibility for the operation of the looms and when from time to time a loom stopped because the yarn had broken they would walk unhurried to it to join the yarn and set it running again. In mills where the yarn was unsuitable and the looms not running smoothly, stoppages were so frequent that the weavers were justified in protesting against the undue speed and strain involved if they attempted to keep the looms working, upon which output of cloth and therefore their earnings depended.

In this example, the number of looms which a weaver may reasonably be asked to operate depends not only upon his efficiency but upon the conditions of work and particularly the quality of the looms and the yarn. A change or difference in these conditions implies a change in the number of looms controlled. Similarly if a time study is made to set a standard of output, the standard is appropriate only if the machinery, materials, and other conditions remain the same as those during the study. Allowance should be made for any appreciable change in conditions.

THE BEDAUX SYSTEM OF WORK MEASUREMENT

Reference must be made to a system of work measurement originated by the late Charles E. Bedaux who established an organization to apply it in any firm wishing to adopt it. During the interwar years it was introduced by a considerable number of firms in North America and Western Europe. The system is discussed at this stage because it is based on time studies, although it also includes wage schemes and could therefore have been reviewed later in this volume in the chapter on Methods of Wage Payment. Its main feature is the measuring of the work done by every worker, whether labourer, skilled artisan, or supervisor, by what the Bedaux Organization claims to be a common unit, and relating the results to a standard which any normal worker in each class of work respectively should be able to reach. By applying the scheme to different occupations and industries, the productive efficiencies of workpeople engaged in various kinds of work are related to a common denominator.

The Bedaux unit is made up of work and rest combined in proportions which depend upon the strain involved in the work, and it is claimed that each kind of strain or effort has its own appropriate amount of rest or relaxation following it and compensating for it, and that both strain and rest can be calculated scientifically. In strenuous manual labour such as felling trees with a heavy axe, the pause or rest required after each swing of the axe is considerable, whereas by contrast in an occupation involving quick, light finger movements, for example typing or rapid assembly of small articles, the appropriate associated rest for each movement is small. Consequently the proportion of work to rest within the unit differs for each type of work.

In order to establish the unit for any kind of work, the operation is analysed into elementary movements, and estimates are made of the time required for each movement and of the rest periods considered essential to compensate for each kind of strain. The principles applied in making these estimates are specially related to such strains as lifting heavy weights, applying powerful pressure, and making rapid or complex sequences of movement. Thus the strain from a muscular movement of given power is proportional to the speed and duration of the movement, while for a given muscular effort the length of its proper rest period varies according to the speed of the movement; also speed of movement is greater the less the weight moved or the pressure applied and the shorter the duration of the movement.

The results are calculated in terms of a minute's work which is designated as a "B," and for each operation the "B" is the amount of work which a normal man should do in one minute if working at normal speed under ordinary conditions, and taking the full amount of rest appropriate to the job. The system is based on the fact that for most jobs each performed under defined conditions of equipment and materials an average worker can reasonably produce a given standard output in a given time, and this is then calculated on the basis of one minute's work and the result called a "B." For example, in one occupation a given sequence of movements resulting in a defined production may require 4 seconds of work and 2 seconds of rest, and therefore represents $\frac{6}{60}$th B, or $0 \cdot 1$ B, and the standard rate of production should be ten a minute or 600 an hour. If in another occupation a task done in standard time requires $2\frac{3}{4}$ minutes of work and $\frac{1}{4}$ minute of rest, it represents 3 B, and therefore the standard output in one hour would be 20.

The Bedaux Organization claim that they use a common unit of measure which is applied to different kinds of work, but it must be clearly understood that the "Unit" is different for each occupation. What is done is to find out for many kinds of jobs the amount of work that can be performed in one minute, and by adopting this common time factor the system, as indicated above, provides a common denominator with which to compare the efficiencies of workpeople on different jobs. The "B" for a coal heaver or a blacksmith's striker is quite distinct from the "B" for a post-office sorter or a seamstress. Assuming, however, that the "B" is properly calculated for each kind of work, then workers in any occupation should be able to do 60 B's in an hour, and if, therefore, within an occupation, e.g. bricklaying, one worker does 56 B's in an hour, a second does 59, and a third 62, these totals measure their efficiency in relation to one another and to the standard of 60 B's. Similarly if a bricklayer does 66 B's, a carpenter 61 B's, an engineering fitter 64 B's, and a seamstress 67 B's, the relative efficiency of these workpeople in different occupations is measured. This system can be applied to individuals in the same occupation or in different occupations, and also to groups of workpeople, to departments, and to whole undertakings.

The Bedaux consultants claim that the system can be applied equally well to highly paid mechanics and lower paid labourers, to men and women, to so-called direct and indirect workers, and that the performance of all can be reduced to a common denominator. They say that the "B" is independent of type of manufacture, product, individuals, and money values, and that the system has been successfully applied, sometimes with slight modifications, to diversified industries in different countries with different races and climates. They further suggest that they can offer a scientific solution for determining the jobs for which men, women, and juveniles are respectively most suited. It must be emphasized that similar claims could be made for any other time-study system in which output for different jobs was expressed in terms of a minute's work or an hour's work. Stripped of its complications the Bedaux scheme has a common denominator because it uses one minute's work as its unit, and what is done is to estimate systematically the amount of work that can be done in a minute.

It follows that the Bedaux system is a form of time study, though it is more systematic than some time studies in its analysis of the work done and the apportionment of work and rest, while there is undoubtedly value, not peculiar to the Bedaux system, in adopting a common time unit and nomenclature which enables the relative efficiencies of different individuals, and departments, and even of different undertakings to be measured. This facility for comparing the records of performance for different kinds of work is an advantage which Bedaux shares with some other time-study systems. Like all time studies the Bedaux technique is most readily applicable to repetition work, and its results become less reliable as the work becomes more variable or requires planning and the exercise of much thought, imagination, and judgment. It would be valueless for measuring the painting of masterpieces by a Constable, musical composition by a Beethoven, or the work of a prime minister or a captain of industry, while in the more ordinary tasks of industry it has its greatest use in measuring processes, of which there are many in these days of mass production, in which the same movements are performed time after time and involve a mechanical or semi-mechanical rhythm.

Bedaux experts, together with other industrial consultants, have the advantage of knowledge of conditions and speeds of work in a number of undertakings and industries based on first-hand investigations into standards of output, whereas most time-study specialists employed by an undertaking, though they know its problems intimately, have little opportunjty to learn much about the pace of work outside their own company. The claim made, however, by the Bedaux organization that the apportionment of work and rest in their standards is scientifically based cannot be admitted. The system is systematic but not scientific, and, except for the experience of its consultants and centralized accumulation of data, the Bedaux standards are liable to the same errors as those of any other time-study experts. Any systematic studies of output can enable the relative efficiencies of men, women, and juveniles to be measured, and can therefore indicate whether men, women, or juveniles are most suited for different kinds of work, but the freedom of employers to act on these results is limited by custom, the attitude of trade unions, and differences in wages.

Although an output of 60 B's an hour is considered "normal" by Bedaux consultants, a standard of 80 B's is regarded as attainable where workpeople and management are 100 per cent efficient. B's produced beyond 60 an hour are called premium B's, for which a bonus is paid as an incentive. The bonus for each premium B is $\frac{1}{60}$th of the base rate of wage, and the Bedaux organization recommend that three-quarters of the bonus be paid to the workpeople directly concerned and the remaining quarter to supervisors and to indirect labour whose work has facilitated production in excess of the 60 B standard. Some firms, however, pay the whole of the bonus or 90 or 95 per cent of it to direct labour, as workers object if they do not get full value for additional output and fear that supervisors may be tempted by substantial bonuses to drive the workers to excessive speed. Records of performances are posted daily as a stimulus to the workers, and average output is often 30 to 40 per cent above the standard, this being also the experience with other incentive systems of wage payment related to standards fixed by time studies. This additional output and the Bedaux statement that output under conditions of efficient production should be 80 B's is inconsistent with the claim that a standard of 60 B's is scientifically established by combining work and rest in proportions appropriate for the average worker. Output beyond 60 B's would imply either sacrificing rest considered necessary for the job, which would involve speeding, or improvements in the workers' movements and in the organization and equipment for the work which should have been made before the time studies for setting the standard are taken. Clearly a standard of 60 B's is an arbitrary conventional output to serve as basis for an incentive system of wage payment, and is a standard which, the Bedaux experts claim, average workers should have little difficulty in exceeding by a considerable margin.

In addition to working out standards of output for each operation, the Bedaux consultants offer an analytical method for determining the relative monetary value of each type of work throughout an undertaking.[1] For this purpose jobs are classified on the basis of the skill, training, experience, physical qualities, responsibility, the mental capacity which each requires, and any risks involved. If then a given rate of wage, e.g. £5 a week, is paid to workpeople doing work with the least requirements, then additions or "margins" for superior qualities are paid to workpeople in other jobs according to their relative values. This is a form of job evaluation.[2] The Bedaux organization does not concern itself with the amount of wages, the basic rates being determined by agreement between management and workpeople.

The advantages of systematic estimates of the relative value of each kind of work have long been recognized, and the adoption of more "scientific" methods of determining relative wages is desirable, and is an ideal towards which to move. The practical difficulties should, however, be fully recognized. It may be practicable to arrange various kinds of work according to the skills and other qualities required of workpeople, though the results will become less

[1] The Bedaux system also includes standardized costing.   [2] See Chapter 7.

reliable as the list of occupations increases, and extend to widely differing industries, e.g. nursemaids and soldiers, cooks and policemen. Even if a reasonably satisfactory order is established, A being lower in the scale than B, there is still the problem whether B should receive 5s. a week more than A, or whether it should be 3s. or 10s.

Strong opposition will often be encountered if proposals are made to alter customary wage ratios, even though these do not correspond to the relative values of the different jobs. The ratios may have been reasonable years ago, but the old ratios having been maintained, some jobs may now be overpaid. Systematic studies of the relative values of different jobs are desirable periodically to reveal such anomalies, and clearly adjustments should be made, preferably gradually by stages so that big departures from customary relationships will not be made, thereby reducing the risk of conflict. Often wage ratios are the result of the relative effectiveness of trade unions, some occupations being relatively underpaid because of weak organizations, while conversely others are relatively overpaid. So long as the strong unions remain strong and the weak ones remain weak a "scientific" adjustment of wage rates will have little chance of success. Then the factors of demand for and supply of labour, and the prosperity or depression of undertakings and especially of industries are obstacles in the way of the adoption of the "scientific" wage policy. Thus in the inter-war years 1919 to 1939 wages were unduly low in the British cotton, coal-mining, and other "unsheltered" industries exposed to the full force of foreign competition, but a more appropriate wage ratio could have been quickly established only by heavy direct or indirect subsidies, and a big transfer of surplus supplies of labour away from these industries.

6

Methods of Wage Payment

DISPUTES FREQUENTLY arise over methods of wage payment, and a thorough knowledge of these methods, their suitability for different kinds of work, and the difficulties which arise in their application is necessary for all who deal with industrial relations. Methods of payment must be distinguished from speed of work and from the amount of workers' earnings, though they are all closely related.

Wages are paid for work done and this is sometimes measured by time worked and sometimes by output, the main alternative methods being (1) time rates, payment being at a fixed rate per hour, day, week, or other period, and each worker in a given category receives the same payment irrespective of differences in individual output; (2) piece rates, under which payments depend upon output, and individual workers receive different earnings according to the amount of work done, the system providing an incentive to increase production. There are also various bonus systems to stimulate production. Piece rates, by which the pay of each worker is proportionate to his output, might be thought more satisfactory than time rates, especially from the point of view of the employer and the national economy, and they also seem fair to the workers. As will be seen, however, they are not suitable for all kinds of work, and also the system is liable to abuse if applied unscrupulously. Earnings are usually higher for workers on piece rates than for those on similar work paid on a time basis, and the danger of excessive speeds is not great as workers are not penalized if they fail to reach a given standard or "target." This danger is, however, serious if, as under some bonus systems, attractive monetary rewards are paid for attaining high standards of production, and efforts to reach these standards may involve strain resulting in injury to health, increase in accidents, and damage to materials and machines.

The proportion of workpeople on piece rates or other incentive systems varies greatly from industry to industry. In some industries it is insignificant, but in others, and particularly in some occupations, for example, textile spinning, most of the workpeople are on piece rates. The proportions on incentive systems are considerably higher for women than for men, and in large than in small undertakings. In British industry in 1906, about 72 per cent were time workers and 28 per cent were on incentive pay in the main industries excluding agriculture, while in the exporting industries the proportions were 60 per cent time to 40 per cent incentive.[1] Since then there has been a tendency for incentive work gradually to increase, and this was somewhat accelerated during and after the Second World War, but by 1951 the proportion was not more than about 32 per cent. Industries in which piece work and other incentive systems are widely used include textiles, mining, the metal trades, and engineering, while building, public utilities, and transport are preponderantly on time rates.[2] Some years ago a sample inquiry in the United States covering three-quarters of a million workpeople showed the proportion of time workers to be 47 per cent, the remainder being on piece rates or other incentive systems.

Trade unions tend to prefer time rates, though they are parties to many collective agreements which include piece rates where these are suitable for the kind of work done. In addition to the risk of speeding, and the greater difficulty of regulating piece rates by collective agreements, there may be a tendency for piece rates to weaken the solidarity of the workers because of considerable differences in earnings. Many individual workers, especially those who can achieve high output, favour piece rate or bonus payments which, if reasonably fixed, enable them to earn more. Where conditions are suitable employers prefer piece rates because of their inducement to workpeople to concentrate and do more work. In the following sections indications are given of the suitability of time and piece rates for different kinds of work, together with practical difficulties which arise in their application and the main safeguards needed.

TIME RATES

The time basis of payment is usually adopted when quality is more important than quantity, the work requiring special care and attention, the materials being costly or the instruments delicate and easily damaged if workers were tempted by bonuses to work at high speed. If skilled craftsmanship is needed, time rates are preferable to incentive payment. When the workers' output cannot be measured satisfactorily, whether in skilled or unskilled work, time rates are

---

[1] *Survey of Industrial Relations*, Committee on Industry and Trade, London, 1926, pp. 16 and 105–107.

[2] See *Industrial Relations Handbook*, 1953, Appendix VI.

paid, as otherwise there would be frequent disagreement over the amounts earned. Thus, unskilled labourers and skilled men on maintenance and repair work are generally paid at time rates. If the pace of work and therefore the output is largely controlled by the speed of a machine and the individual worker can do little to increase production time rates are appropriate. They are also often applied where the workers are under close supervision and would have little opportunity for slackness. If work is irregular or liable to frequent interruptions, time rates are used, as the worker would object to incentive payment if, through no fault of his own, he was not able to work steadily. When wages are low, and hours long, and the tools which the worker uses are inexpensive, he is likely, other things being equal, to be paid a time wage, but if wages and overheads for capital equipment are high the employer will tend to introduce incentive methods. It should be noted, however, that this tendency is diminished by the fact that, though a high output must be obtained if a costly machine is to pay its way, the labour cost is likely to be only a small part of the total cost of the product. The method of payment by the hour, half-day, or day has been used for jobs which are casual or liable to be interrupted by bad weather, for example, dock labour and building, so that the workers can be laid-off almost immediately and no wages paid till work is resumed. This, however, involves irregular income for the worker, with hardship for his family, and experiments are now being made to ensure regular minimum time earnings for such workers.

Some of the above types of work for which time rates are fairly suitable may be illustrated. Diamond cutting is the classical example of an occupation highly suitable for time work because much attention and care must be given in cutting valuable stones and increased speed of work resulting from incentive payment would cause damage to the diamonds. Teachers in the old board school days were paid by results, their salaries being adjusted according to the success of their scholars in an examination in reading, writing, and arithmetic, but this not being a fair measure of the teachers' ability and the system also having effects which were educationally unsound, it was replaced by monthly salaries. Engineers on maintenance and repair work, including motor-garage engineers who service cars, are usually on time rates because their work varies frequently and cannot be measured in easily defined units. Printing compositors are normally paid time wages because accuracy of their work is more important than speed. Most railway workers are on time rates, as often the amount of their work cannot be exactly measured and is determined in part by circumstances which are outside their control. Time wages are suitable for workers assembling motor cars or other products on the moving chain system, as once the rate of movement has been determined the workers have no influence on output; they must either keep the pace set or be replaced by workers who can.

Although time workers in the same grade receive the same wages for the day or week for different amounts of work and although the work of each is not measured exactly, they and their foremen have a reasonably clear idea of the amount of work to be done. In other words, they must approximate to understood standards of output or of steady application to their work, and supervision ensures that this standard is maintained. Those who fail to do so are liable to lose their jobs or be put on to a job with a lower time rate. On the other hand, good work can be rewarded by promotion to a higher grade with a better rate of pay. Thus although time rates are properly distinguished from incentive systems they have associated with them the positive incentives of promotion and the negative incentives of demotion and dismissal. Working at excessive speed is usually more associated with incentive methods than with time rates, but one of the worst examples of speeding known to the author was in a foreign undertaking during a period of severe unemployment where, because of fear of unemployment, the workers on low time rates and long hours worked at almost intolerable speed and strain imposed by the management, each man knowing that if he failed to keep the pace there were dozens of men available to take his place. A foreman or manager who is always forcing the pace and finding fault is responsible for much tension and discontent.

PIECE RATES

Piece rates and bonus systems provide a stimulus to output by varying the payments according to the quantity of work done by each worker or by a team of workers. Workers who produce more receive more. These incentive methods are therefore applied when high output is desired, when quality of work is largely controlled by the machine and not by the men, or where quality is of secondary importance or can easily be tested by inspection. As their wages depend upon output the workers in trying to increase production are liable to be careless of quality, and therefore somewhat closer inspection of the product for quality is necessary than with time workers, but less supervision of the men to keep them at work is needed. Usually there are more workmen to each foreman when incentive methods are applied than with time rates, and incentive payments are of special value if the type of work makes close super-vision difficult.

Incentive methods are suitable where easily defined standardized units are produced in large quantities by repetition work and the output of each worker can easily be counted. They are effective under these conditions if the quantity produced depends considerably upon the worker's efficiency, speed, and concentration on the job. If overhead costs are high the use of incentives which result in increased output enables such costs to be spread over a larger production and the unit costs are therefore reduced. The work should be regular and continuous so that the worker is not hampered in his efforts to attain a high standard of output by having to wait for material or because his machine has broken down. Workers on piece rates are likely to protest if their work is interrupted through no fault of their own, and their grievance is legitimate as their earning power is reduced. In fairness to the workers, therefore, the management must either organize the work so that interruptions are rare, or where this is not practicable they must agree to a reasonable guaranteed minimum time payment to cover losses caused by periods of interrup-tion, or abandon the piece work system altogether as being unsuitable for such work.

The textile industries provide illustrations of work suitable for piece rates. Thus, in cloth weaving the work is of defined standard and the output is easily measured by a meter on the loom. The worker can influence the amount produced by quickly repairing breakages in the yarn and by otherwise keeping the looms running well. Quality of work can be controlled by inspection, and where the worker is responsible for defects he can be penalized by a deduc-tion from his earnings, though this should be rarely done, being reserved for repeated carelessness. Textile spinning and many engineering processes are also suitable for piece rates. Coal hewers are usually paid on tonnage rates, their pay being in proportion to their output. Such work at the coal face is difficult to keep under constant supervision, except where a long face is being worked by a big team using mechanized methods, and therefore an incentive system has advantages. Also the product from a seam is reasonably uniform and output is a fair measure of work done. The coal is loaded into tubs to which an identification disc is attached by the hewer, or for each small team working together, and when the tubs reach the surface of the pit they are weighed and the amount credited to the hewer or team. To avoid disputes about the quantity, the weighings are supervised by a representative of the management and by a checkweigher appointed and paid by the union. The loading of a small amount of dirt or stone among the coal is recognized as unavoidable, but if a hewer's tubs contain too much dirt he will be warned, and if this continues a deduction is made from his pay. Not all coal hewing is suitable for output payments, for example, where there is a fault in the seam causing output for a given effort to be less, and for work in such places the hewer will be paid by the hour.

Piece rates and other incentive systems are satisfactory if applied to suitable kinds of work on the basis of fair time studies, but are liable to misuse. They have been abused by fixing rates so that workers could only attain a reasonable level of earnings by working at excessive speeds. Also much discontent has been caused by the practice of fixing a rate on the basis of a time study, and later cutting the rate, which has the effect of lowering earnings or of making the workers speed up in order to secure a level of earnings equal to that before the rate was cut. If this is done the system seems to the workers merely a device for speeding, and they may come to the conclusion that however hard they work their earnings will not be allowed to increase much. A fair relation must be maintained between the earnings of workpeople in different occupations in an undertaking and those in one occupation must not be able, except by working harder, to earn much more than workers in another occupation of similar difficulty, but this should be avoided, not by cutting rates, but by fixing proper rates at the outset on the basis of reliable time studies.

Piece rates should generally remain unchanged, except (1) where a mistake has been made in setting the rate; (2) where the conditions of the work have changed making it easier or more difficult, for example the worker being provided with a better machine or with material more easily worked; and (3) where the basic rate of pay is increased or decreased, whether by collective or individual agreement. Thus, if an employer buys new costly machines which enable the workers to double their output with no greater effort than before, it would be unfair that the piece rate should remain unchanged and workers gain double earnings. These high earnings would be badly out of line with those of other workpeople in the undertaking for whom no improved equipment was available; also, if almost the whole benefit from improved methods went to the workers, there would be no incentive for the employer to spend money on better machinery and organization.

When piece rates or bonus systems are fairly applied, each worker should be free to earn according to his efficiency except where for any reason he sets a pace which would result in strain. This he may do where his need for money is particularly great; for example, if he has to meet heavy expenses because of sickness in his family, or where he is passing through a period of severe emotional stress which expresses itself in excessive effort at work. Otherwise he should not work below his best pace because of fear that his employer will not approve high earnings or that his workmates will resent his getting bigger earnings than they do. In practice many efficient workers are held back for these reasons, and especially the latter, which takes the form of pressure from other workers to induce him not to work much beyond the standard of the shop.

Straight Piece Rates

The straight piece rate system can be applied to individual workers or to teams of workers, and the earnings whether of an individual or a team are directly proportionate to the amount of work done. If, for example, the piece rate is a penny a unit of output, a worker who produces 120 units in a day earns 10s., and another who produces 150 units earns 12s. 6d., and so on. Teams of workers are similarly paid according to the output of the whole team, and the total amount earned is then divided between the members. The total is divided equally if the workpeople in the team are all of the same grade, or it may be divided in agreed ratios if the members of the team differ in skill.

The system, whether the rates are individual or collective (for a team) is simple and easy to understand. The worker can readily calculate what his earnings will be, for he knows hour by hour what he is producing and he, therefore, knows for himself what he should receive in his pay envelope at the end of the week. Consequently, he has more confidence than in some complicated bonus systems involving elaborate calculations which are made in the office and which he may not fully understand. Simplicity in reckoning the workers' earnings is also an advantage to the management, little clerical work being needed.

The system is a good one if applied fairly on the basis of a satisfactory time study. As it tends to result in greater concentration and effort by the worker to secure higher earnings, and as the piece rates and related time studies cannot be controlled by collective agreements but must be fixed for each type of work within each undertaking, the trade unions usually insist in collective negotiations that the average earnings of experienced workers on piece rates shall be higher by a specified percentage—generally between 10 and $33\frac{1}{3}$ per cent—than the time rates paid to time workers in the same occupation. The employer can afford to pay these greater amounts both because output is higher and because overhead or standing costs are reduced per unit produced by being spread over a bigger output.

Differential Piece Rates

The simplest form of differential piece rate is that devised by Mr. Frederick W. Taylor, the "Father of Scientific Management," who set two piece rates the higher of which was paid only to those workers who reached or exceeded a specified standard of output. Whether the system will provide an incentive to work at high speed depends upon the difference between the two piece rates and upon the standard set. Taylor set a high standard of output and the piece rate paid to workers who reached it was considerably above the rate paid to those whose output was below the standard. One of his objects was to eliminate the latter from the workshop by the discouragement of low earnings, and to staff it with quick workers, a policy which earned for him the title of "Speedy" Taylor.

The system can be applied less drastically. An easier standard of output can be set, but with a smaller increase in the piece rate for work beyond the standard. The differential system has been developed by having three piece rates instead of two, the highest rate being paid to workers who reach the standard, the second to those who reach a given proportion, e.g. 80 per cent or 90 per cent, of the standard, and the third to other workers.[1] The system could be further elaborated by having four or more piece rates each related to a different level of output, but the growing complexity would be a disadvantage. Under the straight piece-rate system the incentive to work at unduly high speed is slight as the same rate is paid for high or low production, but the differential system by its special inducement of a jump in earnings if the set standard is reached is more liable to result in speeding and strain for workers of average or under average efficiency. This risk varies according to the rise in the piece rate as the output of the worker increases, the danger of excessive speed being greater if the rise is large than if it is small.

The differential system has been mainly applied in undertakings with costly machinery, the employer being able to afford to pay a higher piece rate to quicker workers because his overhead costs are spread over a bigger output and are therefore less per unit than if the machines are operated by slower workers. This saving in overhead cost per unit of output is the chief attraction of the system and largely determines the difference between the two rates. In

---

[1] This is sometimes known as the Multiple Piece Rate System, and it was advocated by Merrick as a means of giving an incentive to good average workers who could not attain the high standard of the most competent workers.

undertakings where overhead costs are low the saving would be so small that the system would be of little value and the straight piece rate would be preferable.

BONUS SYSTEMS[1]

The straight piece rate has the merit of simplicity but, though offering an incentive, it does not provide any special reward for workpeople who reach a given standard of output. The differential piece-rate system offers such a reward but may lead to excessive speed of work because, though the standard which entitled a worker to receive the higher piece rate may be reasonable, he still has the attraction of earnings at this rate for output beyond the standard. To avoid this inducement while retaining the advantage of setting an output standard, several bonus systems have been devised. Their practical value depends upon the reasonableness of the standard set and of the wages which workers of average ability can earn.

The number of different bonus systems is very great, although most of them are variations of a few types, modifications being usually made to suit the special conditions of production in individual undertakings. Bonus systems are often introduced where a piece rate would not be suitable but an incentive is needed. In effect they combine some of the features of time and piece rates. Many of the systems are of United States origin, and their application has been greatest in engineering and allied industries.

The main features of bonus systems are:

(1) The fixing of a standard time for a given task, this being usually done by time study or on the basis of average daily production. In some systems the task is a difficult one and can be achieved in the standard time by only a small number of workers, while in other systems the task is within the reach of a majority of the workers.

(2) Payment of the full ordinary hourly rate to workers who do not exceed the standard. There is therefore no penalty on workers who do not reach the standard.

(3) Payment of a bonus to all workers who complete the task in less than standard time. The worker receives the hourly rate for the

---

[1] The term "bonus" is here applied to forms of wage payment devised to stimulate increased production other than straight piece rates or differential piece rates. It must be distinguished from other uses of the term which sometimes cover such general additions to wage rates as cost-of-living bonuses or war bonuses, or bonuses for regularity of attendance or even increases in time rates paid to grades of workers above the grade to which the minimum rate is paid.

time he has actually taken, and in addition a bonus the amount of which is usually a percentage of the hourly rate multiplied by the time saved; i.e. the difference between the time he has taken and the standard time. In some systems the proportion of the hourly rate is as low as 30 or 50 per cent, in others it is 100 per cent or even 120 per cent. Usually low percentages are related to fairly easy tasks and high percentages to difficult tasks.

These features may be illustrated by outlining several well-known systems. In the Halsey system workers who do not exceed the standard time are paid an hourly rate, but those who do the task in less than the standard time receive the hourly rate for the time they take and, in addition, a percentage, usually 30 or 50 per cent, of the hourly rate for the time saved. Thus if the hourly rate is 2s. 6d., the standard time for the task 6 hours and the bonus 50 per cent (i.e. 1s. 3d.) for the time saved, then six workers, taking the times shown in column 2 of the table, would earn respectively the amounts shown in column 3. These figures in column 3 are also the labour costs or piece rates paid by the undertaking for each task. The hourly earnings of the six workers and their earnings for an eight-hour day are given in columns 4 and 5.

Worker	Time taken	Earnings for time taken		Earnings for one hour		Earnings for eight-hour day	
	hours	s.	d.	s.	d.	s.	d.
1	7	17	6	2	6	20	0
2	6	15	0	2	6	20	0
3	$5\frac{1}{2}$	14	$4\frac{1}{2}$	2	$7\frac{4}{11}$	20	$10\frac{10}{11}$
4	5	13	9	2	9	22	0
5	$4\frac{1}{2}$	13	$1\frac{1}{2}$	2	11	23	4
6	4	12	6	3	$1\frac{1}{2}$	25	0

These figures show that earnings for the task fall regularly as time saved increases, and this reduces the incentive to speed. It also diminishes the danger of unduly high earnings if the standard time has not been accurately calculated and the task is too easy, this being in contrast with the increasing incentive of differential piece rates. The earnings are also the labour costs or piece rates for the task, and they fall as the time saved increases. Thus, the fast workers who do the task in less than standard time receive a lower piece rate than those who take the standard time or more than standard time to do the task, the firm gaining the benefit of the difference between the rate actually paid and a straight piece rate. The wage cost per unit of output is less for those above the standard than for those below it, and this has been criticized as unfair to the workers, who do not receive the full reward for their efficiency. The system, however, has the merit of being easy to introduce; methods of working need not be changed, the standard time for the task can be based on average daily production in the department, the ordinary time wage is continued, and workers will receive at least as much as they did before, but have the opportunity of increasing their earnings. Halsey usually set fairly easy tasks and small bonuses by contrast with others who favoured difficult tasks with big bonuses.

Rowan's system, which was first used in Clydeside, goes even farther than Halsey's in penalizing fast workers, the object being still more to safeguard management against having to pay big sums in bonuses if a bad mistake has been made in setting the standard time and the task is much too easy. Rowan's opinion was that workers can only increase production by more than 50 per cent above their ordinary output if too low a standard has been fixed. This assumes, however, that the workers concerned are fairly equal in efficiency, but it would not be true if there were considerable differences in efficiency between the slowest and quickest workers.

Rowan devised a scheme of bonuses on variable percentages instead of Halsey's fixed percentages. In his system the percentages are determined by the ratio of time saved to the standard time for the task. For example: if the worker saves one-fifth of the standard time his percentage for bonus calculations is twenty; if he saves one-quarter of the time the percentage is twenty-five, and so on. But unlike the Halsey percentage which is applied to the hourly rate for time saved, the Rowan percentage is applied to the pay for the time actually taken, and therefore though the percentage increases as more time is saved, the sum to which it is applied becomes smaller. The maximum amount of bonus is reached when a worker does the task in half the standard time, and if he saves more than half the time his bonus diminishes.

The Rowan system is complicated because of the variable percentages. Labour cost for the task, and therefore time earnings are considerably lower for the most efficient workers under the Rowan than under the Halsey system. The Rowan system is more favourable for the lower grades of workers, but the incentive declines rapidly with increases in the time saved, whereas the Halsey incentive declines less rapidly. For this reason the Rowan system has been criticized because it penalizes the most efficient workers. Also objections have been raised against both systems because workers who finish the task in less than standard time do not receive full pay for the task.

93

This objection has been removed in some systems by paying a bonus at the rate of 100 per cent of the full time rate for all time saved. Any worker who completes the task in less than standard time is paid at the full hourly rate for the time taken, and in addition receives a bonus at the full hourly rate for the difference between the time he actually takes and the standard time. In effect the system provides a guaranteed minimum hourly rate for workers who do not reach the standard, and a straight piece rate for workers who reach or exceed it. Thus if the hourly rate is 2s. 6d., and the standard time is 4 hours, then the workers who take more than the 4 hours receive 2s. 6d. an hour; a worker who does the task in just 4 hours, receives 10s., which may be regarded either as a time wage for 4 hours' work or a piece rate of 10s. for the job. All workers who do better than standard time receive a time wage and bonus which together amount to 10s., so that essentially they are paid a straight piece rate for the job. Thus, a worker who does the job in 3½ hours receives 8s. 9d. as wages and 1s. 3d. as bonus (i.e. half an hour's pay at 100 per ce. t of the hourly rate), a worker who does the job in 3 hours also receives a total of 10s., made up of 7s. 6d. as wages and 2s. 6d. bonus, and these workers have half an hour and an hour respectively in which to earn additional wages. The system is simpler than the Rowan and even than the Halsey system, and seems fairer to the workers because the full rate is paid for time saved, or in effect a straight piece rate is paid to all who do the job in standard time or less. However, workers may earn less than under the Halsey or Rowan systems, as what they receive depends more on the standard set for the job and on the rate of pay than on the type of incentive.

Gantt, who was an associate of Taylor, adopted Halsey's methods of a guaranteed minimum time rate and a bonus calculated as a percentage of the full time rate for time saved, but like Taylor he set a difficult task and offered a high reward to efficient workers, his percentage being 120. Unlike the 100 per cent bonus system which gives a straight piece rate to efficient workers, Gantt's piece rate increases as more time is saved. Firms can afford these higher rates because overhead costs per unit are reduced by the high output of the efficient worker. The foreman is also paid a bonus based on the number of his workers who do the task within the standard time, this being a recognition of the part he can play in eliminating delays and interruptions and in arranging conditions favourable to production. As the bonus is big the standard is high, and can only be reached without undue fatigue by efficient workers who concentrate on their work and adopt the best methods, these being indicated in instructions given to the workers.

With the high standards set by Gantt and also in the 100 per cent system, the average worker is not able to save much time, whereas with Halsey and Rowan the tasks are usually easier and more workers can earn a bonus. One of the objects of the Gantt bonus, like Taylor's differential piece rate, is to eliminate slow workers, who cease trying to reach the difficult standard set them and are discouraged by their low earnings. The incentive therefore applies only to highly efficient workers.

The following table illustrates the declining piece rate under the Halsey system of a 50 per cent bonus for time saved, the straight piece rate of the 100 per cent system and the increasing piece rate of the Gantt system of a 120 per cent bonus. The figures are based on a standard time of 4 hours for the task and a wage rate of 2s. 6d. an hour.

Worker	Time Taken	Halsey		100% System		Gantt	
		Earnings for Time Taken	Earnings for 8-Hour Work Day	Earnings for Time Taken	Earnings for 8-Hour Work Day	Earnings for Time Taken	Earnings for 8-Hour Work Day
	hours	s. d.	s. d.	s. d.	s. d.	s. d.	s. d.
1	$4\frac{1}{4}$	11 3	20 0	11 3	20 0	11 3	20 0
2	4	10 0	20 0	10 0	20 0	10 0	20 0
3	$3\frac{3}{4}$	9 $8\frac{1}{4}$	20 8	10 0	21 4	10 $1\frac{1}{2}$	21 $7\frac{1}{2}$
4	$3\frac{1}{2}$	9 $4\frac{1}{2}$	21 5	10 0	22 $10\frac{2}{3}$	10 3	23 $5\frac{1}{4}$
5	$3\frac{1}{4}$	9 $0\frac{3}{4}$	23 3	10 0	24 $7\frac{5}{13}$	10 $4\frac{1}{2}$	25 $5\frac{6}{13}$
6	3	8 9	23 4	10 0	26 8	10 6	28 0

The figures show that Halsey provides the least incentive and a diminishing one, while Gantt offers the greatest incentive and one which increases. Conclusions about the incentives are the main ones which can be drawn from the table, and it must not be assumed that the Gantt system yields greater earnings than that of Halsey. It does if, as in the table, the standard set and hourly rate are the same, or even if they are somewhat less favourable to the workers than Halsey's, but as already indicated, the task is usually considerably easier with Halsey than with Gantt. With a difficult task a small number of highly efficient workers may earn more under Gantt, but workers who are only a little above the average may do better with Halsey's easier task.

As already indicated, workers whose efficiency is only average or slightly better than average are discouraged if they fail to reach the standard. Systems have been devised to give some recognition to workers who, though below the standard, have made a reasonable effort and only miss it by a small margin. They also make some allowance for failures due to minor interruptions or materials difficult to work. In one of these systems used in the U.S.A., a minimum hourly wage is succeeded by a straight piece rate as in the 100 per cent bonus, but the piece rate begins when production reaches 70 per cent, or sometimes 80 per cent of the standard. The production level at which the piece rate begins is varied for different jobs, being lower or higher for standards of greater or less difficulty.

In the well-known Emerson Efficiency System the bonus begins at a specified level of production, for example, two-thirds, 70 or 75 per cent of the standard. Workers who do not reach the specified level are paid at the ordinary time rate, but above that level, instead of a straight piece rate, payment is on a graduated scale providing what is essentially a time rate which increases slowly at first but more rapidly as workers approach 100 per cent efficiency. From 100 per cent production onwards payment is almost a straight piece rate but with a slight decline for high outputs, as in the Gantt system. Emerson set an easier task within the reach of more work-people than Gantt, but with a lower bonus. These systems, which enable a small bonus to be earned by workers who do not reach the full efficiency standard, are more encouraging than the Taylor and Gantt incentives to workers of average efficiency.

Usually incentives are applied to individual workers, but group incentives can be used where the product is the work of a number of workers and the contribution of each individual cannot be measured separately. The amount of bonus, which depends on output, is divided in specified proportions between the members of the group. Group bonus incentives are most frequently applied to small teams of four or five to ten or a dozen workers, but sometimes to all the workers of a department, and occasionally to the whole of the workers of an undertaking. Group incentives have the advantage that keen members of the group will put pressure on potential slackers to make a fair contribution to output.

Any of these bonus systems can be satisfactory if the standard is fairly fixed and the rate of bonus reasonable, and each can be abused if the standard is too difficult for the average worker, even if the bonus is big. Although the "pull" of each incentive differs, the average earnings of the workers, as distinct from the spread of earnings, depend essentially on the difficulty of the standard set and on the rate of pay, and therefore average earnings may be higher under a system with a lower incentive than under one which has a higher incentive. Thus average earnings of workers on a 100 per cent bonus or Gantt's 120 per cent incentive, may be less than under the Halsey 50 per cent bonus.

One of the main difficulties in applying bonus and other incentive systems of payment is to keep a fair relation between earnings for different kinds of work in the undertaking, and particularly between workers on incentive systems and those on time wages. Discontent and unrest often arise because the wages of efficient skilled workpeople on hourly rates, for example, on maintenance and repair work, are considerably below the earnings of workers on incentive systems who may be doing less skilled work. Another difficulty is that of maintaining unchanged the conditions of work which prevailed when the task and the rate of payment were set. If the machines run less smoothly, or the materials are less suitable, the workpeople may be unable to earn reasonable wages.

The main advantage of incentive systems is that the pay of each worker is related to his efficiency, and increased effort usually brings additional reward. Also it is generally speaking true that the more a worker earns the more profitable he is to his employer. The type of work mainly determines the suitability of the particular incentive system, but a simple, easily understood system is preferable to more complicated ones, while the incentive should not be so powerful as to result in excessive speed of work. The straight piece rate has considerable advantages, but where it is unsuitable the 100 per cent bonus system or some other system which combines a guaranteed time rate for those below a specified output, with a straight piece rate for those above it, should usually be satisfactory. One of the main merits of these bonus systems is that they are based on time wages.

7

Job Evaluation, Merit Rating, and Non-Wage Incentives

INCREASING ATTENTION is being given in many countries to job evaluation and merit rating, the first being concerned with the grading of jobs and the second with the grading of individual workpeople. Many examples can be found throughout industry of jobs which, for historical and other reasons, are graded and paid more highly than other jobs requiring equal or superior effort and skill. For example, a job which formerly required well-trained, highly paid craftsmen may now be done by less skilled men using easily operated machines, and yet the old grading and pay are still retained. The purpose of job evaluation is to assess the qualities required by each job, and then to try to bring grading and pay into line with the results of the evaluations. These adjustments will often be difficult because of resistance by workpeople whose jobs have been down-graded, and the changes may have to be made gradually over a considerable time.

Among the criteria used in job evaluation are time and cost of training, skill and experience, effort, difficulty, unpleasantness, and danger. A "points" system is applied, a number of points being given for each of the qualities for each job. Disagreements will arise over the points to be given, but the results of this method provide a better basis for grading jobs and fixing relative wages than the unsystematic methods usually in operation.

Although job evaluation has some resemblance to merit rating they must not be confused. Whether a job has been "valued" or not, the workpeople employed on the job will differ in their efficiency and value to the undertaking. Merit rating is a method of measuring these differences systematically as a basis for making corresponding variations in pay. Incentive methods of payment go a long way in rewarding merit, promotions are usually based on merit, and employers have other methods of rewarding good work. Often, however, the choice of individuals for recognition is based on rather crude general estimates of a person's qualities. Merit rating attempts to make the choice more systematic and objective by listing all the qualities which should be considered, giving to each quality a maximum number of points according to its relative importance and then awarding to each individual the number of points he is considered to merit. Alternatively, each individual may be classified for each quality as excellent, good, average, or poor.

The criteria include skill and efficiency as shown by quantity and quality of output, reliability, care in avoiding accidents, adaptability in adjusting to variations in the job, initiative, personality, and co-operativeness where team work is required. Good judges of men have always assessed merit by these criteria, without using an elaborate system of points, but in large undertakings systematic assessment has advantages. Merit rating with appropriate adjustments of pay can usefully be made in many kinds of work at intervals of six or twelve months, and it is desirable that independent assessments should be made by at least two people who are in a position to judge the workmen's qualities. A workman who does not maintain his previous rating loses part or the whole of the merit pay which he had been receiving.

NON-WAGE INCENTIVES

In addition to the incentives already reviewed, which provide money payments directly related to the output of the individual worker or of a team of workers, there are others with the monetary factor more remote or even non-existent. They include pride in craftsmanship, responsibility for doing a job satisfactorily, recognition and prestige, opportunity for promotion, loyalty to the undertaking, and patriotism, which can be especially effective in times of national emergency. These apply to workers whether on time work, piece rates, or bonus payments, and management should make continuous effort to apply such incentives. These non-wage incentives increase in value as wages rise and become sufficient to provide adequate standards of living.

Craftsmanship and Interest in the Job

Most people have an urge to do constructive work and an instinct for craftsmanship, and if work is interesting they like to do it for its own sake, apart from remuneration, though they would not continue at work so long as present hours of work in industry. Satisfaction results from acquiring skill and doing a skilled job well, whether it be in sport, in a hobby, or in industrial work, and the exercise of judgment, the planning of materials, and the co-ordination of complicated movements to achieve a desired end, such as making a beautiful piece of furniture, are in themselves incentives to effort.

99

Although growth of mass production, with specialization of process and standardization of product, has involved loss of craftsmanship in many occupations, nevertheless vast opportunities have been opened up for highly skilled work, especially in the making of semi-automatic machines used in mass production processes. Also, workpeople with a high order of technical ability are in great demand, and so much heavy work formerly done by physical toil has been taken over by machinery that the "slaves" of the modern world are machines, and man is increasingly the master.

Not infrequently modern industry is compared with the domestic system of the Middle Ages and the greater attractiveness of the latter is emphasized. We tend, however, to see the past through a golden haze and neglect to remember that in the Middle Ages there was a great amount of drudgery and monotony involving heavy physical strain which is nowadays taken over by power-driven machinery which gives the worker satisfaction to control. Also, in the period of domestic industry, few workers were highly skilled craftsmen, and the corresponding group is proportionately greater to-day in highly skilled crafts and in technical and scientific work.

However, though industry requires more intelligent and better educated workpeople than ever before and offers a vast range of interesting work, large numbers of workers are employed upon monotonous repetition work, in which it is easy to lose interest and feel a sense of boredom, with a consequent lowering of the rate of output. Some workpeople indeed prefer simple repetition work to tasks involving variety and intricate movements, but this does not prevent them from experiencing boredom. This tendency towards lack of interest can be counteracted by introducing conditions and incentives for securing the workers' effective co-operation, but this is one of the difficult problems of personnel administration. For this class of work the incentive method of wage payment is particularly useful, and is often widely applied, but other incentives are also needed, and there is great value in improving the general amenities of the workplace.

Responsibility

Whenever possible, work should be arranged so that each individual has definite responsibility and an essential part in the undertaking, or alternatively specific responsibility may be given to small teams of workers. Thus, a target or standard may be set which workers are expected to reach, and if the standard is reasonable most workpeople will make the necessary effort because they wish to be considered competent and desire the approval of those for whom they work. Performance records which are immediately available to the worker as the work proceeds or at the end of each day have been found to arouse the worker's interest in his rate of production and provide a stimulus to increased output. The incentive of responsibility has hitherto been applied more widely to supervisory grades and clerical staff, but there are many opportunities for its application to manual workers. Instead of giving vague, ill-defined tasks, the work to be done should be exactly defined. Thus, an unskilled worker could be required to keep a specified number of skilled men supplied with raw materials, or a cleaner could be made responsible for a given floor space. One undertaking employing a large number of women, having tried various monetary incentives without adequate response, adopted the plan of fixing a task for the day, and each worker was free to leave as soon as the task was done. It was then found that almost all workers were able to do the task in something less than the full normal working day, and some of the quickest workers gained several hours. The inducement of additional leisure was more effective than increased earnings, and the firm gained the advantage of standard output.

Recognition for Competent Work

Workpeople mainly work for money, but most of them like to be known among their fellows for competence and reliability, and they appreciate recognition by the management. Special efforts should never be taken for granted. Qualities of leadership are shown if work of merit is acknowledged and encouragement given, by contrast with the foreman or manager who ignores good work but who frequently finds fault. This does not mean that poor work should be overlooked; management must be fair in both directions, and in the last resort a worker can be transferred to a lower grade or even lose his job, and there is no doubt that degrading and fear of unemployment are powerful negative incentives.

A spirit of emulation if applied with discretion can sometimes be used as an incentive and may counteract boredom. A competitive attitude is outstanding in games, and within limits can be usefully applied in industry whether between individuals or between groups or departments in the undertaking. The results may be recognized by some form of reward which need not be a monetary reward. Thus some firms compare the accident records of different departments, and arrange for a shield or flag to be displayed by the department which during the previous month or quarter had the best record. This introduces a valuable element of *esprit de corps*, keeps the problem continuously before the workers, and maintains their interest. Emulation and recognition were the essence of the Stakano-vite movement in Russia.

Prestige of the Job

Noteworthy "class" distinctions are established among work-people, and their status and precedence among themselves are in many ways as significant as in the aristocracy. Different jobs within an undertaking carry greater or less prestige, while in the outside community in which the worker lives, his trade and industry and the reputation of the firm for which he works affect his standing among his fellows. Workers wish to feel that they are contributing to a worth-while result and that the value of their work is appreciated by the community in which they live, otherwise they suffer from a sense of frustration and dissatisfaction. Hence they prefer some industries to others, and some firms within an industry have a better reputation than others. In any district, each firm, industry, and occupation has its rank or status, and those which stand high in public estimation are able to attract and retain the best workers. The amount of wage which a worker receives is largely, though not entirely, a measure of the prestige or social status of his job, and consequently demands for wage increases are often powerfully sup-ported not merely because they represent more purchasing power but are some index of industrial status. The amenities of the work-place, including good organization and health and welfare facilities, react favourably on production not only directly but also by en-hancing the worker's status, giving him a greater sense of well-being and of working in a satisfactory setting.

Although, however, within given types of work a difference of a few shillings a week has a significance out of proportion with the higher purchasing power which the wage yields, there are noteworthy differences in status between distinct categories of employment which are not measured by money income. Thus clerical work has long had a higher prestige than many manual occupations, and frequently people will prefer a clerical, "white collar job" with less pay because of its higher social status than that of manual work. Where this distinction is merely snobbish it should be broken down. Usually, however, there are real differences in amenities and conditions of work which make some jobs more attractive than others, even though their rates of remuneration are lower. They include prospects of promotion, shorter hours of work, regularity of hours, and work-ing in co-operation with others and not in isolation. Thus, there is a tendency among girls to classify domestic service near the bottom of the scale partly because of irregularity of hours and lack of the companionship with fellow-workers. For a variety of reasons they rate factory work higher, employment as shop assistants higher again, while office work is still more attractive in their estimation, and within this group a distinction is drawn between working in a factory office and working in the office of a bank or doing clerical work for professional people, such as doctors.

In addition to preference shown for certain industries, firms, and occupations, workpeople within an occupation do better work if their immediate associates are congenial, and there is an incentive if a worker is working among people who are temperamentally compatible. Many investigations have shown that where a group of people get along well together, the output of the group is increased, while a disturbing element causes lower production. Hence in personnel management the membership of groups working together should be studied and readjustments made to ensure the most harmonious relationships, and people should be arranged so that those alongside one another are not antagonistic or irritating but friendly.

Promotion

Full use should be made of promotion as a positive incentive, transfers can be used as a stimulus, while the possibility of demotion or discharge provide negative incentives. In many manual occupations the number of workpeople in British industry who reach the highest level of their industrial career and their highest rate of pay at the age of 20–25 years is far too great. There are, of course, opportunities for promotion as foremen or managers, but other chances of advancement should be increased. Thus, instead of relying, as many firms do, upon three homogeneous grades, skilled, semi-skilled, and unskilled, the practice should be much more widely adopted than at present of having several subdivisions within each grade. This would provide more opportunities for promotion, with suitable wage increases. In some countries this system is widely applied and enables promotion and wages to be more closely adjusted to the qualities of each worker. Though this method is more useful for time workers it can also be used for those paid on piece rates. It might be supposed that the incentive of promotion differs little from that of increased wages, but there is a clear distinction. To many workers, promotion gives satisfaction which is not measured by the increase in earnings, and it makes a special appeal to ambitious people.

Where promotion involves responsibility for organizing and directing the work of others, there is the special incentive of leadership. As has already been indicated when considering training for foremanship, promotion should be systematic on the basis of records of performance combined with other information on suitability for leadership. The problem of leadership does not usually arise where workers are advanced from one category to another while still remaining as operatives. Some workers do not want promotion to jobs involving leadership or responsibility. This has been experienced both in military service and in industry, and quite large numbers prefer to remain "in the ranks." This is because they wish to continue on a basis of equality of comradeship with their fellows, but others dislike taking responsibility or exercising authority. Responsibility applies to control of material conditions as well as leadership of men. For example, the tapping of a blast furnace requires considerable judgment on the part of the workman in charge. He has to decide the moment when the metal is ready, and a mistake on his part in judging the various factors may result in loss. Workmen who undertake this responsibility are paid much more than their assistants who, however, have good opportunities of learning the job. Nevertheless, some assistants are unwilling to assume full responsibility even though their pay would be greatly increased.

Recognition of length of service could be more widely given to manual workers in industry. Workers are paid mainly for the work they actually do, and the output of a worker who has been with a firm ten years may be no greater than that of a worker who has only been there a year or two, yet in other ways he may represent an asset to the firm which is not measured by his output. In occupations involving heavy physical strain, output falls as men become older and allowance must be made for this, but even in such cases one of the elements in determining remuneration should be seniority. This recognition of experience would be appreciated, and would act as an incentive.

Loyalty to the Firm

Although it may be thought unlikely that workpeople will show much loyalty to the firm for which they work, there are undoubtedly large numbers of workpeople who have a high regard for their undertaking if it is well managed and treats them fairly. This is an incentive of real value, is an element of goodwill to the firm and increases the satisfaction which the worker derives from his work. It repays cultivation, particularly by establishing relations of mutual confidence. These can be developed by joint consultations about working conditions and other questions of common interest, particularly constructive methods of improving the efficiency of the undertaking. Works councils are useful for these purposes, and their organization and methods are considered in Chapter 9.

Service of the Community

Better work is often done if a worker realizes that he is serving a larger purpose in addition to his own interests and those of his firm. Workpeople feel satisfaction if they believe that the work they do is useful to the community, and this shows itself in the quantity and quality of their work. In war-time the patriotic motive undoubtedly serves as an incentive to greater production. In peace-time it is more difficult to maintain this spirit, and many workpeople may feel that they are working only for themselves and to make profits for the firm, but it is often possible to give to workers a realization that their work is also of service to the community.

Possibly in certain industries, e.g. coal mining, where demands for nationalization are based in part upon solidarity among the workers, the national ownership and control of the industry give them greater satisfaction in working for the state than for private companies. However, in the regular routine of daily labour, no great difference in output is likely to result from such a change of ownership. Whether under private or State ownership, production is largely dependent upon efficiency of organization and equipment, and upon fair working conditions, though political and social factors may also influence attitudes towards work.

8

Profit-Sharing and Co-Partnership

WORKPEOPLE ALMOST inevitably share in the prosperity of the undertaking in which they are employed. If it is doing well, their earnings are likely to be higher, their employment more stable, and their working conditions and amenities better than if it is doing badly. In this sense, they share in its profits. Usually, however, profit-sharing is understood to be a distribution to workpeople, in addition to their wages, of a part of the amount which otherwise would have gone wholly to the owners of the capital. In a rudimentary form profits are shared if, at the end of a good year, an employer in a generous mood decides to pay to his workpeople from profits a cash bonus in addition to their regular wages, but without committing himself to such payments in the future. He might instead have increased wages, but it would be more difficult to reduce them than withhold a bonus if prosperity declined.

Such *ad hoc* payments at the whim of employers or boards of directors must, however, be distinguished from profit-sharing schemes. In these, an essential feature is that the method of sharing shall be known beforehand. Also, profit-sharing as a factor in industrial relations must cover all or a large part of the main body of workpeople in an undertaking, and not be limited to the payment of bonuses from profits to some or all of the managerial staff only. Both these points were included in the definition adopted as long ago as 1889 at an International Congress on Profit-Sharing held in Paris, which defined profit-sharing as payments made in accordance with a freely agreed scheme, of a share, determined in advance and not variable year by year at the discretion of the employer, of the profits of an undertaking to a substantial proportion of its ordinary employees. The question has sometimes been discussed that if employees share in profits they should also share in losses, and a few schemes have been devised for this purpose. In effect they bring about reductions in the remuneration of employees when a firm is experiencing trade depression or other difficulties. This is essentially what profit-sharing does in bad times, but with a limit at the level of customary or agreed wage rates, as only the additional pay derived from profits is reduced or ceases altogether when profits fall.

Loss sharing would result in different remuneration from firm to firm, with lower rates paid by the less efficient firms, and it would undermine standard rates of wages agreed on a local or industry-wide basis.

Wages at current or standard rates are a charge which industry must meet, and they differ from payments to equity capital, which are dependent on the residue after all other charges have been met, but the residue may be small or there may be losses, with the consequence that equity shareholders receive little or nothing in dividends and the capital value of their shares will fall. Such lack of success will also cause losses to workpeople by short time, unemployment, and wage reductions, but at least they can leave a firm which is losing money and seek employment elsewhere, but the capital invested in buildings and machinery is fixed, and its value could fall to what they would be worth as salvage.

TYPES OF SCHEME

As almost all schemes of profit-sharing and co-partnership have been adopted at individual firms, there is wide variety of method to suit the conditions of different companies and industries, and the outlook of employers responsible for their introduction.[1] Firms and industries vary in the proportion of labour costs to total costs of production, while some industries experience much wider fluctuations than others and need bigger reserves in times of prosperity to meet periods of poor demand. Because of such variations in conditions it would be impracticable to devise a uniform pattern.

Distinction must be drawn between three main classes of scheme: profit-sharing alone, profit-sharing combined with some kind of co-partnership through ownership by workpeople of shares in the company, and share-holding without any element of co-partnership.

Profit-sharing schemes usually provide that each year after all working expenses have been paid, adequate provision made for depreciation and reserves, interest paid on debenture and preference stock, and a specified rate of dividend declared on ordinary shares, the participating employees shall have a defined share in the surplus profit.[2] The specified rates of dividend on ordinary shares which

[1] In a *Report on Profit-Sharing and Labour Copartnership in the United Kingdom*, published in 1920, the Ministry of Labour classified schemes into fourteen main types ranging from simple profit-sharing to full co-partnership.

[2] In some schemes the dividends from subsidiary companies are excluded when reckoning net profits. In order to prevent profits being reduced by big salaries, one scheme provides that the total remuneration of any employee, including directors, shall not be greater than five times the wage of the lowest-paid adult male full-time manual worker.

must be paid before profit is available for profit-sharing varies in different schemes, often being 5 or 6 per cent, but sometimes the rate is as high as 10 per cent, and in some schemes the rate is cumulative.[1] The share of surplus profit paid to participating employees may be a fixed proportion of surplus profits, or it may be an amount not exceeding a specified sum, say £50,000. Thus some schemes provide that surplus profits shall be divided equally between employees and shareholders, the half for the employees being distributed among them in proportion to their wages, and the half for the shareholders being distributed as additional dividends. In one company an amount equal to the dividend on ordinary shares is paid as a dividend on annual total wages.

A variation is for the profit available for distribution (after paying, say, 5 per cent on ordinary shares) to be divided at a uniform percentage rate on capital and on the year's total of wages and salaries, so that for every 1 per cent more paid on capital, a dividend of 1 per cent is paid to labour (on wages and salaries). Another arrangement is for half the surplus profits to go to the workpeople, one-tenth to the management, and two-fifths to capital; or again, one-third to capital, one-sixth to active partners, one-sixth to the travellers and the general manager, and one-third to other employees, in proportion to wages and salaries. One company, with capital costs forming a big part of total costs, first pays 6 per cent on ordinary shares, and then only 10 per cent of the residue is distributed to the employees. Some companies after paying a fixed dividend on ordinary shares pay a specified amount, say £100,000, to the employees. One firm pays the whole of the residue to them. A variant is for, say, £17,000 to be distributed to employees for every 1 per cent that ordinary dividends exceed 12 per cent. A special feature was adopted by a number of British gas companies before the industry was nationalized, three-quarters of surplus profits being used to reduce the price of gas to consumers, one-eighth as bonus for employees, and one-eighth as additional dividend for ordinary shareholders.

For an employee to be entitled to share in surplus profits a qualifying period of employment is generally fixed, this being frequently twelve months, but in some schemes it is only three months, and in others several years. Employees who have been with a firm for only a few weeks or months have not helped it much to earn profits. Also a qualifying period may have some effect in reducing

---

[1] In some schemes a specified rate (e.g. 5 or 6 per cent) must be paid on the estimated capital employed in the business before funds are available for profit-sharing, the capital including undivided profits.

labour turnover. Length of service is recognized in many firms by a bigger share of profits. Some schemes give big additions for length of service, and in one scheme its importance is so great that an employee with ten years' service receives five times the share of an employee with one year's service; usually, however, the increase is much less, some schemes providing that employees with three or five years' service shall receive twice as much as those who have been with the firm only one year, and in one firm an addition of only one-quarter of a share is paid to employees with more than fifteen years' service. In another scheme one and a half times the basic rate is paid to employees who have completed ten years' service with the firm, and a double rate after twenty years' service.

Continuity of service is generally required but often interruption because of sickness up to two or three months does not disqualify, while in some schemes temporary suspensions up to similar periods are allowed without losing right to participate. Employees who leave voluntarily or are dismissed usually lose their right to a share of the profits, and any amounts for the part of the year they had worked are generally credited to a provident, sickness, or super-annuation fund for the benefit of all the employees. Lateness is penalized in some schemes, the share being reduced by, say, 20 per cent if twenty times late during the year, 30 per cent if thirty times late, and loss of the whole share if fifty times late. In one scheme one-tenth of the share of any employee is deducted for each time he is late over forty times in the year.

In some schemes participation is limited to adults while in others it extends from the directors and managers to errand boys, with lower rates for juveniles than adults. Directors, senior grades of managers, and also travellers and agents are excluded in some schemes. In others the shares to the salaried staff are paid at a higher rate than that for workpeople; if, for example, workpeople receive a bonus of 6 per cent on wages, the rate on salaries may be 8 per cent. This practice is based, no doubt, on the belief that the salaried staff have a bigger influence than manual workers on the amount of profit, and this reason applies also to schemes in which foremen's shares are at a higher (e.g. double) rate than that applied to manual workers.

The usual method of dividing up the amount available is to base it on each employee's wages or salary, so that those receiving higher pay get a proportionately higher share than those with less pay.[1]

1 In some schemes employees in the lowest paid grade are allotted one unit, and additional units are allotted to higher paid employees for, say, each ten shillings more they receive in wages. The profits available are then distributed in proportion to the number of units for each employee.

This in itself ensures that people will share in profits roughly in relation to their value to the firm, with unskilled workers receiving less than skilled, and so on. The proportions based on wages and salaries are, however, modified in many schemes, as indicated above, by supplements for length of service, grade or status, and by deductions for bad time-keeping. If the profit shares are based solely on the remuneration of employees, the first stage in the calculation is to relate the profits available for division, say £60,000, to the total of wages and salaries paid during the year to all employees, say £1,000,000, in order to find the percentage (i.e. 6 per cent for the figures given). Then each participating employee would receive that percentage of his total remuneration during the year. Allowance can readily be for length of service and other factors where these are features of the scheme.

Some schemes exclude piece work and overtime earnings from the calculations, no doubt, because many salaried employees have no opportunities of increasing their remuneration by such work; also many manual workers are on time work, and other manual workers do not have equal opportunities of overtime. The shares for piece workers are calculated on the basis of the wages they would have received if they had been on time work. Other schemes, however, include overtime and incentive earnings. A few schemes apply a policy of fixing a maximum salary and wage on which the bonus percentage is calculated, e.g. £750 for salaried staff and £400 for manual workers.

Share Ownership

Employees of a company are in the same position as other people in buying its shares on the Stock Exchange, but some companies have introduced schemes with special shares which can only be held by employees. These schemes vary greatly, though all of them are methods of saving, and are also intended, like profit-sharing, to increase the interest of employees in the success of the undertaking. Where profit-sharing and share ownership are linked together, the whole or part of the amount due to an employee may be invested in the special shares. Acquisition of shares may be voluntary or compulsory. In some schemes the decision is left to the employee how much he will take in cash and how much he will invest, but in other schemes the employee is required to invest the whole or a specified proportion, often one-half, of his share of profits.

In some companies, shares can be bought by instalments paid by deductions from wages or they may be bought out of personal savings. Usually the shares are sold to employees at par, this practice having advantages, disadvantages, and restrictions which are indicated later. Another inducement is to pay an increased rate of dividend, in some schemes a double rate, to employees who own shares equal to a year's wages or half a year's wages. Inducements may be given for employees to buy shares by offering them at less than market price. An alternative to the purchase of shares is for the whole or part of each employee's share in profits to be put into a savings account and a fixed rate of interest paid on the credits accumulated.

Schemes which enable employees to build up substantial amounts in a savings fund or in shares are more effective than those in which only cash bonuses are paid.[1] Thrift is encouraged and many workers with twenty or thirty years' service accumulate several hundred pounds, which increases their interest in the business and tends to reduce labour turnover. It is sometimes argued that employees should not "put all their eggs in one basket," and that if their savings are accumulated in the company where they work they may in bad times lose both their savings and their jobs. This is one of the reasons why some schemes provide safeguards to maintain the value of employees' shares. Because of their smaller risk of capital loss, businesses which are stable are more suitable for share-holding by employees than businesses which are risky or experience wide fluctuations.

The rate of dividend paid on special shares is usually the same as that on ordinary shares, and is therefore variable. In some companies, however, special preference shares are issued, with a specified rate of interest (e.g. 6 or 8 per cent); they may be cumulative or non-cumulative, and may or may not participate and receive additional interest if dividends beyond a given rate are paid to ordinary shareholders. Where a company has profit-sharing and share ownership, the employees receive their share in the profits and also interest or dividends on the shares they hold. Some schemes provide for higher dividends to be paid on employee shares than on ordinary shares.

The total number of special shares which may be issued for employees is fixed in some companies, for example, 100,000 preference or ordinary shares of £1 each. In some schemes a fixed number of notional shares or certificates of no par value and unsaleable is issued and the dividends on these shares are distributed to the employees, but this is essentially a method of determining the amount of profits to be distributed rather than a system of share-holding by employees.

---

[1] Workpeople are enabled by these schemes to invest in industry as an alternative to their more usual practice in Britain of putting their savings into the Post Office Savings Bank, Government Savings Certificates, and building, insurance, and co-operative societies.

Some schemes limit the number of shares that any employee may hold. Thus, in one scheme the maximum holding by men is 200 and by women 100 shares, and in another the maximum holding is 250 shares. Alternatively, the maximum holding of an employee may be related to his annual wages, e.g. the holding not to exceed double or four times this amount. Allocation is arranged in some companies so as to prevent a small number of the better-paid employees from holding a large proportion of the shares. In some companies the special shares may not be held by the better-paid employees, holdings being restricted, for example, to those whose pay is not more than £750 a year. In a few companies, "good conduct" is a condition for the allotment of shares to enable employees to become co-partners, recommendations being made by their foremen or the heads of their departments.

Where special shares are held by employees, restrictions are imposed on the holders. Usually the shares must be relinquished to the company on death or on leaving the company's service whether by resignation or dismissal. Some schemes allow holders to retain their shares when they retire.[1] In general the shares being for the benefit of employees, they must be returned to the company as soon as the holder ceases to be employed by it, except that some schemes treat the shares as savings for old age. Usually when shares are sold back to the company or to trustees appointed under the scheme the price paid is the par value, but in some schemes the market value is paid. The first method has the advantage of protecting these savings of workpeople against loss, but it weakens the value of the scheme as an education in the risks run by investors of capital. Funds are often put in reserve as a guarantee of the par value of the shares and are administered by trustees. When shares are thus protected against capital loss they represent a stake in the business as measured by dividends but not by changes in the capital value of the shares.

Employees who hold special shares are generally precluded from selling their shares whenever they may wish, as ordinary shareholders are free to do. The latter can therefore exercise their own judgment when to sell so as to make a profit or avoid loss, but as employees holding special shares are not able to do this they are given the safeguard of par value. Thus, some rules provide that employees shall not transfer or sell shares, or pledge them as security for loans.

[1] One scheme provides that an employee who is over fifty years of age when he leaves the company may retain the shares for life and leave them to his widow or to a descendant employed by the company. If he leaves before he is fifty years of age or wishes to sell the shares at any time he must offer them to the directors at par.

Others allow an employee to sell some of his shares if the value of his holding is more than the amount of his year's wages, but then only the surplus beyond that amount. Some schemes give greater freedom, for example by the company or the trustees undertaking to buy shares or authorizing holders to sell them to other qualified employees. In some companies, the directors can require employees to sell back their shares, and this could be used to terminate a scheme. In the event of a company itself being wound up, some schemes provide that employees' shares shall rank equally with ordinary shares in the distribution of the assets, but in others they participate in the assets only up to the par value of the shares.

Co-partnership with employees implies that they have some share in the management of the business. This may range from consultation in works councils, and participation in partnership committees, to attending and voting at general meetings of the company, and electing employee representatives to the board of directors, though this last method is exceptional. Many companies supply information regularly to their employees about the financial position of the company, its problems, policy, and prospects. Addresses on these matters are given periodically by the managing director, and summaries published in the works' magazine. Representatives of the employees take part in many firms in the management of welfare schemes and social activities. In these various ways the status of employees is raised and their understanding, interest, and influence in the business in which they work is increased.

Some schemes exclude holders of employee shares from any direct part in the management of the company, provision being made that they have no voting rights or rights to attend meetings of the company. In some companies, even where as a result of the operation of profit-sharing and employee share ownership over many years the employees own more than half the capital, the employees are not given such rights. In other schemes employees who own shares have the same rights as other shareholders to attend and vote at general meetings, though these rights are sometimes limited to those who hold at least fifty or a hundred £1 shares. A few schemes go farther and provide that employee shareholders shall be represented on the board of directors, though usually their representatives are in a minority and therefore control over policy does not get into the hands of the employees.[1] Only those employees who have consider-

---

[1] Before nationalization of the gas industry in Britain, many gas companies had profit-sharing and co-partnership schemes which provided that employee shareholders would elect three representatives on the board of directors, but that there would be at least five other directors, thus leaving in a minority the directors representing the employee shareholders.

able service with the company, for example ten or twelve years, and who hold a specified minimum number of shares, can be nominated for election as directors.

Various ways are adopted for the administration of profit-sharing and co-partnership schemes. Some are controlled by the directors of the company, and others by a joint committee half of whom are nominated by the directors, and the other half elected by the employees from among employees. Candidates for election must usually have had not less than a specified period of service with the company, often five years, and in co-partnership schemes must hold at least, say, 25 shares. In some companies, the number of votes by each employee varies with the number of shares he holds, e.g. one vote for every 10 shares up to 100, an additional vote for every 25 shares from 100 to 300, and one more for every 50 after 300. Some joint committees merely decide what amount of the available funds shall be distributed and how much shall be carried forward for equalizing dividends over several years. Often provision is made that a company can terminate its profit-sharing or co-partnership scheme at any time.

DEVELOPMENT

An early successful scheme of profit-sharing was started in 1842 by E. J. Leclaire, the head of a house-painting business in Paris. This initiative was followed by other employers in France, and, attracting attention abroad, the system gradually spread, especially in Britain, the British Dominions, Switzerland, Germany, Belgium, Holland, and the United States. The rate of growth was slow, and in no country has the system been applied in more than a small part of industry. In Britain, less than 2 per cent of all workpeople are employed in firms with schemes of profit-sharing and co-partnership, and the proportion is even less in the United States.

According to the most recent information more than 400 British firms had profit-sharing or co-partnership schemes about the time of the Second World War. These firms employed altogether some 430,000 workpeople, of whom about 264,000 or rather more than three in five participated, the remainder not having acquired shares or not having satisfied age or length of service conditions. At that time an average bonus of about £12 10s. 0d. a year was paid, which was then equal to nearly 6½ per cent of average annual wages or equivalent to the pay for more than 3½ weeks' work. Unless a scheme can give an average yield equal to at least two weeks' work the benefits are too slight to sustain interest. Some schemes have been in operation for several decades, have survived the storms of depression, and have been remarkably successful. Several firms have each paid out money totalling £400,000 to £700,000 during periods of one to two decades, representing additions of 5 to 6 per cent to wages each year. For all schemes surviving in 1937 the average rate of bonus for the years 1910–1937 was 5·3 per cent of wages. One of the oldest British schemes is that of the textile firm of J., J. T., and J. Taylor, Ltd., of Batley, the employees of which own more than three-quarters of the firm's capital and in their dual capacity as shareholders and profit-sharers they receive the greater part of its profits. Schemes have been introduced by firms in a wide range of industries. The most extensive application was by the gas companies until the industry was nationalized in 1948. At that time about fifty-eight gas undertakings had schemes and paid annually about £400,000 in bonuses equal to about 6 per cent on wages to upwards of 52,000 employees, but the schemes were terminated under nationalization, though payment of compensation was arranged for workpeople who would otherwise have been worse off.

Profit-sharing is applied not only by ordinary companies but also by a number of workers' productive co-operative societies. Productive enterprise by workpeople has been much less successful than the co-operative movement in wholesale trade and consumers' societies in retail trade. In Britain, according to the most recent information, some forty to fifty workers' productive societies have profit-sharing schemes. They are mainly in boot and shoe manufacture and the clothing industry, where capital equipment costs are not high and wage costs form a large part of cost of production. About 40,000 workpeople benefit, and the average amount distributed was equal to an addition of about 4 to 5 per cent of wages.

The starting and abandonment of schemes are affected by the state of trade. Schemes are usually started in periods of business prosperity, while during trade depressions many schemes are ended because of reduced profits or of losses. Some schemes have also been started in times of industrial unrest in the hope that they would contribute towards better relations. Stable trades and mature businesses have proved more suitable than risky ones or those which experience wide fluctuations or are growing rapidly.

Proposals are sometimes made for legislation on profit-sharing and co-partnership, but with little support. It would be difficult because of the wide variation in conditions from firm to firm and industry to industry, to do more than outline a few basic principles. This has been done in New Zealand and New South Wales by permissive legislation which empowers companies to issue shares to employees and distribute all profits to them after capital has received interest and a "risk-rate" which varies from industry to industry. No obligation is imposed on employers to introduce co-partnership, and few firms have applied the legislation. In Venezuela, profit-sharing is compulsory, and the law provides that specified proportions of profits shall be shared with employees up to a maximum equal to two months' wages in large firms and one month in small firms. The proportion ranges from 12·45 per cent of the profits of large firms to 2·05 per cent in small firms.

Well-devised schemes of profit-sharing and co-partnership, if extensively applied, would seem, theoretically, to provide a remedy for two of the main causes of industrial disputes, namely, clash of interests over division of the products of industry, and the workers' status in industry. Yet in practice they have been introduced in only a small part of industry, and many schemes have been abandoned after a few years.

Although some existing schemes have continued successfully for periods of thirty to fifty years or even more, the "death rate" has been high especially in periods of depression. Many schemes have been terminated after five to ten years. In Britain not far short of half the schemes in existence in 1912 or started after that date had ceased to exist twenty-five years later, and the death rate was even higher in the United States. Some schemes have been abandoned because of dissatisfaction of employers with results, apathy of workpeople, especially when profits were small or there were losses, the winding up or amalgamation of firms, or because businesses came under the control of new management unfavourable to profit-sharing. As a result of experience gained, there is a tendency for more new schemes to survive. In some firms shareholding has been replaced by pension schemes, and in others an increase in wages has been substituted for the sharing of profits. Indeed, if the share in profits is fairly stable over a period of years, the workpeople tend to count upon it as a regular part of their remuneration, and sometimes demand that profit-sharing shall be replaced by an increase in wages.

TRADE UNION ATTITUDES

For many years the trade union movement was hostile to profit-sharing and co-partnership partly because some employers introduced schemes as weapons in the fight against trade unionism, arguing that their workpeople would benefit more from these schemes than from trade union action to raise wages. Some of these employers, in addition to influencing their workers and putting obstacles to hinder them from joining the unions, showed their attitude by ending profit-sharing schemes if their workers went on strike in support of higher wages and other trade union demands. Other employers had no intention of using profit-sharing as a weapon to defeat trade unionism, but even so the unions opposed profit-sharing because they believed it would increase the loyalty of workers to the firm, make them more satisfied with their conditions, and weaken support for trade unionism. They also suspected that schemes were designed to keep wages down. The unions have preferred to work for standard rates of wages throughout a craft or industry, whereas with profit-sharing the workers' incomes would vary from firm to firm according to the profits which each made. With standard rates of wages paid by all firms in an industry, the most efficient firms may be able to make high profits, but although the unions wish to secure as much as possible of the profits of prosperous firms for the benefit of their members, they have preferred to demand high taxation instead of supporting profit-sharing schemes which would result in different remuneration for their members in different undertakings. Also, profit-sharing and co-partnership schemes have been introduced by employers in individual firms, the workers receive benefits which the unions have not won for them, and the unions have not found a satisfactory way of bringing these schemes within the framework of collective bargaining.

Many workpeople, including individual trade unionists, appreciate the monetary and other benefits they derive from the profit-sharing and co-partnership schemes applied in their own firms. They receive wage rates at the same levels as workers in other firms, and are entitled also to a share in the profits. In recent years the hostility of the unions has diminished, largely because of growing confidence as their strength increased and they won recognition by employers, and because employers generally ceased to use profit-sharing as a weapon against the unions. Employers now often consult representatives of the unions before starting a scheme, and unions though still not favourable to profit-sharing and co-partnership, do not obstruct schemes if, judging each on its merits, they are satisfied that the employer is acting in good faith and without ulterior motives. They will acquiesce without giving positive support.

VALUE AS AN INCENTIVE

As a direct incentive to production, profit-sharing, and co-partnership are much less effective than piece rates and other systems of payment by results applied to individual workers or small teams who receive their reward within a week or two after the effort was made. Shares in profits are much less closely related to the effort of each worker, being paid at uniform rates to all or most of the workers in the undertaking, many of whom may have made no effort to increase the firm's profits. Also the payments are too remote and often too infrequent, being made usually once a year after the annual meeting which may be several months after the end of the financial year, long after the work which contributed to the profits was done. They therefore have little effect upon the day-to-day output of individual workpeople. If the amount available for distribution is adequate, some firms pay the shares in monthly or quarterly instalments, rather like interim dividends, as a more frequent reminder of the value of the scheme.

Another weakness as an incentive is due to the fact that the profits earned by a business often result largely from factors not influenced by the rank and file workpeople. If profits depend largely on such factors the sharing of profits can have little value as an incentive. If workpeople did better work because of a profit-sharing scheme, their expectations could be disappointed because the industry to which they belong was hit by depression, or because a change in fashion or greater severity of competition caused a fall in demand for the company's products. For such causes of failure to realize expectations, neither the management nor the workpeople may be in any way responsible. Mistakes by management may, however, cause profits to fall. They might, for example, misjudge market conditions and buy large stocks of raw materials in the belief that their prices would rise, whereas in fact they may fall heavily and involve the company in big losses. In brief, there is no close relationship between the efforts of the workpeople and the profits of the undertaking. A temporary stimulus may result when a scheme is introduced in a period of good profits, but the novelty soon wears off and hopes of a considerable permanent increase in effort by the workers are often disappointed.

The main value of profit-sharing and co-partnership is indirect, by promoting better industrial relations, and there is some evidence that firms with schemes have less labour trouble. To share in the prosperity of the undertaking gives to the workpeople a greater sense of justice, a better status, and often leads to a more co-operative attitude towards the management. It strengthens the common interests of capital and labour. Workpeople also tend to become more interested in and to have a better understanding of the economic problems of the undertaking. Profit-sharing employers have been willing to sacrifice part of profits in the hope of securing such intangible benefits as better co-operation, less suspicion of management, and less resistance to changes which will increase efficiency.

Formal schemes of profit-sharing and co-partnership are not the only ways of enabling employees to benefit from the prosperity of the undertaking in which they work, and the adoption of alternatives is, no doubt, one of the reasons why such formal schemes have not been more widely applied. Many employers prefer other methods of sharing prosperity with their workpeople by spending substantial amounts on welfare and factory amenities, including recreation and social clubs, or on pension funds. Some pay wages at higher rates than those required by collective agreements, while others consider that workpeople share in good times by more stable employment, and opportunities for increased earnings. In firms where profit-sharing and co-partnership have been most successful they are only one feature of a broadly based programme for improving industrial relations, each part of which supports the others in securing good-will and mutual understanding.

9

Joint Consultation at the Workplace

THE BASIC purpose of all sound policies and action throughout the whole field of industrial relations is to secure maximum co-operation between management and workpeople in production at the workplace. This requires the establishment of standards of wages, hours, and working conditions which are fair not only between different grades of workpeople, but between the workpeople as a whole and the needs of capital for organizing the business, covering its risks, and for maintaining the efficiency of its plant. Such conditions depend in part on economic and social forces outside the individual workplaces, and need collective agreements and State intervention to prevent sweating and unfair competition in labour standards between different firms. But although action is necessary by trade unions, employers' organizations and the State in these wider aspects of industrial relations, and such action attracts much public attention, the unobtrusive day-to-day relations at the workplace are the alpha and omega of the problem. There the wider agreements and regulations have their detailed interpretation and application, there a spirit of harmony and mutual confidence or of suspicion and distrust is generated, and there the workers are disposed to work well if satisfied with their conditions and their relations with the management, or they deliberately or subconsciously put a brake on their output because of discontent and sense of frustration.

The initiative for successful joint consultation rests primarily on the management. Unless management is convinced of its value no scheme can succeed, and this conviction must permeate the whole of management from top to bottom. It is not enough for the managing director to be keen if there is scepticism at lower levels. In particular, foremen must be favourable, as they are closest to the operatives, to whom indeed they *are* the management for practical purposes of detailed day-to-day instructions. Yet in some joint councils foremen and other junior supervisors have been criticized without opportunity to reply, and have even been "by-passed" to such an extent that the first they hear of some information or decision affecting their department is from one of their own workers who has a seat on the council.[1] Success also depends on the goodwill and co-operation of the workpeople, and they should, through their recognized spokesmen, take part in devising the constitution, purposes, and methods of joint relations. Often the main difficulty in securing their support is to overcome suspicion based on harsh and unfair treatment in the past. The evil that men do lives after them, and a long time may be necessary in the operation of joint consultation before mutual confidence is secured. During this period, management may suffer many disappointments and must show much patience in order to establish co-operative relations. The development of co-operative attitudes by all concerned is more important than the machinery and methods adopted for bringing management and workpeople together.

Consultation in some form takes place in all undertakings. Even in an autocratically managed firm the directors must know the probable reactions of the workers to changes they propose to make, and "snoopers" have sometimes been used to find out and report on what the workers' attitudes are likely to be. Apart from such extreme examples, consultation ranges from informal talks with the individual workers during the course of the day's work, through systems by which representatives of the workers, sometimes shop stewards, can put their point of view before the management from time to time, to regular formal representative meetings of works councils and joint production committees. With growth in the size of undertakings it has become increasingly necessary to supplement the direct individual and informal relations by systematic representative consultation. The practical impossibility in large undertakings of maintaining adequate direct personal contact between the higher management and the main body of the workpeople has created the need for organized channels of communication. In regular formal meetings the representatives of management and workpeople get to know one another, learn to appreciate one another's points of view, and evolve recognized procedures which make easier the handling of difficult issues.

In this chapter, the focus of attention is on these representative meetings, which, in the writer's opinion, are essential for securing the best relations in large and medium sized firms, but such formal consultations must be combined with continuous informal contacts throughout the undertaking. In small works, employing less than 200 to 250 workpeople, the employer can usually maintain direct

[1] Some schemes provide that questions shall not be brought before a joint consultative body unless it has been discussed with the foreman or departmental manager concerned.

informal contact, individually and collectively, with all his employees, and in such circumstances regular representative meetings are unnecessary. Individual problems can be settled directly, while questions affecting all the workpeople can readily be discussed informally and the workpeoples' views be put before the management by one or two recognized spokesmen acting on their behalf.

In some countries works councils have been established by law. Thus, shortly after the First World War, laws were passed in several European countries requiring works councils to be set up in all undertakings employing, in Germany and Austria 20 or more work-people, in Czechoslovakia 30 or more, and in Norway 50 or more, provided this was requested by at least a quarter of the workpeople. In Germany, for example, these councils were not joint bodies but consisted only of workers' representatives, numbering 3 in small works to 30 or more in large works, who discussed among themselves questions affecting their employment and conditions of work which they wished to raise with the management. The councils had no right to interfere with the management of the works, but the employer was required to meet the council at regular intervals and to consider with them their grievances, proposals, and suggestions.

In other countries, including Britain, joint consultation at the workplace has been a voluntary development in private industry, though in Britain the Ministry of Labour has fostered interest in and has advised firms on methods and problems.[1] Also in more than a dozen British industries, the national organizations of employers and trade unions have agreed to recommend firms to establish joint consultative bodies along the lines of an approved model constitution. A model based on the experience of many firms can be a useful guide in setting up a new scheme, but must be adapted to the special conditions of each undertaking. In British nationalized industries legislation requires the adoption of systems of joint consultation at the workplace as well as regionally and nationally. Compulsory joint consultation by legislation is of doubtful value in private industry. Legal authority cannot create in management and workpeople that genuine desire for joint consultation which is necessary for success, and merely to comply perfunctorily with legal requirements would do more harm than good. It should not be overlooked, however, that some undertakings, which would not have introduced a scheme voluntarily or would have allowed a voluntary

[1] With the support of the National Joint Advisory Council, the Ministry in recent years has held Regional and National Conferences on joint consultation and related questions, and its personnel management advisers are available to assist firms in devising suitable systems and in dealing with practical issues.

scheme to lapse because of disappointments with results in the early stages, may make a success of a compulsory scheme which could not be abandoned in the initial period of difficulties, misunderstanding and frustrations, and having survived its "growing pains" may evolve into a useful instrument of industrial relations.

PURPOSES AND SUBJECTS OF CONSULTATION

Joint committees provide opportunities for management to explain the policy of the company, including changes in machinery, organization, processes, and products. These changes should not be announced as decisions already taken, but submitted as projects which can be adjusted in the light of suggestions made by representatives of the workpeople. Such a procedure enables workshop changes to be made more smoothly and harmoniously, as they do not come upon the workpeople suddenly without warning, but have been discussed beforehand with them. Information should be given about the prospects of the firm, market conditions for its products and their effects on the processes of production and on employment. Such information made available to the workers' representatives and also to the main body of the workpeople will be likely to increase their interest in their work because they see the significance of their own part in a complex co-operative enterprise.

Joint consultation is, however, a "two way" relationship. Workers' representatives can interpret the attitudes and ideas of the workers to management as well as provide a channel of communication from management to workers. Workers increasingly claim the right to influence their working conditions not only by collective agreements but more intimately at their workplaces. In many countries their standard of education is much higher to-day than at the beginning of the present century, their political and social status has been raised, and they seek improvements in their industrial status. Systematic joint consultation is one of the means to this end.

The range of subjects which may be covered by joint consultation is wide; they include positive measures for increasing production directly, and welfare arrangements which increase production indirectly and ensure greater satisfaction among workpeople with their conditions of employment. Favourable effects on production are also obtained by removal of grievances. Wages, hours of work, and other subjects covered by collective agreements are excluded, except for the detailed application of their provisions within the undertaking where these are not arranged directly between the employer and the local representative of the trade unions.

123

More specifically the subjects include the formulation and revision of works rules, removal of grievances, improvement of welfare, health and safety, workshop application of collective agreements, establishment of schemes for training and promotion, time-keeping and absenteeism, regulation of dismissals in times of redundancy, short-time and overtime arrangements, increased output, and elimination of waste. These objects will be considered in turn.

A recognized procedure for removal of grievances is necessary in every works. Otherwise discontent smoulders and can easily be fanned into a flame of conflict. Many grievances, whether real or imaginary, are trivial and should be dealt with immediately on the workshop floor by direct discussion between the workers and their foreman. Too often they are magnified beyond their merits and are submitted to formal discussion either in the works council or through trade union intervention. Some individual workpeople are unable to state their grievance effectively and prefer to rely on the shop steward or other spokesman in the workshop, but it should be the purpose of such spokesmen to settle simple grievances by the easiest and quickest method available, thereby keeping more elaborate procedures free for the discussion of problems involving questions of principle. They should also refuse to take up complaints which have no foundation; they should do this in their own interests, as their influence with management and with fair-minded workers will be undermined if they raise imaginary or trivial grievances which can easily be shown to be groundless or settled on the spot.

Grievances not settled at the lowest level will go forward successively to higher levels. This should be by a recognized procedure, and usually grievances should not be taken over the heads of a foreman or supervisor directly concerned until he has had an opportunity of trying to reach a settlement. To neglect this is likely to increase friction. In the last resort the managing director or his representative, often the personnel manager, should be accessible for the consideration of serious grievances. Alternatively, if the grievance raised a question of principle, it may be considered by the works council for settlement or for making an advisory recommendation to the higher management.

Where the penalty of dismissal is imposed, some works councils participate in defining the general conditions or principles to be applied, but do not deal with individuals, this usually, though not always, being a sole responsibility of management. In a few works, a semi-judicial procedure is adopted for dealing with individual grievances and discipline, including dismissals, tribunals consisting of a representative of management, a representative of the workpeople, and an impartial chairman being given final authority, and any worker is free to bring a personal grievance before the tribunal. Where dismissals are necessary not for purposes of discipline but because of trade depression, works councils are often consulted about the methods to be adopted for selecting those who will lose their jobs, and in particular whether age, length of service, and family responsibilities will be considered.

Welfare and amenities and the promotion of health and safety are usually prominent in works council agendas, though in many firms separate accident prevention and safety-first committees are set up to concentrate on this subject alone, especially in undertakings where the risk of accidents is considerable. Application within the works of the terms of collective agreements differs from other forms of joint consultation, as such terms involve the direct responsibility of the trade unions and are wider than the domestic affairs of a single firm. Usually, therefore, any questions of interpretation which arise within a works are discussed between the management and representatives of the trade union, whether the shop steward or officials of the union outside the works. Piece rates of payment, bonus systems, time studies, and job evaluation, which apply the general provisions of agreements to the special conditions of the works are, however, often discussed in works councils or joint production committees.

Many factory rules are purely domestic arrangements which are independent of the terms of collective agreements, and such rules are very suitable for consideration by works councils. In making or altering these rules, the views of the workers should be taken into consideration. Such rules are essential for good organization, being of value both to management and workpeople in defining the duties and responsibilities of each. While flexibility in some things is an advantage, in others the clearer the rules the better. This is especially true in big undertakings employing large numbers of workpeople, and discipline will be facilitated if representatives of the workpeople have shared in drafting the rules.

Training and promotion also vitally affect the workpeople, and many works councils discuss these subjects. Usually the councils take part only in formulating principles and methods to be adopted for promoting or up-grading of workers by systematic merit rating or by other ways, but some councils or committees of the councils are consulted about the individual workpeople under consideration for promotion, including promotion as foremen. Criteria for merit rating, including the efficiency of a worker in his job, all-round ability, co-operativeness, initiative, and leadership, are assessed mainly by a worker's own supervisors.

Welfare, safety, and the removal of grievances at the workplace are all incidental and complementary to production (including trade and transport), which is the only reason why capital, management, and labour are brought together. Each needs the others, and all are engaged in a common co-operative effort, though this is often forgotten in the clash of sectional interests over the distribution of what is produced. The complexities of modern industrial and economic life also tend to conceal the common interest in efficient production; for example, the spectre of unemployment has convinced many operatives that there is a limited amount of work to be done, a sort of "work fund," and that if they increase production now, they will soon work themselves out of a job. This is a pernicious myth, far more employment being lost by slow and inefficient production than is gained by a policy of "spreading the work." A policy of obstruction and of going slow brings its own Nemesis in unemployment and low standards of living because of the inevitable impact of competition including international competition from those who are more productive. Yet workers are not easily convinced, for the effects of these forces are more concealed, remote, and less easily recognized than the direct loss of employment often experienced when a job is finished, for example, by builders when a contract ends or by dockers when a ship is unloaded. A big contribution can be made to productive efficiency if in each undertaking and in the wider organization of the economic system, every effort is made to prevent workpeople from losing their jobs because of increased output, whether from greater effort by the workers or by more efficient machinery and organization. Only in this way can the myth be destroyed.

Joint consultation for increased production and reduction of waste can be one of the activities of a works council, but many undertakings prefer to set up a separate body, often known as a joint production committee. This has the advantage of focusing attention on production, for which the qualities needed, especially by representatives of workpeople are different from those suitable for dealing with grievances and welfare. Also, if a works council has been established for several years it may have developed attitudes and methods unsuitable for dealing constructively with production problems, and better results are likely to be obtained by forming a new committee.

The contribution which joint consultation can make to increased production depends not only on the attitudes of management and workpeople, but on the type of work and of workpeople. Thus, where the work is mainly unskilled and the processes are largely controlled and only fully understood by highly trained technicians, few constructive suggestions are likely to be made by workers' representatives, and the setting up of a joint production committee may be undesirable. On the other hand, if highly skilled workers are numerous, many valuable ideas may come from them, and they may also propose useful changes in schemes prepared by management, and their interest and goodwill may be secured if schemes are discussed jointly before introduction in the works. Many representatives of management express disappointment at the few practical suggestions made by the workpeople's representatives for increasing output, but even then there are often important intangible benefits in improvement of understanding and in a more favourable attitude to changes in productive organization which result from joint consultation.

Suggestions for improving productive efficiency should be encouraged from all workpeople and not merely from those who serve as representatives in joint consultation. In the past the attitude of management to workpeople who made suggestions was often discouraging, to say the least, and the workpeople were made to feel that this was none of their business. They therefore kept their ideas to themselves, and constructive co-operation was suppressed. Yet in the interests of better relations and of productive efficiency, their suggestions should not only be welcomed but positively stimulated and fostered. Many valuable devices which would not occur to management can be thought out by the more intelligent among the main body of operatives, especially in the skilled grades, during their day-to-day work at the bench, and the developing of these ideas gives satisfaction to the men themselves and benefit to the firm.

The making of suggestions should be promoted by systematic schemes, which may include the putting of suggestion boxes in convenient places in the works. All suggestions should be carefully examined either by management or by a joint body, those who have made them should be thanked, assistance should be given in the development of an idea, and monetary rewards based on the value of the suggestions should be paid. Joint production committees or works councils, as well as management itself, can be used to stimulate interest in suggestion schemes throughout the works.

Joint councils and committees vary greatly in the range of subjects and the success achieved. A recent survey of joint consultation at a number of works in the United States showed that the greatest success was in accident prevention, and this was followed, in order of success, by giving workpeople a better understanding of the

127

policies of the companies, elimination of waste, better attendance, insurance schemes for workpeople, control of quality, job evaluation, maintenance of tools, working conditions, and health.

POWERS OF JOINT COUNCILS AND COMMITTEES

Considerable thought has been given to the questions whether works council and joint consultation committees can have any real power, whether they reach decisions or merely offer advisory opinions, and what their effect may be on the authority of capital and management. Some regard them as the thin edge of the wedge of syndicalism or other forms of workers' control, and many employers are unfavourable to them because of this fear. Others see little more in them than a channel for communication to workpeople of decisions already taken by management, and a system for the consideration of grievances. If they are no more than this, they cannot secure sustained interest from either management or men. Then they are also criticized because they rarely reach decisions which have executive force, except on minor questions of welfare, but are restricted to making recommendations which management is free to accept, modify, or reject. Clearly they cannot succeed if the workers attempt to use them as instruments of social revolution, because such designs to usurp the authority of management will destroy the basis for co-operation, while equally clearly the workers will consider the meetings a waste of time and will become apathetic if little action results from them and management goes its own independent way. Some schemes have run into heavy weather because of misunderstandings about their authority, functions, and methods.

Management's freedom is restricted by Government controls, and by the provisions of collective agreements involving the joint responsibility and authority of employers' organizations and trade unions. Subject to such restrictions, efficient productive organization at the workplace requires that management shall have final executive authority, otherwise confusion or even chaos will result, and this authority is essential whether management is appointed by the Government, as in nationalized undertakings, or by the owners of capital as in private enterprise, or in other ways. There must be no weakening and undermining of management's responsibility.

In British nationalized industries, in which joint consultation at all levels is obligatory, it was hoped by many that the ending of the profit motive would lead to much higher productive efficiency because of better co-operation between management and workpeople in a joint enterprise. Up to the present, however, the old attitudes of distrust and hostility have persisted, and managements have feared a weakening of their authority. Even so, many differences have been adjusted, and in particular, where uneconomic coal-mines have been closed and the workers transferred to other areas, these changes have been made more smoothly because the arrangements have been based on joint discussion.

However, in the exercise of management's authority, what force have the recommendations which result from joint consultation? Are they merely advisory or have they more authority. There is no doubt that management gives effect to recommendations submitted by efficient joint councils and committees. These recommendations result from interplay of ideas between management and men, and represent, as in so many other organizations, a concensus of opinion or highest common factor of agreement rather than the outcome of a vote between conflicting interests. On practical matters of common interest, agreements can be hammered out, the process must be one of compromise—give and take—and although formally the higher management are not bound by the recommendations they will usually adopt them or refer them back for revision. Such processes of negotiation demand skill and patience, and these can be developed by training representatives in the problems and methods of joint consultation, a task in which management and trade unions can each take part. Consultation can be of great value in policy making, and must be clearly distinguished from the executive functions of management in applying policy decisions.

If the system is conducted along these lines, it becomes irrelevant to try to define precisely the powers of joint bodies and the limits of managerial authority. The main result is the development of co-operation based on fair dealing, mutual respect, and understanding. The status of the worker is raised. Though he remains subject to discipline, which is essential for efficient organization, the discipline and also the productive methods and organization become increasingly a joint affair. The workpeople are associated, through their representatives, with decisions determining working conditions and the policy and prosperity of the undertaking to which they belong. They will observe rules and instructions more willingly if they have been consulted about them, and management will find their authority more effective and discipline better if they know the workers' point of view and have adopted suggestions which are reasonable and practicable.

REPRESENTATION OF MANAGEMENT AND WORKPEOPLE

The selection of management's representatives is simpler than that of workers' representatives. They are chosen by the directorate, and usually include the personnel manager, the works manager or his substitute, and several departmental managers and foremen. It is desirable that most of those selected should attend regularly so as to ensure continuity and that they and the workers may get to know one another, but the management's representatives will include some who only take part when items are under discussion which specially interest them and about which they can make useful contributions. Usually management can be adequately represented by smaller numbers than the workers, and unequal representation is no disadvantage, as decisions and recommendations are not the result of majority votes but represent a general concensus of opinion after problems have been examined from various angles. In many councils, the number of representatives of management is three to five, whereas the workpeople may have twice or three times as many. In undertakings where the works council or joint production committee deals with a wide range of important questions, the managing director should give considerable attention to its development, and should frequently attend its meetings, or if not able to do so he should be represented by another director.

In a fully developed system the workers' representatives are elected by ballot by their fellow-workpeople, usually for one year, or for three years with one-third retiring each year. Those who have been employed by a firm for a specified time, e.g. not less than one or three months, have the right to vote, while a longer period of employment by a firm, sometimes a year, is required of candidates for election. The number of representatives depends on the size, structure, and complexity of the undertaking and the groups which require separate spokesmen. Each of the main departments or shops has its own representative or representatives, and there should be a reasonable balance between the various skilled occupations and unskilled workers. Women if they are employed in considerable numbers should have adequate representation; in a few undertakings which employ many women, separate men's and women's councils have been set up. In some works separate councils are set up for manual and for clerical and technical workers respectively.

It is not practicable to specify the number of workers to each councillor, but where a councillor represents more than fifty or sixty workpeople it is difficult for him to keep proper contact with them. Yet in big undertakings employing several thousand workpeople, this proportion would imply a council of forty, fifty, or more workers' representatives, and such a council may be too large for the most effective work. This difficulty may, however, be overcome by doing most of the work in standing committees, on production, accidents, welfare and other subjects, which follow general policies defined by the works council and submit their recommendations to the council. Departmental and other committees, which may include members who are not on the council, are useful in bringing consultation closer to the rank and file. In some large works the workers' representatives on departmental committees are elected by the rank and file, and they then, by the method of indirect election, select the workers' representatives on the council.

In the choice of workers' representatives and also in the functioning of joint consultation, the trade unions usually exert their influence, and if they are strong enough they manage the nominations and elections, and dominate the workers' policy. The unions aim to be the only body to protect and represent the workers' interests, and are suspicious of or hostile to any other method of representation. They therefore tend to react unfavourably to proposals by employers to form works councils, unless they are sure that they can control the representation of the workers. Their fears of works councils have certainly not been groundless. This was particularly true in the United States in the 1920's and 1930's where in many industries trade unionism was weak and still struggling to establish itself. Among the weapons which many undertakings adopted to fight the trade union movement was the formation of works councils, often called employee representation schemes or company unions. While some employers used these methods for genuine consultation and co-operation, others introduced them in the hope that their work-people would accept them as an alternative to trade unionism, and tried to persuade the workers that company unions were better for them than trade unions, and the benefits would be obtained without money cost.[1] Such unions lack the independence of trade unions, and particularly the support of workpeople in other undertakings which a trade union can bring, and by rousing the suspicions and hostility of the workers they destroy the basis on which effective co-operation can be built.

[1] In 1933, company unions were formed in many undertakings in the United States by employers who claimed that this form of representation would satisfy the requirements of President Roosevelt's New Deal legislation, which gave workpeople the right to bargain collectively through representatives of their own choice. The trade unions, however, raised strong opposition, calling them "company dominated unions."

Where trade unionism is weak the workers in an undertaking are likely to elect many non-unionists to the works council or joint consultative committee. Strong unions, however, sometimes go so far as to insist on nominating the candidates from whom the workers' representatives are elected, or if some non-unionists are nominated the unions do all they can to ensure the election of a large majority of union candidates. Thus in the British coal-mining industry during the first two years after its nationalization, the joint consultative committee at each pit included men freely elected by the miners, but some of those elected, though trade unionists, were not fully acceptable to the union, and some local officials even feared a challenge to their leadership. The National Union of Mineworkers therefore demanded successfully that the independent elections should be replaced by a system in which the local branches of the union nominate men from whom the miners will elect their representatives. This method removes any possible rivalry or conflict of authority between the union branches and the miners' representatives on the joint committees, but it is less democratic and may prevent many highly suitable men from being elected.

Men most active in trade union work are not necessarily the most effective in the work of joint consultative committees, especially on questions of production and discipline. A thoughtful skilled worker keen on his job may make many constructive suggestions for increasing output, but may lack the fighting attitude which is still a passport to trade union leadership. Also, such representatives may be firmer in supporting penalties for absenteeism and other breaches of discipline than would those active in the management of the local branch of the union. Trade union methods and leadership have been based largely on a "two-sides" attitude of conflict, whereas the success of works councils and joint production committees depends on recognition of common interests, and this should be kept in mind in the selection of representatives, and in the policy they adopt. Their job is mainly constructive co-operation and not class conflict.

Workers through their representatives can indicate their attitudes on matters which affect their conditions of work, and can make useful suggestions for improving the organization and methods of the jobs they do, but they lack the wider knowledge and range of outlook necessary for the effective discussion of many of the larger issues of policy. Here they can reasonably expect the managers, who are trained and experienced in management, to devise the best solutions, taking into consideration any practicable proposals made by the workers. Even in the field of their own jobs, workers are often unable to put their ideas forward effectively. To meet this defect, some firms give training to workers' representatives in the scope and purposes of joint consultation, its procedures and methods, and assist them in preparing their suggestions especially on technical processes. Trade unions also train shop stewards and other selected members on time and movement studies, job evaluation, and other subjects which are discussed in joint production committees and works councils.[1] Such training can have valuable results not only on technical but on human and economic aspects of production, and there is scope for big developments in this field.

Some workers' representatives harbour a suspicion that they will be victimized if they take a prominent and vigorous part in joint consultative work. There is little, if any, evidence in recent years to support this view, and on the contrary effective work in joint consultation not infrequently leads to promotion. However, management must scrupulously avoid anything which might appear to foster this fear and thus weaken or destroy the foundations of joint consultation. Workers and management should meet on terms of equality, and workers should be encouraged to speak freely and with confidence on issues about which they feel strongly. On the other hand, obstructive, non-co-operative tactics by workers, and attitudes of arrogance and superiority by management must be persistently discouraged.

Contact with the Rank and File

In industry, as in politics and trade unionism, the apathy of the rank and file is notorious. If joint consultation stops short at the workers' representatives and fails to interest the main body of workpeople, it can only claim a partial success. Efforts must be made both by management and by workers' representatives to extend the influence of joint consultation throughout the undertaking. The workers' representatives and shop stewards can do this effectively only if the number of workpeople each represents is reasonably small, and for good contact the number, as already suggested, should not be more than fifty or sixty. Yet not infrequently several hundred workpeople have only one representative. In some works where the number of workpeople to each representative is too large for effective contact, several workers are chosen in each department to act as links between its representative and the main body of workers, each liaison worker being responsible for contact with not more than forty or fifty of the rank and file.

Representatives should inform the workpeople about the subjects

[1] Courses organized by technical colleges and conferences arranged by such bodies as the Industrial Welfare Society also give training in these subjects.

under discussion and obtain their views, and they should explain to them the main recommendations adopted. Bulletin boards and works magazines are useful for spreading information. Also, great value can result from statements at intervals by the managing director, giving an account in simple terms of the present position of the undertaking, its prospects, pending changes of policy and methods, and showing the relative amounts paid in wages, salaries, raw materials, other costs, and in profits.

Communications

The complexity of modern industry including the use of more intricate machines and technical processes, together with the growth of negotiation and joint consultation, have increased the need for all in managerial positions to be able to express themselves clearly and effectively both in speech and writing. Much confusion and wasted effort can be saved if instructions are clear and systematic, while complaints and grievances can be dealt with effectively only if vagueness and ambiguities are avoided. Systematic statements in well-chosen words provide an essential basis for mutual understanding, and speakers should watch their listeners to see whether they have understood and how far they agree.[1]

In training courses for foremen and junior managers opportunities should be given for spoken and written statements, by discussions and the preparation and presentation of reports by small groups or syndicates who have considered some problem submitted to them. Some firms use tape recorders so that each individual can listen to the reproduction of his own speech and can thereby realize his mistakes.

---

[1] A "two-way" system of communications is necessary for the best results. Opportunities must be available to workpeople to express their views and make suggestions, and management must be ready to listen and to give heed to what is said. These opportunities include direct access to management by individual workpeople, and the representative method of joint consultation.

PART II

Collective Relations

10

Trade Unionism

TRADE UNIONS are essentially associations of manual and/or non-manual workpeople, including professional grades, formed to safeguard and improve the working conditions of their members and more generally to raise their status and promote their vocational interests. The structure, status, cohesion, and strength of the movement depend partly on recognition of common interests by the workpeople and their determination to combine together to formulate and attain their objectives, but also on the political, economic, and social conditions of each country. There is therefore great variety from country to country. The attitude of the Government and of public opinion towards the movement is often a powerful and even a decisive factor. In totalitarian countries the movement either is a creature of the Government performing the functions allotted to it, or, as in Nazi Germany, is forcibly suppressed except for such vestiges as can be maintained "underground." In democratic countries it has the right to exist, subject to some legal limitations, it may be viewed favourably or unfavourably by the Government, and its power and authority are largely dependent upon the quality of its leaders, the efficiency of its organization, and the interest and loyalty of its members.

The status of British trade unionism after the Second World War can be used as an illustration of a movement which, after more than a century of struggle, attained great authority in the affairs of the nation. It had succeeded in establishing a nation-wide organization with a total of more than nine million members in all the main industries and occupations, it employed a large staff of full-time officials to undertake work of organization, administration, and negotiation, and it had accumulated powerful financial resources. Its influence extends beyond its membership. As a result of collective bargaining with employers' organizations it shared with them the responsibility for an elaborate system of industrial codes for regulating working conditions throughout the greater part of industry, and it took part, especially at the highest levels, in shaping the political, economic, and social policy of the nation. Being closely associated with the Labour Government, the movement was consulted by Ministers of the Crown who were greatly influenced by it on all important questions of policy and legislative proposals, including foreign and financial as well as industrial and social affairs. It continued to be a powerful pressure group when later a Conservative Government came into office. Any attempt, however, to use its industrial power to coerce Government would be an intolerable interference with democracy and would endanger the foundations of the constitution. In addition to its influence on new legislation, the trade union movement had gained a recognized place in the administration of existing legislation, being represented on a wide range of statutory boards, tribunals, wage councils, and other authorities, and influencing those responsible for the management of the coal-mines, railways, and other nationalized industries.

It must not be assumed that trade unionism in democratic countries, even where it has grown to giant's stature in Britain and the United States, is a unified or highly integrated movement either in its structure or policy. The lack of solidarity is particularly evident in the United States, with sharp differences of organization and outlook between the American Federation of Labour and the Congress of Industrial Organizations. In Britain, the rifts are not so wide and are bridged in places by the Trades Union Congress to which most of the unions are affiliated, but nevertheless there is much rivalry in organization and sectionalism in industrial action which contrasts with an appearance of solidarity in criticizing private capitalism and in supporting nationalization of industries and other political and social aspirations. Also, as in other organizations, only a small minority of the members are active and keen, while the majority of the rank and file are largely passive, rarely attend meetings, and give little thought to questions of policy except when some vital decision, such as possible strike action, is put before them and rouses them temporarily from their usual inertia.

In order to gain its objectives both industrial and political action are essential to trade unionism. Industrial action is the staple of the movement, while the emphasis placed upon political action has varied in different periods within a country and in different countries. Both are facilitated by the setting up of such co-ordinating bodies as the Trades Union Congress, the American Federation of Labour, and the Congress of Industrial Organizations. In some countries the trade unions have associated themselves closely with one political party, for example, many British trade unions now being linked with the Labour Party which largely depends upon them for financial support and on which the trade unions exert a powerful influence by their participation in the counsels of the Party. During the nineteenth century, however, British trade unionism avoided party affiliations, preferring instead freedom to obtain the best terms from any party. This is the policy also of trade unionism in the United States. The dangers of close party attachments are considerable; in particular there is risk of intensifying national disunion, especially when the party with which the movement is identified is rejected at the polls. The movement itself might become divided as, though the members might agree on the main lines of industrial and social policy, they might split on the foreign or fiscal policy which their party should adopt.[1] A split in the Labour Party, and most political parties split sooner or later, would cause divisions within the trade unions. Also the movement might be weakened if its best leaders and much of its energy and resources were diverted from industrial into political channels.

Although in practice trade union movements, as in Britain, generally approve or acquiesce in the principle that, as they represent sectional interests only, the responsibility for decisions must rest upon the Government of the State whenever differences on policy arise, some trade unionists and especially some intellectuals who support trade unionism disagree with this principle. They do so on grounds of political theory. They deny the complete sovereignty of the State and the assumption that the rights and powers of individuals and of groups within the State are all derived from and are dependent upon the State, and can only be exercised at the pleasure of the State.[2] They deny that an autocracy or even the majority in a democracy has the right in all circumstances to command the obedience of the whole community. Instead, they regard the State as only one of the ways in which individuals group themselves together for common purposes, and that other groups, e.g. religious organizations and trade unions, have a "natural" right to an existence and to work for the attainment of their own purposes even if this brings them into conflict with the State. They envisage the possibility of a conflict of loyalty between the State and other forms of human association and deny that such other associations are

[1] At the Trades Union Congress at Brighton in 1946 a substantial vote was cast against the Labour Government's foreign policy, especially towards the Soviet Union, though a majority was secured for the policy.

[2] Thus the Osborne judgment in Britain in 1909 on the question of the use of trade union funds for political purposes has been criticized as being based on the view that trade unions were bodies whose objects were defined by statute law, with political purposes excluded, and that they could not add to the specified objects, whereas unions should be considered as having "natural" rights of association and be free to add any lawful purposes to their activities.

inferior in any moral sense to the State, however supreme the legal sovereignty of the State may be.

This pluralist view of society has greater practical significance in an autocracy than in a democracy. Thus, in 1933 when the Nazi Government decided to abolish trade unionism the unions had a "natural" right to resist, and there were potentialities of civil conflict which failed to materialize because of the real weakness of the unions behind an imposing façade and because of the ruthless strength shown by the Nazis in "liquidating" the few who attempted resistance. In a true democracy, associations within the State usually recognize the reasonableness of constitutional methods, and minorities acquiesce in Government policies which they dislike, as they have only to win the support of the electorate in order to be able to secure the application of their own policies. Measures are necessary, however, to safeguard genuine conscientious objectors who claim on certain questions to have allegiances which prevent them from obeying the authority of the State. In this connection it may be noted that those who hold the pluralist view of society could not logically support a "closed shop" policy by which workpeople could be coerced into joining a trade union.

Although in the main trade unions tend to be law abiding and to avoid clashes with State authority, there have been occasions when unions have claimed that their members must obey the union and not the State. Thus, in the United States, the coal-miners, members of the United Mine Workers under the leadership of J. L. Lewis, challenged both the Roosevelt and Truman Administrations though claiming that they were taking part in ordinary labour disputes, while a number of "general" and other strikes in Western European countries both shortly before and in the early years after the First World War were a form of direct action to put political pressure on Governments with a view to coercing them to change their policies.[1] Such situations could arise in nationalized industries if the unions concerned failed to gain their demands by negotiation and resorted to strikes against the Government which was responsible for the application of policies in the national interests. Such conflicts should be rare in a democracy and should be avoided altogether by referring to arbitration differences not settled in negotiations between the unions and the authority operating the industry on behalf of the Government.

When trade unionism evolves into a powerful political, economic, and social force in the community, as in Britain, a new type of leader

[1] Mention may be made of the threat of British coal-miners in 1919 to stop work if the Government persisted in taking military action against the Bolshevics.

is needed, quite different from the agitators of the early years of struggle to organize the workers and secure recognition, and distinct also from those who pursue only the sectional interests of their own unions. The leaders of such a movement have responsibility for taking a broad view of economic and social questions, and in formulating their policies must consider the effects upon the national interests. They must recognize that the interests of trade unionists are closely related to the nation's interests, that good working conditions can only be secured and maintained if the national economy is healthy, and that higher standards of living depend upon increased output. They must, therefore, support production incentives, improvements in industrial efficiency, and removal of restrictions, and must avoid the dangers of inflation which may result from successive wage increases first in one industry then in another without relation to production.

Such leadership calls for high qualities, together with knowledge of relevant facts and ability to take the long view, and requires strength of personality to resist the unreasonable demands of agitators, to curb hasty, ill-considered moves, and to prevent action being based upon prejudiced views and ignorant clamour by irresponsible elements among the rank and file. Close contact is needed with the rank and file especially to explain sound policies to them and also to ensure that the leaders and statesmen of the movement are well aware of the views of their constituents. This is not easy, especially as the leaders are required to give an increasing part of their time to the work of boards, committees, and conferences dealing with economic and industrial policy and administration at national and regional levels. Yet insufficient contact leads to misunderstandings among the rank and file, resulting in unofficial strikes, while balanced and farsighted leaders acting with a sense of responsibility, fairness, and moderation may encounter criticism for weakness and lack of vigour, and find their position undermined, with the danger that more extreme and less capable men may seize control. These dangers should be met by more systematic association between all levels throughout the unions, including the appointment of national and regional officers whose main job would be to ensure liaison by interpreting the opinions and aspirations of the rank and file to the leaders and the policies of the leaders to the branch officials and members, thereby establishing better mutual understanding.

FREEDOM OF ASSOCIATION

The right of people to form associations for any lawful purpose is one of the essentials of a democratic community. To deny this right is to take away one of the main foundations upon which the State itself is built, as the formal or tacit agreement of its citizens to associate together for purposes of government lies at the basis of democracy. The State defines what objects are lawful, and it is only logical that these objects may be pursued whether by individual citizens or by voluntary associations of citizens. In defining what purposes are lawful the State may be liberal or restrictive according to circumstances, but, if the purposes have been defined by democratic constitutional procedure, and if they can be amended by the same method, no obstacle should be put in the way of collective association to achieve these purposes.

Legal Freedom

It might be generally supposed that in the twentieth century the legal right of workpeople and of employers to form associations for the protection of their respective interests would be universally recognized. Yet some States have refused it, and others have imposed restrictions. Demands for the general establishment of this right led the authors of the Peace Treaties in 1919 to include freedom of association among the purposes for which the International Labour Organisation was set up; frequent reference has been made to it in the course of the Organisation's work, and its continued importance was recognized by the prominence given to it in the charter adopted by the Philadelphia Conference of the Organisation in 1943. It has been an issue of outstanding significance in various countries during recent decades. Thus the abolition by the Nazi Government of freedom of association, first among workpeople and then among employers, was an early indication of the undemocratic and repressive nature of the regime. Limitations upon freedom of association were also imposed by the State in Fascist Italy and in other countries with corporative systems. In the U.S.A., on the other hand, the State under the New Deal adopted measures with a view to ensuring that legal freedom of association among workpeople should become effective and that unfair practices by employers against the free formation of workers' associations should be prevented. In Britain the State has also been liberal but more neutral.

Freedom of association for the purpose of influencing working conditions must be secured equally for workpeople and for employers. Any discrimination in favour of or against the one or the other would cause discontent based on a sense of injustice. In avoiding discrimination the fact must be taken into account that an employer may represent a bargaining power equal to that of the whole body of the workpeople he employs, and the negotiating strength of a few large-scale employers may be at least equal to that of many thousands of workpeople. Also tacit agreements on common policy may be readily reached by such employers without setting up a formal association. A system which permitted such agreements but denied the more formal organizations necessary for collective action by the workers would be discriminatory in fact if not in form.

The right to form an association carries with it two significant implications. The first is negative; it is the freedom of individuals not to become members of an association and also freedom to terminate their membership of an association. The second is freedom to form new associations alongside existing ones, including freedom to withdraw from an organization in order to set up a rival one. The laws of the State should not restrict these freedoms, though in practice individuals may find it expedient to join an organization whose members exert social pressure or coercion upon him to do so, and effective freedom may be denied him. Further reference is made later on to these implications.

Certain categories of people are usually not allowed freedom of association. Thus, persons serving in the armed forces are generally denied freedom of association, though there have been exceptions, for example, in the early days of the Soviet Revolution, when Workers' and Soldiers' Councils were formed in support of the new Government. Usually also members of police forces are subjected to restrictions. In Britain, for example, they are prohibited from joining any trade union or any association having as one of its objects the control or influence of the pay, conditions, or pensions of the police force. Various opinions are held about the position of civil servants, some arguing that they should have full freedom of association while others favour restrictions. Some civil servants differ in certain respects from workpeople in private industry. Officials in the higher grades are in close contact with their political chiefs, and they are required to serve with equal loyalty chiefs of different political parties as Governments change. Difficulties might arise, however, if an official actively participating in the work of an association with political objects was serving under a chief of another political party. There would be danger also of official secrets being revealed, inadvertently or otherwise, by a civil servant of high rank, who participated actively in the work of a political association. These difficulties are, however, unimportant or non-existent among the rank and file of civil servants and especially among people employed in State mines, railways, post and telegraph and similar services. There is a strong tendency nowadays for the number of persons employed by Governments to increase particularly in industrial or quasi-industrial work, and the possibility must be envisaged of still greater numbers of workpeople being thus employed. The problem of local government employees, including those in public utility undertakings, also arises.

There do not appear to be adequate reasons to support considerable restrictions upon the legal freedom of association of public servants. It may be convenient, especially for purposes of negotiating, for civil servants to have their own organizations, instead, for example, of clerical grades joining an association with membership open also to clerical workers in private industry, commerce, and banking; and under conditions of freedom of association they would usually be likely to form their own organizations. They should have liberty to decide this question on grounds of convenience, and legal freedom of association for public servants is desirable; discretion should be left to individual officials to decide according to the nature of their work and responsibilities whether they should join an association or not and whether, if they join, their membership should be active or passive.[1]

The State in dealing with freedom of association may merely permit freedom by the negative method of removing legislative restrictions upon freedom, as when the British Combination Acts were repealed in 1824, or it may take the positive course of providing for freedom of association by specific enactment. Thus in the United States the National Industrial Recovery Act, 1933, stipulated that every code of fair competition issued under the Act should include the following much discussed provisions: "(1) that employees shall have the right to organize and bargain collectively through representatives of their own choosing, and shall be free from the interference, restraint, or coercion of employers of labour or their agents, in the designation of such representatives or in self-organization or in other concerted activities for the purpose of collective bargaining or other mutual aid or protection; (2) that no employee and no one seeking employment shall be required as a condition of employment to join any company union or to refrain from joining, organizing or assisting in a labour organization of his own choosing."[2]

It will be noted that these provisions mention only the right of employees to organize and bargain collectively, no corresponding clauses being included for employers. But freedom of association had long been a legal right both for employers and for workpeople. The

[1] The British Act of 1927, since repealed, made it unlawful for a public authority to require an employee to be or not to be a member of a trade union.

[2] Section 7(a) of the National Industrial Recovery Act. These provisions, with modifications, were maintained in subsequent legislation.

legislators in 1933 were, however, clearly convinced that, in the conditions then prevailing in the United States, the employees, though legally free to organize, were often prevented from doing so by the interference of employers. The clause was, therefore, designed to strengthen free association among workpeople, and to weaken company unions of workpeople, which were usually controlled or dominated by the firms. There was no need, the legislators thought, to safeguard the position of employers. Following the passing of the Act, many difficulties arose in the interpretation of freedom of association and of collective bargaining and in securing effective action to the workpeople of the United States.

Actual Freedom of Association

A distinction must be drawn between legal freedom of association as reviewed above and the actual freedom of the individual to join or not to join an association. If legal freedom is not accorded, any associations which are formed are illegal, as were trade unions in Britain before the repeal of the Combination Laws, and persons who join them are acting against the authority of the State and are liable to penalties for violation of the law. A frequent consequence is the formation of secret associations, though sometimes the State is negligent in enforcing the law and associations are openly formed.

Legal freedom alone may be of little value if individuals are subjected to economic or social pressure not to exercise their rights. This difficulty is usually greater among workers than among employers, as they are generally less able to withstand economic pressure and are more affected by mass psychology. Pressure by their fellow-workmen upon a small minority to join a trade union may be so strong that it is difficult to withstand. Undue influence, threat of dismissal, or employment only on condition of signing a "yellow dog" contract not to join a trade union are measures by which some employers, especially in periods when trade unions were weak, have made legal freedom of association of little practical value to workpeople. Among employers, pressure, which is sometimes difficult to resist, is exerted to bring non-members into the employers' associations. There is, however, little likelihood of a trade union taking action which would interfere with the freedom of an employer to join an association of employers.

If the State accords legal freedom to form associations, has it any responsibility for ensuring that this right can be effectively exercised? Certainly it has. The main responsibility, it is true, rests with the workers and employers, and the State cannot be expected to set up elaborate machinery for hunting out interferences with freedom of

145

association. But where disputes result from such interferences, as they frequently will, the State must, in the operation of its system of labour relations use its influence and authority to ensure effective freedom of association and to secure redress where victimization is proved.

These tasks are not easy, as often the facts are difficult to establish where victimization or undue influence are alleged. Some of the problems which arise may be illustrated from the experiences of workmen, as it is almost entirely on their behalf that State intervention is needed to establish effective freedom of association for the purpose of influencing working conditions. Examples are given below of action by employers to prevent workpeople from joining a trade union, and of action by a trade union to bring non-members into the organization. Any organized body of workpeople or any employer is fully entitled to use fair means for the purpose of persuading a workman to join or not to join a union. This is consistent with, and is indeed essential to, democracy, but it is often difficult in practice to draw the line between fair and unfair means.

An employer does not take away freedom of association if he suggests non-union arguments for consideration by his workpeople. If, however, he requires his workpeople to sign a "yellow dog" contract, or if he otherwise refuses to employ union labour he has restricted freedom. He may persuade but not coerce. In the U.S.A. the object of many employers in requiring their workpeople to sign a "yellow dog" contract was not to be able to sue their workpeople for breach of contract if they joined a union, but to enable them to secure injunctions to prevent labour organizers from trying to unionize their workpeople. This similarly represents an unfair interference with freedom of association.

Some employers introduce favourable conditions of work and make good provision for the health and welfare of their workpeople in the hope that they will decide not to join a union. This is not unfair though if the motive becomes known it is likely to cause suspicion and distrust among the workpeople, thereby causing a deterioration of industrial relations. But it is unfair if an employer bribes individuals or groups of workpeople not to join a union. In imposing a non-union condition, freedom is denied, though it must be admitted that workpeople who would accept such inducements would be of little value to a union. This category of inducement includes making participation in a profit-sharing scheme conditional upon not joining a union.[1]

[1] More frequently participation in profit-sharing schemes has been made conditional upon the workpeople not going on strike.

An employer may reasonably refuse to allow trade union leaders to enter the works for the purpose of recruiting members. If, however, by his control of a "company" town he prevents genuine union organizers who are not subversive agitators, from putting their arguments before the workpeople he is unfairly hampering freedom of association. Differences of opinion about who can be regarded as "genuine union organizers" cause difficulty. Again, there is no unfair interference with freedom of association if an employer decides to set up a "company union," even if he hopes that this will result in many of his workpeople not responding to appeals to join an independent union. The workers are still free to participate as much or as little as they wish in the work of the company union and may also become members of an independent union. The employer's action, however, becomes unfair interference if his workpeople are required to be members of the company union only, or if the existence of the company union is used as a pretext for his refusing to have any relations with an independent union which includes among its members a substantial number of his workpeople.[1]

Victimization of workpeople raises difficult problems and is a cause of much bitterness. An employer usually has the right to dismiss any of his workers on grounds of inefficiency, lack of work, serious breaches of discipline or criminal offences, and such dismissals do not undermine freedom of association. Similarly he may dismiss a workman who is a disruptive agitator, persisting in creating friction and dislocation by unreasonable obstruction.[2] But he menaces freedom of association if he uses the pretext of inefficiency or lack of trade to get rid of a workman who has been an effective leader of the men and has used fair methods in demanding improvements in working conditions, however strongly the firm may be opposed to granting these improvements. Acute situations frequently arise after a protracted stoppage of work if the firm refuses to reinstate workmen who have been specially active in the dispute, or if these men are singled out for dismissal a short time after resumption of work.

Attention must now be directed to unfair methods adopted by trade unionists to recruit or retain members. As already indicated, freedom of association implies freedom not to join an association.

[1] Reference has already been made to the provision of legislation in the United States that no employee and no one seeking employment shall be required as a condition of employment to join any company union.

[2] It is assumed throughout this volume that any changes made in the economic system will be by democratic evolutionary methods and not by revolt, sabotage, and non-co-operation.

Members of a trade union may use methods of persuasion to induce non-members to join; in particular, they may point out all the advantages of membership, including improvements in working conditions which the union has secured, together with its power of protecting individual workmen against victimization and unfair dismissal. They may emphasize that the union members have paid for these improved working conditions by their money and efforts, and that they resent outsiders enjoying these benefits. But they should not use threats or intimidation. Yet it is often difficult to decide where persuasion ceases to be peaceful and involves intimidation. The problem is as difficult as that of defining peaceful picketing.

Trade unionists may refuse to work alongside non-members. This frequently occurs in workshops where trade unionism is strong and non-members are few. An employer may accept this closed shop condition rather than face a stoppage, or in the circumstances he may prefer that all his workpeople shall be union members.[1] Some employers may, however, insist upon their right to select workpeople because of skill and experience without considering whether they are members of a trade union or not, and a strike may result. If the union wins the outcome is a closed or union shop. This is an undemocratic victory, won by force and not by persuasion, and it can be of little value to the union; it may gain a few unwilling members, but effective power with all the workers in the union can scarcely be greater than when membership was as high as 90 or 95 per cent of those employed by the firm. If the dispute is not settled by the two parties but is submitted to arbitration by an impartial State tribunal, a "closed shop" award may be given on grounds of expediency and convenience, though it would be a violation of the principle of freedom of association.

Operation of the closed shop principle tends to restrict the right of workpeople to withdraw from the union in the future if they become dissatisfied with its policy or leadership, and also stands in the way of the formation of rival unions. To exercise the right to set up a rival or break-away union may often result in conflict and make the processes of collective bargaining more complicated, and it may therefore often have to be abandoned in the interests of

[1] The terms "closed shop" and "open shop" are used with different meanings in Great Britain and North America. Here a "closed shop" is understood to be one which is closed to non-union labour; an "open shop" is one which is open to both union and non-union labour, though it may happen in fact that all the workers are union members, or all non-union, or there may be a proportion of each. The closed shop principle may be applied by a particular craft in a firm or workshop, while large numbers of workpeople in other categories may not be members of any union.

industrial peace. Yet restrictions upon freedom of association may weaken the vitality of the trade union movement. Groups of workpeople hold different views on trade union policy and methods, and if they feel too strongly to reach a compromise they can scarcely be prevented from forming a separate union. Thus, in some European countries Catholic and Socialist unions have been organized side by side, the former being more conciliatory than the latter. Again, where only one union has hitherto operated some of the members may consider that its policy and leadership have become too extreme and aggressive or too complacent and spineless, and if they are unable to bring about a change from within, they may cease to be members or may decide to form a rival union.

Criticisms have been directed against the method adopted in Fascist Italy and in other corporative States of recognizing only one union of workpeople and one organization of employers in each branch of industry. If other unions were allowed to exist in these countries they had no place in the corporative system, and were therefore likely to decline and disappear. Now it is often more convenient in joint negotiations if there is only one union representing the workpeople and one representing the employers. But this is true only if one organization on each side really represents the employers and workpeople respectively. If it conceals substantial differences of cpinion within its membership, or if it speaks for only a proportion of the workpeople or employers and considerable numbers are not represented, the joint negotiations will be hampered or inadequate. In such circumstances to have a more complex mechanism for joint negotiation is preferable consisting of representatives of two or more unions of workpeople and of employers based upon recognition of freely formed associations. There are, however, practical limits to the number of separate unions which should be represented in joint negotiating machinery; participation should be restricted to unions with memberships which are substantial and also reasonably stable over a period of time.

Official recognition by State authorities may be given to certain unions without weakening freedom of association. This is practicable if recognition is not exclusive, but is extended to new unions when they have established their claim to represent a substantial number of workpeople. Thus in Australia, for example, only registered unions may appear before the Commonwealth Court of Conciliation and Arbitration, and the privileges of registration are usually granted to only one union for any defined category of workpeople. But the system is usually applied with such flexibility that, if an unregistered union becomes representative of a considerable number of workpeople in a field in which a union has already been registered, the field will be divided and a new category defined to enable the new union also to be registered.

Instead of applying the exclusive policy of a closed shop or a single union, arrangements are often made to give preference to unionists. This often takes the form of an agreement between a union and an employer by which the employer undertakes that whenever he has a vacancy he will first apply to the union, and only if the union is unable to find a suitable worker among its members does the employer become free to employ a non-unionist. In the interests of industrial peace preference for unionists is sometimes included in the awards of arbitration tribunals, for example, in Australia and New Zealand. Although preference for unionists does not strictly interfere with freedom of association it is a powerful inducement for non-members to join the union. This is especially true in periods of depression when the union has enough unemployed members on its books to fill every vacancy which is likely to occur. In such circumstances a non-member would have little chance of getting a job. Where the State or a tribunal set up by the State requires compulsory unionism, freedom of association is no longer maintained. A worker may still be free to decide which of several unions he prefers to join but he is no longer free not to join any union.

PURPOSES OF TRADE UNIONS

The main objects of trade unionism vary from country to country and from period to period and can be grouped as follows: (1) protection of workers and provision for their security; (2) improvements in standards of living and working conditions; (3) raising the vocational status of workers. Provision for workers' security can be made directly by unions out of their own resources, while this and all the other purposes can be achieved both by industrial action leading to collective agreements with employers or by political action resulting in legislation.

In the early years of the movement many unions, especially those of craftsmen, though having in one form or another all the aims and aspirations indicated above, concentrated a considerable part of their energies on immediately realizable objects. They provided club rooms where members could meet not only to co-ordinate policy and action for improving working conditions, but also for social and to some extent educational purposes. Of outstanding importance was the building up of funds to provide "friendly" benefits for their members, the unions thus resembling in this respect the many sick clubs and mutual benefit societies formed among the workers.[1] In return for their contributions, members were entitled to sickness, accident, unemployment, old age, and funeral benefits, compensation for loss of tools, travelling expenses for unemployed members in search of work, and maintenance at their own convalescent homes. Some unions provided a greater range of benefits than others. These thrift and provident activities were of great value in increasing the security of the workers at a time when there was no State social insurance and when the only other means of relief were dependence on relatives, private charity, and the hated pauper system of the poor law authorities. Sturdy independence was a marked characteristic of these pioneers, mainly skilled men, who could afford to pay high contributions to unions when circumstances were favourable and whose tenacity in maintaining their membership when times were difficult so as to hold on to their right to benefits ensured the stability and continuity of the unions in a period when employers were bent on their destruction and public opinion was largely hostile. Provision of friendly benefits has remained an important activity of unions of skilled workers in Britain, North America, and other countries, and where State insurance schemes have been introduced the union benefits supplement those provided by the State.

Unions of skilled craftsmen tended to be conservative. The accumulation and administration of large friendly benefit funds demanded detailed attention and a cautious policy. Many union officials found that they were operating a business resembling that of insurance companies, and in order to ensure that the promised benefits could be paid they were reluctant to spend much of their money on strikes. Indeed, one of their leaders, William Allan, in his evidence on behalf of the unions before the British Royal Commission of 1867, said: "We believe that all strikes are a complete waste of money." The moderation shown, the reasonableness of their demands, and the efficient organization of the unions caused public opinion to become more favourable to them in this period, and this led to legislation giving them greater freedom of action.

The unions in this period paid little attention to politics except to secure better legal status, but along with their friendly benefit work they persisted in their efforts to secure recognition by the employers, and as they gradually gained this objective progress was

[1] An indication in Britain of the prominence of friendly benefits among trade union activities is the fact that the Chief Registrar of Friendly Societies is the government official responsible for registering trade unions and receiving reports from them.

made in improving working conditions by a growing code of collective agreements. The building up of this network of agreements
regulating in great detail working conditions, industry by industry,
is the outstanding contribution made by trade unions and employers'
organizations. By collective negotiations the unions have gone a
long way towards securing standard conditions of work in many
industries instead of the wide variety which would result if each
employer were free to fix conditions for his own workmen either
independently or by individual agreements. The unions have attached
importance to standard conditions which enable them to secure the
best general level attainable whether in good or bad times: unions
would be ineffective if conditions varied widely from one undertaking
to another, and there would be danger of competitive lowering of
conditions. It is one of the main purposes of unions to prevent such
undercutting.

The unions have used their bargaining strength to secure standard
time rates of wages, and have sought to raise them whenever economic conditions have been favourable, claiming for the workers
their share in economic and industrial progress, so that they would
gain adequately from increases in the productive efficiency of
industry, and also claiming compensation by higher money wages
to meet rises in the cost of living. The time rates are regarded as
minima, not maxima, but the practice varies considerably, in some
industries the actual rates paid to most workers being above the
agreed minima, whereas in other industries few workers receive more
than the agreed rates. In periods of depression the unions have
striven to minimize wage reductions, while at all times they have
fought against exploitation and have put pressure on inefficient firms
paying low wages. Piece rates are more difficult to regulate by
agreement because of variations in type of product and conditions
of production from firm to firm, but in some industries, e.g. cotton
textiles, highly elaborate lists of piece rates have been drawn up to
cover all the main varieties of work, and these have been incorporated
in collective agreements. Where, as for example in engineering, the
variety of processes and products is too great to be covered by a
schedule of standard piece rates, unions have secured some control
through agreements providing that piece rates in any undertaking
shall enable workmen of average ability to earn not less than a
specified percentage, often 25, but in some agreements $33\frac{1}{3}$ per cent,
above time rates, and that piece rates shall not be altered unless the
method of manufacture is changed.

Prominent among the objectives of trade unionism mainly by
collective agreements, but also by legislation, have been reduction

152

in hours of work, limitation of overtime, regulation of shift working, and paid holidays. Other purposes are the exclusion of unqualified workers from skilled occupations, demarkation or allocation of defined jobs to specified categories of workers, limitation of the number of apprentices and regulation of conditions of apprenticeship, regulation of other juvenile labour, and preference for unionists when employers are in need of more workpeople. Particularly valuable to the individual worker is the protection which the unions give against unfair dismissal and against victimization for taking part in union activities.

Employers have claimed and exercised the right to dismiss workers for inefficiency, for indiscipline or other conduct injurious to the operation of the undertaking, and when work was not available. These rights have often been abused, workpeople having been dismissed for trivial offences, or even for some difference with a foreman of manager without any opportunity of putting their case before a higher authority or an impartial tribunal. Frequently also, employers have refused to reinstate workpeople who have been out on strike, or those who have been specially active in the conflict or effective in supporting the union's demands. Sometimes such men have been reinstated on demands of the union at the end of the strike, but have henceforth been marked men and later on they have been dismissed in circumstances which made a charge of victimization difficult to prove, however strongly it might be suspected.

Unions have consistently sought to protect the workers against these insecurities and interferences with their legitimate freedom of action in trade union or political work. Where such tyranny persists the workers are kept in a state of servility, and many strikes have been called as a protest against wrongful dismissal and victimization, and to ensure fair play. Even where dismissal is due to shortage of work, unions have pressed for a period of notice, e.g. a week, to be given, and have also succeeded in securing a guaranteed week in some industries. Many employers in their desire that workers shall have a fair deal or because of the trouble that can result from wrongful dismissal have themselves arranged for the case to be reviewed before a worker loses his job, while some collective agreements with unions require an impartial hearing before a tribunal in which the workers are represented. In many agreements on the terms of resumption of work after a strike, the unions insist that there shall be no victimization, that strikers shall be reinstated as soon as possible, and that workers temporarily employed in their place during the strike shall be dismissed or if retained shall not be the means of preventing the strikers from resuming their work. By

153

some agreements or by legislation in certain countries, e.g. the United States, the general principle is laid down that workpeople shall not be dismissed or in any way penalized because they are members or officials of a trade union, or because they have taken part in a strike or in any other lawful activity on behalf of their union.

In addition to direct provision of friendly benefits, action to safeguard members against victimization and unfair dismissal, and collective bargaining and promotion of legislation for improvement of working conditions and greater security, the trade union movement has given much attention to the status of workpeople and to the ownership and control of industry. Indeed, a widely held view is that participation with capitalists in collective bargaining and progress by legislation in capitalist countries represent only a transitional stage pending the ownership and control of the instruments of production by the State or by the workers. Negotiation and legislation within the existing economic order are supported because they give immediate practical results, but the ultimate aim towards which trade unionism in many countries directs its efforts is socialism.

From the early days of the industrial revolution workers' organizations in Britain nurtured aspirations for a different economic system. In most occupations the workers no longer owned the machines and implements used in production as they had done in the preceding domestic system. They saw businesses which were started on a small scale sometimes by enterprising workers grow to undertakings of considerable size, with factory buildings, machinery, and power representing substantial capital, and from Robert Owen's time or earlier they were attracted by the idea of forming producers' societies of workers owning their own capital, managing production, and marketing and sharing the profits among themselves. They would compete on equal terms with capitalist industry and by their efficiency they would hope to gain an ever greater share of production. Many experiments were tried both in Britain and in continental Europe, but though the initiators were often competent workers and were actuated by high ideals they did not understand the complexities of productive organization, technical developments and finance, and the schemes failed by contrast with the success of co-operative societies in retail and wholesale trading.

Then, as private capitalism grew from strength to strength, the workers in Britain and Western Europe became increasingly class conscious and began to drink the heady wine of Marxian socialism and the overthrow of capitalism. It took some time for the new doctrines to penetrate trade unionism, especially as standards of living in the second half of the nineteenth century were rising with increased production and avoidance of devastating wars, and as the membership of the most powerful unions was mainly among skilled workpeople whose policy, as has been noted, was *laissez-faire*, cautious, and conservative. However, during the last decade of the century and subsequently, trade unionism began to spread among unskilled workers, who had hitherto been considered by the craft union leaders to be unsuitable for union membership. New leaders with a more aggressive policy based on socialist doctrines preached the need for solidarity of all workers in the struggle against capitalism and advocated independent political action, both in Parliament and in local government councils. Gradually the more conservative leaders of the craft unions modified their attitude as the new unionism gained ground, but the conservative and radical streams have never completely united. They can still be distinguished in the trade unionism of the present day and clashes of policy result from time to time.

The membership of the new unions of semi-skilled and unskilled workers was much less stable than that of the craft unions, and for a time many of them were of mushroom growth. Sometimes waves or organization such as those by the Knights of Labour and the Industrial Workers of the World, which were particularly prominent in North America, would gain huge membership, followed by heavy declines through inefficient organization, hostility of employers, and the impact of depression and unemployment. Support was forthcoming during a vigorous campaign for better conditions, but membership fell rapidly when the excitement was over, though gradually greater stability was achieved. Subscriptions were low so as to be within the means of workers whose incomes were small, and union funds were used mainly for purposes of organization and to support strikes. Friendly benefits, which would have involved much larger subscriptions than the members could afford, were often not provided, and the unions looked to the State to meet the social security needs of the workers. The new unions, however, imitated the craft unions in demanding recognition by employers and in negotiating collective agreements with them.

In the trade union movements of each country extremist agitators acting without a sense of responsibility have urged dislocating strikes, arguing that capitalism is disintegrating and if weakened by organized unrest would break down altogether, and in the resulting chaos the workers could take control. This revolutionary or syndicalist policy has gained wider support in some countries than in others. The methods of evolutionary trade unions are roundly condemned by those who believe in revolutionary force as the only means of dislodging and destroying powerfully entrenched capitalism. Thus in *Leninism* by Joseph Stalin the opinion is expressed that in the fight against imperialism, which is described as the omnipotence of monopolistic trusts and syndicates, of banks and the financial oligarchy, the customary methods of the working class—trade unions and co-operative organizations, parliamentary parties and the parliamentary struggle—have proved to be totally inadequate; opportunism, compromises with capitalism, political bargaining and parliamentary scheming are criticized as showing weakness in practical policy.[1]

Most movements, however, have supported evolutionary policies and have made agreements by negotiation and conciliation with capitalist employers. These agreements, as has been noted, are an important part of their work, though the unions also strive for their long-term objective of abolishing or greatly modifying private capitalism. Supporters of this policy consider that the unions should get the best possible bargains out of the present system, they recognize that they would bring great misery to the workers if they made the system unworkable and would arouse determined opposition if they tried to do so, and they are convinced that it would be much preferable to take over an efficient industrial system in good working order than one which has been driven to a state of collapse.

Yet trade union leaders who take part in frequent negotiations and many agreements with employers refer to capitalists as the common enemy, and some unions preface their rules with statements indicating that there are only two classes, the possessing masters and the producing workers, that the interests of these classes are opposed to each other, and that, while the unions' immediate objects are to improve the material conditions of their members and to raise them from being beasts of burden to human beings, their ultimate object, expressed somewhat emotionally, is the emancipation of the working class, a goal towards which the unions are marching steadily and irresistibly.

In Britain the movement was rapidly converted to socialism, and since the early years of the present century the Trades Union Congress has supported demands for nationalization including the mines and railways. The implications of nationalizaton were not, however, always thought out clearly, and there was confusion in the minds of many trade unionists about participation of the workers

[1] The claim is made that in the Soviet system of government the replacing of territorial electoral constituencies by industrial units, factories, and mills, enables the workers to be linked directly with the apparatus of State administration and to be taught how to administer the country.

in the control of industry. Some believed that nationalization would satisfy all their aspirations, including elimination of the profit motive, so that they would no longer be exploited but receive the whole product of their labour. Others, however, saw that nationalized industries might be controlled by Government and operated by a bureaucracy unsympathetic or hostile to the workers and that their position might be worse than under private capitalism. Consequently, as long ago as 1914, the National Union of Railwaymen in advocating national ownership of the railways demanded that under nationalization the railwaymen should be guaranteed their full political and social rights, a due measure of control and responsibility for the efficient operation of the railways, and a fair share in the benefits likely to result from State ownership; and they indicated that without these conditions no system of State ownership would satisfy them.

Policies for ownership and operation of industries by the workers employed in them now have little support, and experience of industrial management by the workers in the Soviet Union in the early years of the revolution is a warning against such methods. Instead many unions in Britain and other democratic Western European countries favour ownership and control of basic industries, including public utilities, by the State, which should be responsible for their management on behalf of the community. They consider that, as the community is largely made up of workers by hand and brain, the influence of the workers will be strong enough to ensure the application of policies acceptable to them. They also demand participation by people who have been trade union leaders in the management of State-owned industries, both at the workplace, and at district, regional, and national levels.

Trade unions and their members have hitherto shown much more interest in working conditions than in technical and financial aspects of production and marketing. This is partly because these questions have been claimed as the prerogative of the employers. Some union leaders have given attention to problems of production, but the unions will need to develop a new outlook and include new types of leaders and advisers on their staffs if they are to make useful contributions to industrial management. Also their participation in management calls for many adjustments in industrial relations whether in nationalized industries or in private industries, by developments in the working of national and district joint industrial councils, works councils, and factory production committees. Hitherto, the scope of such consultations has been limited mainly to working conditions, these being defined in some agreements, e.g. in that reached in the British engineering industry after the lock-out in 1922 caused because the employers claimed that shop stewards and other union officials were encroaching on the functions of management. It is essential for productive efficiency and discipline that management's functions and responsibilities should be clearly defined. Participation by workers' representatives can be effective in the formulation of policy and in some aspects of its application, but executive control must rest with the management.

One of the main reasons for the strength of the unions' demands for national ownership and control of industry is the desire of workers for an improvement in their status. Many workers feel that they are treated like pawns, and must do as they are told without having any influence on policy. They feel frustrated and stultified because production, commercial and financial policies are controlled entirely by the employers, and are rarely explained to them and often kept secret from them. In democratic countries the position of the autocratic employer is being increasingly questioned, and a growing number of people hold the view that autocracy in industry must go as it has gone in political life. In the regulation of wages and working conditions it has largely disappeared because of the use of collective bargaining, and an attack has begun on autocracy in the field of productive organization.

With improved standards of education the workers claim a higher status and more recognition of the dignity of human personality. It is admitted that the ordinary skilled or unskilled workers, often working on a narrowly specialized job, cannot make any considerable direct contribution to the larger questions of policy. They can, however, be encouraged to use their intelligence by making constructive suggestions in their own field of work with valuable results in production and in improving industrial relations. Also they will feel greater satisfaction and have an enhanced status if their representatives take part at all levels in the formulation of policy. In political life most voters are neither Ministers of Government, Members of Parliament, nor civil servants, yet they know that they exert a general influence over national policy. Similarly in industry, though political methods would be inappropriate and vocational representation through trade unions is preferable, such influence would do much to enhance the dignity of labour. They could thus take part in regulating the policy of their industry, and share in the application of that policy in their own undertaking.

In the past, trade unions thrived on grievances, they had much justification for using the methods of industrial warfare to remedy the grim conditions which prevailed as the factory system developed, and many of the restrictions demanded by unions were necessary for protecting workers against exploitation. A strike was often the only way to secure recognition for the union or removal of grievances. To-day a new outlook and orientation of policy are needed, with more co-operation and less conflict, and with greater emphasis on increased production and less on restrictions. This is particularly true in Britain where industrial relations have reached an advanced stage of maturity, with much of the former exploitation gone, considerable mutual respect, understanding, and fair dealing between the leaders of employers and workpeople, comprehensive joint machinery for consultation and peaceful settlement of differences, and an elaborate code of agreed working conditions in all industries.

In some countries, e.g. the United States, misunderstandings and distrusts are still the cause of bitter, costly conflicts, but in Britain the prospects for constructive advance.are favourable. Many of the early objects of the unions have been or are in course of being gained, including strong organization, recognition, a comprehensive national system of social security, minimum or standard conditions of work, and nationalization of basic industries. In these circumstances new objectives must be sought, and a main future task of trade unions, in co-operation with employers and Government, is to work for productive efficiency of industry. Studies of inefficiency and waste which have been made in Britain and other countries show the great possibilities of raising productivity and standards of living by a widespread application of the best processes and methods of organization. In the past the workers and their representatives were unwilling to suggest more efficient methods, as they were likely to be told that this was none of their business. Also, the workers believed that the results of improved efficiency went unduly to the shareholders, leaving the workers little or no better off, while labour-saving methods caused unemployment.

To-day the unions are strong enough to secure for their members a fair share of the fruits of industrial progress, and, with the co-operation of the State and employers, can largely safeguard them from the worst effects of technological unemployment. Many leaders and members having been trained in the school of conflict find it difficult to see the possibilities of new policies and to change over to new methods. Yet conflict in present British conditions is largely out of date, and if resumed would undermine industrial prosperity and leave the workers and the whole community poorer. Losses would outweigh any gains from fighting over the division of industry's product, whereas constructive co-operation throughout industry would accelerate considerably the rate of increase in the national income and provide the basis for more rapid rises in standards of living.

11

Bases of Trade Union Organization

TRADE UNIONS are formed because workpeople feel the need to join together in order to further common interests on the basis of common employment. But what is common employment and what are common interests, and what is the best form of organization for furthering them? The answers to these questions in highly industrialized democratic countries are so varied and complex that a simple logical plan of trade union organization has proved impracticable and is incompatible with effective freedom of association, with its implication of freedom for workpeople to form different types of unions and to choose which union they will join and have to represent them if they are eligible to join several. In the older industrial countries industry is so intricate and its parts so much interwoven that a complex trade union structure is inevitable. Some of this complexity is the result of historical factors, the movement being a slow, unplanned growth from small beginnings with opportunism leading to the adoption of almost every conceivable principle of organization. The difficulties have been aggravated by the rapidity with which industrial processes and techniques have been changing and new industries and occupations growing up in recent years.

By contrast, in some countries with authoritarian Governments where the trade union movement is not the result of independent growth over a long period, but is a recently established centrally planned system, a simple structure has been devised. Thus, in the Soviet Union the basis of organization is the undertaking and industry and not the craft, and there are about fifty industrial unions, each with its local, district, regional, and State committees and an All-Russia Central Committee. There are also local, district, regional, and State congresses or assemblies and councils in which representatives of the different unions meet together, and at the apex of the highly centralized structure is the All-Russia Trade Union Congress, which meets once in two years, and the All-Russia General Council of Trade Unions.

In Fascist Italy a comprehensive integrated structure both of trade unions and of employers' organizations was established as basis for the corporative system controlled by the Government. The workers, and likewise the employers, were represented by local or district associations, and these were grouped into regional associations and national trade federations, and only one workers' federation and one employers' federation was given recognition for each industry or other category of economic activity. Freedom of association was not prohibited, and no person was required to become a member either of a recognized association or of any other association, but the legally recognized bodies had exclusive rights of representation. The national federations were combined into confederations covering mainly the four great branches of economic activity—industry and transport, agriculture, commerce, and banking, credit and insurance; thus twenty federations representing the workers were grouped together in the Confederation of Industrial and Transport Workers, and four in the Confederation of Agricultural Workers. Agreements were binding on all persons whether members of the federated associations or not, and as strikes and lock-outs were prohibited, disputes not settled by negotiation or conciliation were referred to arbitration. While the organization could act in defence of the occupational interests of their members, these were to be brought into harmony with the national interests. The safeguarding and furthering of the national interests were undertaken by twenty-two National Corporations to which the trade associations grouped in each corporation nominated representatives of employers and ·vorkers in equal numbers, while other interests, particularly the National Fascist Party, were represented.

Such co-ordinated systems have not been introduced in the Western industrial countries both because their industrial structure is more complex and because they have preferred democratic liberalism to authoritarian controls, the advantages of freedom, even though involving some confusion and waste, being considered to outweigh the benefits of more centrally disciplined structures. The authoritarian systems have taken the various industries as main basis for their organization, other bases being used only within the framework of the industrial classification. This is an advantage if the State exercises a substantial control over industry, but in countries where a more limited view is taken of the functions of the State and where greater freedom is given for organization of vocational interests in ways which the people concerned consider best, diversity predominates, with advantages and disadvantages which are indicated in outlining the various bases.

Organization by Craft

Members of a craft are those who are engaged in a fairly clearly defined skilled occupation with its own distinct requirements based upon a considerable specialized training and experience. The most characteristic crafts are those in manual work, for example, fitters, blacksmiths and electricians in the engineering industry, bricklayers, carpenters, and plumbers in the building industry, printing compositors, and so on, but the term can be extended to cover non-manual workers, including clerks, technicians, teachers, and other professional workers. The differences are in the type of work and training, but each is a skilled specialized occupation. Members of the same craft have many common interests, including the establishment and maintenance of adequate standards of training and skill for admission to the craft, exclusion of unqualified persons, and improvement of working conditions and wages by common action.

The training required to reach the necessary qualification or standard of craftsmanship may take the form of apprenticeship or systematic learnership. By collective agreements or other means the number of entrants is limited, and this benefits the members of crafts as they have a monopoly position which, along with their skill, makes them into the "aristocracy of labour." In safeguarding their employment, conditions of work and standards of skill, the craft unions are ever watchful to prevent encroachment by "dilutees," i.e. workpeople who have not gone through the recognized training but have acquired some knowledge of the craft. The problem of dilution becomes specially acute when processes are simplified or more specialized machinery is introduced which can be operated by less skilled workpeople. This weakens the position of the craftsmen who face loss of employment and lower wages because of the competition of outsiders, and conflicts arise, especially in engineering, between unions of craftsmen and unions to which the less skilled workers belong, the latter claiming that their members should be admitted to certain jobs which the craftsmen regard as exclusively their own.

It is natural, therefore, that members of the same crafts will form unions for purposes of mutual aid and to present a stronger front in negotiations with employers. Being skilled they have higher wages than other workers and can afford to pay bigger contributions to the unions for sickness, old age, unemployment, and other friendly benefits provided out of union funds, for strike pay when in conflict with employers, and for the cost of organizing and administering the union. Having acquired right to friendly benefits they will not lightly allow their membership to lapse. For such reasons the craft

162

unions in Britain, the United States, and other countries are the oldest stable elements of modern trade unionism, for which they have provided the foundations, and they have some features in common with the mediaeval guilds.

The simplest form of craft union is one consisting of members of one craft only. Frequently, however, two or more crafts whose work is closely related are joined together in a multiple craft union, usually by amalgamation of unions for single crafts. Thus the Amalgamated Engineering Union, although it now includes some semi-skilled and unskilled grades, is essentially a multiple craft organization covering fitters, turners, planers, borers, electricians, patternmakers, and other categories. Organizational conflicts arise between multiple and single craft unions if the former open their doors to members of a craft for which a union for a single craft exists. Those who support multiple craft unions claim that the common interests of the crafts concerned are more important than the special interests of each craft, and that they are stronger and therefore more effective if combined together. Against this it is argued that bargaining strength depends more on the importance of a craft in the processes of production than upon numbers, and that a single key craft can represent its own interests best without having to water down its demands by making concessions and compromises to meet the needs of other crafts. Also employers may agree to pay considerable increases in wages to members of a small essential craft, though they would reject similar demands if made by a larger body of workers. In the last resort a strike by an essential craft may hold up production as effectively as a bigger strike covering several crafts. The possibility should not, however, be overlooked of finding some substitute for or of "by-passing" the labour of a small number of workers in one craft, and where this risk exists the case for a multiple craft union becomes stronger.

Some crafts form part of one industry only; for example, shipwrights work in the shipbuilding industry and no other. Many crafts, however, extend over two or more industries. Thus, plumbers, painters, and carpenters work in the building industry, railway service, and shipbuilding, and may also be employed on construction and maintenance work by the chemical, iron and steel, and other industries, by municipal authorities and by universities. Again, fitters and turners are employed in engineering, shipbuilding, railway workshops, textile factories, road transport services, and other industries where machine construction or maintenance is needed. Though each industry has its own special requirements, such craftsmen are mobile between industries and can readily adapt their skill to meet the needs of different industries. Employment opportunities are therefore open to them in several industries, and if one industry is depressed they may be able to find jobs in another. Consequently craft unions have an interest in establishing good wages and conditions by agreement with employers in all the industries in which their members are distributed, and the members in one industry have much more in common with their fellow-craftsmen in other industries than they have with those in other occupations working alongside them day by day in their own industry. Thus a fitter in a textile factory has stronger occupational ties with fitters in engineering plants or in railway workshops than with the spinners and weavers whose machines he daily maintains. This linking of craft interests across the lines of industry involves clashes with other types of association.

Organization by Industry

Just as workpeople become specialized in the performance of particular processes, so undertakings specialize in the products they make or in the services they render, and industries consist of undertakings making similar products or rendering similar services. Thus undertakings engaged in mining coal make up the coal-mining industry, undertakings producing leather form the tanning industry, those producing engines and machines make up the engineering industry, undertakings providing transport services form the transport industry, and so on. Some industries are relatively homogeneous and others are much more complex. For example, though in coal-mining subdivisions can be made for anthracite, lignite, and ordinary coal, and for underground and open-cast mining, the industry is less complex than engineering, which includes general engineering, marine engineering, aeronautical engineering, motor engineering, electrical engineering, and such specialized sections as the making of textile and agricultural machinery. Similarly transport consists not of one industry but of several—rail, road, water (river, lake and canal, and ocean), and air transport. For the purpose of organizing workers into trade unions by industries, circumstances determine whether there should be a separate union or not for each of the main subdivisions of a complex industry.

All persons are employed either to produce goods or render services, and if therefore such production and services can be grouped into separate industries a comprehensive basis would be available for trade union organization to cover all employed persons without overlapping. In applying this basis workpeople in a given craft spread in two or more industries would be separated from one

164

another by being members of the unions for the industries employing them. Thus maintenance engineers employed by a textile company would be members of the union for workers in the textile industry and not of the union for the engineering industry. The union for an industry would be open to all workers of the industry, whether craftsmen, semi-skilled, or unskilled. In Britain, the National Union of Railwaymen, and the National Union of Mineworkers are examples of organizations which approximate closely to the industrial type.

The difficulty of making a clear-cut classification of industry is a complicating factor. Industries overlap one another and their boundaries are blurred; some undertakings are wholly within one industry but others have a foot in two or, Manx-like, in three. The British nationalized railways, in addition to having workshops for the construction and repair of locomotives, carriages, and wagons, and their own hotels, may operate docks and ships, and undertake other ancillary work. Originally the British railway companies bought their locomotives from engineering companies as still do the railways in colonial areas and some foreign countries. The work is clearly engineering whether it is operated by a railway company or separately. Yet the National Union of Railwaymen competes with the engineering unions for members among the workpeople in the railway engineering workshops. Such rivalries would complicate the adoption of a simple industrial structure for trade unionism, quite apart from the clash between the craft and industrial principles of organization. Another example of a vertical combination cutting across the lines of several industries is an iron and steel company which has its own coal-mine and coke ovens and sells surplus gas to a neighbouring town.

Even if a scheme of industrial unions were adopted, changes in production with creation of new industries and decline or modification of old ones would involve difficult adjustments of trade union structure. Thus, plastics will be used for a whole range of products from motor-car bodies to cups and plates. Should it be considered as a new industry for purposes of trade union organization, or be split into parts and distributed over the older industries such as the pottery and motor industries with which it has little affinity? Again, one part of artificial silk production is closer to chemicals than to textiles. Oil from coal, synthetic rubber, and many other new processes are disturbing older industries, while the industrial consequences of atomic energy cannot yet be forecast.

Having reviewed difficulties which arise in defining industrial boundaries, consideration must now be given to factors which tend towards the formation of industrial unions. Although some

165

undertakings in an industry are more prosperous than others, they are all affected by changes in demand for its products or services and by the introduction of labour-saving inventions. Wages throughout the industry rise or fall under the influence of these changes, which also determine working conditions, and skilled craftsmen, semi-skilled and unskilled workpeople are all liable to be affected by prosperity or depression of the industry. Also one industry may be enjoying good trade with opportunities for wage increases at the same time as another is suffering from poor demand for its products and is faced with lower wages. Trade unions organized by industries can adapt their policies to the economic conditions of each industry, without the complications which must arise when unions cut across the boundaries of several industries. Also employers are often organized by industries, as they are free from the alternative of craft organization, and the structure of collective bargaining is simplified and the chances of reaching agreement may be increased if the workers are similarly organized.

Members of a craft union may argue that they do skilled work of the same standard for each of the industries in which they are employed and that, therefore, they should receive the same standard rates of wages irrespective of the industry in which they work and whether it is depressed or not. This is why union scales of wages have been drawn up which the union tries to secure by agreement with employers in each industry in which its members are employed. However, the economic conditions of different industries prevent uniformity of rates and conditions, and where differences arise, craftsmen will become more inclined to seek the support of other grades of workpeople in their own industry and to rely less on common action with members of their own craft in other industries. This tendency is, nevertheless, kept in check by the mobility of the craftsman, who will try to move from the lower-paid to the better-paid industries, thus restricting wage divergencies and strengthening the craft against the industry as basis of organization.

Some trade unionists favour industrial unions because they believe that the main purpose of organization is to strengthen the workers in the "class" struggle and that negotiations with employers about working conditions are subsidiary. They regard such unions as the best instruments for this purpose, the exclusive sectional interests of the craft unions being avoided and solidarity of all grades of workers fostered. If industry is to be owned and controlled by the workers or if they are to have a substantial share in its management, the most convenient and practical type of union is one which conforms closely with the pattern of industry. Industrial unionism,

166

though associating skilled and unskilled workers together, is not, however, free from the risk of supporting sectional interests, as a strongly organized union in an industry vital to the country might secure advantages for its members which weaker unions in less essential industries could not gain, and in certain circumstances it might do so in collusion with the employers who would pass the cost on to the consumers by raising prices.

The formation and development of industrial unions are easiest where there is no clear-cut line separating skilled from semi-skilled and unskilled workers. In some industries, in building, for example, large numbers of labourers are unable to become craftsmen as they have not gone through the necessary apprenticeship, whereas in others, for example, coal-mining and railway service, the line is not so sharply drawn and unskilled workers can gain promotion into the higher grades as vacancies occur. Industries of the latter kind are those in which industrial unionism has made most progress among the main body of workers, though in each of them there are some groups of workers whose work is so distinctive that they have preferred to remain apart in craft organizations. Other industries again, for example, the woollen and worsted, cotton textile, and clothing industries, have few unskilled workers, for the great majority in varying degrees are skilled, and in such industries the formation of industrial unions is facilitated, though in some of them long established unions for separate grades have retained their hold for traditional reasons.

Changes in industrial processes involving greater use of semi-automatic machinery, mass production, and increased specialization have reduced the importance of craftsmanship among the main body of workers of some industries. This has led to the formation of industrial unions with large memberships, and to the decline in importance or even the entire break-up of some of the crafts under the pressure of semi-skilled machinists and other types of dilutee labour. This has been outstanding in the mass-production industries of the United States, for example in motor-car manufacture, and the rubber, oil, and iron and steel industries, as well as in coal-mining, and has facilitated the rapid recent growth of industrial unionism co-ordinated by the Congress of Industrial Organizations as a rival on fairly equal terms to the old-established, craft-based American Federation of Labour for the leadership of the workers of the United States. In Britain also the clash of principle exists, though it has been somewhat moderated by the influence of the Trades Union Congress, to which all the main craft and industrial unions are alike affiliated.

167

The conflict between the craft and industrial principles of organization is likely to persist long in democratic countries. They represent alternative and in many ways irreconcilable methods of furthering the interests of distinct groups of workers. Given freedom of choice some will continue to favour craft and others industrial unions as best suited to their respective purposes. The trends of productive processes are increasing the numbers of semi-skilled specialists in industry, and the strength of industrial unions measured by numbers is likely to grow substantially, but skilled craftsmen and technicians with high qualifications will always be needed, as they are essential both for the operation and progress of industry, and many of them will wish to have their own unions for maintaining high standards of competence and satisfactory working conditions. If they joined in with other grades they would be in the minority and therefore they often decide that they can best safeguard their interests by remaining independent. In the trade union movement as a whole they will be a minority, but their effective power in industrial relations will be greater than if measured by their membership alone. In national political issues the bigger membership of industrial unions will give them the greater power in elections and as pressure groups on labour policy and legislation.

Organization based on Type of Employer

Some organizations define the scope of their membership to conform with the field of employment provided by certain classes of employer. Strictly speaking, industrial unions do this, but the kind of organization which will now be considered differs from industrial unionism by extending beyond the boundaries of an industry. The British National Union of Railwaymen has been mentioned as an example of an industrial union because it aims at recruiting all workpeople engaged in the railway industry and because the main body of its members consists of railway workpeople. As, however, it also recruits engineers in the railway workshops, and workpeople in hotels and steamships and at docks owned by the railways, it is really basing its membership not on the railway industry but upon the personnel employed formerly by the railways companies and now, since nationalization, by the British Railways. This has advantages in collective bargaining as the wages and working conditions of all the personnel depend upon the prosperity or otherwise of the railways, which also have special conditions of service of their own.

A union open to all persons employed by the railways represents only a small departure from a true industrial union, as the members

168

outside the railway industry proper form only a small minority in ancillary services. Some unions based on the type of employer differ widely, however, from industrial unions, for example, unions bringing together persons employed by the Co-operative Societies, or by municipal and other local authorities, or civil servants employed by central Government departments. The main work of the Co-operative Societies is in retail and wholesale trade, and logically persons employed in this work could join with those doing similar work for other employers in an industrial union of workers in the distributive trades. The Co-operative movement also engages in production, particularly food preparation and boot and shoe manufacture, and the workers in these productive undertakings could combine in industrial or alternatively in craft unions with workers in the respective industries or crafts who are not employed by the Co-operative Societies. However, the Societies have a special outlook which distinguishes them from other employers, and many workers employed by the Societies have found it convenient to form unions among themselves only, but open to both distributive and productive workers.

Central Government departments and local authorities also form a distinctive class of employers, with special conditions of service and systems of negotiation. In the past they have differed from any private undertakings in giving greater security of employment and in providing pensions for those on the establishment. Much of the work has been non-profitmaking, and although wages, salaries, and other conditions, are influenced by the standards of private industry, they have been sheltered from the direct effects of business prosperity and depression. Some of the work has, however, been run on a modified economic basis, for example, the Post Office services and the electricity, tramway, and other public utilities, and the importance of this type of public employment has been much increased by the nationalization of great basic industries.

Although the central Government administrative, clerical, and manual personnel are broadly similar to those in private industry, with whom they might have combined along professional, craft, and industrial lines, they have found it practical to form unions or associations of civil servants, largely because of the distinctive character of their employer and their conditions of service, and of the growth of Whitley Joint Councils for negotiation between representatives of the personnel and of the departments as the immediate employer. The formation of such unions was made inevitable in Britain during the years 1927 to 1946 by legislation which prohibited civil servants from joining any union which was not restricted

169

solely to persons employed by the Crown. The Government employs so great a number of persons in so wide a range of departments and occupations that the number of unions and associations of Government employees is very considerable. Some, within the limits of Government service, are of the "craft" type with members in a number of departments, e.g. the Civil Servants' Clerical Association, while others are restricted to a single department, e.g. the Ministry of Labour Staff Association; others again are of the industrial type, e.g. the Union of Post Office Workers. Indeed, there is almost as great a variety of types of unions within the Government service as outside. The Postmaster-General's Department may be taken as an illustration of the ways in which the personnel might be linked along craft or industrial lines if it had not proved so convenient for them to form the "employment" type of union; its clerks might have joined with clerks in private employment, telephone operators with those doing such work outside, and similarly with skilled engineers and electricians, while some counter clerks do work so much like that of shop assistants that they could appropriately combine with them! Alternatively it might be argued that the postal services are so distinctive that, whether operated by Government or by private capital, the main body of the workers should be members of an industrial union.

The special features of local authorities as employers have similarly led to the formation of unions of the "employment" type. The membership of the National Union of General and Municipal Workers includes a large number of semi-skilled and unskilled workers employed by local authorities in a wide variety of occupations, They are linked by common employment and not be similarity of work, whether in craft or industry. There are also unions of more specialized workers, e.g. tramway workers, while the National Association of Local Government Officers uses the basis of common employment combined with that of "craft," to bring together clerical, technical, and administrative grades of officials.

Other examples of the employment type of union are associations of bank clerks and of the personnel of insurance companies. From some points of view, however, each of these occupations could be regarded as providing a special service, and the associations, therefore, could be classified as craft or industrial unions, except where the membership is limited to a particular company. Such a body as the Association of University Teachers is somewhat of the employment type, being limited to teachers employed by universities, but within these limits it is a kind of "craft" or professional rather than an industrial union; only a union open to all persons employed by universities, including administrative, clerical, and manual, would be of the employment or the industrial type, but a carpenter employed permanently on maintenance work by a university would have little in common professionally with members of the academic staff.

It must be emphasized that, whereas almost all employed persons could be classified into one industrial union or another, the employment type of union is not a comprehensive basis for organization, but has limited though important fields of application such as have been indicated above. As has been already noticed, some of the unions of the employment type are also based on the craft and others on the industrial principle.

Organizations of General Workers

The earliest stable unions in Britain were along craft lines to protect the interests of skilled workpeople, and they were followed by industrial unions covering skilled and unskilled workers alike in separate industries. In some industries, however, trade unionism was almost non-existent, and it played little or no part among semi-skilled and unskilled workpeople where craft unions were established. The trade union movement, like nature, abhors a vacuum, and from the last decade of the nineteenth century a growing recognition of the claims of hitherto neglected low-paid workers led to a wave of organization among the semi-skilled and unskilled. This began with unions in particular industries, and sometimes the industry basis was maintained, but a process of consolidation and amalgamation resulted in the formation of unions which recruited members in any industry. These became known as general labour unions, and they set out to organize workpeople in any industry who were not members of a union. They have, however, invaded territories claimed by craft or industrial unions. In Britain, the Transport and General Workers' Union and the National Union of General and Municipal Workers are of this type.

In theory a general workers' union, being open to workpeople in any industry or occupation, including skilled craftsmen, clerical workers, and supervisors, could if wholly successful take the place of all other unions and become "one big union" representing all the workers. In practice, however, industrial and craft unions are usually strong enough to defend their own territories, and agreements or understandings have sometimes been reached by which recruiting rivalry is restricted; in particular general workers' unions have agreed not to seek members in certain skilled crafts. Consequently, the membership of general workers' unions consists mainly of semi-skilled and unskilled workers, and they are therefore the

171

counterpart among labourers and semi-skilled workers of the craft unions for skilled workers, cutting across the lines of industry. Their members include labourers working with unionized craftsmen, e.g. builders' and engineers' labourers, and also workpeople of all grades in industries in which other unions had been ineffective or had been able to organize only a part of the field. In addition to manual workers they have gained membership among clerical, administrative, technical, and professional workers, both in private employment and in Government and other public services.

The success in Britain of the general workers' unions which grew rapidly during the inter-war years, both by gaining individual members and by attracting other unions to amalgamate with them, is sufficient evidence that they have met a real need. They have brought trade union protection to workers who had been neglected by the older unions, and they undertook collective bargaining on behalf of these workers in a wide range of industries and occupations. Many of the members either have a general skill, for example that of clerical workers, which can be adapted quickly to many different kinds of work, or are semi-skilled or unskilled and can similarly learn in a short time the special needs of a new job; they are therefore readily mobile between different industries and occupations, and consequently have an interest in establishing a reasonable equality of wages and conditions for equivalent work throughout the whole field of employment open to them. A general workers' union can do this more effectively than separate unions for each industry, as it is more likely to apply common principles and has the advantage of unity of organization and action.

Unity is, however, qualified by the necessity for providing substantial autonomy for each of the distinct classes of workers. Thus, the Transport and General Workers' Union, with almost 1,200,000 members, representing a fourfold increase in less than thirty years, has many separate trade committees with considerable freedom of action for such diverse occupations as dock labour, road transport workers, engineering and shipbuilding labour, chemical workers, agricultural workers, flour mill workers, clerical and administrative workers. The autonomy of these various sections is inevitable because each has its own distinct problems which require separate treatment in the determination of policy and in negotiations with employers. Sometimes autonomy is the result of arrangements made when unions with memberships in separate occupations have amalgamated with the Transport and General Workers' Union. The system of government is outlined later, in the section on trade union structure and government.

The success of unions of this kind depends upon the ability with which their national leaders can keep in touch with the rank and file and upon the effectiveness with which the special needs of each section can be met. Unless both these conditions are satisfactorily covered, some of the more powerful sections will become restive, may decide that they can do better for themselves by having their own separate organizations, and the union will begin to disintegrate. There is no reason, however, why a general workers' union through its national and district trade committees should not be able to deal efficiently and promptly with the problems of each of its sections, as a question raised locally can be sent on from branch to district and from district to the national executive as rapidly as in a national craft or industrial union. For this to be achieved and delays avoided, the system must be flexible, and provide for considerable devolution of administration and autonomy of action for each trade group. Such a union can bring more powerful support to the various occupations than they would have if each had a separate union, and this advantage is particularly great for workers in some of the smaller industries and for others whose economic strength would be small if they acted alone. It can build up an efficient central organization with a large staff of specialists, and its wealth of information and wide range of contacts with many industries enable it better to judge the opportune time for action and what demands are likely to be successful than could separate unions for each section, whose outlook, experience, and resources would inevitably be much more limited.

As already indicated, general workers' unions have been effective in gaining membership in a wide range of occupations where trade unionism had hitherto made little progress, and they have therefore satisfied a need not met by other unions and have filled many gaps in trade union ranks. Without them, many of these workers would not be members of any union. The very success of general workers' unions bring them to the territories of other unions, and conflicts are inevitable with old-established craft and industrial unions, though these can sometimes be restrained or avoided for a time by understandings about boundaries. However, the clash of organizational principle is so complete, especially between the industrial basis and the general labour basis, that some gradual evolution of structure is likely. One possibility would be for the general workers' unions to break up into separate industrial unions or for members to be transferred to other unions organized on industrial lines. A second alternative would be for general workers' unions to consolidate their position in clearly defined industrial fields so that they would mainly

173

represent workers in a range of industries by absorbing certain industrial unions. They would then become what they are already to a considerable extent—multi-industrial unions for semi-skilled and unskilled workers and for some other categories. This seems the more probable evolution and would in the main be a continuation of present trends. It would still leave unresolved their relations with craft unions, which might be regulated by defining boundaries on the basis of "professional" qualifications. There would also be certain powerful single industrial unions, for example, of coal-miners and railwaymen, which would remain independent of the multiple industrial unions. Whatever direction the evolution may take there will be difficult adjustments to be made in shaping the structure of trade unionism so that it may best meet the needs of the future.

Other Bases

In addition to the four main bases of trade union organization reviewed above there are others, some of which are variations or combinations of the four and therefore need not be discussed here, while others leading to subdivisions or groupings within the main types may be briefly mentioned. Among these are the material used, the process, the product, sex, and religion. There are also unions based on grades of workers such as foremen and supervisors, technicians, and professional and semi-professional categories, but these in principle closely resemble the craft unions.

The material used sometimes tends to the formation of broadly based unions, for example metal workers and woodworkers, which clash with unions based on other principles of organization. In textiles, although fibres of different kinds are often woven together, separate unions are formed for the cotton industry, the woollen industry and the silk industry, and there are also subdivisions by processes, e.g. spinning, weaving, and dyeing. In flour milling, the process and product together provide the basis of a distinct industry, while iron-moulders form a craft based on material and process.

Most unions are open to men and women, except where by custom or the nature of the work women are not employed, for example, in the crafts in engineering, building, and printing, or in heavy work in mining, quarrying, and iron and steel. In circumstances where women consider that their interests require special organizations or where their work is quite distinctive separate unions for women only have been formed. This is rare in manual work, and women's organizations are mainly set up in some of the secretarial grades and in the professions, including teaching. In Britain the tendency to form separate organizations for women was relatively strong during the years of agitation for votes for women and representation in Parliament, and a feminist bias was noticeable, but more recently women have joined the same unions as men, their special interests being cared for, when necessary, by women's sections or committees and by provision for their representation on district committees and the national executives of the union.

Although religious doctrines play their part in the policies and politics of the British trade union movement, they have not led to the formation of separate unions. In some European countries, however, the outlook of many Roman Catholic workers has differed so much from that of members of the socialist unions that they have formed separate unions often in the same industries and crafts as the socialist unions. These Christian or Catholic unions have not approved the doctrines of syndicalism and the policy of the class struggle, they have adopted a conciliatory and co-operative policy towards the employers, both they and the employers have based their relations on Papal encyclics dealing with social policy, have sought peaceful methods of settling disputes, and have avoided the use of strikes and lockouts. Catholic unions have been active in the Netherlands, Belgium, Luxemburg, and in parts of France and Germany.

Enough has been said to show the great variety and complexity of the trade union movement in countries where it has grown spontaneously, any group of workers with common interests being free to form an association. The common interests of a craft differ, however, from those of an industry, and yet again from those of general labour, and consequently rivalry develops. Once powerful unions have been established on different principles of organization, great difficulties are experienced in trying to simplify the structure of the movement, and the most that can be attempted is a process of gradual amalgamation.

STRUCTURE AND GOVERNMENT

A study of trade union structure and government in any industrially developed democratic country reveals problems of great interest and complexity which closely resemble those of national government and international relations. Yet they have not received the attention which they deserve from political scientists. Unions provide in their constitutions for local, regional, and central government, for systems of election, and for the degree of authority to be exercised locally and centrally. Each union has its own system and practices, with, therefore, wide variety in the movement as a whole corresponding to differences in the franchise, local autonomy, or centralization, democracy, or dictatorship in the government of States. Though most unions have democratic constitutions, some of them reveal features of dictatorship in their practical operation.

Then among unions, as among States, there are great or first-class powers, second-class powers, and small States, and relations between them may be friendly, neutral, or hostile. Rivalries and boundary disputes with frontier incidents lead to conflicts, small unions may come under the domination of big ones and may be invaded by them, territories are disputed and minorities in one union may be supported by an outside power acting in its own interests. Civil wars break out within unions and revolutions sometimes result in secessions. Diplomatic relations may be cordial or strained; treaties, *ententes*, and alliances are arranged. In favourable circumstances federations are formed, some loose with much autonomy for the constituents and others highly centralized, while complete amalgamations may be arranged by processes resembling the unification of Germany in the nineteenth century or the earlier formation of the United Kingdom.

Nor does the structure of trade unionism end at the frontiers of the States. For many industries there have long been international trade secretariats, for example, for miners, metal workers, transport, textiles, and at the apex is the International Confederation of Free Trade Unions which for the Western countries is the movement's equivalent to the United Nations, and faces many of its problems.

For purposes of organization and government, the basic unit of trade unions is the branch, which is a local grouping of members small enough to enable them all to meet together for the transaction of union business. Branches are of two main types, one of them consisting of workpeople of a particular craft or employment category living in the same locality but working for different employers in separate factories or workplaces. The second is based on the place of employment; for example, the most convenient unit for the organization of tram drivers and conductors is at the tramway depots, and of bus drivers and conductors at the garages, as their homes may be widely scattered and there may be no other good meeting-place. Both types are local, but the latter has the advantage that all the members of the branch are in daily relations at their workplace, where they work under the same conditions and have common problems. A branch headquarters away from the workplace has, however, the advantage that the affairs of the union are conducted entirely away from the employer and his influence, but meetings of the branch may be held only once a week or once a fortnight, whereas problems requiring attention may arise from day to day in the works. At each workplace or shop one member is appointed as collector to collect subscriptions, keep in touch with members, and report to the branch any conditions of work which do not conform with union rules, and may adjust minor differences with the employer.

The shop steward movement is strong in engineering and other industries in which the union branches are based more on the place where the members live than on the workplace. The shop steward represents union members at the workplace and deals with problems as they arise. If in the future trade unions take more part in productive efficiency, the most suitable basic organization of the workers will be the workplace. Sometimes union branches are based *both* on where the members work and where they live, for example, in a mining village where the miners are all employed at the local colliery. Such branches are simple and compact, though they sometimes suffer from isolation from which branches with members from several works are free.

Branches are grouped into districts, and as these district groups were often independent unions before amalgamating to form national organizations, some of them retain considerable autonomy. In unions with fairly homogeneous membership, district affairs are controlled by district committees, but if membership is complex because it includes several distinct trades with special interests separate committees are appointed for each trade. Central or national control is exercised by general conferences of delegates of the whole union, these being usually held annually to decide on major questions of policy and on the rules of the union. Then there is a central executive council or committee which meets frequently to deal with the main current affairs of the union; it is a powerful body and usually consists of one representative from each district, and, in complex unions, one representative from each trade group. Members of district and trade committees, of the central executive, and of the general meeting or conference are elected by ballot of union members, the single transferable vote sometimes being used.

Usually the central or national executive committee is responsible for negotiations on changes in rates of wages and working conditions, it controls the work of organization, deals with appeals from branches and districts, and decides when levies should be raised. When suspension or expulsion of a member for breach of the union's rules is proposed the executive committee considers the case, giving the member concerned an opportunity of making his defence. Incidentally this power of unions to expel members implies that, where

177

a union has won the closed shop, a member who is expelled is prevented from working in the occupation. The executive committee directs the policy of the union in disputes, but decisions to take strike action are usually reached by a ballot of members, a two-thirds or sometimes a three-fourths majority being required.

As an illustration of the structure of a complex union the constitutional arrangements of the British Transport and General Workers' Union may be given. After the Second World War this union had a membership of about 1,200,000 in many different industries, it had more than 4,000 branches, and an annual income of about £1,400,000. The problem in such a union is to secure cohesion and efficiency by central control, while giving effective autonomy in collective bargaining to each of the trade groups comprising the membership, and to decentralize the administration so as to avoid cumbersome arrangements. The method adopted is based on two principles of organization, by trade groups, and by geographical areas. The membership is formed into six trade groups, each with a national trade group committee, and an area trade group committee in each of thirteen areas of the country, and these committees are mainly concerned with the special problems affecting their trades, including negotiations about working conditions.[1] In addition, each of the thirteen areas has a committee covering the whole membership of the area irrespective of trade and consisting of representatives of each area trade group committee, and these area committees are responsible mainly for organization and administration.

Central control is exercised by a general executive council consisting of one representative elected by ballot from each area and one from each national trade group committee; officials of the union are not eligible for election to any area or trade committee or to the executive council, which therefore consist only of lay members. The final authority of the union is a biennial delegate conference, the delegates being chosen by the area trade groups.[2] The union does not adopt the practice of many other unions of electing all the main officials by ballot of the members, only the general secretary being chosen in this way; other officials are appointed by the executive council, but only those who have been members for at least two years of the trade group with which they will work may be appointed. The main structure of the constitution has remained unchanged since

[1] The trades comprising the groups are docks; waterways; professional, technical, clerical, and administrative; road transport (passenger); road transport (commercial); general workers; there are also several trade sub-sections.
[2] The constitution provides for national trade delegate conferences.

it came into operation in 1922, and during that time the union's membership has quadrupled, largely by amalgamation with many other unions.

As already indicated, the rates of contribution to union funds vary greatly, some unions having big contributions in return for substantial friendly benefits as well as "trade" benefits, while others have small subscriptions to provide "trade" benefits only. In some British unions with mainly unskilled and semi-skilled members the minimum weekly contribution is 6d. or 7d. for men and 3d. for women, with additional amounts varying according to benefits, while in unions of skilled craftsmen the rate is much higher, members of the London Society of Compositors, for example, paying 4s. 6d. a week, of which 3s. 6d. is reserved for superannuation. The average weekly contribution in British unions is between 1 and 1½ per cent of an average weekly wage. Often contributions to friendly benefit funds are optional, and there has been a marked tendency for the numbers contributing for these benefits to decline since the establishment of a comprehensive system of social insurance. In addition to regular contributions, a small entrance free is often required, while the rules of many unions authorize the raising of special levies, a power which is exercised only to meet emergencies, particularly to maintain strike pay or friendly benefits. The wide differences in rates of contribution and of benefit among unions organizing similar classes of labour are a hindrance to amalgamation.

The biggest item of union expenditure is usually organization and management, this representing in British unions an average of more than 50 per cent of the revenue from members' contributions, though the percentages are considerably higher in those unions in which friendly benefits are small. Expenditure on friendly benefits comes next with an average of more than 40 per cent of the total. Strike pay during the seven years before the Second World War was only 2 or 3 per cent of total expenditure, and was smaller still in the seven years after the War; it had been considerably higher in the 1920's. Expenditure from the political fund has also been relatively small, only occasionally being more than 2 per cent of total expenditure.

The work of unions is conducted largely by their full-time national and district officials, under the general control of executive, district, and trade committees, and the more senior officials usually wield great power as they have the widest knowledge of the union and its problems. In most unions the main district and national officials are elected directly by the members, though in some unions they are appointed by the executive committee. The method of direct election

179

tends to develop too great an independence and insufficient co-operation between officials, as each knows that he relies individually on members' votes. Also the qualities required from those who administer the affairs of a great union are not always those likely to capture the support of members, who may have little conception of the complexities of the union's business. Consequently, selection is haphazard, and though some unions have arranged for the systematic training of young officials, great extension of such opportunities would be of value, both to full-time officials and to workshop representatives and officers of branches, as mostly they acquire experience as best they can "on the job."

The full-time officials, numbering only a few thousands in Britain, form the "civil service" of the movement. Many of the leaders after years of struggle have emerged as skilled negotiators with strong personalities. The salaries paid to the senior officials of British trade unions are too low in relation to the responsibilities borne, though men of ambition and ability within the movement, who would have few other channels of advancement open to them, are attracted by the power and prestige which high office in the union gives, and also because it may facilitate election to Parliament or appointment to the boards of nationalized industries or other public bodies. A few British unions have efficient headquarters staffs not only with skilled accountants and a professional solicitor, but with a trained research staff of statisticians and economists. In many others, however, even in powerful unions with large memberships the headquarters organization is weak, inadequate for the responsibilities, and unable to provide the data necessary for formulating sound policies and conducting collective negotiations. These defects are no doubt due to a distrust of experts and bureaucracy by the rank and file, a preference for the amateur and a reliance on opportunism in negotiations, but with the changed conditions and responsibilities of to-day, a more up-to-date mechanism should be devised. In the United States many of the leading unions have more developed headquarters organizations, especially on the research side, than most British unions, and they pay more adequate salaries.

As each union represents a separate craft, industry or other group of workers, the policy of each union is based on the sectional interests of its own members, and although attention is paid to trends of wages, hours, and employment in other industries, and to general economic conditions, there is no adequate central co-ordination in the interests of the workers as a whole. Union officials as the servants of their unions, therefore, have a sectional outlook. Thus, no union authority can call a halt to the demands of powerful unions for wage increases at a time when the country faces inflationary risks which would be injurious for the main body of workers. Each union hopes by isolated action to get the best bargain for its members, whatever the effects may be on workers in other crafts or industries. The Trades Union Congress in Britain through its General Council exercises a valuable general influence on policy, but each union remains sovereign in bargaining about wages and conditions. With the growing integration of national life there is increasing need for methods by which, while maintaining reasonable flexibility, sectional interests can be modified in the interests of the workers as a whole and of those of the community. Yet the unions are still as unwilling to commit some of their sovereignty to a central authority as are the Great Powers to transfer part of their sovereignty to the United Nations.

In most highly developed industrial countries a few powerful unions represent the main strength of the movement both in membership and influence, but alongside them is a large number of quite small unions. Thus in Britain at the end of 1951 the number of unions was 704 with a total membership of 9,480,000, but 15 only of these unions each with 100,000 or more members accounted for almost two-thirds of the total and these unions together with 28 others each with memberships of 25,000 or more, covered about 85 per cent of the whole movement. By contrast with these 43 big unions there were left 661 unions with only about 15 per cent of the membership, and of these unions about two-thirds had less than 1,000 members each, and together covered under 2 per cent of the total.[1]

The existence of large numbers of small unions is due partly to historical reasons, many local unions of craftsmen and other specialized groups being formed in the early days of the movement or at the time of its extension to occupations previously unorganized, and once formed they have believed that their interests are better served by remaining independent than by merging in a larger union. However, many small unions have seen advantages in amalgamation, or have submitted to the pressure of powerful unions to join them. Consequently in Britain there has been a steady reduction in the number of unions from 1,384 at the end of 1920 to between 1,100 and 1,000 in the 1930's, followed by a further substantial fall to 704 at the end of 1951.

Consideration only of the number of separate unions is liable to

[1] The statistics are based on data compiled from the records of the Chief Registrar of Friendly Societies and published by the Ministry of Labour and National Service.

give a misleading impression, as many local and other unions work together in federations, and some unions are in two or more federations. Each union in a federation maintains its own membership and organization for collecting subscriptions and paying benefits, but frequently the federation acts for the affiliated unions in negotiating with the employers about wages and working conditions. Sometimes the term "confederation" is used, especially for great organizations affiliating for certain common purposes powerful national unions and federations of unions.[1] Some federations are merely loose associations for advisory purposes, with the affiliated unions retaining almost complete autonomy, while a few federations are so highly integrated that, for practical purposes, they differ little from complete amalgamations. Not infrequently federations prepare the way for amalgamation of the member unions. Thus, the Miners' Federation of Great Britain, with which were affiliated the miners' unions in the various coal-mining districts was the forerunner of the National Union of Mineworkers.

The formation of great national unions and federations for separate industries leave the trade union movement sectional in outlook and action, with risks of independent policies being applied which may injure the interests of other sections of workers and the whole community. Attempts to solve this problem have been made in different countries, but have had only a limited success. The two main methods are co-operation between branches or other local trade union organizations in each industrial centre, and the formation of a national organization in each country to which the unions affiliate for specified common purposes, though in some countries two or more national organizations are established because of fundamental differences of policy between distinct groups of unions.

In Britain, bodies known as trades councils or trades and labour councils have been established in hundreds of cities and towns for co-operation on industrial and political questions. They are, in effect, associations of trade union branches and of any independent unions in each locality, and are an expression of labour solidarity. Their functions are rather narrowly limited, their general purpose is to promote the interests of the affiliated unions and to improve the economic and social conditions of the workers, and they may organize support for any union involved in a strike or lock-out, and

[1] For example, in Britain the Confederation of Shipbuilding and Engineering Trade Unions is an organization bringing into association some 2,000,000 members in the engineering, shipbuilding, and ship-repairing industries, including railway workshops.

try to settle differences between the unions. Unwillingness has been shown by the unions to giving important industrial tasks to the councils, and although proposals have been made that the councils could be developed into agencies of the Trades Union Congress for giving effect in the localities to its policies, no progress along this line has been made.

The Trades Union Congress

Nationally, trade unions co-operate through such bodies as the British Trades Union Congress, the American Federation of Labour, and the Congress of Industrial Organizations, and the French Confédération Générale du Travail. The Trades Union Congress was formed in 1868 and its functions in general terms are to promote the interests of its affiliated organizations and to improve the economic and social conditions of the workers. For the achievement of these purposes it supports public ownership and control of natural resources and of services, particularly the nationalization of land, mines, minerals and railways, and extension of State and municipal enterprise for the provision of social necessities and services, together with adequate participation of the workers in the control of public services and industries. Its programme also includes a working week of forty hours, a legal minimum wage for each industry or occupation, payment for holidays, adequate State pensions for all at sixty years of age, suitable maintenance for the unemployed, extension of training facilities for both juveniles and adults unemployed, adequate housing, compensation for industrial accidents and diseases, pensions for the infirm and for widowed mothers and dependent children, the raising of school-leaving age to sixteen with adequate maintenance allowances, abolition of overtime for all workers under eighteen years of age, and State educational facilities extending from the elementary schools to the universities.

The Congress exercises its authority mainly by influence and not by formal powers, and its affiliated unions retain complete autonomy over the regulation of wages and working conditions. It has, however, made steady progress, especially since the end of the First World War; it has acquired great prestige, and has become effective as the central representative of trade unionism, expressing its views and co-ordinating its policy. Effect is given to Congress decisions by its General Council which is composed of thirty-two members, twenty-seven of whom represent seventeen trade groups, and remaining members representing women workers. The Council, like Congress, has no authority to enforce its decisions, but proceeds by the method of counsel and consent.

The powers and duties of the General Council have been summarized as follows: "to keep a watch on all industrial movements and where possible to co-ordinate industrial action; to watch legislation affecting labour and to initiate such legislation as Congress may direct; to adjust disputes and differences between affiliated unions; to promote common action on general questions such as wages and hours of labour; to assist any union which is attacked on any vital question of trade union principle; to assist the work of organization and to carry on propaganda for strengthening the trade union movement; to enter into relations with the trade union and labour movements in other countries; and to take, if necessary, trade union legal cases to the House of Lords as the Court of Final Appeal for decision."[1]

The affiliated unions act independently in negotiations with employers about working conditions, and no plans are made by the General Council for common action to secure general increases in wages, such as those launched in the United States by the Congress of Industrial Organizations. Nor does the Council normally intervene in an industrial dispute unless requested to do so by the affiliated union or unions concerned, but such unions are required to keep the General Council informed about disputes. However, the Council may intervene on its own initiative where there is no probability of an amicable settlement by direct negotiation and the dispute is likely directly or indirectly to involve other affiliated bodies of workers in a stoppage of work, or involves a menace to wages, hours, or other working conditions. In these circumstances, the Council must organize all such moral and material support as appears justified, and it has acted in this way on a number of occasions, notably in 1926 in support of the coal-miners. The Council is also empowered, upon application by affiliated unions, to investigate disputes between them, whether on demarkation or other questions. In such cases, or in exercise of its power to investigate the conduct of an affiliated union, failure to give effect to its decisions may lead to disciplinary action, which may include suspension or expulsion from Congress.

In addition to its work at home, the Trades Union Congress and its General Council have shown great activity in entering into relations with the trade union movements of other countries. The Congress is affiliated to the International Confederation of Free Trade Unions, and its representatives take a leading part in its work. The General Council nominates the British workers' delegate and advisers to the International Labour Conference.

[1] *The Trade Union Movement of Great Britain*, published in 1926 by W. M. Citrine, then Secretary of the General Council.

THE PROBLEM OF THE CLOSED SHOP

Different meanings are given to the term "closed shop," and in considering problems which arise it is necessary to distinguish between three main alternatives. A shop is closed if the trade unionists employed there refuse to work with non-unionists, while leaving each workman free to join any union he pleases, and in consequence though all the workpeople are trade unionists they may be members of several different unions. A second alternative is that all the workpeople in the shop must be trade union members, but instead of being free to join any union they are required to be members only of what may be called "good" or recognized unions. Thus, workpeople in the shop may be required to be members of a union affiliated to the Trades Union Congress, this policy being adopted to destroy breakaway unions or other independent non-affiliated unions which are pursuing policies disliked by the main body of workers in affiliated unions. The most strict form of closed shop is where only members of one particular union may be employed. Many agreements providing for this form of closed shop have been reached between employers and unions in the United States, while in undertakings in Britain it has been established *de facto*, not by agreement with the employers but because trade unionists have refused to work with non-members. By contrast an open shop is one which is open both to union and non-union labour, and usually there are some union and some non-union workers in the shop, though it may happen that all the workers are union members or all are non-union.

A closed-shop policy may be applied within only one shop or occupation, or to several, or sometimes throughout a whole undertaking. Usually demands for a closed shop are made by strongly organized trade unionists comprising the great majority of the workers concerned, and they refuse to work alongside non-union members of their trade or occupation, though there may be many non-union workers in other shops, occupations, or grades in the undertaking with whom they are willing to work. In most cases the demand comes from strongly union-conscious workers faced either with a few individuals who refuse to join or with a small rival union pursuing an independent policy with which they disagree. If the closed shop in its strictest form were applied to a whole industry, it would follow that a workman, who for any reason was refused admission to the union or was expelled from it, would be prevented from gaining employment in that industry anywhere in the country. The closed-shop demand in its widest application raises the major

185

issue of the advantages of freedom for individuals or minorities compared with the benefits, including the smoother running of industry, which may result from complete organization of the workers.

In the nineteenth century in Britain and much more recently in the United States and Canada large numbers of employers refused to employ trade unionists, but the wheel has turned full cycle and now, instead of fighting for freedom of association and the open shop, powerful demands are made by trade unionists for the closed shop and under threat of strikes or as a result of strikes many employers have acceded to these demands. When employers were fighting to prevent the growth of trade unionism their tactics were unfair, unscrupulous, and oppressive, one of the methods adopted being the "yellow dog" contract already mentioned, by which a worker as a condition of his employment undertook not to join a trade union, while victimization for trade union activities and the use of violent methods of strike-breaking were frequent. Such tactics are rightly condemned as an interference with the freedom of workpeople to form associations for protecting and furthering their interests. In Britain such practices gradually diminished and were abandoned, while in the United States the New Deal legislation, promoted by the Roosevelt Administration in 1933, provided that employees have the right to organize and bargain collectively through representatives of their own choosing; it made yellow-dog contracts illegal, and denied to employers the exercising of discrimination against a worker because of his membership of a trade union.[1]

To-day the reverse danger must be faced of trade unionists refusing employers the right to employ workpeople, however competent, unless they are members of the union, and coercing workpeople to join the union by denying them opportunities of employment unless they do. The point of view of the trade unionists is easy to understand. They have banded together, paid contributions, and used time and effort to secure improved working conditions, and they resent outsiders enjoying advantages for which union members have had to struggle. Yet the rates of pay, hours of work, and other conditions provided by collective agreements apply to unionists and non-unionists alike in the undertaking, and relations become strained and embittered between them. The non-unionists do not, of course, receive any friendly benefits or strike pay which the union may provide, but the influence of a strong union is a genuine protection against victimization or unfair dismissal, even though the union would not act in defence of a non-member.

[1] Yellow dog contracts had already been made illegal in the United States by legislation in 1932.

When workpeople, having had the advantages of membership put before them, fail to respond to peaceful persuasion, there is danger of threats, intimidation, and other pressures being directed against them, and peaceful persuasion is at least as difficult to define as peaceful picketing. Non-members protest against these pressures; claim that freedom of association implies freedom not to join an association; and assert that their employment and pay depend on their own efficiency and not on trade union action. Employers also demand the right to employ people because of their efficiency and suitability for the job independently of whether they are members of a trade union or not. The unionists reply that refusal to join the union is based on obstinate prejudices and shows an unfriendly attitude of non-co-operation with their fellow-workers. If then the union members insist that they have the right to decide with whom they will work or not work, and if they refuse to work with non-unionists or with members of a break-away organization, the problem becomes the clash of a complexity of rights and freedoms; the chances of peaceful settlement by persuasion recede and the stage is set for conflict.

The use or threat of the strike weapon to compel all workpeople of a certain grade to join the union is usually made only where trade unionism is strong and non-members are few. The strike or threat is directed mainly against the employer to require him to employ only union members, although it also brings pressure on the non-unionists who, fearing that the employers will give way, decide to join the union when they see how determined the union members are. The employer, though disliking the closed shop as an interference with his own freedom and with that of some of his employees, may be unwilling to fight the main body, perhaps 90 per cent or more of his workpeople, on a principle which is of interest mainly to a very few of his men. He knows that his own freedom in choosing some workpeople from outside the union is restricted within very narrow limits by the strength of the union and is therefore of little value to him, and he realizes that any gain from maintaining the open shop will be heavily outweighed by the loss resulting from unrest in his works. He also sees advantages in dealing with representatives who can speak on behalf of all his workpeople, though these advantages disappear if the discipline of the union is weak and unofficial strikes occur. Being a realist he will probably decide that expediency is preferable to principle and will acquiesce in a closed-shop agreement.

Such a result is a victory for the union but an undemocratic one, the additional membership being secured by force and not persuasion, and it gives to the unions a potentially dangerous power over its members. The union leaders may be less considerate of their members' interests if workers no longer have the safeguard of leaving the union and still be able to find work. Nor is the victory likely to be of much value to the union, for, although it gains a few unwilling members, its bargaining power can scarcely be increased thereby. A union which has a membership of 90 per cent of the workers of a shop and which has built up this membership by persuasion is strong enough to be tolerant and does not need to coerce the non-union minority. Though the unorganized minority may be a cause of irritation to trade union members, it is in many ways better to have a 90 per cent organization voluntarily than a 100 per cent compulsorily.

Employers may, as already indicated, accept the closed shop for reasons of expediency, and some may even approve it, while an arbitration tribunal appointed by the State may decide in the interests of industrial peace to make a closed-shop award as the only means of settling a dispute on this issue. The State, however, should hold the scales in balance in its legislation on freedom of association, neither adopting compulsory unionism nor supporting employers in demands for a non-union policy. The abolition of trade unionism by the Nazi Government in Germany in 1933 is a sufficient warning of one menace to freedom of association, and the danger to democracy and also to the character and vitality of the trade union movement itself are just as great at the opposite extreme. One aspect of the problem was regulated in Britain by the Trade Disputes and Trade Unions Act, 1927, which, as is indicated in Chapter 12, made it unlawful for any local authority or other public body to require any person they employed to be or not to be a member of a trade union.

Operation of the closed-shop principle denies the right of workpeople to withdraw from a union in the future if they have become dissatisfied with its policy or leadership. It also stands in the way of the formation of rival unions. Yet the right to set up a rival union is included in freedom of association, and to take away this right could weaken the vitality of the trade union movement. Groups of workpeople may hold quite different views upon trade union policy and methods, and if they cannot reach agreement they are likely to form separate unions. This explains the existence in some European countries of separate Catholic and Socialist unions each having members in the same industries and occupations. Again, where only one union has hitherto operated some of the members may consider that its policy and leadership have become too extreme and aggressive or too complacent and spineless, and if they are unable to bring about a change from within, they may cease to be members or may decide to form a rival union. Differences may arise not only on the industrial policy of a union but also on the question

188

of the union identifying itself with a particular political party. At the present time in Britain the trade union movement is closely linked with the Labour Party, but political issues cover much more than industrial issues, and circumstances could easily arise in which the trade union movement might be so sharply divided on some non-industrial question, for example foreign policy, that the ranks might be split even though there was a large measure of support for the industrial policy of the Labour Party. When feelings run high and sharp differences develop involving large numbers of people the closed-shop principle would be swept aside.

Thus the problem of the closed shop is not merely whether all workers of a given grade or occupation shall be trade unionists, but is often whether they shall be required to join a particular union. If one union is strong enough it may use the closed-shop policy to destroy its weaker rivals and consolidate its position. This may be illustrated by the action of the Transport and General Workers' Union in securing from the London Passenger Transport Board a decision announced in August, 1946, to apply the closed-shop principle by not continuing in its service any employee in grades covered by its agreement with the union who was not a member of that union. This decision, which would have been illegal under the Trade Disputes and Trade Unions Act, 1927, was mainly the outcome of determination by the Transport and General Workers' Union to destroy the National Passenger Workers' Union formed after the big London bus and tram strike in the Coronation period, 1937. This was a breakaway union from the Transport and General Workers' Union, and in its view the proper work of a union is to obtain better conditions for its members by industrial action without dissipating its energies in party politics as it believed the British trade union movement to be doing. Its membership among employees of the London Passenger Transport Board remained very small compared with that of the Transport and General Workers' Union, it was not recognized by the Board, nor had the Board entered into agreements with it, but had always dealt with the Transport and General Workers' Union. In these circumstances, therefore, when the latter union informed the Board that they would not work with employees who were not members of their union, the Board decided that it would not continue in its service any employee in the grades concerned who was unwilling to join that union.[1] The Board evidently

[1] The decision should be considered in relation to the policy of the British National Union of Mineworkers that membership of the union shall be a condition of employment by the National Coal Board in the nationalized coal-mining industry.

189

believed that only by ending the friction resulting from rival unions by deciding in favour of the long-recognized and much more representative union could it properly perform its duties to the public of providing an efficient transport service. Refusal to agree to the closed shop would have involved the danger of a strike with dislocation of London's passenger transport system. The Board's decision involved both the closed shop and the frequently related question of the recognition of only one union, and each is a restriction of freedom of association.

In Fascist Italy and in other corporative States a policy was adopted recognizing only one union of workpeople and one organization of employers in each branch of industry. If other unions were allowed to exist in these countries they had no place in the corporative system, and were therefore likely to decline and disappear. Now, it is often more convenient in joint negotiations if there is only one union representing the workpeople and one representing the employers. But this is true only if one organization on each side really represents the employers and workpeople respectively. If it conceals substantial differences of opinion within its membership, or if it speaks for only a proportion of the workpeople or employers and considerable numbers are not represented, the joint negotiations will be hampered or inadequate. In such circumstances it is preferable to have a more complex mechanism for joint negotiation consisting of representatives of two or more unions of workpeople or of employers based upon recognition of freely formed associations. There are, however, practical limits to the number of separate unions which should be represented in joint negotiating machinery; participation should be restricted to unions with memberships which are substantial and also reasonably stable over a period of time.

Official recognition by State authorities may be given to certain unions without removing freedom of association. This is practicable if recognition is not exclusive, but is extended to new unions if they establish their claim to represent a substantial number of workpeople. Thus in Australia, for example, only registered unions may appear before the Commonwealth Court of Conciliation and Arbitration, and, as already mentioned, the privileges of registration are usually granted to only one union for any defined category of workpeople. But the system is usually applied with such flexibility that, if an unregistered union becomes representative of a considerable number of workpeople in a field in which a union has already been registered, the field will be divided and a new category defined to enable the new union also to be registered.

Instead of applying the exclusive policy of a closed shop or a single union, arrangements are sometimes made to give preference to unionists. This often takes the form of an agreement between a union and an employer, by which the employer undertakes that whenever he has a vacancy for a worker he will first apply to the union, and only if the union is unable to find a suitable worker among its members does the employer become free to employ a non-unionist. In the interests of industrial peace, preference for unionists is sometimes included in the awards of arbitration tribunals, for example, in Australia and New Zealand. Although such preference does not strictly interfere with freedom of association and does not result in the closed shop, it is a powerful inducement for non-members to join the union. This is especially true in periods of depression when the union has enough unemployed members on its books to fill every vacancy which is likely to occur. In such circumstances a non-member would have little chance of getting a job. The shop becomes closed if an agreement provides that any non-unionist taken on by the employer shall be required to join the union.[1]

TRADE UNION RIVALRIES

The trade union movement is often assumed to have a solidarity and unity which it does not in fact possess, and it suffers from internal stresses, strains, and tensions which weaken its structure. Many of the difficulties arise from competition and rivalry between unions applying conflicting bases of organization, while other divisions result from differences of policy. An extreme example is the great cleavage in the United States between the American Federation of Labour and the Congress of Industrial Organizations, the rift being due to divergencies both of structure and policy, accentuated by clash of personality between the leaders, and resulting not only in internal hostility but in conflict with employers on the question of recognition. The division in some European countries between socialist unions and Catholic or Christian unions has already been noted. In Britain the Trades Union Congress has succeeded in achieving a considerable measure of co-ordination, but has to tread warily amid a welter of conflicting interests.

Each union in its drive to gain as many members as possible finds

[1] Where the State or a tribunal set up by the State requires compulsory unionism, freedom of association is no longer maintained. A worker may then sometimes be free to decide which of several unions he prefers to join, but he is no longer free not to join any union. In New Zealand the Industrial Conciliation and Arbitration Act, 1936, provided that all workers subject to any award or industrial agreement registered under the Act must become members of a union.

itself in competition with other unions because of conflicting basis of organization or jurisdiction along the lines already indicated. This results in poaching for members or in "border raids," and in some ways the problem is akin to struggles about boundaries between States in international affairs, with two or more claimants for disputed territories. Such conflicts seem to be solely internal to the trade union movement and of little concern to employers, but in reality each of the rival unions, in addition to trying to attract members by claiming to be able to serve the workers best, strives to gain its ends by demanding that employers shall recognize it and it only to represent the workers it claims to organize. Where two or more unions make this demand the employer is faced with unrest which reduces productive efficiency and often leads to strikes. These are sometimes specially bitter, and employers become the victims of circumstances for which they are not responsible and which frequently cannot be overcome by the ordinary processes of negotiation and concession such as enable settlements to be reached in disputes about wages or hours of work.

So long as several distinct principles of organization are applied no permanent stability can be achieved which would prevent competition and overlapping, although agreements may be reached which for a time may reduce the severity and limit the field of conflict. The problem may be illustrated from British experience. Two great unions, the Transport and General Workers' Union and the National Union of General and Municipal Workers, each with more than a million members, are open to accept members from any industry and occupation, though actually the main body of their membership consists of labourers and of semi-skilled workers employed as machine tenders in many industries. These unions are inevitably in competition with one another for membership over the whole field of industry, and this struggle must continue until either one of them is absorbed by or amalgamates with the other or they break up into industrial or other sections. If they coalesce, then the basis of organization would be one big union, open to all, along the lines of the short-lived Grand National Consolidated Trade Union fostered by Robert Owen in the 1830's, and of more recent broad-based unions such as the Knights of Labour and the Industrial Workers of the World. They must also be in actual or potential competition with every other kind of union, and the Transport and General Workers' Union has been described as an octopus by leaders of small unions which have experienced its encroachments and its attempts to destroy them or to persuade or coerce them into amalgamation. It would be possible theoretically to avoid much inter-union conflict if all labourers and semi-skilled workers were organized in one great union, and skilled workers were organized by crafts, but in practice the boundary between skilled and semi-skilled work would be difficult to define, and is continually changing because of changes in industrial processes and techniques. Also segregation of workpeople into the two main divisions of skilled workers and others would accentuate and develop class divisions within the trade union movement, probably leading to new forms of conflict as well as involving undesirable social repercussions.

Industrial unions find themselves in competition with general unions and also with craft and other occupational unions. Thus, membership of the National Union of Mineworkers is open to all coal-mine workers, and it is the policy of the Union to secure a closed shop with all mineworkers in the Union and to be the sole representative of the workers in the industry. However, among other unions of which some workers in the industry are members there are Winding Engineers' Associations which though numerically small are in a key position because the safety of the men and the operation of the mines depend upon these engineers who control the lowering and raising of the cages. These associations could therefore hold up the industry almost as effectively as could the National Union of Mineworkers, and they could scarcely be coerced into merging with the National Union. The policy of the National Union is, however, to persuade the other unions to join it by amalgamation or affiliation.

The position is somewhat similar in railway transportation, the National Union of Railwaymen being an industrial union open to all workpeople employed on the railways; but largely outside its ranks are two occupational groups essential for the operation of the railways and organized independently in the Associated Society of Locomotive Engineers and Firemen and the Transport Salaried Staffs' Association. The attempt to bring all railway workers into one industrial union is further complicated by the many ancillary services, including railway workshops for constructing engines, coaches, and wagons, building and maintaining stations and bridges, operating railway hotels, restaurants, and buffets, docks, shipping lines, and printing plants owned and operated by the railways. Here the field is open for the "catch-as-catch-can" methods of "all-in wrestling," with the N.U.R., the Amalgamated Engineering Union, the National Union of Foundry Workers, the general workers' unions, and unions of builders, printers, catering trade workers, and many others all involved in the scramble. The engineering industry shows even greater complexity. The Amalgamated Engineering Union is the biggest union with a membership which includes some of the main categories of craftsmen, semi-skilled workers, and women, but some forty other unions are concerned in the industry. Among them are craft unions for foundry workers, boilermakers, patternmarkers, electricians, sheet metal workers, and coppersmiths, while the general workers' unions recruit mainly unskilled workers, and there is overlapping between the engineering and shipbuilding unions.

The above examples suffice to show the complexity of trade union structure resulting from the use of different principles of organization and causing rivalry within the ranks of unions affiliated to the Trades Union Congress. Other kinds of conflict have taken place between unions affiliated and others not affiliated to the T.U.C., or break-aways from affiliated unions, and they may be illustrated from the outbreak of disputes in the autumn of 1946 over the inter-related questions of rivalry between unions, accentuated by this question of affiliation, and demands for exclusive recognition and for the closed shop. Reference has already been made in the section on the closed shop to the demand of the Transport and General Workers' Union, which was successful without a stoppage, that the London Passenger Transport Board would not continue in its service in certain grades any employee who would not join that Union, a main purpose of the demand being to destroy the break-away National Passenger Workers' Union. Somewhat different was a dispute involving more than 3,000 meat porters and other members of the Transport and General Workers' Union employed at the Smithfield meat market who went on strike in support of their demand that non-unionists and members, numbering several hundred, of the Smithfield Guild of Clerks and Salesmen, which was not affiliated to the Trades Union Congress and which they regarded as not being a genuine trade union, should join the Transport and General Workers' Union or some other organization affiliated to the T.U.C. They refused to work alongside men who were not members of an affiliated organiza-tion. The Guild, unlike the National Passenger Workers' Union, was not a break-away union, and had been recognized by the employers at Smithfield Market.

More complex and showing other features was a decision of the Aeronautical Engineers' Association to call a strike at one of the airports because it had been refused recognition by the British Overseas Airways Corporation. The Association claimed recognition on the grounds that it had 1,600 members or more than double the combined membership at the airport of ten unions including the Amalgamated Engineering Union and the Electrical Trades Union, all of which had been recognized by the Corporation. It had been formed during the war to protect the interests of aircraft maintenance engineers, including ex-service men from the Royal Air Force and the Navy, who had become highly skilled, although they were regarded as "dilutees" by the Amalgamated Engineering Union because they had not had a recognized apprenticeship training. The Association was not a break-away union, and many of its members had never been in any other union. It had, however, been in continuous conflict with the big unions, and was not affiliated to the T.U.C. This was, no doubt, the reason why the Corporation refused recognition, as it preferred to remain on good terms with the big affiliated unions even though the Association claimed to have a large majority of the engineering employees at a number of airfields who would be able by going on strike to hold up a considerable number of air transport services. The ten unions with T.U.C. affiliations and recognized by the Corporation decided to set up joint negotiating machinery comprehensive enough to cover every grade of employee at the airfields.

While the Transport and General Workers' Union members were trying to establish closed shops at the Smithfield meat market and elsewhere, a group of Liverpool dockers, with support from dockers at several other ports, started a movement to break away from the Transport and General Workers' Union, and form a separate organization for dockers as formerly instead of remaining only a section, though an important one, of the huge composite union in the formation of which it had taken a leading part a quarter of a century earlier under the leadership of its then general secretary, Mr. Ernest Bevin. They evidently believed that a separate union would be better able to fight for the dockers' demands than if they remained part of a giant union which had many other interests to consider. In the autumn of 1945, they had taken part in an unofficial strike of dockers, were dissatisfied that the union had not held out for their full demands for a wage of 25s. a day, a 40-hour week, and no overtime, and they, therefore, took the initiative for a break-away, which, however, they abandoned after several weeks of agitation.

One other example may be given. The Union of Post Office Workers and the Civil Service Clerical Association, though not seeking a closed shop, decided to claim exclusive rights to negotiate with the Postmaster-General and the Treasury respectively, and to ask them to withdraw recognition from other unions. The Union of Post Office Workers desired to be the sole officially recognized representative of the manipulative grades, with exclusion of several small unions hitherto recognized.[1] Withdrawal of recognition would be likely to cause collapse of these unions, as they would be able to do little for their members. These demands were opposed by the Federation of Civil Servants, which represented 40,000 members in nine unions or guilds not affiliated to the T.U.C. and opposed to political attachments.

Most of the disputes were between big, old-established unions affiliated to the T.U.C. and small, usually recently formed unions independent of the T.U.C. with its Labour Party associations. Some forty-five of these independent unions with a total membership of about 400,000 were affiliated to a newly formed Federation of Independent Trade Unions which favoured political independence and an open-shop policy with the right of individuals to join whatever union they preferred. Some of these unions had not secured recognition as employers wished to avoid conflict with the big unions, which were responsible for negotiating about working conditions on behalf of the main body of the workers. Mention must be made of the National Association of Local Government Officers which has joined neither the T.U.C. nor the Federation of Independent Trade Unions, but is long-established, is recognized by local authorities as a negotiating body, and with 145,000 members in the service of local authorities and public utility undertakings is the most powerful of the independent unions. It has not experienced difficulties when some local authorities exercised the freedom restored to them by the repeal of the Trades Union and Trade Disputes Act, 1927, of applying the closed-shop principle, as the condition of employment has usually been defined to require membership of recognized unions without specifying that the unions must be affiliated to the T.U.C.

A comprehensive solution of trade union rivalries cannot be found by application of the closed-shop principle in its strictest sense of requiring all workpeople in an occupation or undertaking to be members of the union which has a majority of the workpeople. Some of the most powerful unions affiliated to the T.U.C., for example the Transport and General Workers' Union, have only a minority of the workers in many undertakings, and their organizations would be so seriously undermined and weakened by such a policy that they would inevitably oppose its general application,

[1] The Union of Post Office Workers had about 146,000 members throughout the country, while the small unions, e.g. the Guild of Telephonists, the Guild of Sorters, and the Association of Counter Clerks, had memberships in London ranging from 3,000 or 4,000 down to about 1,000. The Civil Service Clerical Association asked for recognition to be withdrawn from the National Association of Women Civil Servants and the Association of Ex-Service Civil Servants.

even though they might fight for a closed shop where circumstances were favourable to them in particular undertakings.[1] This is one of the main reasons why the T.U.C. has not made the closed shop a part of its policy. To secure 100 per cent membership by persuasion is a policy which most trade unionists would support. An attempt to apply a closed-shop policy widely could not be successful so long as, in many occupations, only a minority of workpeople are members of any union, while where there are several competing unions in an undertaking each would be uncertain which of them would gain most from requiring all workpeople to join one or other union. No doubt many unions affiliated to the T.U.C. would support the restriction, wherever practicable, of employment to members of affiliated unions, but the trade union movement is well aware that large organized groups are not easily coerced on a question of social principle and so long as associations like N.A.L.G.O. and other unions, including those catering for some of the clerical and supervisory grades, decide to remain independent it would be impracticable and unpolitic to force the issue. Almost inevitably, therefore, the T.U.C. has preferred to leave the field open for the evolution of recruiting, for opportunism, and for the gradual development of co-operative relations between unions.

CO-OPERATION AND AMALGAMATION

It would be wrong to assume from the above review of competing interests that the British trade union movement is rent with bitter feuds. Many working arrangements are made and co-operative relations established between different unions. Some unions have agreed to mutual recognition of membership cards and to a system of transfer of membership when members move to new employment in an occupation, industry, or locality involving change from the jurisdiction or territory of one union to that of another. Then the processes of negotiation with employers have led to meetings between representatives of a number of unions to formulate a common policy on wages and working conditions, and these consultations have often resulted in close and systematic co-operation. Some unions in related occupations are linked together by affiliation. Thus the National Federation of Colliery Enginemen, Boilermen, and

[1] During the closed-shop controversy in the autumn of 1946, Mr. Arthur Deakin, General Secretary of the Transport and General Workers' Union, stated that his union stood for the principle that every worker should be a trade unionist, but not that all should be members of the same union, and it had rejected the closed-shop policy—evidently in the strict sense.

Mechanics is affiliated to the National Union of Mineworkers. The latter union in pursuing a policy of becoming the sole representative of the coal-miners does not contemplate fighting Winding Engineers' Associations, deputies' associations, and other unions in the industry, but hopes by negotiation and agreement with them to arrange some form of combination, perhaps on a federal plan, which would secure the benefits of common action while safeguarding the interests of the various groups. Many federations have been formed and provide in varying degree for the autonomy of the member-unions. For example, the Confederation of Engineering and Shipbuilding Unions brings together a number of craft unions, and was greatly strengthened in 1946 by the decision of the powerful Amalgamated Engineering Union to affiliate to it. Unions in the building industry are affiliated to the National Federation of Building Trade Operatives, in printing there is the Printing and Kindred Trades Federation, and so on for other industries. The formation of federations and amalgamations of unions has made great progress, especially since the end of the First World War.

The Trades Union Congress plays a central part in restricting rivalry between its affiliated organizations and in fostering consolidations and simplification of structure. Already the unions affiliated to it cover so wide a range of crafts and industries that scarcely any part of the whole field of employment is not catered for by one of them, and often by several. Consequently Congress rarely accepts new unions for affiliation, knowing full well that they would be considered by one or more of the already affiliated unions to be rivals. Some of the independent unions mentioned in the previous section may have preferred for political reasons to remain outside the T.U.C., but if they had requested affiliation it would probably have been refused. No union which was a breakaway from an affiliated union would be allowed to affiliate.

The T.U.C., like the American Federation of Labour and other central organizations, deals with jurisdictional disputes which unions bring before it. These occur where one union is accused of entering territory claimed by a second union with a view to "poaching" some of its members or recruiting non-members. Such poaching must be clearly distinguished from demarcation disputes which arise not from rivalry over the recruiting of members, but from two or more unions each claiming the exclusive right for its members to undertake defined kinds of work. These disputes are mainly between unions of skilled craftsmen. Among classical examples, mention may be made of disputes between joiners and shipwrights over certain jobs in shipbuilding which each regards as belonging to them, and

198

disputes between plumbers, fitters, and heating engineers about the sizes of pipes which each craft should fit. The introduction of acetylene welding has caused many conflicts in various industries, including shipbuilding, because the new process has reduced the demand for riveters, drillers, and other categories, each of which has claimed to do the welding as it serves the same purpose as the old method, though the work itself is entirely different from that of the old crafts. Similarly the development of new industries, for example, motor-car and aeroplane construction and maintenance, raises the question whether the old-established engineering, coach building, and other crafts should do the work or whether new specialized occupations will be formed.

Demarcation disputes have sometimes been bitter and prolonged as members of a union which loses ground in a contested field of work may suffer from unemployment. Though custom has settled the main jobs done by each craft, there are uncertainties at the frontier owing to the complexities of processes and products and to industrial changes resulting in new methods and new products. This disputed territory becomes a kind of no-man's land in which raids, attacks, and counter-attacks take place, or, to change the analogy, each union accuses the other of "gate-crashing." In their way such disputes resemble that over Trieste between Italy and Yugoslavia, or over Germany between the Soviet and Western Powers. Each union is trying to safeguard the field of employment of its members and to stake out its claim to as big a field as possible but in the zone of conflict the issues may be so confused that fair and logical solutions may be possible but only arbitrary compromises. Attempts to draw a line of demarcation are made by the unions, while some disputes are referred by the unions to a form of arbitration in which the employers concerned may also take part. Where a federation has been formed to which the unions in dispute are affiliated it will try to find an acceptable solution by submitting the issue to a tribunal of disinterested people, though sometimes the difficulties in selecting a tribunal which will be approved as impartial are almost as great as in appointing a boundary commission in international affairs.

Thus, many trade union rivalries, including those due to poaching and demarcation questions, are more easily solved or are reduced in severity by the formation of federations and amalgamations, while collective bargaining is facilitated and trade union forces consolidated. The advantages of amalgamation and of simplifying the structure of the movement have seemed so great to many trade unionists that, as long ago as 1924, a resolution was passed by the Trades Union Congress declaring that the number of unions should be reduced to an absolute minimum and instructing its General Council to draw up a scheme for organization by industry and for a scientific linking up of unions to secure unity of action, without merging of unions. After a comprehensive investigation, the General Council reported to the 1927 Congress that as it was impossible to define any fixed boundaries of industry, it was impracticable to formulate a scheme of organization by industry. Nor could it propose any scheme for a scientific linking up of unions, though it thought that groups of unions with related industrial interests which desired closer working might find it possible to prepare their own schemes. The ramifications of trade union organization were seen to be so complex and the differences in conception as to the best form of structure so great that no agreed principle could be found. The .affiliated unions had divergent policies on organization because each had carved out its own special field of action often during generations of unplanned growth. Amalgamations and other adaptations of structure could not, therefore, be forced but would depend on the desire of the individual unions to co-operate. Though the vested interests of the various unions seem to imply that changes in trade union structure can only be gradual, scientific progress is rapidly creating new industries, demanding new techniques, and breaking down or modifying old occupational skills and industrial boundaries in ways which inevitably disturb or even disrupt the organizations of to-day and demand new groupings to meet the needs of to-morrow.

Amalgamations generally depend upon the members of two or more unions agreeing that there are mutual advantages in combining their forces, though sometimes a big union may virtually coerce a small one into merging with it. Amalgamation of local or district unions into national unions is relatively easy if they cover the same craft or category of workpeople, but other amalgamations involve combining two or more crafts unions or craft unions with unskilled workers' unions, or unions in two or more industries, and each group has to be convinced that it will gain more from the merger than from remaining free to pursue its own purposes independently. If members of a compact key craft believe that their needs would not be understood or their demands supported by unskilled workpeople, they will decide against amalgamation with a union of unskilled workers. The difficulties are greatest when attempts are made to bring together highly skilled craftsmen, technicians, specialized clerical workers, or foremen and supervisors with unskilled workers.

Even where the members of two unions are satisfied that there would be advantages to each in the future from amalgamation,

200

financial obstacles have to be overcome, for one union may be financially much stronger than the other, with big reserves and high rates of benefit, and it may be difficult to make a fair adjustment. Again, amalgamation favoured by the rank and file may be resisted by officials whose positions might be adversely affected; for example, there will be only one general secretary instead of two. Provision can, however, be made to ensure continuity of employment for all officials with at least the same salaries as before.

It must be noted that in Britain, amalgamation of unions is subject to legislative regulation. The law provides that unions can amalgamate only if in each of the unions at least 50 per cent of the members vote on the amalgamation proposals, and if of the votes recorded, those in favour are at least 20 per cent more than those against.[1] These provisions were somewhat modified during the Second World War to facilitate amalgamations.

[1] This is required by the Trade Union (Amalgamation) Act, 1917. Methods have sometimes been adopted of effecting mergers of unions without having to comply with the requirements of the Act. Thus, a small union may dissolve itself and, by agreement, transfer its funds and members to a big union with which it desires to combine. An ingenious device was adopted in the iron and steel industry which avoided the necessity of conforming with the Act, and made unnecessary the immediate extinction of the original unions. The scheme, which was evolved between 1915 and 1917 and was supported by three of the main unions in the industry, involved the setting up of a new society responsible for organization and benefits—The British Iron, Steel, and Kindred Trades Association—in which all new members were enrolled and to which members of the original unions could transfer. Ultimately the new organization absorbed the whole membership, while the original unions declined and were dissolved. From the start of the scheme another body known as the Iron and Steel Trades Confederation was established to conduct negotiations on wages and working conditions on behalf of the unions and the Association. Other unions later joined in the scheme.

12

The Legal Position of Trade Unions

ALTHOUGH THE main interest in the trade union movement of any country lies in its membership, structure, policy, and power, a knowledge of its legal position is essential for a full understanding of its place in the community and of the attitude taken towards it by the legislature and the judicial authorities. In the present section an account is given of some of the main features of the legal position of British trade unions, but the problems reviewed are common also to other countries, each country, however, having its own system of regulation. The position at the time of writing is outlined, without tracing the historical evolution of trade union law through its many changes after 1824 when unions ceased to be unlawful as criminal conspiracies.

The legal status of British trade unions is complex, being based upon a number of Acts of Parliament, including laws dealing specially with trade unions and trade disputes, but also laws of general application on conspiracy and protection of property. The law has not been codified and is obscure on a number of points, with possible alternative interpretations if cases arising out of some provisions were brought before the Courts. The basis of the present status of British trade unions is the Trade Union Act, 1871, which enables unions to manage many of their internal affairs free from legal jurisdiction, so that in this respect they resemble voluntary associations. By this Act, unions were no longer subject to the common law principle by which action in restraint of trade is illegal. Other Acts, however, define the principal purposes of a trade union and grant certain rights and privileges, so that trade unions have some of the characteristics of a statutory corporation. In view, therefore, of the "mixed" attitude taken by the legislature, British trade unions can be regarded as quasi-corporations. As is indicated below, the term "trade union" is defined in British law to cover both unions of workpeople and associations of employers.

Legal Definition of a Trade Union

General indications have already been given of the purposes of a trade union. British legislation defines the principal objects of a trade union to be the regulation of relations between workmen and masters, or between workmen and workmen, or between masters and masters, or for imposing restrictive conditions on the conduct of any trade or business, and also the provision of benefit to members.[1] In order to be recognized as a trade union a combination must have these as its principal objects. It may include in its constitution any other lawful objects and use funds for these purposes, e.g., the publication of a magazine or newspaper, but if it undertakes political activities it must comply with special conditions which are reviewed below in the section on "Political Action."[2] In British law the definition of a trade union includes organizations either of workpeople or of employers, whereas in ordinary parlance the term "trade union" is applied only to organizations of workpeople.

Restraint of Trade

For many years British trade unions were hampered by the application of the common law doctrine that acts in restraint of trade are illegal. Thus it was argued that if trade unions made successful demands for higher wages, or shorter hours, restraints would be imposed on trade. The Common Law doctrine is that any trader shall be free to carry on his business according to his own discretion and choice, this being in harmony with the widely approved *laissez-faire* principles of the nineteenth century. Restraints upon trade can, however, be authorized by Statute Law, which overrides Common Law, and the trade unions succeeded in securing in the Trade Union Act, 1871, a provision that the purposes of a trade union would not be regarded as illegal because they involved restraint of trade, and that agreements in restraint of trade would not be illegal.

Freedom of Internal Affairs of Trade Unions

Trade unionists in Britain have always desired that the internal affairs of trade unions should be free from legal control, although they demanded and secured legal rights for the protection of their property. The Trade Union Act, 1871, which gave this protection also provided that no court of law shall have jurisdiction for

[1] The definition is mainly given in the Trade Union Act Amendment Act, 1876, and is repeated and supplemented in the Trade Union Act, 1913.

[2] The provision that a trade union must have the statutory objects as its principal objects, and may include in its constitution other lawful objects is given in the Trade Union Act, 1913, which also defines the special conditions to be observed if political activities are undertaken.

directly enforcing or recovering damages for breach of any of the following agreements by unions whose purposes are in restraint of trade:[1]

(1) Agreements about the conditions on which members shall or shall not be employed, including agreements between two or more unions;

(2) Agreements to pay subscriptions or penalties to a trade union;

(3) Agreements to pay benefits to members from trade union funds.

Such agreements are quite lawful, though not legally enforceable. It must also be noted that, in addition to purely internal affairs, for example the payment of trade union contributions by members and of benefits to members, a collective agreement between a trade union of workpeople and an employers' organization (legally a trade union of masters) has no legal standing and cannot be enforced by any legal action. Collective agreements, therefore, are "gentlemen's agreements" which depend for their application on the word, good faith, and authority of the contracting parties over their members. These are the most effective guarantees of observance, and in most British industries the standard of application is remarkably high. In periods of severe depression, however, actual conditions in some industries may be less favourable than those in agreements, both sides neglecting to insist upon enforcement, which would result in more unemployment, but this relaxing of conditions is often followed by a new agreement with lower standards, or a recovery of prosperity may take place and enable a high standard of observance of the original agreement to be restored. If the terms of a collective agreement are put into the contracts of employment between an employer and individual workpeople, actions could be brought to the courts claiming damages for breaches of such contracts.

THE RIGHT TO STRIKE

The problem of making strikes or certain kinds of strikes illegal has been widely discussed, but no satisfactory solution has been found. The fundamental issues are the desire of Governments to protect themselves against coercion and to safeguard the community against inconvenience and loss, and the demand of workers that they should be free to withdraw their labour collectively if they are dis-

[1] Agreements are enforceable if made by unions whose purposes are not in restraint of trade.

satisfied with their working conditions. The resultant of the forces represented by these attitudes varies greatly in different communities, freedom to strike being usual in peace-time in most democratic communities, whereas Governments in dictatorship countries frequently refuse this freedom to workpeople. In war-time the Governments of democratic countries declare strikes and also lock-outs to be illegal, all sections of the community regarding these methods, which are approved or tolerated in ordinary times, as being quite inappropriate in periods of grave national crisis.

The most constructive approach to the problem is the development of systems which ensure such a fair and acceptable regulation of working conditions that disputes become rare. The development may be the result of voluntary arrangements, of Government initiative or a combination of both, and if successful the prohibition of strikes and lock-outs becomes relatively unimportant. Voluntary methods for the collective regulation of working conditions are outlined in Chapter XV, and compulsory arbitration, which is often combined with prohibition of strikes and lock-outs, is reviewed in Chapter XXIV. Prohibition of strikes should be considered in relation to the right which is widely recognized, of an industrial worker to withdraw his labour if he considers the working conditions to be inacceptable. When a number of workpeople act together they are in one sense exercising their individual rights simultaneously. Such collective strike action is usually legal in democratic countries, except under certain compulsory arbitration systems, as in Australia and New Zealand. In war-time, however, collective strike action and also the rights of individuals to withdraw their labour may be prohibited or restricted. In such circumstances certain rights have to give way to necessities or obligations which are more important, the obligation to serve the country in times of peril being more vital than maintenance of the right to strike. This attitude is supported by public opinion, including that of most workers, and acts as a powerful deterrent to those inclined to strike, greatly reinforcing respect for the law.

In ordinary times local strikes and lock-outs involving small numbers of workpeople are "private" quarrels between the parties, and, except when they are at public utility undertakings, they cause little inconvenience to the community, as supplies of goods or services are continued by firms not stopped, and can be brought in from other districts. The problem, however, changes if a stoppage is extensive, covering the whole or a large part of an industry, or even several industries. Such stoppages if prolonged have repercussions throughout the whole national economy because the goods or services, e.g. coal, steel, or transport, of the industries stopped, are required by many other industries, which must soon curtail production when the raw materials or services upon which they depend are not available. Yet to make a strike or lock-out illegal because it is national and causes serious dislocation in other industries would take away from workers their freedom to withdraw their labour if unwilling to work under the conditions offered. Special restraint is, however, called for in negotiating, and the leaders and members of great national organizations of employers and of workpeople must make every effort to avoid a stoppage.

Should workers in an industry where conditions are acceptable and they have no disagreement with their own employers have the right to strike in support of workers in another industry where there is a dispute about conditions? It is sometimes argued that strikes should be restricted to the trade or industry in which there is a dispute, and that sympathetic strikes should be illegal. The trade unions reply that wages and working conditions in different industries are inter-related, and that a defeat by the workers in one industry will be likely to result in a deterioration of conditions in other industries. Therefore, by taking part in a sympathetic strike the workers are fighting their own battle in addition to supporting workpeople in another industry. Their action is an expression of solidarity and community of interest among workers in different industries. The trade union movement claims the right of unions to assist each other by direct industrial action or by moral support in any strike or lock-out.

This view is reasonable, but it must be realized that if sympathetic strikes are legal the extent of an industrial conflict may be very wide. Some sympathetic strikes would be limited to one or a few industries closely allied to that in which the dispute arose, but others might cover some or all of the main industries of the country. Thus a general strike called to support workers in any industry in their struggle to maintain or improve the terms of their employment would be legal. The trade union movement believes that the whole movement should, if necessary, act together to prevent unjust conditions being imposed on any part of its membership. At the time of the General Strike in Britain in 1926, the trade unions and their supporters claimed that the strike was legal, arguing that its objectives were only industrial, that its main purpose was to support the coalminers in their efforts to resist wage reductions, and that if the miners were defeated lower wage standards would be forced upon workers in other industries. Counter arguments were advanced to show that the strike was more than an industrial dispute about conditions of labour, that it had political aims, being designed to coerce the Government, and that it was therefore illegal.[1]

Along these lines, lawyers gave conflicting opinions about the legality of the 1926 strike, but the question was not tested in the courts. The following year Parliament attempted to remove the uncertainty by declaring in the Trade Disputes and Trade Unions Act "that any strike is illegal if it (i) has any object other than or in addition to the furtherance of a trade dispute within the trade or industry in which the strikers are engaged; and (ii) is a strike designed or calculated to coerce the Government either directly or by inflicting hardship upon the community."[2] Only if a strike had both these purposes did it become illegal. The first condition applied to work-people on strike who were supporting workpeople in a dispute in another trade or industry, but such strikes would not have been illegal unless it could be shown that they also had the object of coercing the Government as defined in the second condition. It would not have been enough to show that a strike inflicted hardship on the community; all strikes do this to a greater or less extent. It would have been necessary to prove that it was designed or calculated to coerce the Government; this purpose being a deliberate intention of those responsible for the strike. A big sympathetic strike in a number of essential industries may have an industrial aim, and yet it so profoundly affects the life of the community that the Government is compelled to take steps to safeguard the public by maintaining essential supplies and services, and it must also try to bring about a settlement. In these circumstances the strikers may act in ways at variance with the Government's policy, and many people may, therefore, believe that the strikers are trying to coerce the Government.

Although the 1927 Act was repealed by the Labour Government in 1946 and the terms in which the Act defined illegal strikes are no longer in force the problem of distinguishing between industrial strikes and those which have a political object still remains. In the debate in the House of Commons on the repeal of the 1927 Act, Sir H. Shawcross, Attorney General, drew a distinction between

[1] The Trade Disputes Act, 1906, defined a trade dispute as any dispute between employers and workmen or between workmen and workmen, which is connected with the employment or non-employment or the terms of employment or with the conditions of labour of any person, and the expression "workmen" was defined to mean all persons employed in trade or industry, whether or not in the employment of the employer with whom the trade dispute arises. By this definition a general strike would appear to be legal provided it was purely industrial and had no political aims.

[2] An illegal lock-out was defined in similar terms.

revolutionary strikes and industrial strikes, arguing that the former always had been and always would be illegal but that the latter should be legal.[1] A purely industrial strike should, he claimed, be legal, though inflicting hardship on the community and though having political repercussions, provided these were not purposes of the strike. If, however, men have political objects in view, for example, to coerce or overthrow the Government, or upset the Constitution, and they use the existence of a trade dispute to further these objects by organizing a strike, such action would be illegal. These generalizations may be accepted, but the practical difficulty is to decide which disputes are industrial and which are political or revolutionary against the Government.[2] As was indicated in the previous paragraph, a general strike represents a national crisis in which the boundary between industrial and political may easily become blurred, and a general strike could only rarely be solely industrial.

If millions of people feel so strongly about a principle which they believe to be essential to their interests as to be willing to take part in a general strike they are not likely to be prevented by a legal prohibition. It is true that the great majority of people are generally law-abiding, and responsible leaders would not lightly plan action which is illegal. But they would not lightly organize a general strike even if it were legal. Also the deterrent effect of a law making general strikes illegal is likely to be slight at a time when powerful demands are being made for mass action in the defence of a vital principle. Furthermore, owing to the difficulty of drafting appropriate legislation, the law is likely to be uncertain and open to different interpretations. Though a general strike could be made illegal, there would be the practical difficulty of imposing penalties.

During the Second World War when public opinion and trade union official policy were strongly opposed to industrial disputes, there were numbers of unofficial strikes, but though these were followed by many prosecutions and many sentences of fines or imprisonment the penalties could not be effectively enforced. In peace-time the difficulties in dealing with a widely supported general strike would be much greater. The Government could, of course, use the military forces and civilian volunteers to ensure the essentials

[1] He indicated that, in his opinion, an industrial strike might in certain circumstances be illegal under the 1927 Act. It is doubtful, however, whether this would be a correct interpretation.

[2] Sir H. Shawcross considered that no further legal definition was needed, but that the courts should determine the facts, which should be submitted to a jury.

of life to the community by maintaining transport, food distribution and supplies of water, fuel and light.[1] It could not, however, effectively bring criminal prosecutions against millions of citizens; nor could it prevent such mass movements unless it abandoned democracy and became a dictatorship ruthlessly applying repressive measures and taking away the fundamental freedoms of the people. It must, however, be emphasized that, although the problem has been discussed in some detail, general strikes are very rare indeed and quite outside the main stream of industrial relations, and they never need occur in a democratic country if Governments, employers, and workpeople are led by men who are reasonable and are willing to apply those methods of fair dealing and compromise which are essential for the solution of great social questions.

Although the Conspiracy and Protection of Property Act, 1875, and the Trade Disputes Act, 1906, legalized trade disputes, a strike devised for political objects such as attempting to overthrow the Constitution or to coerce the Government would, as already indicated, be illegal and the organizers and participants indictable for criminal conspiracy. A strike might, however, be justifiable in circumstances where the Government was itself unconstitutionally assuming powers which interfered with the fundamental freedoms of the people and violated the principles of democratic government. From the Government's point of view such a strike would be illegal and it would use every means to meet this challenge to its authority, but democratic interests might desire the success of the strike as a means of defeating a Government which had acted unconstitutionally. Such a strike should never be supported in a democratic country so long as the Constitution functions democratically.

Proposals have been made that strikes which are likely to cause injury to life or property or to lead to danger or grave inconvenience to the community should be illegal, but not only would this interfere with the reasonable rights of workpeople to refuse unacceptable labour conditions, there would be difficulty in drawing a line between industries and occupations involving these risks and others free from them. In British law, the act of striking is not a criminal offence, but if in striking workpeople *both* wilfully and maliciously break a contract of service, and are aware that by doing so they are likely to cause these injuries or dangers, they become liable to prosecution. This is a powerful deterrent to sudden, irresponsible stoppages which might have serious consequences endangering or causing grave

[1] In Britain, the Emergency Powers Act, 1920, gives the Government authority to set up and operate the organization necessary for these purposes. These powers were used at the time of the 1926 general strike.

inconvenience to the public, e.g. if railway signalmen went on strike without warning, or if railway engine drivers went off, leaving trains crowded with passengers stranded in the middle of the night at a remote place. But once they have completed their contracts of service, workpeople are not responsible for the consequences of a stoppage of work. Also, by giving due notice of termination of the contracts, the employers are given time to arrange ways of avoiding injury to life and property.

As is indicated later, a breach of contract by workpeople employed by water, gas, or electricity undertakings renders them liable to criminal prosecution if they know that it will deprive consumers of their supplies. Apart from this legal liability, a special moral responsibility rests upon workpeople in these and other public utility industries to maintain services essential for the life of the community.

Merchant seamen are also in a special position because of the risks to life and property which might result from indiscipline or desertion. By British merchant shipping legislation a lawfully engaged seaman is liable to criminal prosecution for continued wilful disobedience, deserting his ship, absence without leave, or failing without reasonable cause to join his ship as required. The liability is for breach of contract or terms of service, but where there is no breach of contract the act of striking, whether by seamen or any other category of worker, is not a criminal offence. If seamen in going on strike break the terms of their engagement each is liable to individual criminal prosecution for this breach but not for going on strike.

Members of police forces are under special discipline and are subject to restrictions which do not apply to other categories of workers. Thus, police strikes are prohibited in England and Wales by the Police Act, 1919, which provides that anyone who causes or attempts to cause a member of a police force to withhold his services shall be liable to fine, or imprisonment, or both, and if he is a member of a police force shall be disqualified from being a member of any police force. The same Act provides for the establishment of a Police Federation, which must be entirely independent of and unassociated with any body outside the police service, and the purpose of the federation is to enable members of the police service to consider and bring to the notice of the police authorities and the Home Secretary any matters affecting their welfare and efficiency except questions of discipline and promotion affecting individuals. Regulations governing the pay, pensions, and conditions of service of the police forces of England and Wales are made by the Home Secretary, but before making any regulation a draft shall be submitted to a Council which includes representatives of the Police Federation, and the Home Secretary shall consider any representations which the Council may make. Thus, there is consultation and also opportunity for negotiations akin to collective bargaining. Except for the Police Federation it is unlawful for a member of a police force to be a member of any trade union or association having for its objects, or one of its objects, influence or control over the pay, pensions, or conditions of service of any police force, and contravention involves dismissal from the service and may cause loss of pension rights. A member of a police force who was a member of a trade union before joining the force may continue his membership if his Chief Officer of Police gives his consent. This enables him to maintain any rights to benefits to which he had contributed, but consent could not be given if the trade union included among its objects the influence of police service conditions.

THE POSITION OF CIVIL SERVANTS

The position of civil servants differs from that of persons employed in private undertakings, a main difference being that action taken to enforce demands which the Government is unwilling to grant would be an attempt to coerce the Government. The Government may feel compelled to refuse the demands because they are in conflict with public policy, which is based upon a vast complex of considerations, and acceptance of the demands might involve consequences injurious to the public interest. Collective bargaining, in the sense in which this is understood in private industry, is scarcely possible in the civil service. The Government has the last word. Also the civil service works in turn for Governments each representing a different political party or group of parties, and the loyalty of the service to the Government of the day, irrespective of its party, must be unquestioned. Does this mean that civil servants should keep out of politics?" Difficulties would certainly arise if a senior official took an active part in politics in his spare time and during his daily work was in close relations with a minister whose political party was different from his own. Also in his daily work a senior civil servant may obtain confidential information, and it would not be easy for him to avoid being influenced by it if he also engaged in politics, and even if he did not disclose it the knowledge would give him an unfair advantage.

Large numbers of other civil servants, however, including many clerical workers, have no such contacts and have few opportunities to see highly confidential documents; therefore the difficulties indicated above would not apply to them, and could not be used as a reason to make undesirable their participation in politics. Thus, civil servants in the lower and intermediate grades, including those in the postal, telegraph, and telephone services, totalling the great majority of civil servants are free from this difficulty.

Subject to limitations upon collective bargaining by organizations representing civil servants, it is reasonable that they should be free to join trade unions, including unions not restricted to the civil service, and that if unions so restricted are formed there should be no barrier to their affiliating with outside trade unions if they desire to do so. In almost all countries the State is only one employer among many, it must compete with private employers for personnel and it certainly does not invariably give the best conditions. There is inter-relation of conditions inside Government service with those in comparable occupations outside, and civil servants have common interests with persons employed in similar work in private industry, and they can assist one another to improve their conditions of service.

Restrictions have sometimes been imposed upon the freedom of association of civil servants, and have applied both to industrial and political action. Thus, in Britain the Trade Disputes and Trade Unions Act, 1927, provided that established civil servants should be subject to regulations prohibiting them from joining any organization the primary object of which was to influence the pay and conditions of its members unless its membership was limited to persons employed by or under the Crown; also organizations so limited in membership were to remain completely independent of any association with outside trade unions or federations, were to have no political objects, and were not to associate directly or indirectly with any political party or organization.[1] Subject to a few minor qualifications, established civil servants who broke these regulations became disqualified from remaining in the service.

With the repeal of the 1927 Act by the Labour Government in 1946, civil servants in Britain became free again to join trade unions which include members working in private industry, even if these unions have political objects, and unions with a membership wholly or mainly of civil servants can have political objects and can affiliate with outside unions or federations with political objects, including the Trades Union Congress and can thereby be associated with the Labour Party. The arguments in favour of freedom of association

[1] These conditions did not prevent an established civil servant from maintaining his membership of an outside trade union under specified conditions in order to retain his rights to superannuation or other friendly benefits, provided he had been a member of the union for more than six months at the coming into force of the Act.

212

for industrial purposes are stronger, along the lines indicated above, than those for freedom of political affiliation and of political action. Though the civil servant is a citizen and has political rights he also has, as already mentioned, special responsibilities to serve impartially the Government of the day. On balance it seems preferable to maintain the principle of freedom in the political field with the reasonable expectation that discretion will be exercised by individuals and organizations in the actions they take. If freedom were abused then restrictions could be introduced to meet the particular issues raised.

The infrequency of strikes by civil servants is an indication that great discretion is exercised in negotiations about conditions of service. The law in Britain does not forbid civil servants to strike; even the 1927 Act did not do that. Yet the Government may take disciplinary action against those who go on strike, and might thereby take away partly, or wholly, the value of the right to strike. During the debate on the repeal of the 1927 Act, the Attorney General, speaking on behalf of the Labour Government, stated that they, like any other Government, would take whatever disciplinary action any strike situation demanded and in illustration indicated that if some special section of the civil service (e.g. prison officers) went on strike, the Government would undoubtedly exercise their right as an employer of instant dismissal without hope of reinstatement. Prison officers are subject to special discipline and the penalty of dismissal would be appropriate, but the Attorney General did not indicate whether such a penalty would be limited to a few special categories of civil servants or would have wider application. Private employers may have the right to dismiss strikers without hope of reinstatement, but in practice they usually agree with trade unions on reinstatement as one of the conditions of ending a strike.

Employers have often considered that they should be free to decide for themselves whether or not they would employ trade unionists or would employ both trade unionists and non-trade unionists, and that they should have the right to make it a condition of employment that they would not employ trade unionists or would employ only trade unionists. This is the legal position in Britain, though in practice the legal right is restricted by demands of strong trade unions, which as already indicated, have in some industries secured priority of employment for their members or by their pressure have made it expedient for employers to employ only members of trade unions. During the period from 1927 to 1946, however, it was unlawful for any local or other public authority to require any person they employed to be or not to be a member of a trade union, or to put any employees at a disadvantage because of their membership or non-membership of a trade union.[1] This provision was included in the Trade Disputes and Trade Unions Act, 1927, to prevent the practice which had grown up for the Councils of some local authorities with Labour majorities to make it a condition of employment by the authority that workpeople in various occupations should join approved trade unions. It was criticized because it imposed a legal restriction on public authorities from which other employers were free. It lapsed when the Act was repealed in 1946, but it would be unsatisfactory if public authorities changed their policy on this question with every change in the political party in power.[2]

In the United States freedom to refuse to employ trade unionists which many employers had exercised was withdrawn by the New Deal Legislation under the Roosevelt Administration with a view to the development of collective bargaining. In some other countries, particularly Australia and New Zealand, preference for trade unionists or compulsory unionism has been introduced either by legislation or by legally binding awards of arbitration courts.

PICKETING AND INTIMIDATION

In conducting a strike or lock-out, workpeople or employers may commit acts which are violations of criminal or civil law. Thus, pickets of workpeople organized to dissuade non-strikers from working or strikers from giving up the struggle may interfere with freedom and be guilty of acts of intimidation or violence, the risk of which increases as the strike continues. Employers may hire "thugs" who threaten or commit acts of violence against the strikers. These acts involve criminal liability. Again, workpeople may commit a crime if, in breaking a contract of service by going on strike, they cause danger to life or property, while civil action may be taken against them for damages to cover loss caused by breach of contract.

A general principle which is reasonably applicable, and which is the basis of British law, is that an act which is not criminal if done by an individual does not become criminal because it is committed in a trade dispute by a number of people acting together. This

[1] Similarly public authorities were forbidden to make it a condition of any contract that any person to be employed by a party to the contract should be or not be a member of a trade union.

[2] After the repeal of the Act the Durham County Council tried to impose trade union membership on all its employees. This was strongly resisted, especially by doctors and teachers. The Labour Government and later the Conservative Government took action to prevent the Council from giving effect to its policy, and the trade union movement indicated that it was for unions and not employers to deal with problems of membership.

principle was applied by the Conspiracy and Protection of Property Act, 1875, and by the Trade Disputes Act, 1906.[1] The earlier Act made peaceful picketing legal, but the right was specifically included in the Trade Disputes Act, 1906, which provided that a person or persons acting on their own behalf, or for a trade union, or an employer, may go to a person's house or workplace for the purpose of peacefully persuading any person to work or abstain from working.[2]

When tempers are frayed in an industrial conflict, it is easy to pass from peaceful persuasion to the use of threats, intimidation, or even violence. These are always criminal whether done in an industrial dispute or not, and whether they are the acts of one or of more persons. By the Conspiracy and Protection of Property Act, 1875, it is illegal to commit such acts for the purpose of compelling anyone to abstain from doing anything which he has a legal right to do, specific mention being made of violence or intimidation to a person or his wife or children, injury to his property, persistently following him about, hiding his tools, clothes, or other property, or depriving him of or hindering in the use of them, or watching or besetting his house or place of work or the approaches to them. No definition of intimidation is, however, given, and to draft a good one is not easy, as a nervous person may feel intimidated by acts which would cause no uneasiness to another. Intimidation causes a mental condition, and this was the basis of the definition given in the Trade Union and Trade Disputes Act, 1927, which stated an act of intimidation to be causing in the mind of a person a reasonable apprehension of injury to him or any member of his family or his dependents, or of violence or damage to any person or property.[3] Although that Act has been repealed it is still the responsibility of courts of law to decide

[1] The Conspiracy and Protection of Property Act, 1875, provides that any agreement or combination by two or more persons to do any act in furtherance of a trade dispute between employers and workmen shall not be indictable as a conspiracy unless such act committed by one person would be punishable as a crime. In the Trade Disputes Act, 1906, the provision is that an act done in pursuance of an agreement or combination of two or more persons, if in contemplation or furtherance of a trade dispute, shall not be actionable unless the act without any such agreement or combination would be actionable.

[2] The full provision is that it shall be lawful for one or more persons acting on their own behalf or on behalf of a trade union or of an individual employer or firm in contemplation or furtherance of a trade dispute, to attend at or near a house or place where a person resides or works or carries on business or happens to be, if they attend merely for the purpose of peacefully obtaining or communicating information or peacefully persuading any person to work or abstain from working.

[3] The expression "injury" includes injury to a person in respect of his business, occupation, employment, or other source of income.

whether such fear has been caused, taking into account the temperament of the person who complains of intimidation.

BREACH OF CONTRACT

Breach of a contract of service is a crime, involving liability to a fine or imprisonment, if a person does it wilfully and maliciously knowing or having reasonable cause to believe that it will probably endanger human life or cause serious bodily injury or expose valuable property to destruction or serious injury.[1] Special provisions are usually applied to persons employed in certain public utility services, and in Great Britain if any person employed in gas, water, or electricity supply breaks a contract of service knowing that his action either alone or in combination with others will deprive consumers of their supply, he is liable to criminal prosecution.[2] This liability is limited in British law to gas, water, and electricity, these being supplied into the homes of many millions of town dwellers and essential for their health and welfare.

Interruption of other public utility services, e.g. tramway, motorbus, railway, telephone and telegraphic services, causes grave inconvenience to large numbers of people, and it might be argued that similar liability for breach of contract should apply to persons employed in such undertakings. Once, however, a process of extension begins it is difficult to know where to stop. By the Trade Disputes and Trade Unions Act, 1927, which was repealed in 1946, criminal liability for breach of contract involving risk of injury or danger, or grave inconvenience to the community was applied, in similar terms to those given above for gas, water and electricity, to any person employed by a local or other public authority. Such application to persons employed by a public authority was not satisfactory for purposes of limitation as many services by private undertakings, e.g. food distribution, are more essential than some of the work done by public authorities. Also, with the tendency to increase the economic activities, including nationalized industries, controlled by public authorities, one large part of the employed population would be subject to criminal liability for breach of contract leading to serious consequences, while the remainder would be free from it. There would be no adequate reason for this discrimination.

[1] This is provided by the Conspiracy and Protection of Property Act, 1875.

[2] For gas and water supply, this liability is provided in the Conspiracy and Protection of Property Act, 1875, and for electricity supply, by the Electricity (Supply) Act, 1919.

The question arises whether a civil action can be brought against a trade union or the officials of a trade union for inducing workpeople to break contracts of employment and take part in a strike. Formerly in Britain and, in recent years, frequently in the United States, the courts have, on application, issued injunctions to restrain trade union officials from inducing workpeople to go on strike in breach of their contracts of employment. In Britain the question was settled by the Trade Disputes Act, 1906, which provides that any act done in contemplation or furtherance of a trade dispute shall not be actionable merely because it induces a person to break a contract of employment.[1]

IMMUNITY AND SECURITY OF TRADE UNION FUNDS

When trade union members pay their contributions they do so mainly to meet the cost of organization and administration, to accumulate reserves for strike pay, and in many unions to provide friendly benefits. If, however, civil actions could be brought against a union for wrongful acts alleged to have been committed by it or by its members acting on its behalf, damages might often be awarded against it, and a succession of such actions would cause its funds to be drained and its effectiveness would be destroyed, as almost anything it might do in a trade dispute might lead to an action for damages. To employers who would not trouble to bring actions against individual members of a union because these workmen would not be able to pay much in damages, a wealthy union would seem "fair game."

This issue became prominent in Britain in 1901 as a result of the famous Taff Vale Judgment. Until then it had been widely believed for many years that trade unions could not be sued for activities in a trade dispute. In that year, however, the Taff Vale Railway Company brought an action in tort for damages against the Amalgamated Society of Railway Servants, alleging that during a strike against the company, some of the union's members had conspired on behalf of the union to induce workmen to break their contracts of service and unlawfully to interfere with the traffic of the company.[2] The House

[1] Also any act done in contemplation or furtherance of a trade dispute is not actionable on the ground only that it is an interference with the trade, business, or employment of some other person, or with his right to dispose of his capital or his labour as he wills.

[2] Torts are civil wrongs, i.e. violations of a general duty imposed by law, and are not merely breaches of contract or of trust or other obligations made by the parties themselves. Torts include libel, slander, defamation, nuisances, fraud, trespass, threat of violence, and false imprisonment, and the remedy for a tort is an action for damages. An act may be both a tort and a crime, or a tort and a breach of contract.

217

of Lords as final court of appeal decided that a trade union could be sued in its registered name for torts committed by its authority, and the Amalgamated Society had to pay damages amounting to £25,000 and costs totalling £17,000. After several years of controversy and agitation the trade unions succeeded in 1906 in securing the passing of the Trade Disputes Act, which gave them immunity from such civil actions. It provided that a trade union, whether of workmen or masters, or any members or officials of a trade union could not be sued for any tortious act alleged to have been committed by or on behalf of the union. Though unions are free from civil liability and their funds are therefore protected, their officials and members can be sued and are personally liable.

The immunity of trade unions is not limited to activities in contemplation or furtherance of a trade dispute, and the 1906 Act seems to place them "above the law," unions not being like corporations which are responsible for the actions of agents or servants done on their behalf. There is, however, one qualification of this in the 1906 Act, which provides that, except for tortious acts in a trade dispute, the trustees of a union are liable to be sued for tortious acts concerning the property of the union, and therefore in such circumstances claims could be made against the union's property controlled by its trustees. It is likely, therefore, that the courts would consider claims for damages against a union's property in the control of its trustees, e.g. for libel in a publication of the union, or for nuisances in the union's premises. It must be repeated, however, that such actions could not be brought against the trustees if the torts were committed in connection with a trade dispute.

Until after the middle of the nineteenth century trade union funds in Britain were insecure because unions had no legal right to bring an action against defaulting officials. An attempt to provide protection was made in the Friendly Societies Act, 1855, which enabled unions registered with the Registrar of Friendly Societies to bring such actions before the magistrates. Some years later, however, it was found that the intended protection was inadequate, and it was not until the passing of the Trade Union Act, 1871, that proper protection was established on a permanent basis, legal status to bring actions being acquired by registration with the Registrar of Friendly Societies.

13

Political Action by Trade Unions

MEMBERSHIP OF trade unions is open to persons irrespective of their political views or associations, and during the nineteenth century many British trade union leaders believed strongly that the movement should keep to industrial action and leave party politics alone. They considered that this would preserve the unity and ensure the effectiveness of the movement, both in its membership and concentration of effort. This did not prevent trade unions from influencing measures before Parliament which directly affected the interests of the workers, and by having no party affiliations they could, according to circumstances, support whichever Government or party would promise them the best terms. This is still the policy of trade unions in the United States, whereas in Great Britain the nineteenth-century attitude has been abandoned and the trade union movement has been closely identified with the Labour Party. In Australia and New Zealand the evolution has been similar to that in Great Britain.

A problem which has arisen is whether trade unions should be treated as corporations whose field of action is defined and limited by Statute, or as voluntary associations which may undertake any lawful activities including participation in politics if their members so decide. In various ways trade unions in Britain have an intermediate legal status and receive certain privileges by statute. It would be quite impracticable as well as undesirable, however, in a democratic community to try to prevent trade unions taking political action, while any attempt to restrict such action to industrial issues of special interest to their members would be ineffective, as standards of living and conditions of work are inextricably related to the whole of economic life, both national and international. The solution adopted by law in Britain from 1913 onwards seems reasonable, that in order to benefit from statutory privileges and protection a trade union must direct its main activities to improving working conditions and providing friendly benefits for its members, but if these are its principal objects it may add any other lawful purposes which its members authorize it to undertake, though participation in political objects is subject to restrictions which are outlined below, and therefore in this respect trade unions are not so free as voluntary associations or clubs.

The reason for the restrictions is to satisfy workpeople who wish to be members of trade unions for industrial purposes but have conscientious objection to contributing money for political purposes of which they disapprove.[1] A trade union which undertakes political activities has many members who support such action, others who disagree perhaps strongly with the political policy of the union or the party which it supports, and a large number who are not politically minded, or who do not object to the union using for political purposes some of the funds to which they contribute, believing this may lead to better conditions for workers in industry though they may vote for another party. It has been argued that if a majority of trade union members desire to support a particular party and give the union authority to use funds for this purpose the minority should be bound by this decision and either contribute like everyone else or leave the union. But leaving a union is not the same as resigning from many voluntary associations or clubs, and a worker who did so would lose the industrial benefits of membership and would be unlikely to find another union suitable for him to join; nor would he and others who thought like him be likely to find conditions favourable for starting a new union of their own.

A reasonable solution, therefore, is to introduce a conscience clause enabling a worker to be a member of a trade union without having to contribute to its political fund. This is applied in Great Britain by the Trade Union Act, 1913, which provides that a trade union shall use funds for specified political purposes only if it complies with the following conditions:

(a) A resolution approving political action as an object of the union has secured a majority of those voting in a ballot of the members. The rules applying the Act provide that the ballot shall be secret.

(b) Any payments for political objects are to be made out of a separate fund, known as the political fund.

(c) Any member can obtain exemption from contributing to the political fund, without losing any benefits of union membership. This is known as "contracting-out."

[1] This issue was raised in Great Britain by the famous Osborne Case in 1909, and the House of Lords, on appeal, decided that trade unions had no legal right to spend money for political purposes such as supporting a Parliamentary candidate or paying a Member of Parliament, because the law mentioned specific objects and a trade union was not entitled to add political or other unspecified objects. This decision led to an amendment of the law in 1913, the Trade Union Act of that year legalizing political activities by trade unions subject to certain restrictions.

The political objects which can be undertaken only if the above conditions are complied with are mainly payment of expenses of political candidates or prospective candidates, holding meetings or distributing literature in support of such persons, and maintenance of Members of Parliament or of local government authorities. Political objects not specified in the Act can be undertaken without observing the above conditions, and these would, no doubt, include "lobbying" and other political action to support legislation on working conditions or other matters of particular interest to workers in the industry or trade to which the union belongs.

By the 1913 Act, it is assumed that persons joining a trade union will pay the political levy unless they take action to obtain exemption. The onus is upon the individuals who object to paying the levy to act. There are, however, many people who because of inertia will not take the trouble to fill up a form claiming exemption, especially as the amount involved is small, averaging only about 1s. a year. Some of them are not politically minded and give no thought to the question, others are willing to contribute because a majority has voted for political action, and yet others pay the levy because they will not take the risk of incurring the odium of their fellow-members by standing out against participation in the political work of the union. Therefore, in practice, only a relatively small number of members who have strong political convictions against the union's policy contract out of the levy.

By the Trade Disputes and Trade Unions Act, 1927, the contracting-out system was replaced by contracting-in, and, instead of every member paying the levy unless he had taken action to secure exemption, no member paid unless he had filled in a form expressing his desire to do so. Inertia then acted against contributing, and the political funds of the unions suffered seriously in consequence.[1] For the purpose solely of safeguarding political consciences there is no theoretical difference between contracting-out and contracting-in, but their practical effects are very different owing to inertia, and the psychological factors already mentioned. Also it is argued that if an association decides to spend money for a specified purpose the minority are usually expected to conform to the will of the majority, but if in any organization the minority has the right to exemption it would seem reasonable that the onus should be on the minority to claim the exemption. The system of contracting-out, which is based on this argument, was restored when the 1927 Act was repealed by the Labour Government in 1946.

[1] The effects on contributions were illustrated by the Attorney General, Sir H. Shawcross, in a debate in the House of Commons, February 12, 1946, on a Bill to repeal the 1927 Act.

221

14

Employers' Organizations

THE CONSUMERS of the goods they produce are the real, though indirect, employers both of workpeople and of managers, technicians, enterprisers, and suppliers of capital. By their purchases they pay wages, salaries, interest, and dividends. This is recognized more clearly by firms than by workpeople, and firms compete strongly against one another to win customers and gain a larger share of the market. In periods when labour is scarce they also compete for workpeople by offering higher wages or other inducements. It follows that this rivalry tends to keep firms, who are the direct employers of labour, from joining together in associations until they find it in their interest to unite so as to face the attacks of trade unions.

Employers' organizations are formed for several distinct purposes, (1) to protect themselves against demands by trade unions which they consider to be impracticable or undesirable; (2) to prevent unfair competition amongst themselves by regulating the volume of production, allocating markets and fixing selling prices; (3) to organize jointly various commercial, legal, and other services of mutual interest; (4) to express the views of employers on economic, financial, labour, and social policy to the Government, to appoint representatives on public bodies, and to influence public opinion. Only the first of these purposes and those parts of the fourth which concern labour are relevant to industrial relations. Some employers' organizations specialize on matters within the field of industrial relations, but others have wider scope.

So long as employers have to deal severally only with their own workpeople in regulating wages and working conditions, they have no need to form associations for mutual support. Each employer has a bargaining power equal to that of the whole of his workpeople. Employers are, however, faced with a very different situation when their workpeople in a number of firms form a trade union and use the "strike in detail" method, that is, try to gain their demands by going on strike against one employer at a time, the strikers being supported by contributions from the wages of union members at work in other firms. By this method a strike can be prolonged until the employer concerned is forced to give way. If the union attacks only those employers who have been competing unfairly by low wages and poor working conditions, the action of the union will be welcomed by other employers, who will not interfere. Where, however, each employer may be attacked in turn, they have a powerful incentive to combine.

For the reasons indicated, organizations of employers for the regulation labour conditions have usually been formed after trade unions have been set up. At first, organizations consisted of only "tacit combinations," to use Adam Smith's phrase. The employers would reach a general understanding about the wages and conditions they considered proper in the locality, and undertake to support financially and in other ways any employer against whom the union called a strike to secure better wages and conditions than those agreed upon by the employers. They would also exchange information about trade union "agitators," and refuse to employ them. From these beginnings more formal organizations often evolved, with constitutions, defined conditions of membership, regular subscriptions, elected officers, and staff.

Not all employers' organizations are formed because of trade union pressure. Sometimes Government intervention in the regulation of working conditions is a reason. For example, when the British Government set up Trade Boards for the regulation of minimum wages in industries where organizations of employers and workers were too weak to regulate wages and conditions effectively, employers' organizations were formed largely in order to get agreed policies and to nominate representatives for the employers' side of the Boards. Again, in Australia and New Zealand, although the main reason for the establishment of employers' organizations is to meet trade union pressure, an additional inducement is to secure registration by the arbitration courts so as to be able to present their case in court hearings. Central organizations such as the British Employers' Confederation are usually set up to formulate general policies, to express the views of employers on national consultative bodies set up by the Government and on international bodies, for example the International Labour Organisation. Usually each member association retains the right to make direct representations to Governments on proposed legislation and other matters which specially affect its own industry; also collective bargaining on wages and working conditions is undertaken by the association or associations within each industry.

The task of building up an employers' organization is very different

223

from that of recruiting and maintaining trade union membership. The organizers of a union must win the approval and support of large numbers of individual workpeople, and this requires publicity and mass appeals. Relatively to workpeople the number of employers in an industry is small, and once a nucleus has been formed, other employers are approached separately and privately by one or two members who indicate the advantages and conditions of membership. Often the first approach to an employer is made by a member who knows him personally and is likely to win his support. Those who join do so because they feel the need for the greater strength which can be shown by an employers' association in resisting trade union demands, or because they see advantages in fixing standards of labour by collective agreements. Some employers, however, remain outside the organization because they prefer to deal with the unions independently, and are opposed to standardization of labour conditions. They may be small-scale employers who wish to be free to pay lower wages than those fixed in collective agreements, while some progressive firms remain outside because their wages and conditions are better than the agreed standards, and they do not, therefore, expect trouble with the unions.

Not only is recruiting for membership conducted privately without publicity, but also the business of employers' organizations is similarly conducted. There is usually no equivalent to the annual conventions and congresses of the trade union movement where publicity is sought and where cleavages of opinion are revealed in public debates and votes. Such publicity has a propagandist value to trade unions in recruiting members and sustaining interest which employers' organizations achieve in other ways. Nor do employers' organizations usually publish figures showing their membership and the state of their finances.[1] Memoranda on policy are circulated privately to their members, and only occasionally do they publish documents on policy, though the main lines of policy are indicated in statements submitted to Government commissions, committees, courts of enquiry, and advisory councils, and in the processes of collective bargaining with trade unions.

One of the reasons why little has been written about the history, structure, and policy of employers' organizations, by contrast with the vast literature on the trade union movement, is the smaller amount of information available because of the privacy with which

[1] In Britain large numbers of trade unions, including the biggest ones, are officially registered under the Friendly Societies Acts and supply information about their objects, constitution, and membership, whereas none of the great employers' organizations is registered.

their affairs are conducted. Another reason, however, is that their defensive and conservative attitudes have proved less attractive to writers on social problems than the more novel political and social theories that lie at the foundation of trade union policy. Nevertheless, their development and activities are of equal significance in industrial relations to those of the trade unions.

Employers are largely free from the complexities caused among workpeople by the craft *versus* industrial basis of organization and by divergent interests of skilled and unskilled workers. The interests of an employer of several thousands of workpeople are usually linked with those of the industry to which he belongs, whereas his workpeople may consist of several groups with different interests. Organizations of employers are usually based on the industry, but industries range from relatively homogeneous ones, for example, coal-mining, to complex ones, such as engineering, and textiles, and these differences result in considerable variety in types of organizations. Thus, in Britain in some complex industries the many distinct parts have their own associations, but these join together for purposes of collective bargaining into a great "omnibus" federation; for example, the Engineering and Allied Employers' National Federation. In other complex industries several organizations remain independent. Thus, employers' organizations in the British textile industry are divided first by the material used, cotton firms being organized separately from woollen firms. Within these main divisions firms which specialize in spinning may be separately organized from those specializing in weaving.

Usually for each division of an industry there are district or regional associations, and these combine into national federations. Generally, the national federation affiliates only associations and not individual firms; the firms join the association in their district. The rules often provide that member firms shall not negotiate directly with a trade union, but must refer differences and disputes to the district association or its local branches. Member firms generally undertake not to employ, during the continuance of a dispute, any workpeople on strike or locked out by other member firms. Some federations provide that member firms before engaging a worker who had previously been employed by another member firm shall obtain specified information from the former employer.

The funds of employers' organizations consist mainly of entrance fees, annual contributions, and special levies. The basis of payment varies according to industry. In organizations where member firms do not differ much in size, equal amounts are contributed by each firm. Usually, however, contributions are based on the size of each firm or, for national federations, on the size of each district association. Size also determines the number of representatives on the councils of national federations and the voting power of member firms and district associations on major questions.

Various criteria are used to measure the size of firms and district associations for the purpose of fixing the amount of contribution. In many associations the number of persons employed is taken as basis. Some use the wages bill during the last financial year or average of several years, the contributions being fixed at so much for each £100 paid in wages. Output is the measure adopted by some organizations, for example, tonnage of coal produced, while equipment is found suitable in some industries, for example, the number of spindles and looms is used in some branches of the textile industry, and gross tonnage of vessels by shipping organizations.

General meetings are held usually once or twice a year of member firms of district or regional associations, and committees meet more frequently. Some national federations also hold general meetings which any member firm may attend. Federations are generally managed by a council, an executive committee, or board of management, and by various standing committees. The councils are usually large bodies, consisting of representatives from each district association, the number of representatives being based on the relative importance of each association. Regular meetings are held, often once a quarter, to decide general lines of policy. Executive committees are much smaller; they usually hold monthly meetings and are responsible for policy within the general framework adopted by the council. Details of policy and administrative matters are dealt with by an administrative or general purposes committee. Other committees include a finance committee, a legal and parliamentary committee, and a labour committee, which deals with labour policy and often represents the federation in negotiations with trade unions.

National federations vary considerably in the degree of autonomy retained by the federated associations in the districts, but the tendency is to increase the powers of federations. Some constitutions provide that certain major questions shall be decided by a general meeting of members, or by a referendum to all the federated associations. For example, in many federations decisions leading to a lock-out may not be taken by the National Council until the matter has been referred to the affiliated associations; often a two-thirds majority of the recorded votes of members in the various districts is required before a lock-out may be ordered. Conversely, provision is usually made that a district association shall take no action of general importance to the industry without previous consultation with the federation.

OBJECTS AND POLICY

During a substantial part of the nineteenth century in Britain the usual policy of employers and employers' organizations was to secure collapse of the trade unions. In various industries employers refused to employ union labour and gave jobs only to those workpeople who would sign what came to be known as the "Document," binding themselves as a condition of employment not to join a trade union. Employers and their organizations often refused to recognize the unions and bargain with them. Trials of strength by strikes and lock-outs were frequent, and it was not until unions were firmly established that collective bargaining became frequently accepted as the normal way of regulating working conditions. In the United States in steel, coal-mining, and other industries, the struggle between unions and employers on the question of recognition continued during several decades of the present century, being marked by intimidation, violence, and bloodshed on both sides. It was not until President Roosevelt's New Deal legislation imposed the obligation on employers to recognize trade unions and to bargain collectively with them that this method, supported by the Government, came into general use in the mass production industries.

In summarizing here the main objects and policies of employers' organizations, it is assumed that trade unionism is well established and that the unions are recognized for purposes of collective bargaining. Employers' associations differ considerably in the emphasis they place on the promotion of good relations with workpeople, the development of joint machinery for conciliation and arbitration, and the fixing of reasonable working conditions. Some associations place emphasis on resistance to demands by unions which they consider unfair or impracticable, while others appear more constructive and include among their objects the establishment and maintenance of friendly relations with workpeople and their unions.

The main objects and policies are:

(1) To safeguard the interests of the association and its member firms.

(2) To take such action as may be necessary for the satisfactory regulation of wages and working conditions, and for the

227

avoidance and settlement of disputes between member firms and their workpeople, including methods of voluntary conciliation and arbitration.

(3) To provide mutual support and uniformity of policy in dealing with demands made by trade unions, to resist demands for wages and conditions likely to be injurious to the industry, and to protect members by financial, legal, or other means against strikes by workpeople and against losses incurred by acting in accordance with decisions of the association.

(4) To promote or oppose legislation affecting the interests of the industry, to make representations to Government departments, and to give evidence before Government committees on matters affecting the industry.

Private enterprise is preferred to nationalization or public control of industry. Preference is also shown for the flexibility of collective agreements compared with the rigidities of legislation for regulating working conditions, and extensions of interventions by Government are often opposed. While recognizing trade unions for purposes of collective bargaining, employers' organizations usually support the "open shop" principle, that is, the right of an employer to give employment to any worker whether a trade unionist or not. They try to secure removal or relaxation of trade union practices which restrict production, and they oppose participation by workpeople in the functions of management, except by joint advisory or consultative committees which leave the employer free to make decisions. They also often advocate economy in Government expenditure as a means of reducing the burden of taxation on industry.

15

Collective Bargaining

COLLECTIVE BARGAINING takes place when a number of work-people enter into negotiation as a bargaining unit with an employer or group of employers with the object of reaching agreement on conditions of employment for the workpeople concerned. This definition would include bargaining by workpeople acting together temporarily for this purpose, but developed systems of collective bargaining are based upon greater continuity of organization among workpeople. The definition also includes bargaining by so-called "company" unions, or employee-representation arrangements, which were frequently established in the inter-war years especially in the United States of America. Often in the early stages of organization amongst workpeople employers have refused to discuss working conditions except with their own workpeople. This company basis of negotiation is, however, defective because the spokesmen of the workers are in a weak position. Being themselves employed by the firm, they are dependent upon the employer for their pay and are not so free to take a strong line in negotiation as would be officials of a trade union who are paid from union funds. Collective bargaining is therefore only likely to be conducted on equal terms if the spokesmen of the workers are trade union officers and are dependent upon the union and not upon the employer for their position and pay.[1]

If workpeople negotiate by means of a "company" union and not by a union with members in a number of companies, the bargaining is collective to the employer in the sense that he is dealing with more than one worker. From the workers' point of view, however,

[1] This aspect of trade union recognition was raised before a Court of Inquiry in Great Britain during consideration of a dispute in 1941 at Briggs Motor Bodies, Ltd. The court noted that the management of the company dealt with certain of their own engineering workers whom they knew to be members of the Amalgamated Engineering Union and shop stewards chosen by members of that union, but had no dealings with the officials of the union unless they were also employed by the company. The court recommended that the normal procedure should be adopted for discussions and settling disputes "which procedure necessarily involves the recognition of those unions who fairly and largely represent their workpeople."

they are bargaining with an individual firm, and are not able to demand standardization of working conditions in a number of firms. A trade union can do this, and can often secure agreements which go a long way towards eliminating competition in labour standards between firms.

RECOGNITION OF TRADE UNIONS

Collective bargaining can begin only when an employer or employers' organization recognizes a trade union or other body representing the workpeople. In the early stages in the growth of trade unionism many employers resisted the movement by using the "yellow dog" contract to prevent their workers from joining a union, and they also refused to recognize and enter into negotiations with representatives of a union.

An employer may properly refuse recognition to a union which is so weak in membership that it is not representative of the workpeople. Also, before giving recognition to a union, an employer will want to be satisfied that the organization is likely to be permanent, stable, and well administered. It is because many unions in colonial territories and under-developed countries lack stability and sound leadership that employers refuse to recognize them. Again, an employer may reasonably refuse to recognize a body which is "subversive" in its aims and objects, or is in the hands of extremists.

In Great Britain recognition of trade unions by employers has been achieved throughout almost the whole of industry without legal authority, whereas in some countries, for example the United States, recognition and the right to bargain collectively has been generalized by law. By New Deal legislation in the 1930's, workpeople were given the right to bargain collectively through representatives of their own choosing, and in various Canadian provinces employers are liable to penalties if they refuse to bargain collectively with representatives of their workpeople.

A problem arises where there are two or more rival unions each claiming to represent the same workpeople, and difficulties would result if two or more of such unions were recognized for bargaining purposes by an employer or employers. It would be possible to have meetings for negotiation attended by representatives from each union, the number of representatives of each union being proportionate to its membership, but in practice the rivalries of the unions and their conflicting policies would usually lead to bitter struggles between themselves which would be no concern of the employers, but would be likely to render collective bargaining ineffective and to break down completely. It is desirable, therefore, that one union only should be recognized for any given group of workers.

The question then arises how the employer should decide which one of two or more unions is most representative of the workpeople concerned. Sometimes employers have adopted the policy of recognizing a union which has a membership of not less than a specified percentage of all the workpeople. For example, in the British Post Office shortly after the Second World War, a formula provided that a request for recognition would be considered from any association which had a membership of not less than 40 per cent of the workpeople in a given grade. Often, however, this would be an unduly high percentage, and many unions with a smaller percentage have been effective in collective bargaining. On the other hand, even with a 40 per cent membership there may be two rival unions each claiming to satisfy this standard, and therefore the fixing of a percentage may not solve the problem. In practice, the formula led to the formation and recognition of many small unions each representing a special section or grade of workers, and this made difficult the reaching of broadly based agreements.

The question of deciding which one among rival unions should be recognized has received more attention in recent years in the United States and also in Australia and New Zealand than in Great Britain. When, under the National Labour Relations Act, 1936, workpeople in the United States were given "the right to bargain collectively through representatives of their own choosing," employers were faced with claims by rival unions to represent the workpeople, and in order to settle this issue a system of elections by secret ballot was arranged, the elections being conducted by labour officers appointed by the Federal Government. Where two or more unions satisfied these labour officers that they had a sufficient membership they were included in the ballot, and all the workpeople concerned, whether union members or not, were given the right to vote. The union which obtained the largest support was then designated as the recognized agency for collective bargaining, but if after a time it lost membership and a rival union grew in strength, a new election would be held to give the workpeople an opportunity to alter their earlier decision. In Australia and New Zealand the Arbitration Courts recognize only one union for any specified grade of workers, and this union is the one which can appear before the court to present the claims of the workers concerned. The courts decide between rival unions on information about the strength of the unions, particularly the paying membership of each union. Sometimes unions have memberships which do not cover exactly

231

the same grade of workers, and in such circumstances two or more unions may be recognized, provided it is possible to regard each union as representative of the interests of a distinct category of workpeople.

Experience of collective bargaining shows that one or both sides may adopt unfair practices. In Britain these have, in the main, been brought under control by a growing sense of responsibility, but in some countries steps have been taken to define unfair practices, and laws have been passed making them illegal. In order that collective bargaining may have a reasonable chance of success, employers and workpeople must negotiate "in good faith," and this includes willingness to make concessions. No bargaining is possible if an employer or employers merely listen to claims by workers and then reject them and refuse to discuss them further. Similarly there is no genuine negotiation if workers' representatives make their demands with a "take it or leave it" attitude, and threaten to call a strike if their demands are not fully met. Unless the two sides make a serious attempt to find a common solution of their differences collective negotiations can be of little value. Collective bargaining requires the adoption by both sides of an enlightened and disciplined sense of responsibility if it is to be successful. In the United States a Federal Board has been appointed to secure good faith in bargaining.

Where irresponsibility is shown and unfair practices are adopted by either side, legislation may become necessary to make such practices illegal. This was done, for example, in the United States by the Labour-Management Relations Act, 1947, known as the "Taft–Hartley" Act. The following are some of the practices made illegal by this or other Acts: "Yellowdog" contracts are not enforcible in Federal Courts, and other interferences with or coercion of work-people in the exercise of their freedom of association are illegal. So are attempts to cause an employer to discriminate against a worker in order to encourage or discourage membership of a labour organization.[1] Jurisdictional strikes were made illegal, such strikes being those which arise because each of two or more unions claims the right to organize the workpeople in a given occupation or grade. Strikes or lock-outs in violation of the terms of an agreement are unfair, and can lead to actions for damages. Again, although it is within the power of a union to expel members, it is an unfair practice

[1] Except for non-payment of union dues or initiation fees under a "union shop" agreement.

for a union to try to compel an employer to discharge such workers. Threats, intimidation, and the use of bribes in labour relations are also illegal. Such unfair practices associated with collective bargaining must be distinguished from others, often known as restrictive or obstructive practices, which are related to production rather than to organization and negotiation. Injunctions can be issued requiring cessation of any illegal practice, and failure to observe injunctions involves contempt of court by the responsible organizations or individuals, who then become liable to fine or imprisonment.

BARGAINING MACHINERY

In the early stages of trade union development collective bargaining was often between a trade union and one employer, and many collective agreements in Britain in the nineteenth century were of this kind. As trade union organization and collective bargaining developed, an increasing number of agreements were on a regional or nation-wide basis. In some countries, however, differences of conditions and traditions have resulted in a continuation, after collective bargaining had become well established, of negotiations between trade unions and individual firms. Such negotiations and agreements are still frequent in many industries in the United States, though in steel, anthracite, and some other industries there are tendencies for regional standardized agreements to be concluded. Although formally the terms of agreements apply only to the contracting parties, in practice employers apply agreed conditions to all their workpeople whether trade unionists or not, except where agreements specify certain privileges for union members. Also the terms of agreements are often observed by or substantially influence employers who are not parties to the agreements.

Where collective bargaining is well established, highly developed constitutions and rules of procedure for meetings and negotiations have evolved between employers' organizations and trade unions. These arrangements include the ways in which employers and workers respectively are represented, the calling of conferences, the choice of a chairman, and procedure at meetings. They also include provisions for conciliation and arbitration when direct negotiations break down. Often, when collective bargaining is in an early stage of development, meetings are *ad hoc* and no provision is made for subsequent meetings, but, as systematic relations develop, arrangements are made for meetings to be called whenever changes in agreements are demanded or there are other matters in dispute. Many agreements may provide that they shall be in operation in the first instance for a year, but that they will remain in force afterwards until either side gives notice that they want a revision.[1]

If employers and workers meet in conference only when differences have arisen between them, they always meet in an atmosphere of controversy or even conflict. Yet there are many subjects of common interest which do not unnecessarily divide them into two sides, and on which joint discussion can be of much value. It was for this reason that the Whitley Committee in Britain towards the end of the First World War proposed the setting up in each industry of joint industrial councils which would hold regular meetings, for example, once a quarter, to consider matters affecting the progress and well-being of the industry, including means of ensuring to the workpeople the greatest possible security of earnings and employment, methods of fixing and adjusting earnings, technical education and training, improvements of processes, industrial research, elimination of waste, and standardization of products. Such regular meetings provide the basis for a better understanding of the difficulties of each side, and enable representatives to get to know one another and establish mutual respect. This system of joint industrial councils was widely adopted in the civil service, local government, and in some private industries. In many of the most strongly organized industries, however, the scheme was not adopted, but the previous well-established arrangements for meetings to negotiate agreements on working conditions were continued, the meetings being held only when necessary to settle differences which had arisen about wages and other conditions of work. Since the Second World War, however, the establishment of development councils in some of these industries provides a means for considering general questions concerning the progress and prosperity of the industries in regular meetings, and these councils, together with the conferences for negotiating about working conditions, go a long way towards dealing with the same needs as those for which joint industrial councils were proposed.

Systems of joint negotiation vary greatly from industry to industry. They have evolved to meet the special needs of each industry, and are often highly complex. Some industries are localized, while others are widely distributed in all parts of the country, some consist of many small and medium-sized undertakings but others mainly of a few large firms, in some the structure of organization of workpeople and employers is simple, but in others it is highly complicated. All these varying circumstances result in wide differences in bargaining

---

[1] When conditions are stable, agreements may remain in force for several years, especially if they provide for cost-of-living or other sliding scales for the adjustment of wages.

machinery. In some industries workpeople and employers are each represented entirely or largely by one trade union and one association. In others the two sides may be represented by federations. In some British industries the workers' side is represented by twenty or more unions, some of which are craft unions, others industrial, and others general labour unions. The basic agreements establishing these systems of negotiation were sometimes reached three or four decades ago, and the original provisions remain substantially in force.

In compact industrial countries in Western Europe many agreements are national in scope. These usually provide uniform standards for hours of work, length of overtime, and paid holidays, but basic wage rates fixed in the national agreements vary from place to place, though there is a tendency for the differences to be reduced. Alternatively, national agreements deal with general matters, and these are supplemented by district or local agreements which apply the national provisions in accordance with the varying needs of each area and also include matters not covered by the national agreements. Systems of joint negotiation differ considerably in the extent to which disputes that arise locally are referred to national level. Unless they raise national issues, such reference involves delay and sometimes the risk of not allowing sufficiently for variation of conditions in different localities.

PROVISIONS OF AGREEMENTS

In countries where collective bargaining is highly developed, the provisions of agreements can be regarded as industrial codes which go into great detail in the regulation of working conditions. They somewhat resemble legislation, but are negotiated by people from within the industry concerned who know its conditions and problems, and they have the advantage of flexibility as they can be adjusted when necessary to changes in conditions. Many provisions remain in force with little or no alteration for long periods, while others, particularly rates of wages, are adjusted at frequent intervals especially in times of rapid changes in economic conditions and the cost of living. In order to avoid the danger of frequently throwing into the "melting pot" of controversy the whole of a complex agreement each time wages scales and other details are revised, the practice is sometimes adopted of having two agreements, one containing provisions which remain unchanged for long intervals, and another on wages and other matters which are frequently changed. This practice has much to commend it. There is, however, some danger that several agreements may be adopted for the same trade or industry, and this may lead to confusion and lack of co-ordination because of the application of conflicting principles in the different agreements.

Indications are given below of the wide variety of questions with which collective agreements deal. They are essentially matters which directly affect workpeople. The terms of agreements inevitably restrict the freedom of action of employers, and a line is difficult to draw between questions which are properly included in collective agreements and those which are the sole responsibility of management. Employers are, however, alert to prevent encroachments by trade unions upon managerial functions. A protracted lock-out was organized by British engineering employers in 1922 to prevent shop stewards from interfering in the management of the industry.[1]

Wages

The complexities of collective agreements may be illustrated by outlining the many features in the regulation and payment of wages. The agreements may fix time rates of wages and wages based on output. Time rates may be either minimum rates, leaving employers free to pay higher rates than those fixed in the agreement, or they may be standard rates which are usually understood to be the rates which employers will actually pay. In an agreement covering a whole country or a region, rates may be uniform throughout, or there may be differences by localities, separate rates for each being fixed in the agreements. Thus, cities and towns may be graded by population, with higher rates in the bigger centres. Some agreements divide the workpeople into a few main grades, for example skilled, semi-skilled, and unskilled, with a separate rate for each, while other agreements give a detailed list of many occupations each with its own rate. There are also differences by sex and age, the rates for juveniles usually providing for annual increments. Such increments are also provided in occupations where seniority and longer experience are of value, for example in the civil service and the teaching profession. In some manual occupations the agreements provide for higher rates for workpeople employed on unhealthy jobs, unpleasant work, or work in high temperatures or high humidity. Agreements may also make provision for the adjusting of wage rates by cost of living and other sliding scales. Some agreements prohibit the use of piece rates, this having been done in the building industry in Britain

---

[1] In 1953 the Austin Motor Company, Ltd., refused to be coerced by a trade union into giving preference in re-employment to a shop steward who, along with many other workpeople, had been laid off in a period of redundancy.

up to the Second World War. This prohibition is usual for juvenile workers.

Where wage payments are based on output, there are often difficulties in completely regulating the system by collective agreements because the piece rates and bonuses depend on processes and products which vary from firm to firm throughout an industry, and can only be fixed at factory level. Also, piece rates or other incentive rates must be adjusted whenever changes are made in processes or products, and these may occur frequently. In some agreements, for example in the cotton textile industry, piece rates, sometimes known as piece price lists, are fixed in great detail, with differences according to kind of yarn, structure of cloth to be woven, and type of machine, and indeed these lists are often highly intricate. In other agreements no attempt is made to fix the piece rates, but provision is made that they shall be fixed in each undertaking at levels which shall enable average workpeople to earn not less than a specified percentage, for example, 15 per cent, 25 per cent, or 33⅓ per cent above the rates fixed for time workers doing similar kinds of work. Provision is made in some agreements for a small joint committee to be set up at each works to decide upon incentive rates when agreement is not reached directly between the management and the workpeople concerned. Some agreements require equal piece rates to be paid to men and women, but others fix different rates. In order to give protection to piece workers from loss of earnings due to breakdown of machinery, shortages of materials, or other causes, agreements often provide that they shall receive a guaranteed time rate if their piece-work earnings fall below that amount. Alternatively piece workers may be put on time rates during temporary interruptions. Where teams of workers are paid according to the output of the group, the agreements may provide for total earnings to be shared either equally or in specified proportions by members of the team. Many agreements provide that incentive rates shall not be altered unless changes are made in the processes or in the product. Where work is defective, the worker is held responsible by the terms of some agreements and he is not paid for such work, but provision may be made for a joint committee to give decisions if disputes arise.

In communities where a "cash" economy is well developed, wages in kind are of little or no importance in most industries, but in certain industries some payment in kind is made. Thus, coal-miners may receive allowances of coal either free or at cheap rates, and agricultural workers may receive free or cheap housing and free or cheap potatoes, milk, corn, and other foods. Some workers, for example bus and tramway drivers and conductors, receive uniforms.

Where such payments in kind are made, agreements specify them.

Many agreements regulate frequency of payment, some indicating that they shall be paid weekly, and others fortnightly or monthly, and the day of the week on which wages shall be paid is often stipulated. Provision is often made that payments shall be during or immediately after working hours, and if after working hours, some agreements require that the whole time involved shall not be more than is specified in the agreement, for example, ten minutes or thirty minutes, and if longer, the worker shall receive payment for the excess of time. Some agreements provide that when payment is made the employer must supply a statement showing the gross wage, how it is made up, and the amounts of deductions. Certain agreements prohibit any deductions from wages other than those specified in the agreement.

Agreements may provide that the workers shall be under no obligation to buy goods from their employer or from any shop specified by him. Such obligations often led to grave abuses, and are prohibited by Truck Acts in many countries. In some industries employers are required to provide tools or to pay allowances to workers who provide their own tools. Payments for journeys and maintenance when working away from home are regulated. Certain agreements specify that deductions of a limited amount, for example, up to 5 per cent of the wage may be made for loss of tools, damage to materials, breakages, or faulty work for which the worker is responsible, but fines as a penalty for breaches of discipline are prohibited in many agreements. In industries subject to interruption because of bad weather, for example building and quarrying, provision may be made that workers who assemble at the workplace but are prevented from working by bad weather, shall receive at least part payment for the half-day or day involved.

Hours of Work

Regulation of hours of work is prominent in collective agreements and also in legislation. Laws may apply to certain industries only, for example, to underground mining, road and rail transport, or to certain classes of persons, e.g. women and juveniles. Some laws lay down general principles, leaving details to be settled by collective negotiation. Hours are usually fixed on a daily or weekly basis, and provision is often made for a shorter working day on the Saturday or for the distribution of weekly hours over a five-day week. In industries with continuous processes, for example steel and chemicals, agreements provide for shift working, including rotation of shifts and arrangements for changing shifts, the timetable being planned so that each worker shall take an equal share of night and Sunday work; provision may also be made so that each shift worker shall be free for twenty-four hours on one Sunday in every three weeks. Agreements frequently provide for shorter hours if work is done in high temperatures or in atmospheres with high humidity. In mining, the hours of underground work are carefully defined by agreement and legislation; in some countries, these are from "bank to bank" so that all time underground is included.[1] In the building industry in some countries the working day is somewhat longer in summer than in winter, thus allowing for better weather and longer daylight. In many industries the agreements fix the length of break in the middle of the day. Special regulations in legislation and agreements apply to night work, which is often prohibited between specified hours for women and young persons.

Overtime, Short Time, and Paid Holidays

Some agreements stipulate that overtime shall be exceptional and temporary, and prohibit the regular working of overtime. Where overtime is permitted, the amount is usually restricted to a specified number of hours a week, a month, or another period, and overtime may be worked on not more than, say, two days a week. Usually sufficient notice shall be given to the workers that they will be required to do overtime on certain days, or provision may be made for overtime to be arranged by agreement between the management and representatives of the workpeople. Higher rates of pay for overtime are usual, the addition over ordinary time rates being from around 15 to 25 per cent up to 100 per cent. Such double rates are frequently laid down for work on Sundays and public holidays. Many agreements provide for a lower rate of increase for the first few hours of overtime and higher rates subsequently, for example, an increase of 20 per cent, for the first two hours, and of 50 per cent afterwards.

In industries subject to short time, agreements may provide that advance notice shall be given, and that short time shall be systematically organized on a rotation system unless it applies simultaneously to all workers. Systematic short time provides a means of sharing the work available instead of dismissing some workers

[1] In British coal-mining, the "bank to bank" system is not used, and, in order to calculate the average time underground, there should be added to the specified hours the duration of one winding time, which averages about half an hour for the whole of the industry. This is because the hours of work of underground miners are reckoned from the time when the last man in a shift leaves the surface until the first man in the shift returns to the surface. No arrangement is made to ensure that the men come up in the same order as that in which they went down.

and keeping others on full time, and is a useful temporary expedient for keeping the working force together. Sometimes arrangements are made for some compensation to be paid to heads of families for loss of earnings. Some industries adopt a guaranteed minimum week of, say, 30 or 36 hours, while in seasonal industries, for example clothing, some agreements guarantee minimum employment for a specified number of hours, for example 730 hours, in each period of six months.

A distinction is usually drawn between public holidays and regular annual leave. Public holidays are usually defined by legislation, though agreements often provide for payment of wages for such holidays. There is a growing tendency in many countries for paid annual leave, usually of a week or a fortnight, to be provided for manual workers by collective agreements. For non-manual workers the period of holiday is often longer, though in some industries there is a tendency to reduce the differences between the two categories. Workers become entitled to the full period of leave only after having been in the service of the firm for a year. Those who are dismissed before a holiday period, except for a serious offence, often receive holiday pay, or a proportion of it based upon length of employment during the year. Provision may be made for the holiday to be taken at times convenient to the management, but usually in a part of the year when the weather is likely to be good, for example April to September. Some agreements prohibit workpeople from doing work during the holiday period, this being stipulated in order to ensure that they shall benefit from the leisure which is the essential purpose of the holiday. Workers on time rates are paid at these rates during their holiday period, while the holiday pay of piece workers is often based on their average earnings.

Other Provisions

The period of notice which must be given to a worker before dismissal is often specified, though workers may be dismissed immediately if guilty of serious offences. Some agreements provide that in times of slack trade non-unionists shall be dismissed before unionists, but others apply the principle of "last in, first out," though this may be modified by taking into consideration efficiency, the age of the worker, and the number of his dependants. Compensation for dismissal may be paid, except where dismissal is for a serious offence, the amount of compensation being based upon length of service.

Many agreements provide for a system of training for apprentices and fix apprenticeship rates of pay according to age. Agreements

240

often prohibit the employment of more than a certain proportion of apprentices to skilled workers in any firm, for example one apprentice to every seven skilled workers, the object being to prevent the supply of skilled workers from becoming too great.

Demarkation of the kind of work which may be undertaken by each category of skilled operative is often strictly regulated by agreements, as demarkation problems have led to sharp controversy. Some agreements provide that if work in their usual occupation is not available, workers may temporarily be required to do some other suitable work.

Some agreements deal with the status of the union and its members. Thus the union concluding an agreement may be recognized as the sole bargaining agency for the workers whether union members or not; this excludes rival unions and company unions from recognition by the employer or employers who are parties to the agreement. Alternatively, a union may be recognized only for its members. Then, agreements may provide for a closed shop, or that employers needing additional workpeople shall give preference to union members, and if they give employment to non-members these shall be required to join the union. Where workpeople are not required to be members of the union, agreements may provide preferential treatment for union members; for example, that in a slack period not only shall trade unionists be the last to be dismissed, as already indicated, but that when trade improves they shall be the first to be re-employed. By some agreements, employers deduct union dues from the wages of workpeople and pay them to the union. This is known in the United States as the "check off," the deductions being made from the wages of those union members who authorize the employer to do so. Many agreements provide that employers shall allow employees who are union officials to have reasonable time from their work to deal with union affairs, and that they shall not be dismissed, victimized, or otherwise discriminated against because of their union activities. In specified circumstances, trade union officials who are not employees may be given right of access to the workplace. The functions of shop stewards may be defined, and in some agreements there are provisions to prevent shop stewards or other trade union representatives from interfering with managerial responsibilities.[1]

Provisions for the settlement of disputes by voluntary conciliation and arbitration, which are prominent features of many agreements, are reviewed in the last section of this chapter.

[1] This was done, for example, in an agreement in the British Engineering Industry in 1922, following a lock-out in the industry on this problem.

SOME LEGAL ASPECTS OF COLLECTIVE
AGREEMENTS

A collective agreement is not a contract of employment between the parties, as neither employers' organizations nor trade unions pay wages or render services to each other. Legally these organizations are "imperfect personalities," and their agreements regulate the conditions of employment for third parties. Clauses defining relations between the signatory parties, e.g. procedure for giving notice to terminate agreements, are direct obligations between the contracting organizations.

In some countries, including Britain, collective agreements are not regulated by law but are applied by mutual consent.[1] In other countries, collective bargaining and agreements are regulated by legislation, which may lay down general principles on the representation of employers and workpeople in the negotiation of agreements on procedure, on the rights and obligations of employers and workpeople towards each other, and on the contents of agreements, together with provisions on the legal validity and enforcements of their terms. Some laws provide that for a collective agreement to be valid it must be in writing, and a copy registered with a specified Government authority. Many laws make the terms of agreements binding in the sense that no individual labour contracts shall be inferior to those terms. Terms more favourable to the worker are permitted, but any provisions of an individual contract which are less favourable are automatically replaced by the terms of the agreement.

Ordinarily, collective agreements are binding only on those who are parties to the agreements, that is, the employers and workpeople who are members of the signatory organizations, but legislation has been passed in various countries to make the provisions of sufficiently representative agreements binding on all employers and workpeople in the industry covered by the agreement. Such extension, known as the "common rule," has been adopted, e.g. in some Canadian provinces and in South Africa by legislation, and in Australia and New Zealand by arbitration awards; in Britain the

[1] Because the terms of collective agreements are not legally binding in Britain and employers' associations and trade unions are free to alter them at any time, the Government has been unable to ratify some of the Conventions of the International Labour Organisation, even where the standards provided in the agreements are as high as or higher than those of the Conventions. As the Government has no responsibility for the terms of the agreements and their application it cannot undertake the necessary international obligations for their enforcement.

method was authorized for the cotton manufacturing industry by legislation passed in 1934.[1]

Collective agreements which are legally enforceable are in the nature of special laws for an industry or occupation, adopted by the parties and not by the legislative, and are of limited duration. They are a form of labour legislation. In Britain and some other countries, Government departments in arranging contracts with private firms require, by a "Fair Wages" clause, the firms to pay rates not less than those fixed by collective agreements in the industry and district where the contract work will be done.[2]

Whereas in most countries the parties to agreements are free to fix wages and conditions by negotiation, taking into account all the circumstances, in the Soviet Union the Government fixes the total amount available as wages for each industry. The parties to collective agreements then allocate this amount between the undertakings and occupations in accordance with specified criteria, particularly the relation between wages and output.

INDUSTRIAL DISPUTES

During the course of collective bargaining, circumstances often make agreement difficult and call for great skill and patience in negotiation if a breakdown is to be avoided. In the background is the possibility of the use of force in the form of a refusal of workers to work if their "final" demands are rejected or a refusal of employers to offer work if their final demands are not accepted. Restraint shown by both sides in negotiations is not so much due to the frequent use of the weapon of the stoppage as to the possibility that it may be used.[3] Breakdown of negotiations may take place on a question of principle on which each side believes itself to be right and on which

---

[1] The law provides that if organizations representing the majority of the employers and workers in the industry make joint application to the Minister of Labour to issue an order giving statutory effect to any agreement between them on rates of wages, the Minister may refer the application to a Board consisting of three persons not connected with the industry. If they are unanimous that the proposal is desirable the Minister is empowered to issue an order giving statutory force throughout the industry to the wage rates in the agreement.

[2] Where emergency work is done to relieve unemployment, some Governments have authorized payment of rates lower than those in agreements.

[3] The strike weapon is frequently used in the struggle to build up trade union membership and to win recognition. When trade unions have become well established and there is adequate machinery for negotiation and a sense of responsibility on both sides, strikes and lock-outs between trade unions and employers' organizations are rare.

neither will compromise. Or a conflict may arise from misunderstandings or ignorance about the present conditions of an industry, its profits and prospects of employment. Again, there may be failure to estimate the balance of forces between the two sides, or a clash of personalities may be responsible, or a demand may have been made in such a way that agreement on less favourable conditions would involve "loss of face" and be interpreted as weakness. In most disputes there is a margin or range between the two sides within which agreement can be reached, but these limits may not be recognized, or there may be lack of skill in making a concession on one issue in return for an equivalent concession on another. Sometimes conditions are unfavourable because of uncompromising tempers resulting from an accumulation of real or fancied grievances.

The factors which affect the severity of disputes vary from industry to industry, country to country, and from period to period. The greatest losses are in periods when the "climate" of industrial relations is bad, that is, when there are class antagonisms or other profound differences between employers and workpeople, with each side distrustful of the other and unwilling to make concessions in their negotiations, when the leaders of one or both sides in some of the big industries are aggressive, obstinate, and take up irreconcilable attitudes, when the machinery for settling disputes is defective, or when employers are determined to resist encroachments on what they regard as the functions of management. Severe losses occur when unions are fighting for recognition and for an improved status for workers and when employers are determined to oppose such developments. In such circumstances of hostility the struggles are often marked by bitterness on each side.

Such periods of severe conflict were experienced in Britain during the years immediately before the First World War and the seven or eight years immediately after. Employers, who had long enjoyed almost automatic control of their undertakings, were unwilling to make considerable concessions to their workpeople, while the workers, who were rapidly strengthening their trade union organizations, were embittered by past injustices and bad working conditions and were not prepared to give way on their main demands. During the years 1919 to 1921, the average annual loss from disputes was 49 million worker-days, and in the year 1926 alone it was 162 million worker-days, this being the year of the General Strike and the prolonged stoppage in the coal-mining industry. Subsequently there was a remarkable change in the climate of industrial relations, and during the whole period from 1927 to 1952, the annual losses were around $2\frac{1}{2}$ to 3 million worker-days; in the last five years of this period they averaged only 1,725,000 worker-days a year. Thus, in this period of a quarter of a century, long disputes involving many workers were rare, and the total losses were equivalent to less than $2\frac{1}{2}$ hours annually if spread over the whole of the industrial workers.[1] By contrast, the climate of industrial relations was bad in the United States especially during the years 1933 to 1939, and in several years during the first decade after the end of the Second World War, when widespread and bitter disputes took place in major industries including coal-mining, steel, the railways, and among dock workers. The growing-pains of collective bargaining which was so widely extended by New Deal legislation in the 1930's was partly responsible, as many industries had little experience of the system and its implications.

It is interesting to review the main causes of the changed climate of industrial relations in Great Britain during the second quarter of the present century. First, there was growing recognition that British goods were faced with increasingly severe competition in world markets. In the nineteenth century, Britain had been foremost in using new machinery and techniques in industry, and had found ready markets abroad for her products, but even before the turn of the century her supremacy was challenged by the growth of highly efficient industries in other countries. In consequence, it became no longer possible for British industries to interrupt the supply of goods to foreign customers while employers and workpeople fought one another and then to find those customers still waiting. Competitors abroad were only too glad during a stoppage of British industry to seize, and subsequently to hold, markets hitherto supplied by British firms. Once these changed economic conditions were fully realized, British industrialists and trade unions alike made much more determined efforts to settle their differences without stoppages. This changed attitude, together with the further development of employers' organizations and trade unions, led to better arrangements for collective bargaining and for the settlement of disputes, and these were reinforced by greater activity by the State to promote better relations, especially by conciliation and arbitration, and, in certain industries, the statutory regulation of wages. Other factors were

[1] Since the end of the Second World War around 90 per cent of all stoppages in Britain have lasted less than a week, whereas before the First World War more than 50 per cent lasted longer than a week. In the disturbed years just before and after the First World War the big losses were caused by stoppages lasting two or three months, but in the twenty-five years up to 1952, the biggest strikes usually lasted less than a month. Increase in the number of small stoppages may be partly the consequence of a reduction in big ones, because after a severe conflict workers will not easily be led into other stoppages.

improved standards of living, and better relations and conditions at the workplace through industrial welfare and personnel management.

Causes of Stoppages

The main specific causes of industrial disputes are wages, hours of work, trade union membership, recognition, closed shop, and other "solidarity" questions, and "frictional" causes, including working rules, arrangements and discipline, and the employment of particular persons or classes of workpeople.[1] Immediate or apparent causes may have to be distinguished from others which are more basic or fundamental. Quite often a trivial incident may lead to a stoppage, especially a local unofficial one, but there may be a more serious or underlying cause not easy to discover. Some disputes are difficult to settle because of a complexity of different causes. Large-scale disputes between trade unions and employers' organizations are usually over some question of vital principle or stubborn attitudes on wage standards.

The statistics of many countries show that wages have been the greatest cause of disputes, being responsible for between one-half and two-thirds of the total time lost in all disputes. While remaining the main cause, there is considerable variation in the proportion of disputes about wages. For example, in Britain during the first nine years after the end of the Second World War, though wages continued to be the greatest cause of stoppages, they were responsible for a distinctly smaller percentage than in the inter-war years.

[1] Disputes over wages include demands for increase or reduction of time rates and piece rates, opposition to changes from time rates to piece rates or bonus systems, opposition to wage rate reductions when labour-saving aids are introduced, demand for higher rates when working in abnormal conditions, demands for weekly instead of fortnightly pay, and objections to deductions from wages. Disputes about hours of work include demands for reduced hours, and disagreements about excessive overtime and about shift arrangements, including working an excessive number of night shifts.

Solidarity disputes include refusal to work with non-unionists, refusal to negotiate with trade union officials, objection to discharge of trade unionists, and sympathetic action such as refusal by workpeople to handle goods belonging to firms involved in a dispute. "Frictional" causes include demarkation issues such as employment of plumbers on work claimed by fitters, objection of skilled painters to the employment of unskilled labourers on painting work, objection to the employment of women instead of men, objection to youths taking the place of men on certain machines, restriction on the number of apprentices, reinstatement of discharged workpeople, and demands for the dismissal of a foreman. They also include disputes over working rules and arrangements, for example failure to observe working rules, and objections to changes in processes.

For more examples see Board of Trade *Report on Strikes and Lockouts*, 1912, Appendix 1, Cd. 7089.

The importance of hours of work as a cause of stoppages varies considerably in different periods. Thus, in Britain in the years 1919 to 1922, disputes over hours of work were responsible for 10 per cent of all workers directly involved in stoppages. This was a period when an eight-hour day was introduced in many industries in place of the nine-hour day previously in force. Again, in the years 1947 to 1949, disputes over hours of work were responsible for about 9 per cent of all British workers directly involved in stoppages. When, however, new standards of hours have been adopted in many industries a period of stability follows, and disputes about hours may cause only 3 to 6 per cent of losses from stoppages.

Solidarity disputes over trade union recognition and the employment of union members also vary in importance in different periods. They were particularly frequent in Britain in the two decades before the First World War, and in the United States in the 1930's. In Britain during the decade before the Second World War less than 13 per cent of all workers directly involved in stoppages were in disputes on solidarity questions, and the percentage was about the same in the first few years after the War. During the first few years after the end of the War frictional disputes in Britain were responsible for about 34 per cent of all workers directly involved in stoppages. This was higher than in the decade before the war when the percentage was about 26.

In periods of improving trade and of industrial prosperity, trade unions demand better working conditions, and it might be expected that such periods would show the greatest losses from industrial disputes. However, in times of good trade, employers can afford to grant higher wages and better conditions, and also they are anxious to avoid stoppages of work while "the going is good." The statistics of stoppages show that the *number* of disputes is usually greater in upward than in downward trends of employment, but that these disputes are relatively short and the losses in worker-days are less. This is largely because both sides desire to reach agreement quickly and conditions are favourable for doing so. In special circumstances, however, disputes causing heavy losses occur in periods of prosperity, and sometimes these are due to an accumulation of unsettled disagreements from the past. Some severe disputes occur near the top of a boom when money wages may have lagged behind a rise in the cost of living and the unions try to insist on wage increases at a time when employers believe that they will soon be faced with a decline in prosperity.

During trade depressions, and especially in the early downward stages, the number of stoppages is usually smaller than in prosperous times, and the stoppages are longer. In such periods workpeople are at a disadvantage in trying to secure better conditions or even in opposing demands by employers for reduced money rates of wages. Trade unionists, therefore, do not make many demands for improvements in such periods, knowing that they have little chance of success, while many employers, especially in industries in which wages form a relatively small part of their total costs, will meet depressions which are not severe by dismissing workpeople instead of by demanding wage reductions. When, however, stoppages occur they tend to be longer than in boom conditions because tempers on both sides are strained by the uncertainties of the depression, and also employers with few orders on their books may be much less seriously embarrassed by a stoppage than in prosperous times, and some employers may suffer little hardship in having their works closed for several weeks during severe depression. Workpeople often show stubborn and sometimes grim resistance to demands for lower money wage rates, even though the purchasing power of money may be rising because of a fall in the cost of living. Resistance is often stronger if demands for lower rates come after a long period of prosperity during which workpeople have had successive increases in money wages.

Although there is evidence of a positive correlation between the number of industrial disputes and the swings of prosperity and depression, and of a longer duration of disputes in bad than in good times, the statistics of disputes do not show a consistent relationship between the severity of disputes, measured by worker-days lost, and the fluctuations of trade activity. This is because the causes of severe disputes are complex and include many which are unrelated to the state of trade.

The statistics of industrial disputes show that certain industries and occupations are almost free from stoppages, whereas others are frequently disturbed. In the civil service, banking, insurance, the teaching profession, and in some industries and occupations stoppages are rare. This freedom from stoppage is due partly to the nature of the work, to recognition that stoppages will not do much to settle differences, to a sense of responsibility to the public, and in some of these occupations, to the absence of the profit motive. These reasons have been influential in such essential services as gas, water, and electricity supply, though in some other essential work, the same sense of responsibility has not always been shown, for example, in dock labour and among transport workers engaged in moving food supplies. In serious hold-ups of essential services, the Government may, however, call upon the armed forces to do the work in order to safeguard the welfare of the community, and the knowledge that such action may be taken is likely to be a deterrent to stoppages.

Among industries which in a number of countries have suffered most from stoppages, coal-mining is outstanding. In Britain, for example, this industry has been responsible for more than half of all worker-days lost over a period of many years. Transport, particularly dock labour, is another industry with frequent stoppages, while in engineering and allied trades the loss from stoppages is considerable. In some industries workers and employers are able, both in the period when a stoppage seems likely to occur and especially afterwards, to make good a large part if not all of the loss. For example, after a strike of dock workers at a particular port the ships may still be there to be unloaded when the stoppage ends, and this work often offsets for the dockers a large part of their losses during the stoppage. This may, indeed, make them less anxious to avoid strikes, but it should not be overlooked that some ships may be diverted to other ports, and some work, such as repairing of ships, may be done abroad.

Kinds of Stoppages

The two main kinds of stoppages are strikes and lock-outs, the first being withdrawal of labour by a body of workpeople acting in agreement, and the second being action by an employer or employers in refusing employment to workpeople with whom he is in dispute. Each is the use of economic power with the object of forcing the other side to accept conditions of employment which they had rejected. Thus, workpeople may go on strike to get better terms of employment or to resist a proposal by employers to reduce the standard of working conditions. If cessation of work is a result of a decision of the workpeople the stoppage is a strike, but if notice of cessation is given by the employer the stoppage is a lock-out. However, this distinction is usually of little value as "it takes two sides to make a quarrel." Also, it would be quite unsatisfactory to define a strike as a stoppage due to a demand made by workers and a lock-out as a stoppage resulting from a demand by employers.

Usually strikers expect to return to their jobs with the same employer at the end of the strike, the employers also expect this, and the same applies to lock-outs. The interruption of the relationship between workers and their employers is therefore intended to be temporary. Sometimes a strike is called because an employer has dismissed workpeople who are redundant and he has no intention of re-employing them, or because he has dismissed them for some other reason and will replace them by recruiting new workpeople. Here

249

the purpose of the strikers is to prevent the employer from making a permanent change in his labour force. Often, however, during stoppages, some workpeople find employment elsewhere and do not return to their original employer, and employers engage some new workers during or after the stoppage.

Strikes are official if they are organized by the trade union, and, if the union has funds available, the members receive strike pay. This can be continued for a long time if the strike is at one works or in one locality and the union is a big national organization with substantial resources. Many workpeople who are not members of the union may join in a strike, but do not receive strike pay. Many unions require a two-thirds or three-quarters majority of members or branches before authorizing a strike. Some unions distinguish between an "offensive" strike, which is in support of higher wages or other demands for better conditions, and a "defensive" strike to resist demands made by employers. During conflicts, employers may be supported financially and in other ways by their associations.

Strikes are unofficial if they are not authorized by the union, but are organized by a group of workpeople acting independently of the union and led by an improvised strike committee. There is no strike pay from the union, though funds are often obtained by collections. Some unofficial strikes are supported by union officers without, however, committing the union, but if an unofficial strike is sharply contrary to the policy of the union, the union officers will try to get the strikers back to work, and some unions take disciplinary action against those who continue the strike. Unofficial strikes are usually small local affairs, often at a single works, most are settled within a few days, and the total losses from them are not large. Their numbers may be considerable, especially in periods when official strikes are few and when the machinery of joint negotiation is settling the main differences between unions and employers effectively.[1] Unofficial strikes may then be a protest against delays in the working of the machinery of negotiation, or they may be a result of strong feeling over some local grievance which expresses itself in immediate action to force a quick remedy.

In some disputes, workpeople, instead of staying away from the workplace, use "irritation" strike methods to put pressure on the employers. This may be by "stay-in" or "sit-down" strikes, with the workpeople going to their place of work, but remaining idle or making a pretence of working. Another method is that of "working to rule," which has been used in railway and other kinds of transport,

[1] In the British coal-mining industry in 1951, there were 1,637 stoppages, but in none of these did the strikers receive official union backing.

the workers complying meticulously and in a leisurely way with the elaborate code of rules so that operations are greatly retarded and the work becomes dislocated. Such methods cause considerable loss to employers and are somewhat similar to ordinary strikes in their effects. If settlements are not quickly reached they are likely to lead to lock-out action by employers.

Statistical Classifications

Statistics of industrial disputes are compiled by Governments and usually show their number, size (that is, the number of workpeople involved), and duration in number of days, and these statistics are classified by industries. Information about the number of disputes is useful in showing whether stoppages have been many or few, but a large number of short stoppages involving few workpeople may be much less serious than a few stoppages which continue for a long time and involve many workpeople. In statistics showing only the number of stoppages a strike of two days at a works with only 50 workpeople counts the same as a nation-wide strike of 250,000 workpeople which lasts a month. The figures of size and duration are used to compile aggregates of the number of worker-days lost, and these aggregates provide the best general index of the losses incurred. Such composite figures need, however, to be used with the more detailed information, as a given aggregate, for example, of 400,000 worker-days may be due to a few lengthy stoppages involving large numbers of workers in one or two industries, or to a large number of short stoppages spread over many industries. The average size of stoppages in a given period can be calculated by dividing the total number of workers by the number of stoppages, while the average duration can be calculated by dividing the total number of worker-days by the total number of workers.

Consideration is often given not only to the number of worker-days lost by persons directly involved in disputes, but also to losses from unemployment among other workers because of dislocations caused from the stoppage. The first is a measure of industrial unrest or conflict, and the second is a measure of the economic losses caused by the unrest. There are, however, difficulties in estimating these indirect losses, which include not only those at the establishments directly involved in the stoppage, but also at other undertakings where there is no dispute, but where workers become unemployed owing to shortages of materials. Thus, a stoppage at a spinning factory may cause unemployment in weaving factories, or a prolonged coal-mining or transport stoppage is likely to cause unemployment in many industries, but only rough estimates can be made of such wider losses.[1] The statistics of some countries, for example Britain, restrict indirect losses to workpeople who, though not themselves involved in a dispute, are rendered idle because of a strike or lock-out at the works where they are employed. During the years from 1930 to 1950 the number of workpeople indirectly involved has averaged about one-fifth of those directly involved. A strike of a few men in a key occupation may, however, cause large numbers of other workpeople to have to cease work.

Statistics of disputes are classified by causes, the main divisions, as already indicated, being wages, hours of labour, trade union and other "solidarity" questions, and frictional disputes arising from working rules and discipline, and over the employment of particular persons or classes of workpeople. Classification by causes is defective, as many disputes have more than one cause. In some countries, attempts have been made to give statistics of strikes and lock-outs separately, but for the reasons noted earlier they have been abandoned. Another classification which is no longer used in some countries is that which tries to distinguish between disputes which end in success for the workpeople, those which end in success for the employers, and those with an intermediate result. In fact disputes rarely end in complete victory for the workpeople or for the employers, and there are usually varying degrees of compromise. A useful classification is by methods of settlement, such as by direct negotiation between the parties, by conciliation of specified kinds, and by arbitration tribunals. There are also disputes which end by a return to work without any formal settlement, the workers going back on terms offered by the employers, but without these terms being accepted by the union.

International Comparisons

Figures are given below of the average annual number of workerdays lost in disputes during the twenty-one-year period 1927 to 1947 in various countries per thousand workers employed in mining, manufacturing, construction, and transport.[2] A figure of 1,000 days

---

[1] One estimate made after the strike in the steel industry in the United States in 1952 gave the cost to the nation as about 4,000 million dollars in lost production of one kind or another, including the wages of 1,400,000 workers (beside the steel workers) who were unwillingly made idle by the strike. The loss of steel production was 17 million tons. Large parts of the automobile industry were stopped by shortage of steel, 300,000 of its workers were made idle, and it took four to six weeks for it to get back into its stride again.

[2] They are taken from an article on "The Incidence of Industrial Disputes," by Robert Morse Woodbury, published in the *International Labour Review*, November 1949.

lost means a loss of one day a year if spread over all the workpeople employed in these branches of industry, or reckoning 300 working days in a year it is equal to only one-third of 1 per cent of the full working time in a year. The figures are not strictly comparable because of different methods of compilation in the various countries, but they range so widely that they indicate substantial differences in the prevalence of disputes.[1]

Belgium	..	..	588	Great Britain	..	290
Denmark	..	..	580	United States	..	1,103
France	..	..	776	Canada	..	416
Netherlands ..		..	313	South Africa	..	58
Sweden	..	..	1,460	Australia	..	1,061
Switzerland ..		..	91	New Zealand	..	202

Sweden, the United States, and Australia each had average rates of more than 1,000 days lost per 1,000 workpeople a year or one day a worker a year, the Swedish rate being nearly a day and a half a year. The average for all the above countries is 578 days, equal to about 4½ hours a worker a year or only about one-fifth of 1 per cent. In Great Britain the figure was still less, averaging less than three hours a worker a year or one-eighth of 1 per cent; it was even slightly lower at about one-tenth of 1 per cent during the five years from 1948 to 1952. This means in effect that nearly 99·9 per cent of British industrial activity was free from disputes. The wide variations from country to country are due to differences in the traditions and tempers of labour and employers, the strength of trade unionism, the development of negotiating machinery, the quality of leadership, and in differences in the importance in different countries of coal-mining, dock labour, and other industries in which there are usually big losses from disputes. The exceptionally low rate in Switzerland is no doubt partly due to the absence of coal-mining and other heavy industries. The still lower rate in South Africa can be explained by the docile attitude of coloured workers in that country during the period covered.

Not only are the losses small even in the most disturbed countries but, as already noted, they can often be made good, at least in part, by overtime and other additional work when the stoppages are over, and also, if there is a considerable period of warning that a stoppage is likely, by more intense work in anticipation of a stoppage. The extent to which losses can be made good varies considerably with

[1] For some countries, including Great Britain, the figures cover workpeople made idle by strikes and lock-outs in the establishments where they worked but who were not themselves parties to the disputes. For other countries only those directly involved are included.

the nature of the work and the economic conditions prevailing. If the trade is still there when the stoppage ends, the chances of making good the losses are greater in an industry experiencing unemployment than in one fully employed.[1] Also, losses are more likely to be made good where there are monopoly conditions or little competition than where competition is severe. The protracted stoppage in the British coal-mining industry in 1926 gave opportunities during that period of intense competition in the coal markets of the world, for foreign competitors to obtain long contracts in some markets at the expense of the British industry. In such circumstances, long-term losses after the stoppage is over must be added to the immediate losses incurred during the stoppage.

Relative Losses

Strikes and lock-outs are spectacular and receive much publicity; in consequence many people have a greatly exaggerated impression of the losses caused. Strikes and lock-outs have news value, and the Press rightly gives attention to them because they are an index of discontent in industry, but the public draws conclusions which are out of proportion. The figures already given show the time lost in disputes in proper perspective by calculating them as a fraction of the time worked by all workers throughout industry. The figures for the years 1948–52, showing a loss of only one-tenth of 1 per cent of the total time worked in British industry, may be compared with the vastly greater losses from unemployment, sickness, and absenteeism. During the years 1948 to 1952 the average percentage of unemployment in British industry was at the low rate of 1·5, but even so this was 15 times the rate of loss from industrial disputes.[2] Over a much longer period a more normal rate of unemployment would be 5 per cent or more, which would be 40 times the rate of loss from strikes and lock-outs. The rate of absenteeism in British coal-mining during the period 1948–52 was about 12 per cent, or 120 times the rate of loss from disputes throughout British industry. In 1950–51, the cost of sickness benefits was about 45 times the estimated total of wages lost in industrial disputes, and this makes no allowance for absence from work because of sickness for which

[1] Strikes in an essential industry when stocks of its products are low and demand is keen, will cause more injury to the economy than in the reverse conditions. Thus a coal strike in Britain in any of the years 1945–1953 would have been more disastrous than one in the depressed years of the 1930's.

[2] The losses from industrial disputes do not include those from unemployment caused at other establishments than those at which the stoppages take place. Also the efficiency of those involved in industrial disputes is probably higher than that of unemployed workpeople.

no benefits were paid, or of the much lower rates of sickness benefit compared with rates of wages.

It must be noted that losses from strikes and lock-outs are a sort of index of industrial discontent much of which does not result in stoppages but expresses itself in friction and reduced production at the workplace. Although there is no means of calculating such losses, it is certain that they are very much greater than those caused by stoppages. Most differences are settled without stoppages, but often there is delay during which output falls because of dissatisfaction or a sense of grievance, and in extreme cases the "work to rule" or other "go slow" tactics are adopted, with substantial loss to production.

VOLUNTARY CONCILIATION AND ARBITRATION

Conciliation and arbitration of industrial disputes by systems established by the State are considered in Chapter XXIV. Before, however, legislation made provision for statutory machinery many British industries set up for themselves local, district, or even national boards for conciliation and arbitration. The oldest of these seems to be the Board of Conciliation and Arbitration for the Manufactured Iron and Steel Trades in the North of England, which dates from 1860, and boards along similar lines were set up in this industry in the Midlands in 1872, and in the West of Scotland in 1890. Other British industries in which such boards were set up half a century ago are building, quarrying, textiles, boot and shoe, and the furnishing trades.[1]

Such boards are composed of representatives in equal numbers of employers and workpeople who try to settle differences by conciliation. The agreements, however, provide for the appointment of an arbitrator or an umpire acceptable to both sides to deal with disputes which the parties are unable to settle by negotiation. The decisions of umpires or arbitrators are widely accepted and observed by both sides of the industry, and in some agreements the parties bind themselves beforehand to accept arbitration awards, and in effect have agreed not to use the weapon of strikes or lock-outs. Provision is often made that the parties shall not call a strike or lock-out while an agreement is in force, or until all the procedures of conciliation and arbitration for the settlement of disputes provided in the agreement have been used. Sometimes provision is made that in the event of a strike or a lock-out contrary to agreement the conciliation and arbitration procedure shall be suspended until work is resumed on *status quo* terms, in order that conciliation and arbitration

[1] See *Industrial Relations Handbook*, 1953, p. 23.

can function under favourable conditions.[1] In certain industries, for example the British boot and shoe industry, funds in the hands of trustees have been established by contributions from both employers' organizations and trade unions, and from such funds penalties are paid to the aggrieved side where a party to an agreement fails to observe it and causes a stoppage.

When the State provides machinery for voluntary conciliation and arbitration, some industries conclude agreements to use this machinery. Thus, in Great Britain many joint industrial councils have agreed that any disputes which they are unable to settle by negotiation shall be referred to the Industrial Court set up under the 1919 Act or to other methods of arbitration which the Minister of Labour and National Service can arrange. Many industries, however, prefer to use their own machinery for conciliation and arbitration, which can be adapted to their particular needs and can be changed if this seems desirable. Thus in the British coal-mining industry disputes in the last resort go to a National Reference Tribunal composed of persons who are not engaged in the coal-mining industry. For railway transportation a Railway Staff National Tribunal has been set up, consisting of an independent chairman appointed by agreement between the railway executives and the unions (or, if they fail to agree, by the Minister of Labour and National Service), together with one member selected from a panel previously nominated by the executives, and one from a panel nominated by the unions. The Civil Service Arbitration Tribunal is similarly composed.

In many industries detailed procedures have been arranged to cover disputes arising out of the application or interpretation of existing agreements, and also from failure to reach new agreements. If in the application of an existing agreement a difference arises at the workplace between a worker or group of workers and a supervisor and is not settled directly between them, it may be discussed by the shop steward and a representative of the management of the firm. If still not solved it may be considered in successive stages by the employer or his representative and the local official of the trade union, by local representatives of the trade union and the employers' association, and similarly at district and national levels, and finally by independent conciliation and arbitration. Arrangements for dealing with failure to negotiate the terms of new agreements are similar, except that, in countries where agreements are regional or national, the procedures are at those levels from the outset.

---

[1] Some agreements provide that in the last resort a stoppage may be authorized to enforce the terms of an agreement or award.

PART III

Wages and Hours of Work

16

Wage Bases and Principles

WAGES ARE central to the problems of industrial relations, and more
controversies and conflicts arise about wages than about any other
subject. This is not surprising, as wages provide the workers' standards of living and, in most industries, they form a high proportion
of the employers' costs of production. The issue between the two is
essentially: What, in the last resort, are the workers willing to accept,
and what can employers afford to pay? It is a frequent practice in
wage bargaining for workers to claim more than they are willing to
accept, and at the end of the negotiations they will often agree to
something less than their original demands. Similar tactics are
adopted by employers. Each tries to probe the strength of the other
side, and conflicts may result because of ignorance or insufficient
knowledge on one or both sides. Greater availability of reliable
information on the capacity of industry to pay would narrow the
margin of dispute and facilitate the reaching of agreement.

The main considerations raised in wage negotiations are:

(1) Capacity of industry to pay;
(2) Workers' standards of living;
(3) Relation between the wages of the workers concerned and
    those paid to other workers, including workers in other
    occupations and industries.

Sometimes one argument is used and sometimes another, or two or
more arguments may be used together. As an illustration, the
Amalgamated Engineering Union in 1950 supported its claim for
increased wages both by pointing to the rise in the cost of living since
their wages had last been fixed, and by stating their opinion that
profits in the industry were enough to enable the higher wages
demanded to be paid without raising prices to the consumers of
engineering products. In a court of enquiry in January 1951, into
wage claims made by the three railway unions, all the above arguments were presented, each union emphasizing the arguments most
suited to its claim. The representative of the Amalgamated Society
of Locomotive Engineers and Firemen argued specially that the

responsibilities of its members made it necessary to recover at least a part of the relative advantage they held over lower-paid workers before the war and which had been whittled away by numerous flat-rate increases. The spokesman of the Railway Clerks' Association based his case mainly on comparisons with the salaries paid for similar clerical work in other public employment. The Secretary of the National Union of Railwaymen, which includes the lowest paid categories of railway workers among its members, gave special attention to increases in the cost of living. It was left to the representative of the Railway Executive to point to the heavy losses which railways were incurring, and to indicate that improvements in wages depended largely upon economies, including reductions in staff, and upon greater efficiency.

The three considerations mentioned above are examined in turn in this chapter, which also includes discussions of family allowances in relation to wages, the problem of equal pay for equal work, and the use of cost of living and selling price sliding scales.

CAPACITY OF INDUSTRY

The productivity of industry is the source from which real wages are paid, and neither pressure from powerful trade unions nor any manipulation of State-established systems can, except temporarily, raise real wages beyond the capacity of industry to pay, without bringing painful correctives, usually unemployment or inflation, into operation. For a time the wages in an industry may be forced so high that its capital cannot be fully replaced as it wears out, but this must result in less production and therefore lower wages in future. An industry may pay wages beyond its capacity if it is subsidized, but this implies that directly or indirectly the capacity of other industries is reduced. Temporarily, a firm may pay wages which it cannot immediately afford, when it is going through a period of difficulty from which it expects soon to recover.

Distinction must be drawn between the capacity of industry as a whole and the capacity of single industries and individual firms. This raises difficult questions of wage policy and wage standards. Within a single industry there is often wide variation in the prosperity of its firms, some of which might be able to pay wages 20 or 50 per cent higher than their less efficient competitors. Yet, usually, in collective agreements in Britain the same rates of wages are fixed for all firms in the industry. This is partly because trade unions favour standardized rates for their members, who consequently are all treated alike so far as union policy applies. Unions could, no doubt, obtain a larger total amount for their members if they bargained separately with each firm and gained higher rates from the more prosperous firms. This, indeed, is a widespread practice in the United States, Canada, and other countries but is rare in Britain, not only because trade unions prefer standardization and because of the compactness of the country but because employers are organized on an industry-wide basis and their policy also is to secure standardized rates which put all firms on the same competitive level for labour. Standardized rates are also facilitated by mobility of labour between firms within an industry. Some prosperous firms pay rates higher than those required by the agreements, but this enables them to recruit the better workers, and so they get value for the higher rates they pay. Even if prosperous firms pay no more than the standard rates, their workers have the advantage of greater security of employment and may benefit from better amenities and welfare schemes.

In Britain, the trade unions and employers' organizations, by their processes of collective bargaining, have greatly widened the basis of wage regulation and standardization over a period of many decades from the early days when agreements were with individual firms. These were followed by local agreements with a number of firms within an industry in the same city or district, and then industry-wide agreements for the whole country became usual. The scope of agreements has been widened further by the formation of federations of unions in allied trades, the federations being given power to bargain on wages and conditions for the associated unions.[1] This evolution has, however, not gone beyond single industries or closely related industries and, except for the tentative measures resulting in restraints on wage increases after the war, no co-ordination or standardization of wages has been achieved between industries. In effect, each industry is a law unto itself. Each union strives to secure as much as it can for its own members, and wide variations in wages result because of differences in prosperity from industry to industry.

This is well illustrated from experience in Britain during a large part of the inter-war years. Some industries, known as unsheltered industries, were exposed to the full blast of fierce competition in world markets, and their wages fell heavily and remained for years below the national average. Among these industries mention may be made of coal-mining, shipbuilding, and engineering, all vital for the economy of the country. By contrast considerably higher wages were paid in printing, building, public utilities and other industries work-

[1] An outstanding example is the Confederation of Shipbuilding and Engineering Unions.

ing for the home market, which, by its nature, was sheltered from the direct impact of foreign competition. In such conditions the relative levels of wages in different industries became badly distorted, bearing no reasonable relation to the value of each industry in the national economy, the workers in some industries being seriously underpaid for the skill, training, experience, energy, and other qualities required of them. These disparities tend to be greatly diminished during a long period of general prosperity when employment in all industries is at a high level, whereas in depressions the heavy industries and those producing mainly for world markets suffer more from unemployment than those supplying essential consumer goods. By 1950 wages in British coal-mining, engineering, shipbuilding, and agriculture bore a much better relationship to those in other industries than they had done fifteen or twenty years earlier, if "better relationship" is determined by the relative skills and other qualities required from the workpeople in different industries.

Mobility of labour is a potent factor in reducing wage disparities between different industries, workpeople moving from lower to higher paid industries. This is easier and quicker for unskilled than for skilled workers. A skilled man who has undergone several years of apprenticeship or learnership and has then had a long experience in one industry is loth to undergo a training for skill in another industry, and he is usually unwilling to undertake unskilled work. He therefore tends to cling to the industry in which he is skilled in the hope that better times will come, and this, in a declining or heavily overmanned industry, keeps wages down. In such conditions, mobility of labour among skilled categories operates mainly by reduction in the number of youths entering the industry, and half a generation may be needed to bring about a proper balance between the demand for and the supply of labour in the industry.

If, when an industry is depressed, wage rates are allowed to fall much below the levels in most other industries, the industry will experience somewhat less unemployment than if wages had been kept nearer to the general level. In these circumstances, notwithstanding the attraction of higher wages in other industries, mobility of labour is likely to be retarded. This keeps a larger part of the working force of the industry together, which is an advantage if the industry returns to prosperity after a few months or even in a year or two, though this advantage might be secured even better by working systematic short time during the depression, without much lowering of wage rates. If, however, the industry is likely to experience a long period of decline and must lose a large number of its workers, it may be more effective to maintain wage rates though this will cause more unemployment, than to have heavy wage reductions with less unemployment. With more unemployment, mobility of labour will be greater, and the movement can be accelerated by training for employment in prosperous and expanding industries.

Workpeople who are employed in prosperous industries will inevitably enjoy advantages over their fellows in less prosperous industries, and the advantages will include higher wages. Yet they probably do not work harder or more efficiently than workpeople in other industries, the prosperity of their industry being mainly due to favourable conditions of demand for the goods produced, invention of improved machinery, discovery of better processes, and efficient organization by management. If workers are in short supply in prosperous industries their wages will rise, but if the rise reaches a level far out of line with wages in other industries, there is danger that the greatly increased labour costs will be passed on to consumers in higher prices, to the disadvantage of workpeople in other industries. Also the high wages may, in course of time, attract too many workers to the hitherto prosperous industries, which will then suffer from unemployment and a fall in wages, thus contributing to instability in the economic system. A more farsighted wage policy which avoids grabbing greedily at temporary gains and does not carry wages in highly prosperous industries far beyond those paid for work of similar quality in other industries, is in the long-term interests of workpeople in all industries. Somewhat similarly it would be undesirable for the benefits of an important invention to accrue mainly to the persons, including the workpeople, in the industry to which it is applied; they are likely to gain some increase in wages, but the main benefits should be spread over the whole community by lower prices.

Real wages, that is the purchasing power of money wages over commodities and services, can sometimes be increased at the expense of profits, and this is sound policy where high profits result from underpayment of workpeople. Profits, however, must be adequate to give a reasonable return on investment, ensure maintenance of capital, provision of reserves to cover contingencies, and capital for new developments. If wages are so high that these capital needs cannot be met, the industry will begin to stagnate and decline. Real wages may also be increased in some industries at the expense of consumers by raising the selling price of the product in order to pay the higher wages. If, as is usual, the products are largely consumed by workpeople and their families, the higher real wages in some industries are gained by a lowering of the real wages of workpeople in others.

In Britain in recent years the practicability of raising real wages at the expense of profits has been negligible over almost the whole of industry. The days are gone when big strikes had a chance of securing gains for the workpeople which would compensate them for the losses of the stoppage and leave them better off for the future. In present circumstances, an industry-wide strike could only result in loss for the workpeople. Profits are so heavily taxed to provide foundations for the Welfare State that the residue yields only a moderate return on capital in most industries. Many firms are not able to make adequate provision for maintenance and renewal of plant and equipment at the high level of post-war prices, and they experience difficulties in securing new capital for expansion. Substantial increases in real wages can, therefore, be gained not by conflicts over division of the product of industry but by co-operation to increase the amount produced.

This situation was indicated by Sir Stafford Cripps, then Chancellor of the Exchequer, when, in September 1948, he told the Trades Union Congress that the total amount of corporation profits distributed in 1947 as dividends after deduction of tax was only about one-tenth of the total wages and salaries combined. "So that," he said, "even if corporation profits were reduced by a quarter—a very drastic cut—it would mean an average addition to wages and salaries of not more than 4d. in the pound." This would be equal to a wage increase of about $1\frac{1}{2}$ per cent, representing a rise of only two or three shillings a week for the great majority of manual workers and lower paid salaried employees, or, as was much quoted at the time, an increase less than enough to pay for an additional packet of cigarettes a week. Again, in a speech early in 1949, Sir Stafford Cripps said, "It is most unfair of those workers who think they can bring some particular pressure to bear upon society to demand increases which can only be got at the cost of their fellow-workers. Not only is it unfair, but if such demands were generally indulged in it would wreck all hope of our recovery. . . ."

The relatively small amounts distributed after deduction of tax as dividends to shareholders are shown by statistics published in 1949–50 by a number of companies at their Annual General Meetings. These are summarized below for forty-four companies, including some of the leading companies in seven industrial groups. The figures for each industry make no allowance for the relative size and importance of the firms included, but the averages take account of the number of firms. Though the accountancy methods of the various firms differ somewhat and the number of firms is too small to form a representative sample, the figures are adequate to indicate broadly the way in which the total revenue from the sale of their products is

264

distributed by the various firms. Purchase taxes and duty on beer paid by consumers are excluded. The biggest expenditure group for all the industries covered is for raw materials and manufacturing costs other than wages and salaries; these costs include maintenance of plant and buildings, depreciation allowances, rents, rates, debenture interest, bank interest, and other overhead charges. Payments to employees include national insurance contributions, superannuation, and holiday pay, in addition to wages and salaries.

DISTRIBUTION OF EACH £100 OF REVENUE BY VARIOUS INDUSTRIAL FIRMS, 1949-50

Industry[1]	Raw Materials and General Manufacturing Costs	Re-invested in the Business	Taxation	Dividends to Shareholders	Wages, Salaries, and Other Payments to Employees
	£	£	£	£	£
Iron and Steel (7) ..	66·0	2·5	5·5	1·4	24·6
Engineering (12) ..	60·7	2·7	5·1	1·3	30·2
Chemical and Cement (4)..	66·2	3·1	6·8	2·9	21·0
Textiles and Clothing (5)	71·5	3·0	3·5	1·9	20·1
Food Processing and Distribution (3) ..	86·1	0·8	3·2	1·3	8·6
Brewing (4)	55·3	7·3	11·6	5·8	20·0
Miscellaneous (9) ..	64·7	2·3	4·8	1·9	26·3
Average	65·3	3·0	5·5	2·1	24·1

[1] The figures in brackets are the number of firms included.

The figures show that average wages and salaries together formed about 24 per cent of total revenue, and that dividends paid to shareholders are less than one-tenth of wages and salaries. More goes to the Government in taxation than the combined totals of dividends to shareholders and amounts reinvested in the businesses. Of special significance for industrial relations is the variation between different industries in the proportion to total revenues which goes to wages and salaries. This ranged from 8·6 per cent in food processing and distribution to 30·2 per cent in engineering; for most of the industries tabulated the range is between 20 and 30 per cent. Among the individual firms covered the range is much wider, the wage and salary proportion in one food processing firm being under 5 per cent, while in two engineering firms it was over 40 per cent. These variations are due largely to differences in the cost of raw materials and to a smaller extent to differences in manufacturing costs. Thus, in some of the firms covered, the cost of raw materials was between 30 and 45 per cent, in many of them it was between 50 and 60 per cent, and in a few firms it was between 70 and 90 per cent. The higher these costs, the lower generally is the proportion of wages and salaries. Some industries not given in the table show much higher proportions for wages and salaries. They include mining, quarrying, and services which spend little on raw materials. Thus, in coal-mining the wage proportion is more than 60 per cent. Where the wage proportion is high any considerable rise or fall in the selling price of the product resulting from increase or decrease in demand will quickly raise or lower the industry's capacity to pay, which will lead to early demands for higher or lower wages. Such demands are likely to be much more frequent, and the risks of disputes greater, in such an industry than in one where the wage proportion is small. The high wage proportion in coal-mining is, no doubt, one of the reasons why losses from disputes in this industry are greater than in most other industries.

As increases in real wages depend so largely upon expansion of output it is useful to review the main ways of securing greater production. They may be summarized as follows:

(1) Increase in the amount of capital and power available per worker.[1] This depends upon savings in one form or another, and willingness of investors to undertake risks. In Britain the necessary amount of capital will be forthcoming only if more encouragement is given to investors than in recent years.

(2) Improvements in machinery, the use of new inventions and better manufacturing processes. There is no sign of any slowing down of the rate of invention and improvements in industrial equipment and with higher standards of education and greater opportunities for scientific and technological research, the pace may be accelerated. In order to encourage the more rapid installation of up-to-date equipment, the tax system should be revised to allow of machinery being written off more quickly.

[1] In the United States the amount of capital per worker, allowing for changes in the price level, increased by about 37 per cent during the years 1900 to 1949. To secure this growth of capital with an increasing labour force involved the investment of about one-tenth of the national income for expansion of plant, machinery, and inventories. See *How to Raise Real Wages*, a Statement on National Policy by The Research and Policy Committee of the Committee for Economic Development, New York, June 1950, which outlined methods for the United States here adapted to the needs of Britain.

(3) Better methods of management and industrial organization. The most efficient firms in Britain show standards equal to the best anywhere, but production could be substantially increased if these standards were more widely applied.

(4) Higher standards of education, training and health among the workpeople. These standards have greatly improved during the present century and progress is likely to be continued.

(5) Recognition by workpeople and trade unions of the gains they can obtain from increased output. This would lead to removal or relaxation of restrictive practices, withdrawal of objections to introduction of better machinery and methods, greater willingness to agree to incentive methods of wage payment where these are suitable, removal of social pressures which prevent workpeople from doing their best and producing the most of which they are capable without strain or undue fatigue, and willingness of workpeople on the basis of their practical experience to make constructive suggestions for eliminating waste, increasing output, and improving quality. Another consequence would be less absenteeism. Restrictive practices by workpeople are a greater brake on production in Britain than in the United States, but in recent years with continuation of full employment, better personnel management, and recognition that wage increases are dependent on increased production there are signs of a willingness among the more enlightened trade union leaders to relax restrictive practices and to support co-operation with management to increase productive efficiency.

(6) Maintenance of a high stable level of employment. This implies the avoidance of severe depressions such as that which resulted in low earnings and heavy unemployment in many British industries in the early 1930's. Success depends partly on the Government's financial, currency, and economic policy, and partly on steadiness throughout industry in investment in new capital goods. Owing, however, to her dependence upon international trade, Britain is specially vulnerable to the effects of depressions in other countries and might experience heavy unemployment resulting from causes outside her control.

(7) Reduction of seasonal unemployment. Because Britain has a fairly equitable climate the loss of output from seasonal causes is less than in countries with severe winters. However, a worthwhile increase in output and consequently higher wages could be gained if firms which experience seasonal variations in demand for their goods would spread production more evenly throughout the year. Many firms already do this; for example the printing of Christmas cards is spread over many months before they are sold, and this practice could be more widely used in many industries.

(8) More opportunities of employment should be provided for older people, who should be encouraged to continue to work. In the inter-war years of severe unemployment, there was some justification for lowering the age of retirement and concentrating employment on those in the prime of life. When, however, there is shortage of labour the work of older people is needed, and by increasing national production leads to higher real wages. Also, because of better health resulting from improved standards of living, housing, and medical services, people live to a greater age now than at the beginning of the century and are able to work efficiently for several years longer. Recent investigations have shown that older people, though often unsuited for work requiring great physical strength, are able to do other kinds of work well. They may be somewhat slower but more accurate and reliable than younger workers. With the rapid growth during the next twenty-five years in the proportion of older people in the population it will be essential for industrialists to organize their undertakings to provide openings for older people, and for the conditions of Government and other pension schemes to encourage rather than discourage older people from continuing in employment. At the same time, the prolongation of their employment should be done in ways which will not delay the promotion of younger people to responsible posts.

(9) More opportunities for employment of women, especially on half-time. This would involve difficult problems of organization, but there are large numbers of women who, because of care of the home, would not undertake regular full-time work but would be willing to work for three days a week or for four or five hours a day throughout the week.

(10) Provision of facilities for starting new businesses. For many years people wishing to start new businesses in some industries have found great obstacles in their way in the form of arrangements by established firms which hamper new entrants. These somewhat resemble in intention, if not in method, the restrictive practices adopted by trade unions. No doubt restrictions are needed to prevent unfair, cut-throat competition between firms, but they should not be used to keep out able people with fresh ideas and initiative who would provide a stimulus to industrial efficiency and a safeguard against stagnation. Such men should be helped by advice and provision of capital. Already some assistance of this kind is available, for example, in the trading estates which enable workshops to be rented and other facilities to be obtained for suitable projects. Such assistance could be extended with considerable benefit to the national economy.

These are the main methods by which real wages can be raised and future progress will depend upon the extent to which they are applied.

Reference may be made to a few theoretical considerations. One is whether reductions in the general level of wages would be likely to reduce unemployment in a period of depression or would aggravate it by reducing purchasing power. This was the subject of keen controversy in the inter-war years, and no general conclusion was reached. The answer is likely to be different at different stages of the depression phase of the trade cycle, and no doubt also differs according to the main causes and degree of severity of different depressions.

A second point is that in collective bargaining an element of monopoly arises, and this increases with the strength of organization of employers and workpeople, and it also varies according to the extent to which firms control the market for their products. In circumstances of considerable monopoly, wage increases can be passed on to consumers in the form of higher prices, and this may facilitate agreement between employers' organizations and trade unions. Yet, in the long run, such monopoly power is limited by competitive factors, particularly because consumers will be likely to find substitutes not controlled by the industry. Again, if a strong trade union succeeds in forcing wages too high, there is no obligation on employers to maintain any given level of employment, and unemployment will be likely to increase. Also employers will be stimulated to substitute machinery for labour.

Some trade unions seem to have adopted a policy of raising wages somewhat above the level likely to secure full employment, and in these circumstances some of the less efficient workers will be unemployed. Such unions are in effect sacrificing a small proportion of workpeople in order that the wages of the great majority of workers who constitute the main part of their membership will be increased. It is also argued that the higher rates of wages will stimulate employers to increase their productive efficiency and thereby provide a dynamic factor for a more rapid rise in wages based upon more effective production. Such a policy is likely to be more successful in periods of prosperity than during depressions.

Usually any gains which trade unions secure at the expense of employers or vice-versa over or under the fair rate are usually short-term gains and are liable to be removed by the operation of long-term factors. Monopolies of employers and of workpeople by acting together may gain considerably in the short period at the expense of consumers by restricting supply and by raising prices, but competitive forces and mobility of labour tend to reduce these gains.

THE LIVING WAGE

The principle that workpeople should be paid a living wage in return for their labour commands wide agreement when stated in general terms, but difficulties arise in giving precision to it for the practical purposes of regulating wages. The living wage is related to full-time work, and this implies that workpeople on short time will earn less than enough to meet their needs. It is also understood to be sufficient for a family of average size, often defined as a man with wife and two or three dependent children, but this means that larger families receive less than a living wage and consequently suffer privation if they are entirely dependent on the wage. This raises the question of supplementing the wage by family allowances, a system which is considered later.

Difficulties are encountered in attempting to say what is the amount of a living wage because the concept is vague and there is no objective standard which can be used. If it is defined as an amount sufficient for the reasonable needs of an ordinary labourer, there is still the difficulty of deciding what are "reasonable" needs. Is the amount to be enough only to keep the worker and his dependants in physical health, that is, enough merely for subsistence, or should it enable them to enjoy conventional necessities and comforts? It may be considered "reasonable" to allow for a small expenditure on beer and tobacco, but what if large numbers of ordinary labourers habitually spend so much on these commodities that their families are deprived of essential food and other necessaries? Few would argue that in estimating the amount of a living wage provision should be made for substantial expenditure on non-essentials. Again, large numbers of workpeople including many unskilled labourers regularly spend considerable sums on football pools and other forms of gambling, but no one would claim that such items are to be included in estimating a living wage.

Even if the wage is spent solely on necessaries there are considerable differences in the efficiency with which this is done. Some housewives by careful buying of food, by skill in cooking, by avoiding waste, and by repair of clothing and household goods, can get the best value out of the money available, while others are much less competent. Similarly, some men are handy in the home and do many jobs involving little or no expense which raise the standard of comfort of the household, while others are unwilling or unable to undertake such chores. Consequently there is a wide range in the standards of living which different people obtain from similar wages. In estimating the amount of a living wage it cannot be assumed that the money

270

will be used with maximum efficiency. But although some allowance must be made, the living wage cannot safeguard from privation those who are thriftless, wasteful and incompetent in the management of their incomes.

In view of these difficulties any estimates of a living wage are inevitably crude and open to challenge, including those based on the theoretical method and the family budget method. The theoretical method can be used only for part of the items which must be covered by a living wage, its main value being for food. Calculations are made of the quantities of proteins, fats, carbohydrates, and vitamins required to maintain health. The results of scientific studies show the needs of adults and the smaller needs of children of different ages, and they also show the number of calories or energy units required by people on heavy manual work, light manual work, and sedentary occupations. These can be used to estimate the total nutritive needs of families of different size and occupation. Scientific investigations have also been made into the nutritive values of each kind of food, and from the results a balanced dietary can be built up indicating the quantities of bread, meat, milk, butter or margarine, vegetables, fruits and other foods needed for health. The costs of these quantities at current prices when added together give the amount which should be spent on food.

It must be pointed out, however, that the same nutritive standards can be provided either by a few cheap foods, including say, rye bread, potatoes, and margarine, or by a varied diet of expensive foods, and consequently there are wide differences in expenditure on food. For use in living wage estimates, the foods chosen are the cheaper kinds, but workpeople are conservative in their habits and will continue to buy the kinds of food they are accustomed to eat, even though they could get the same nutritive values or a more balanced dietary at less cost. Only by a slow process of education can habits be changed. Also changes would have to be made in the quantities of different foods produced and marketed. For example, soya beans are highly nutritive and cheap, but in Britain only small quantities are eaten.

Even if such difficulties could be overcome, the theoretical method is of limited use in making living wage estimates, as it has no application to many items which must be covered by the living wage. For food, its main practical value is in providing a standard for measuring the nutrition obtained by workpeople and their families from the foods they actually consume, and where deficiencies are found these may be remedied either by buying more nutritive foods for the same amount of money, by spending less on other commodities, by wage increase, or by some form of subsidy. For housing, calculations can

271

be made of the cubic space per person required for health, and the cost of providing such accommodation estimated for inclusion on a weekly basis in the living wage. Differences in current costs of house building, however, complicate the problem, as does the existence of large numbers of houses built many years ago at much lower than present costs. Then house building is often subsidized, or people with low incomes may pay less than the economic rent of the houses they live in. It follows that the living wage may consist only partly of the money which the worker receives from his employer, but also in varying degree of the value of subsidies for housing, food, and other essentials.

Of only limited value for food and housing, and perhaps for fuel, the theoretical method can provide no standards for expenditure on clothing, furniture, household furnishings and utensils, or for other necessaries. The family budget method has been more widely used but it also is defective for purposes of living wage estimates. Families are asked to give detailed information about their expenditure on each of the things they buy, indicating the quantity and cost of each of the commodities. This is not the place to discuss the difficulties which arise in collecting and checking as far as possible the accuracy of this information. For living wage purposes averages are calculated from data supplied by the families of ordinary unskilled workers. These merely show what, in fact, the workers and their families do consume, and not what they need for health and efficiency, and except for reduced expenditure because of short time or increased expenditure made possible by additional income, they only indicate how the ordinary full-time wage is actually spent. If, however, the quantities of the various commodities consumed are systematically examined an opinion can be formed as to their adequacy or deficiency. It was along these lines that Mr. B. Seebohm Rowntree estimated the cost of providing a subsistence standard and a somewhat higher but still meagre human needs standard.

Several points must be noted about such standards. First, they are subjective, and each investigator is likely to give a different result, although experienced people will not differ widely from one another. Second, the amount considered necessary to provide a living wage may be considerably greater than the wages which many labourers receive, and the standard may therefore be an objective to be attained in the future and not one which is immediately practicable. Too much "generosity" may have been shown in including commodities as necessary which can be done without, or the cost of new articles of clothing and furniture has been used when, in fact, large numbers of poorer families buy secondhand things cheaply, or durable articles are made to last longer than the investigators had thought possible. Investigators when determining what they consider to be an "adequate" standard find it difficult to omit commodities which are, in fact, beyond the reach of large numbers of unskilled workers. Thus, the Australian Royal Commission appointed in 1919 to inquire into the cost of living according to reasonable standards of comfort for a family consisting of man, wife, and three children, collected family budgets and then built up a budget which it considered desirable for Australian conditions. The Commission had no power to fix wages, though it was expected that its findings would be used for the determination of basic wage standards by the wage-fixing bodies. However, the Commission's standard was considerably above the levels of wages being paid in many industries, and when the question of fixing wages at that standard was examined, the Commonwealth statistician stated that it would be quite impracticable as the whole of the national income of Australia, including profits to employers and the revenues required for Government expenditure, would not, if divided up equally among employed persons, yield the necessary weekly amount, nor, of course, would anything have been available to pay higher wages for skill.

It follows that if living wage estimates are to be realistic they must generally be related to the productive capacity of industry, and that in effect there must be reconciliation between the principles of the living wage and the capacity of industry in general to pay. This is not to deny that where Malthusian conditions exist, with population increasing more rapidly than resources, there may be large numbers of workers with less than a living wage, who, with their families, suffer from under-nourishment and consequent ill-health. Nor does it deny the existence of conditions where rich natural resources combined with efficient capital equipment and supplies of power result in such high rates of production that the wages of unskilled workpeople are well above subsistence level. But it does mean that estimates of the living wage vary from country to country and from period to period. These variations are due not only to the effects of climate, geographical position, habits of consumption, and ways of living, but to changes in productivity. In the tropics, housing and clothing needs and the kinds of food eaten differ from those in colder countries, in places near the sea more fish is eaten than in inland regions, while in some countries rice and in others wheaten bread is a staple food, but in addition to these differences, estimates made of the amount of a living wage are higher in, say, the United States, Canada, Australia, and Great Britain than in Southern Europe and in Asiatic countries. This is because their general standards of living are higher, and

273

investigators are thereby influenced in deciding upon minimum standards. Similarly, living wage estimates in Britain to-day are higher than those a hundred years ago because production per worker is greater as a result of industrial progress.

When in the early nineteenth century the subsistence theory of wages was widely supported, the argument used was that increases in the wages of unskilled labourers would result in growth of population with the consequence that wages would fall to a "fodder" standard. There was no realization that minimum standards could be raised progressively, and that, although they would still be regarded as low, they could rise substantially above a mere subsistence level. Where labourers are held in a condition of serfdom, or where there are Malthusian conditions, wages will be at or near a fodder basis, but elsewhere the living wage is relative and may rise substantially above a mere subsistence level.

In Australia where, until recently, living wage estimates were used for fixing legally enforceable basic wages of unskilled workers, the idea was given precise definition for that practical purpose. In Britain and other countries, though no exact authoritative figure has been established, unofficial estimates by specialists do not differ widely. In Britain they are appreciably above the standards used by the National Assistance Board in helping people who are not at work.

Whether a living wage is given precision or is left indefinite, the idea exerts considerable influence in wage regulation. As the living wage is the money expression of specified goods and services, it is used in support of proportionate increases and reductions in money wages as the cost of living rises or falls. These are facilitated by cost-of-living sliding scale arrangements which are discussed later. Such changes in money wages are applied not only to unskilled labourers who are mainly concerned with securing a living wage, but also to semi-skilled and skilled workers. Their wages are above the living-wage standard as this is ordinarily understood, but their higher wages are their living wage, i.e. their customary way of living, and they are committed to rent payments and other expenses which cannot be changed at short notice. They will make great efforts to prevent any lowering of the standard to which they are accustomed.

If the cost of living is higher in some localities than in others, the money wages paid to provide a living wage should differ in similar proportion. One of the reasons why many wage rates including those of unskilled workers are higher in London than in other parts of the country is that rents are higher there.

The living wage expressed in goods and services or their money equivalent is a general standard unrelated to particular industries. With only minor qualifications it is the same in a given locality, region, or country irrespective of the industry or occupation in which the worker is employed. If it is authoritatively fixed and legally binding as a minimum or basic wage below which no workpeople shall be paid, there may be some undertakings, or even industries, in which the wage is beyond their capacity to pay. This has led to the adoption of the principle, for example, by the Australian Commonwealth Court of Arbitration, that the living wage should be sacrosanct, "beyond the reach of bargaining," and that, if any employer cannot maintain his business without cutting down the wages necessary for decent living according to Australian standards, it is better that he should abandon the business. Where, except temporarily in a period of depression, there are such businesses, it is usually because the employer is inefficient or the business is unsuited to the conditions of the country. Where the principle is applied, sufficient time is allowed for such businesses to improve their efficiency, but if they are unable to do so it is preferable that their workpeople should move to more efficient undertakings or to industries more suited to the country than that "sweated" conditions should be allowed to continue.

COST-OF-LIVING SLIDING SCALES

A widely adopted method of wage adjustment based upon an agreed criterion is that of the cost-of-living sliding scale. This can be used appropriately in periods during which there are considerable upward or downward movements in the cost of living and when at the same time conditions of production are relatively stable. It can also be effectively applied, however, in periods when changes both in the cost of living and in productivity are taking place, but it must then be recognized that adjustment to changes in the cost of living is only one of the reasons for adjusting rates of wages, and that the rates must also be changed on other grounds.

Cost-of-living sliding scales provide a valuable means of dealing in a semi-automatic way with one of the factors affecting money wages. Their use can facilitate industrial negotiations and reduce the risks of conflict. The system has been criticized because it merely maintains the worker's standard of purchasing power over commodities and services, but gives no improvement in standards of living. This criticism would be valid only if wage adjustments were limited solely to changes in the cost of living, whereas the purpose of cost-of-living sliding scales is to maintain the purchasing power of wages in periods of price change, and they do not prevent adjustments needed because of other changes affecting wages. Suppose, for example, there has been a 10 per cent increase in the cost of living over a period of three years and an increase of 5 per cent in industrial productivity during the same period, then, leaving aside other factors affecting wages, an increase in money wages of 10 per cent would bring the original wage scale up to date, and then a further increase of 5 per cent could be made to provide an improved standard of living based upon increased productivity.

The greatest application of cost-of-living sliding scales has been during periods of rapid changes in the purchasing power of money, particularly those resulting from war-time conditions between 1914 and 1922, and again for some years after 1939. In such periods, monetary factors and shortages of commodities cause increases in the cost of living, followed after the First World War by deflation and falling prices. In periods of rising prices during a war or in the subsequent reconstruction period, the workers demand wage increases to compensate for increases in the cost of living, but the fundamental problem is shortage of consumers' goods because capital and labour have been diverted to war purposes. This inevitably means a lower standard of living, though this may be unevenly distributed between different sections of the community, and workers in some industries may succeed in maintaining their standards by obtaining cost-of-living sliding scale adjustments of wages, while those in some occupations producing urgently needed munitions may improve their standards because of incentives offered to them to increase output. Such maintenance or improvements in standards are at the expense of other sections of the country, including workers in other occupations. In such circumstances the shortage of commodities is better met, not by increased money incomes but by increased taxation, including taxation compensated by credits payable after the war, by increased savings, whether voluntary or compulsory, and by rationing and price control. These methods were applied with considerable effect in various countries, for example, Britain and Canada, after 1941, although there had been substantial increases in the cost of living and also in wages during the first two years of the war.

It must be emphasized that, during or after a costly war, when there is danger of "runaway" inflation because of monetary expansion and shortage of goods and services, the successive raising of wages of large numbers of workpeople, whether by automatic cost-of-living sliding scales or other adjustments in which increases in the cost of living are largely influential, would seriously aggravate the

276

situation. It would increase the disturbance of economic "balance," and would involve greater hardship to those whose incomes, either from employment or from investment of savings, were relatively fixed. Conversely, in times of deflation with plenty of commodities on the market and rapidly falling prices, the lowering of purchasing power by downward adjustments of wages as the cost of living fell would intensify the depression. This is well illustrated by the collapse of prices and wages in the United States in 1932 and 1933, and President Roosevelt's drastic action to stop the downward spiral.

Increases or decreases in the cost of living may result not only from rapid adjustments of economic conditions to war-time and post-war conditions, which are usually the most disturbing to price levels, but also to fluctuations of the trade cycle. If trade-cycle booms or depressions are severe, changes in the cost of living may be considerable within a short period of two or three years. Then there are smaller changes due to minor fluctuations in trade-cycle conditions, and also long period price trends, such as the gradual upward movement in prices which began in the 1890's and continued until 1914. Index numbers showing changes in the cost of living are valuable as an aid in the adjustment of wage rates to each of these movements, whether the index is used as basis for automatic sliding-scale adjustments or as one of the elements considered in negotiations for wage changes. Sliding scales are more widely used in periods of substantial price change, whereas when price movements are more gradual other factors affecting wages preponderate, including changes in the capacity of industries to pay, and cost-of-living sliding scales tend to be abandoned.

It is of interest to examine the relation between wage changes based upon cost-of-living sliding scales and changes in the capacity of industry to pay. The cost of living is made up of a large number of items of food, clothing, household furnishings and equipment, fuel, light, housing accommodation, and miscellaneous goods and services. When, for example, a pronounced rise takes place in the cost of living, as a result of monetary or other factors of general influence, many industries producing this wide range of consumers' goods benefit together or within short intervals of a few months. In these circumstances many industries are selling their products at higher prices and can afford to pay higher money wages. The application of cost-of-living sliding scales leading to similar wage increases in a number of industries assumes, however, that all the industries benefit in the same proportion, but this is not so. The increase in the cost of living may be the result of fairly similar

277

increases in the prices of all the main commodities and services which comprise the cost of living, or it may be caused by big price increases of a few items and only small rises or even reductions in the prices of others. Also the effect of a given price change upon capacity to pay wages varies according as wages form a large or small part of total cost of production. Then again, changes in the cost of living are often less marked, especially during the course of a trade cycle, than those in the wholesale prices of raw materials. Therefore cost-of-living sliding scales are likely to be less suitable for application in industries producing raw materials and semi-manufactured products for the wholesale market than in industries producing consumers' goods which are important items in the cost of living. It must be emphasized, however, that cost-of-living sliding scales have usually been introduced for the purpose of maintaining the purchasing power of workpeople's wages in periods of rapidly rising prices, and in such circumstances most industries can usually afford to pay the higher money rates involved.

In the application of a cost-of-living sliding scale, it is essential that both employers and workpeople should have reasonable confidence in the cost-of-living index available to measure changes in the cost of living. In the compilation of such an index, there are various practical statistical difficulties, and even if these are overcome, the actual experience of many workpeople and their families when spending their wage is likely to differ appreciably from the general average change shown by the index. Thus, in negotiations, representatives of the workpeople may say that, whereas the index may show an increase of 25 per cent over a certain period, they can bring figures to prove that for themselves the increase is considerably more. This is no doubt true, but it must be realized that the index is representative for the general average covering skilled and unskilled workpeople in different parts of the country, and not for individuals or particular groups.

Another difficulty which has sometimes been experienced is that of realizing that for practical purposes an index may provide a reasonably reliable measure for changes in the cost of living, although the commodities included and the quantities of these commodities used as basis or "weights" in the calculation of the index may represent a standard of living lower than that which most workers enjoy. It is quite possible that such a meagre basis may give as high, or even a higher index of the cost of living than a more adequate standard, and this could be so if the prices of items of considerable importance or "weight" in the meagre standard had risen more during the period than the prices of commodities not included. It is, however, desirable that the standard should correspond reasonably with the average standards of consumption of workpeople in the country, and after a period during which standards have changed considerably the basis or family budget of consumption upon which the index is changed should be altered. Nevertheless, the cost-of-living index published by the British Ministry of Labour which for many years measured changes in the cost of living on the basis of the year 1914 was calculated by using a quite meagre standard of consumption obtained from a small number of families before 1914, and although there had been great changes in standards of consumption since that time, the index gave results which were still of practical value for purposes of wage adjustment. So long as weights are not widely disproportionate and unrepresentative, an index of changes in the cost of living will not show great discrepancies. Subject to this condition that the weights are not seriously distorted, the accuracy of the price data collected for each commodity is much more important and has a greater effect upon the index than variations of the weights.

When cost-of-living sliding scale adjustments are first introduced in an industry, the method adopted is often inadequate. Frequently, for example, in war-time, workers demand an increase in wages because of a rise in the cost of living, but employers are anxious to distinguish between the customary or normal rate of wages and increases, which they hope will be temporary, to meet the increased cost of living. Sometimes in the circumstances mentioned, a cost-of-living bonus or "war" bonus is paid at a flat rate, for example, 5s. a week to all workpeople whether skilled or unskilled. A more developed system is to agree that for a change of say 8 points in the cost-of-living index there shall be an addition or reduction in wages of 4s. a week, again applicable to all workers, both skilled and unskilled. The defect of this method is that though making some allowance for the increase in the cost of living it benefits the unskilled more than the skilled in a period of rising prices, since a rise of 5s. a week for an unskilled worker receiving a wage of £2 10s. is an increase of 10 per cent, whereas the 5s. bonus paid to the skilled worker with a wage of £4 a week represents an increase of only 6¼ per cent. This process of making equal additions to both skilled and unskilled if continued would very much narrow the relation between the wages of skilled and unskilled workers. Some narrowing may be desirable or even inevitable in war-time conditions, as in the circumstances of shortage of commodities the unskilled workers are so near to the minimum of subsistence that very little reduction in their real wages is possible, whereas skilled

279

workers have a greater margin above mere necessaries. To avoid the danger of inflation resulting from serious shortage of goods, while not imposing privation on low-paid workers it may be desirable that increases in the wages of all but unskilled workers should be less than the increase in the cost of living. It would be preferable, however, that any changes in the relation between the standards of living of skilled and unskilled workers should be considered openly whether in wage negotiations or by other means, and not altered in this somewhat "concealed" way by the granting of equal cost-of-living bonuses to skilled and unskilled alike.

In periods when there is no serious shortage of commodities, cost-of-living sliding scale adjustments should be applied so as to ensure that the basic wages of each category of worker are altered in the same proportion. Thus, if there has been a change of 5 per cent in the cost of living, then the money wages of unskilled, semi-skilled, and skilled workers should all alike be increased by 5 per cent, and this will keep their relative wages unchanged. If it is necessary for any reason to change relative wages, this should be done on its own merits and not in the application of the cost-of-living adjustments.

A criticism is sometimes directed against cost-of-living sliding scale adjustments because there is a time lag between a rise in the cost of living and the change in the rates of wages. If, for example, the cost of living in March is 5 per cent higher than in December of the preceding year, the adjustments being made quarterly, statistics showing this change may not be available until the middle of May and wage rates may not be increased until June. This difficulty might be met by making the increase retrospective, but this has not generally been adopted. Owing therefore to the time lag workers begin to receive in June wages to offset the rise which took place some months earlier, but if the cost of living is still rising the June rates of wages will be below that necessary to meet the change in the cost of living. The time lag is greatest in periods of rapid upward or downward movements in prices, and it also involves some reduction in real wages in a long period of steady upward movement in the cost of living extending over a period of years. Where, however, successive periods occur of rises and falls in the cost of living within a comparatively short time there is compensation, as the unfavourable effect on the workers when prices are rising is compensated by the benefit of the time lag which accrues to the workers when prices are falling.

Sliding-scale systems were widely adopted in Britain and other countries during the years of rapid changes in price levels resulting from war conditions from 1914 to 1923 and again after 1939. In such periods almost all wage negotiations bring changes in the cost of living under review, but sliding-scale adjustments operate only if wage changes are made automatically in accordance with a previously established system relating wage rates to changes in the cost-of-living index. In Britain after the outbreak of war in 1939, the cost-of-living index rose by about 30 per cent within two years and was then stabilized by the Government's policy of food subsidies and price control, and most of the wage increases by cost-of-living sliding scales were therefore made between 1939 and 1941. Subsequently, though most of the sliding-scale agreements continued in force the resulting wage changes were small until after the war, but substantial wage increases were obtained for other reasons by agreements or arbitration awards, and by the spring of 1946 wage rates in British industry had increased by an average of about 60 per cent since the outbreak of the war, or about double the rise in the cost-of-living index.[1]

The number of workpeople covered by cost-of-living sliding scales, which had been about 3 million in 1922, was about $1\frac{1}{2}$ million in 1939, but rose during the Second World War to $2\frac{1}{2}$ million in a wide range of industries. Some industries, for example boot and shoe manufacture and building, have had cost-of-living sliding scales in operation under successive agreements since 1921 or 1922. The scales vary considerably in the different industries, the main variables being the number of points of change in the cost of living before wages are altered, the amount of the wage adjustment, and the time interval when wage adjustments are made. Some agreements provide for a change in wages with each change of one point in the cost-of-living index, while others reduce the frequency of wage change by requiring a "step" up or down of several points, e.g. 4, 5, 6, or even 10 or 15, before wages are adjusted. Many scales provide that if the cost-of-living index falls below a specified figure there shall be no further reduction in wage rates, but few scales fix any upper limit.

In most scales a specified alteration, e.g. of 5 points, in the cost-of-living index involves a uniform wage change usually of a flat rate per hour, per shift, or per week whatever the occupations, but the amount is greater for men than for women and young persons. In some scales the wage variation is a percentage of basic rates and is uniform for all occupations and for men, women, and young persons.

[1] Had there been no subsidies to keep the cost of living down, the index in the spring of 1946 would have been about 60 per cent above the 1939 level, according to Ministry of Labour estimates.

A few scales provide smaller changes for the more highly paid workers than for the lower-paid occupations, and for piece workers than for time workers. Many variations along these lines are found in different scales. The timing of wage changes also differs considerably, some scales requiring changes, whenever the cost of living has moved the specified number of points, while others provide that wages shall be adjusted at three monthly or other specified intervals if the cost of living has made the required change. When the latter system is applied some scales base the wage change on the average of the cost-of-living indexes during the preceding period, while others take the last index of the period.

Illustrations of some of the above features from sliding scales in operation in Britain during the war years 1939 to 1946 and the subsequent period of readjustment to peace conditions are of interest.[1] In the building industry a national agreement for England and Wales provided that wage rates would be reconsidered each January, May, and September in relation to the *average* of the Ministry of Labour's monthly cost-of-living index numbers during the preceding twelve months. Standard rates of wages of skilled craftsmen and labourers in each of the grades of towns for which separate scales had been established were related to an average index of 65, that is an index 65 per cent above the cost of living in the period (1914 = 100) on which the indexes were based. Wage rates were increased or reduced by ½d. an hour for each rise or fall of 6½ points in the average index.[2] In the boot and shoe industry, for which cost-of-living sliding scales have been applied by national agreements since 1922, a scale which came into operation at the beginning of 1944 specifies six different levels of the cost-of-living index, namely, over 50 but not over 60, over 60 but not over 70, over 70 but not over 80, over 80 but not over 90, over 90 but not over 100, and over 100 but not over 110. For each of these levels there is a schedule of minimum weekly rates for men, women, and young persons, and the weekly rates vary by 3s. for men, 2s. for women, and 1s. or 2s. for young persons as the level of the cost of living moves up or down a step. There is also a scale for piece workers, additions to basic rates being usually 4½ per cent for each step up or down in the cost of living. Wage adjustments are made whenever the monthly index of the Ministry of Labour moves from one to another of the six levels mentioned above. If the index nears 110 the parties to the agreement have undertaken to consider what

[1] The examples given are taken from the *Ministry of Labour Gazette*.
[2] Cost-of-living sliding scales have been applied in the British building industry since 1921.

wage increases should be made in the event of the cost of living exceeding that figure.

In the heavy steel industry the selling-price sliding scale was suspended by agreement in March 1940, and a cost-of-living sliding scale substituted. Wage changes are determined each month on the basis of the cost-of-living index for the month. By a revised agreement of October 1942, a flat-rate addition of 0·8d. a shift for men, 0·6d. a shift for youths aged 18 and under 21 years, and 0·4d. for boys was paid for each point by which the cost-of-living index exceeded 62. The coal-mining industry introduced a cost-of-living sliding scale in March 1940, as one component of its wage rates. This provided for the payment of a uniform flat-rate war addition per shift, the amount of the addition being calculated by multiplying 7d. for adult workers and one-half of this figure for other workers by the number of points by which the cost-of-living index exceeded 55, which was the figure at the outbreak of the war. The adjustment of this wage addition was considered quarterly, but no alteration was made until the index had moved 5 points or more from the number on which the latest change was based.

In addition to cost-of-living sliding scales provided by collective agreements the system has been applied in a number of industries by wages council orders. Thus in the tobacco trade a war emergency payment of 5¾d. a week for men and 3¾d. a week for women and juveniles was added to the minimum rates of wages for each point which the cost-of-living index rose above 65 but not above 114. In the baking trade in Scotland each rise of 5 points in the cost-of-living index between 55 and 150 resulted in wage increases ranging from 1s. to 2s. a week according to the amount of the minimum wage.

SELLING-PRICE SLIDING SCALES

In the preceding section the relation was noted between changes in the cost of living and changes in the capacity of industry to pay. As hitherto wages have been regulated independently in each separate industry, the adjustment of wages would be facilitated if some "yardstick" could be found to measure changes in the capacity of each industry to pay. Capacity to pay is the result of a combination of many factors, including cost of raw materials, cost of production, quantities sold, and selling price. In the past comprehensive information has rarely been available for a whole industry, partly because firms were often unwilling to disclose these data to their competitors. For many industries, however, the selling prices of products are known, and in a few of them these prices have been found to provide under certain conditions a rough measure of changes in capacity to pay, and selling-price sliding scale systems of adjusting wages have been successfully applied.

The method is unsuitable where an industry produces a wide range of goods of differing quality, or where the products change considerably over a period of a few years. For example, it would be difficult to select representative products and build up an index of selling prices for such complex industries as engineering and woollen textiles. It can, however, be done where a few standardized products represent the main output of an industry. Thus in the iron and steel industry adjustments of wage rates have been made by collective agreements for sixty or seventy years in accordance with changes in the prices of pig iron or of steel rails, bars, and plates. Also in the coal-mining industry for several decades before 1914, wages in some districts were adjusted to changes in the selling prices of specified qualities of coal, but in 1921 a more elaborate system, which is described below, was adopted.

Not only must the industry have a few typical standardized products or varieties of output, but selling prices must be determined in a free or competitive market if the system is to have much value. Prices regulated by a monopoly or by the State would be more stable, and price alterations, being the result of deliberate policy based upon other considerations than capacity to pay, would not provide a suitable index for wage adjustments. It was for this reason that in 1940 the iron and steel industry suspended its selling-price sliding scale, the prices of its products being fixed by Government war-time controls.

In selling-price sliding scale agreements wages are usually adjusted every two or three months according to the latest selling-price ascertainments. The price data for defined products are taken from selected markets and averages are calculated, the work being done jointly by accountants acting on behalf of the trade unions and the employers' organizations. As with all other systems of sliding-scale adjustment there is a time lag or period usually of a month or two between the date for which the selling prices are obtained and that on which the related wage rates are paid, the interval being taken up with the compilation of the price averages, their communication to the interested parties, the formal approval of the appropriate wage change, and its notification to the companies.

Wages adjusted to the selling prices of an industry's products may move in the same direction as wages in other industries, or may move in an opposite direction. Where the products of the industry are widely used by other industries, e.g. iron and steel

284

products and coal, it is likely that trade cycle influences will cause the prices of these products to move in the same direction as the general price trend, though the movements may not synchronize. Consequently wages in the industry will tend to move in the same direction as wages in many other industries, and probably also in the same direction as the cost of living. In these circumstances the system would be more likely to give satisfaction than if the sliding-scale adjustments resulted in falling wages in the industry at a time when wages in other industries were rising.

A basic industry may be depressed and the prices of its products fall when other industries are prosperous because it has been over expanded or the demand for its products is low as a result of competition of a substitute commodity. Falling wages will reflect the condition of the industry and will cause workers to seek employment elsewhere, thus reducing the labour force in the industry to economic proportions. Falling prices in the industry may, however, be due to the wide application of improved methods of production with lower costs, and, if demand for the products is elastic and the lower prices lead to considerably increased sales, the industry may be much more prosperous than before. Yet, although the industry's capacity to pay had increased, the application of the selling-price sliding scale would result in falling wages. Such circumstances would call for a raising of basic wages to a level appropriate to the new conditions of production, and then adjustments to changes in selling prices could be continued.

The system may be illustrated by the agreement in force until the spring of 1940 for adjusting the wages of workers employed in the manufacture of pig iron in the north-east of England (Cleveland area). Standard rates of wages were fixed and these were related to a selling price of iron of 50s. a ton. For each variation of 3d. a ton in the average selling price, the standard rates were increased or reduced by $\frac{1}{4}$ per cent. The price ascertainments were made at intervals of three months and certified by a selected firm of accountants, and any resultant wage changes came into operation about five weeks after the end of the quarter to which the price related. In coke and by-products manufacture in Durham collective agreements providing for sliding scale adjustment of wages to changes in the selling price of coke have been in operation for most of the period since August 1924. The agreement in force in 1944 provided that when the average price of coke at the ovens was not more than 18s. a ton an addition of 30 per cent would be made to the basic rates of wages per shift. This addition would be increased by $\frac{1}{2}$ per cent for every rise of 4d. in the price per ton up to 24s., and by 1 per cent for every rise of 6d. per ton beyond 24s.[1] From April 1941, this selling-price sliding scale was applied in association with a cost-of-living sliding scale, the arrangement being that the scale giving the more favourable result to the workers at any date would be applied.[2] An agreement for regulating the wages of coke and by-product workers in South Wales and Monmouthshire also linked a selling-price sliding scale with a cost-of-living sliding scale, but wages were adjusted to changes in both scales, and not only to the one more favourable to the workers, as in Durham. The standard basic rates of wages were raised by 28 per cent when the average net selling price of coke was 16s. but under 16s. 4d. a ton, and one point was added to this percentage for every increase of 4d. in the price up to a maximum percentage of 75. In addition, a cost-of-living allowance of 0·7d. a shift was paid for each point by which the cost-of-living index exceeded 55 per cent above the level in 1914.[3]

Adjustment to Changes in the Proceeds of an Industry

Selling-price sliding scales, though useful for wage adjustment, are defective as they are based on only one of the factors which determine the capacity of an industry to pay. Attempts have therefore been made to build up a more comprehensive measure which will include costs of production and quantities sold as well as selling prices. Such information is rarely available for a whole industry, partly because of unwillingness to disclose the data, though the fear by individual companies of disclosure to competitors of details of their financial position can be overcome by sending the returns to an independent firm of accountants. It has not, therefore, been possible to test for a number of industries how closely wage rates have in fact fluctuated in relation to an index of proceeds. This method of adjustment is likely sooner or later to be adopted, perhaps in conjunction with other principles, for wage regulation in nationalized industries, for which all the relevant statistics will be available. Its success in such industries would lead to its wider use, although account would have to be taken of the possibility that it might be less suitable in some competitive industries. Also difficulties would

[1] Accountants representing both sides obtained returns from the employers showing the realized value of all by-product coke sold except ballast and coke sent to the producers' works or to companies affiliated with them.

[2] A cost-of-living index of 90 points was equated to the basic rates plus 63 per cent, and for each increase of 5 complete points above 90 in the index an addition of 3½ per cent was made to the 63 per cent.

[3] The examples given are taken from *The Ministry of Labour Gazette*. The South Wales and Monmouthshire system had been in operation since December 1935.

arise in industries with a wide variety of products or where wages were a small proportion of cost of production or where this proportion varied widely between the different undertakings and products.

Practical experience of the system has been gained by British coal-mining where it operated on a district basis from 1921 to April 1944. Detailed information was supplied by the mine-owners showing the proceeds from the sale of coal and costs of production of the industry and this was examined by independent auditors appointed by each side. The proceeds were at pit-head prices, and arrangements were made to prevent proceeds being reduced by sale of coal at less than commercial prices to iron and steel or gas plants owned by collieries or to companies financially associated with them. Costs for the purpose of the scheme comprised timber and other materials and stores used, repairs and renewals, depreciation, rents, rates, and royalties, remuneration of directors, managers, clerical and administrative staff, employers' payments for accident compensation, health and unemployment insurance for workpeople, the miners' welfare levy, and other expenses of production, excluding wages.[1] The miners insisted that costs should in no way be inflated artificially, for example, by the inclusion of items not used in production or by booking them at more than true cost prices.

When the pit-head receipts from sales of coal were aggregated for a district, and the aggregate costs of production other than wages deducted from receipts, the surplus, or net proceeds, was divided between wages and profits in agreed proportions, which varied in the different districts, the part for wages usually being 85 or 87 per cent of the surplus.[2] The total allocated to wages was then used for the adjustment of rates of wages, a percentage corresponding to the total being added to the basic rates, whether day-wages or piece rates. These adjusted rates were then payable during a period usually of two or three months until the results of the next ascertainment were applied, but in each district a minimum percentage addition to basic rates was fixed thus providing a level below which the rates actually paid would not fall even though the surplus (pit-head receipts for coal less costs other than wages) was insufficient to pay them. In these circumstances the deficit was made up by the colliery owners, but the amount of the deficit was carried forward and refunded to the owners out of future surpluses.

[1] During the war costs also included levies under coal (charges) orders, to which reference is made later.
[2] The remaining 13 or 15 per cent was available for profits, but this is no indication of the rates of interest or dividend paid on the capital invested in the industry, most companies paying at much lower rates.

During periods of depression when receipts from sales of coal were small because of low prices and reductions in quantities sold, the deficits carried forward in successive periods grew to such large amounts in many districts that a refunding of the amounts advanced by the owners would have absorbed for years the surpluses of more prosperous times. The effect of this was that the miners would remain at the minimum percentages for long periods, which was discouraging, especially when prosperity was returning to the industry. In order, therefore, that the miners might have a reasonable chance of getting some increases over the minimum the owners in some districts from time to time cancelled the accumulated deficits due to them, while in other districts the amounts were cancelled or reduced by agreement with the unions. This had the effect of making the proportion allocated to wages from net proceeds somewhat greater than the 85 or 87 per cent fixed in the agreements.

The scheme was an ingenious and effective method of relating wages to the capacity of the industry to pay; it was particularly valuable in an industry in which wages form an unusually large part of total cost of production, and made a notable contribution to industrial peace. It was essentially a system of adjusting wages to fluctuations in the prosperity of the industry, but was not profit-sharing as this is ordinarily understood. Percentage additions to basic rates were uniform at all collieries throughout a district, but there was no pooling of profits by the various companies or payment of subsidies by the more prosperous ones, and consequently those with rich, easily worked coal seams and efficient managements were able to earn high profits while others were struggling to avoid loss. Also they could earn profits in periods showing successive deficiencies to meet the agreed minimum percentage on basic rates. This system, with modifications, continued in operation during the war until April 1944, when it was suspended by a national agreement operative for four years which incorporated into the new time and piece rates the percentage additions payable at the time of the agreement in accordance with the ascertainments of net proceeds.

It is interesting to review the main principles applied to coal-miners' wages during the war, including the new agreement, as they provide the starting-point for wage regulation under nationalization. The pre-war method of wage adjustment became artificial as a result of war-time Government control of the industry and the fixing of selling prices for coal. Also wage changes based on the ascertainments were too small to meet the needs of the situation. The main change of principle during the war was the payment of flat-rate national additions to wages, this being a direct consequence of the national control of the industry, and it is also an indication of the inevitability of a national wage policy for the industry under nationalization. Previously the colliery owners had strongly opposed national wage regulation which the Miners' Federation advocated, and one of the demands which the owners made successfully in the 1926 conflict was for district wage agreements, their contention being that economic and geological conditions differ so much that national regulation was impracticable. In this connection it is noteworthy that the miners were organized into district unions loosely linked together in the Miners' Federation of Great Britain until 1945 when the National Union of Mineworkers was formed, a change which has facilitated the regulation of working conditions on a national basis since the nationalization of the industry.

A number of flat rate increases in wages were made on a national basis between 1939 and 1944 to supplement the rates as determined by district ascertainments. Between November 1939 and July 1941 these increases were based on changes in the cost of living, six advances being made in this period, the total amounting to 2s. 8d. a shift. Then the cost-of-living index was stabilized by the Government's policy of price control and the subsidizing of essential foods, and subsequent additions to miners' wages were made for other reasons. By April 1944, the total amount of the flat rate increases was 8s. 8d. a shift, including the cost-of-living additions.[1] These were consolidated in the national agreement of that date, which also continued the fixing of national minimum wages which had been introduced in 1942, the minimum in the 1944 agreement being £5 a week for adult underground workers and £4 10s. for adult surface workers.

The cost of these increases was a burden which some of the poorer companies were unable to bear, and a national pool, known as the Coal Charges Fund, was developed to assist them. The fund, which was controlled by the Government, was maintained by a tonnage levy on coal, the amount of which was increased successively until by March 1945, it was 12s. a ton.[2] By this system the richer and more efficiently managed pits helped the poorer pits, and thus uneconomic undertakings were kept in production. For several years the Government helped the industry by subsidies as coal prices had

[1] Included were an attendance bonus of 1s. a shift, the Greene Award of 2s. 6d. a shift and the Porter Awards totalling 1s. 3d. a shift.

[2] The levy was originally begun voluntarily by the owners in 1940 at the rate of 3d. a ton, the purpose being to provide a sort of insurance for paying grants to companies which had suffered losses because of the war, and help was also given to some of the poorer undertakings. When the Greene Award of 2s. 6d. a shift was made in June 1942, the fund came under Government control, the levy was increased to 3s. 7d. a ton, and a standard rate of profit was guaranteed.

not kept pace with costs and production had declined, but towards the end of the war the Government adopted the policy that the industry must pay its way without subsidies. To enable it to do this, however, the Government has tried to fix coal prices high enough to enable the industry to cover its costs, including wages, and to earn a standard rate of profits. Such a policy of fixing high prices could be regarded as an indirect subsidy at the expense of consumers.

Under nationalization, the fixing of national minimum weekly rates for underground and surface workers was continued after the war. Also wage rates are increasingly determined on principles applied nationally, and district differences in the past due to variations in economic conditions, e.g. districts enjoying favourable home markets compared with those suffering from severe competition abroad, will be greatly reduced if not altogether eliminated. Poor mines and districts are assisted by the richer areas, the resources of the industry being pooled for the purpose, which will enable coal to be extracted from uneconomic pits so long as the yield in relation to costs is considered of value to the nation. Incentive methods of wage payment will be continued for some of the main categories of underground workers, though, with increasing mechanization, the old practice of relating the whole wage to the tonnage extracted may be modified by the fixing of a basic time wage and paying a tonnage bonus for output beyond a stated standard. Wages and working conditions have been raised so as to attract a sufficient number of workers to meet the needs of the country, and the selling prices of coal to consumers have been successively increased so as to meet higher labour and other costs. Any indirect or concealed subsidy from high selling prices will have to be met by home consumers, as the prices at which coal can be sold abroad will be determined by the forces of international competition.

17

Relative Wages

WORKPEOPLE GIVE attention not only to the amount of their own wages but to the relation between their wages and those of other workpeople in their own undertaking and industry and of workpeople in other industries. Indeed, as there is no absolute criterion for deciding whether wages are fair, workpeople tend to judge fairness by comparing their wages with those of other workpeople. If workpeople in one occupation in a factory or industry secure an increase in wages, those in other occupations usually demand increases which will restore their relative wages. Similarly, wage increases in some industries lead to pressure for corresponding increases in other industries. Thus, there is a powerful tendency for wage ratios which have become customary in the past to persist, and frequently when wage changes are negotiated collectively for an industry or undertaking the same percentages are applied to all occupations, leaving relative wages unchanged.

This maintenance of relative wages would be sound enough if the customary or established ratios were fair, and if the skill, experience, and other qualities required in the various occupations and grades into which workpeople are classified within industries and between industries remained unchanged. There is, indeed, a long period tendency, through mobility of labour, towards the establishment of fair ratios. But alongside this trend, the qualities required of workpeople in different occupations and industries are continually being altered, sometimes gradually and unobtrusively, sometimes rapidly. A skilled handicraft occupation may be transformed by machine processes into a semi-skilled job. Even a whole industry may be substantially changed, a noteworthy example being the extensive mechanization of British agriculture in recent years. Where such changes take place it is unsatisfactory to maintain the former ratios, but especially where a skilled craft is "degraded" by changes in methods the workpeople often show great determination to cling to their relative standard, and wage anomalies result. The removal of such anomalies is one of the main difficulties faced in trying to base wage ratios on job evaluations. Again, wage ratios between industries are powerfully affected by differences in relative prosperity, wages rising in a prosperous industry and falling in a depressed or declining one, with the result that workpeople of equivalent skills receive substantially higher wages in the one industry than in the other. Mobility of labour will tend to remove such disparities in the long run, but for skilled workpeople the time required for this to be accomplished may be as long as fifteen or twenty years.

Not only do workpeople and employers in private industry use the relative wages argument in their negotiations, but the fair-wage clause, which in many countries forms one of the provisions of public contracts, often stipulates that the wages paid by contractors shall not be less than the standard trade union or other fair rates paid in the district in which the contract work is performed; some fair-wage clauses require contractors to pay not less than the wage standards of good or reputable employers. Again, in some countries laws which provide for the fixing of statutory minimum rates for certain trades require the wage-fixing authorities to base their rates on those current for similar classes of work in other trades.[1]

The impact of labour standards in some industries upon those in other industries is not limited to wages, but affects hours of work and other conditions. In recent years collective bargaining in some industries has been extended to the provision of old-age pensions, which can in some ways be regarded as deferred wages; to the employer they are a labour cost, while to workpeople it seems only fair that the efforts of their working life should entitle them to adequate pensions on retirement. The close link with wages is shown by occasions when workpeople have bargained for pensions instead of wage increases. Now, if workpeople in some industries secure pension schemes, this will, by the principle of "relativity," lead workpeople in other industries to demand similar schemes. Thus, in Britain the arrangement in 1950 for a special pension scheme for coal-miners to supplement the pensions provided under National Insurance will undoubtedly stimulate demands in other nationalized industries and more generally throughout the whole of industry. Such additional pensions are specially needed for skilled workers, who otherwise would experience a much greater drop in their standards of living than unskilled workers when both are in receipt on retirement of the same flat-rate National Insurance pension.

[1] In several European countries minimum wage legislation for the protection of homeworkers has required their wages to be based on those paid for similar work in factories.

WAGE DIFFERENCES BETWEEN INDUSTRIES

It is of interest to review differences in wages from industry to industry, and also the relative wages of skilled and unskilled workpeople, of men and women, and of workpeople in different localities. Such differences and ratios between industries are illustrated below by British statistics based on data compiled by the Ministry of Labour. The first table gives average weekly and hourly earnings in October 1938, and April 1950, of adult men and women in eighteen groups of industries; they cover all classes of manual wage-earners, skilled, semi-skilled, and unskilled and general labourers, and the earnings include payments for overtime and night work, piece work, and other incentive earnings, but on the other hand, they are affected by time lost by workers during the week.[1] The differences in earnings do not indicate differences in the rates of wages in the different industries for comparable classes of workpeople employed under similar conditions, as the earnings are affected by wide variations from industry to industry in the proportions of skilled and unskilled workers, in opportunities for extra earnings for overtime, night work, and piecework, and also by differences in the amount of time lost by sickness, absenteeism, and other causes. There is, for example, considerable variation in average weekly hours, including overtime and short-time, from industry to industry, the range for men in April 1950 being from 43·9 in the clothing group to 48·8 in the transport group, and for women from 39·8 in Government service to 44·3 in transport. The overall average hours of men in April 1950 was 47 compared with 41·9 for women, which explains why the ratio of women's to men's weekly earnings is lower (55·2 per cent) than the ratio of their hourly earnings (62·1 per cent).

The figures for April 1950 given on page 294 may be supplemented by the average earnings of dock-workers, which in the last pay-week of that month averaged 156s. 4d.,[2] while for adult coal-miners the average weekly cash earnings, together with the value of remuneration in kind, in the week ending March 18, 1950, were 195s. 6d. Thus, coal-miners were the highest paid, and dock-workers were fifth from the top.

In April 1950, the men's weekly average was 145s. 9d., with a range from 117s. for national and local government service to 166s. 3d. for metal manufacture, the difference between the lowest

[1] The industrial classifications used by the Ministry of Labour at the two dates are different, but calculations have been made which give roughly comparable figures.

[2] The weekly average for the three months April to June 1950 was 170s. 3d.

and the highest being 49s. 3d. The women's weekly average was from 72s. 10d. in national and local government service to 101s. 7d. in transport and communication. Omitting this last exceptionally high

AVERAGE WEEKLY AND HOURLY EARNINGS OF ADULT MEN AND WOMEN IN VARIOUS BRITISH INDUSTRIES, OCTOBER 1938 AND APRIL 1950[1]

Industry Group	October 1938, Earnings				April 1950, Earnings			
	Men		Women		Men		Women	
	Weekly	Hourly	Weekly	Hourly	Weekly	Hourly	Weekly	Hourly
	s. d.	d.	s. d.	d.	s. d.	d.	s. d.	d.
Metal Manufacture ..	78 6	20·1	32 2	8·6	166 3	42·0	82 5	23·7
Engineering, Shipbuilding, and Electrical.. ..	72 2	18·1	32 2	9·1	150 11	38·5	82 10	23·5
Cutlery, Tools, etc. ..	76 11	17·8	31 6	8·4	154 6	39·7	77 10	22·7
Vehicles	83 1	20·6	40 1	11·4	162 7	42·4	91 4	26·3
Brick, China, Earthenware, Glass, Cement, etc.	63 2	15·5	27 10	7·8	149 8	37·1	77 1	22·2
Chemical and Allied Trades..	69 3	17·1	32 8	8·9	147 6	37·5	78 6	22·3
Precision Instruments, Jewellery, etc... ..	71 1	17·7	30 8	8·2	154 1	40·5	84 10	24·3
Textiles	57 3	13·2	31 9	8·6	142 1	53·8	82 11	23·5
Leather, Leather Goods, and Fur	64 1	17·7	34 11	9·0	140 7	36·8	75 11	22·0
Clothing	64 3	18·0	32 9	9·9	141 1	38·6	81 11	24·3
Food, Drink, and Tobacco	65 3	16·0	32 11	8·7	134 5	33·6	74 11	20·9
Wood and Cork Manufacture..	66 7	17·0	33 4	9·1	143 2	37·4	82 6	23·9
Paper and Printing ..	84 3	22·2	34 1	9·2	164 0	42·1	79 1	22·2
Mining and Quarrying (excluding coal) ..	60 3	15·8	—	—	141 4	35·9	81 2	23·0
Building and Contracting	66 0	17·1	—	—	140 0	35·6	73 0	21·6
Gas, Electricity, and Water	69 8	16·7	26 6	10·3	136 10	34·8	75 7	22·6
Transport and Communication (excluding Railways) ..	70 0	17·2	34 11	9·2	137 2	33·7	101 7	27·5
National and Local Government Service ..	—	—	—	—	117 0	31·3	72 10	22·0
General Average[2] ..					145 9	37·2	80 6	23·1

[1] The earnings are for the last pay week in October 1938, and the last pay week in April 1950. They are for men 21 years of age and over, and for women 18 years of age and over. The statistics for April, 1950, cover 6½ million workpeople.

[2] Including other manufacturing industries not listed in the Table.

figure, the range was from 72s. 10d. to 91s. 4d., a difference of 18s. 6d. Men's average hourly earnings were 37·2d., and thirteen of the eighteen industries were between 33d. and 40d. Women's average hourly earnings were 23·1d., and twelve of the eighteen industries were within the narrow range of 22d. and 24d.

It would be an interesting study to examine in detail the causes of differences between earnings in these industries at the same date, and also of differences between 1938 and 1950, but such an investigation is beyond the scope of this book. A main cause of differences at a given date is the higher proportion of skilled workpeople in some industries than in others, while changes from one period to another are the result also of changes in the proportion of skilled workpeople in the various industries as processes change, but mainly of changes in the relative strength of demand for the products of different industries.

In forty-eight trades for which wage rates are fixed by wage councils the average in 1950 of the general minimum weekly rates for adult male workers was 88s. 11d., but the range was from 79s. 8¼d. in the trade with the lowest minimum to 97s. 6d. in that with the highest. The corresponding average for women was 60s. 11d., and the range was from 47s. 8d. to 71s. Thus, in the lowest paid trade, the rate for men was 9s. 2¾d. a week below the average, and that for women 13s. 3d. below the average. These are substantial differences and the minimum rates in some of the lowest trades must have involved considerable privation to workpeople with dependants. Only in a few trades, however, were minimum rates more than five or six shillings a week below the average, and many unskilled workers in these trades may have been receiving rates or earnings above the minimum. The wide range from the lowest to the highest minima is the result largely of differences from trade to trade in economic conditions, in location, and in the qualities required from workpeople to whom the minima apply. The considerable dispersion of the minima below the average indicates the impracticability of attempting to fix national minima until rates in a number of trades with the lowest minima have been raised nearer to the average. Sufficient time would be necessary to enable the trades concerned to adapt themselves to such changes without causing serious economic dislocation and unemployment.

WAGE DIFFERENCES BETWEEN SKILLED AND UNSKILLED WORKPEOPLE

The wages of skilled workpeople must be sufficiently above those of unskilled to induce enough people to undergo the manual training and often the technical education needed to qualify for the skilled grades. Yet in some conditions the "margin" for skill becomes too small, and this tends to lower the quality of the goods produced. In periods of inflation the wage rates of skilled workers often rise in less proportion than those of unskilled, thus narrowing the margin. The table below shows the wage rates of skilled and unskilled workers in a number of British industries in October 1949.[1]

[1] In industries in which higher rates are paid in London and lower rates in rural districts than in large provincial towns, the figures given in the table are for large provincial towns.

The figures given from the unweighted average of the wage rates of unskilled workers was 83·4 per cent of those of skilled workers.

WAGE RATES OF SKILLED AND UNSKILLED WORKPEOPLE IN VARIOUS BRITISH INDUSTRIES AT OCTOBER 1949

Industry	Wage Rates of Skilled Workers		Wage Rates of Unskilled Workers		Unskilled Rate as percentage of Skilled Rate
	Weekly Rates				
	s.	d.	s.	d.	
Railway Waggon Repairing	107	6	95	6	89·0
Boot and Shoe Repairing..	107	0	95	0	88·8
Agricultural Machinery ..	107	0	94	0	87·8
Biscuit Manufacture ..	111	0	96	0	86·5
Engineering	107	0	92	0	86·0
Spring Manufacture ..	108	10½	92	6¼	85·0
Railway Workshops ..	110	0	92	6	84·2
Shipbuilding	109	0	90	0	82·6
Drugs and Fine Chemicals	108	0	98	0	81·5
Paper Bag Making ..	114	0	92	0	80·7
Stationery Manufacture ..	122	6	99	0	80·7
Flour Milling	124	0	100	0	80·6
Light Castings	120	9	95	6	78·9
	Hourly Rates				
Leather Tanning	2	5	2	2	90·0
Rubber Tyre Manufacture	2	4½	2	1½	89·5
Shirt Making	2	5	2	1½	88·0
Glove Manufacture ..	2	5	2	1	86·2
Vehicle Building	2	9	2	4	84·8
Furniture	2	8½	2	3½	84·6
Hat, Cap, and Millinery ..	2	4	1	11½	83·9
Glass Processing	2	10½	2	4½	82·6
Road Vehicle Repairing ..	2	7	2	1½	82·2
Electricity Supply	2	11	2	4¾	82·1
Saw Mills	2	9	2	3	81·8
Constructional Engineering	2	9	2	3	81·8
Heating Engineering ..	2	10¾	2	4	80·5
Building	2	10	2	3½	80·0[1]
Jewellery	2	8	2	1¼	78·9
Heavy Chemical	2	11½	2	3½	77·5
Cement Manufacture ..	2	10½	2	2½	76·8

[1] This ratio was raised in July 1950 to 84 per cent, as a result of the adoption of a fixed difference of 5½d. an hour for unskilled workers below the rate for skilled. On this basis a rise in wages results in reducing the percentage difference and vice versa.

This was after nearly a decade of rising prices, and the margin for skill was higher before the war. The smallest difference shown in the table was only 10 per cent, while in the industry with the biggest difference the unskilled workers' rate was 22·5 per cent below that of skilled workers. This range is largely the result of differences from industry to industry in the customary grading of workpeople. In some industries a worker becomes skilled only after a long apprenticeship or period of training, often of five years, while in other industries the term "skilled" may be applied to workpeople who are "experienced" after a few months, or at most a year or two. In the latter industries, "experienced" workers may be doing the same kind of work as unskilled workers who are learning the job, whereas in industries with a long apprenticeship skilled workers do a different kind of work from that of unskilled labourers.

RELATIVE WAGES OF MEN AND WOMEN

Causes of differences in the wages of men and women are considered in the section on "Equal Pay for Equal Work." Here, statistics are given for Britain to show the relationship between the wages of men and women. In July 1950, the number of females in employment in Britain for every 100 males was 45·3, compared with only 37·7 in July 1938. The increase was largely due to greater opportunities for employment of females in a period of keen demand for labour, and to the continued employment after the war of many women who had gone into industry during the war. In the same period the ratio of women's to men's wages rose as is shown by the table below. The hourly earnings give the better comparison, as men's weekly earnings are for a somewhat longer working week than those of women.

EARNINGS OF MEN AND WOMEN IN BRITISH MANUFACTURING INDUSTRIES, 1938 TO 1950[1]

Date	Average Weekly Earnings			Average Hourly Earnings		
	Men[2]	Women[3]	Ratio of Women's to Men's Earnings	Men[2]	Women[3]	Ratio of Women's to Men's Earnings
	s. d.	s. d.	Percentage	s. d.	s. d.	Percentage
October 1938	69 0	32 6	47·1	1 5·4	0 9·0	51·7
1946	120 9	65 3	54·0	2 6·4	1 6·4	60·5
1948	137 11	74 6	54·0	2 11·4	1 9·5	60·8
1950	150 5	82 7	54·9	3 1·9	1 11·6	62·2

[1] The statistics are those compiled and published by the Ministry of Labour for 18 industry groups for the last pay-week of October in each of the years given.
[2] Twenty-one years of age and over.   [3] Eighteen years of age and over.

297

The fact that women's hourly earnings in October 1950 were only 62·2 per cent of those of men has no bearing on the question of the rates paid respectively to men and women for equal work, as the figures for the men include a much greater proportion of highly paid skilled workers, and men do more overtime than women. This element of incomparability can be substantially reduced if not altogether ruled out by comparing the wage rates for similar grades of men and women fixed by voluntary collective agreements or by statutory bodies. The table below gives such rates; where the occupation is stated men and women do the same kind of work, but where only the industry is given the rates are usually for unskilled men and unskilled women respectively, who, though in the same general grade, may do work which is different in kind.

COMPARISON OF THE WAGE RATES OF MEN AND WOMEN IN VARIOUS
BRITISH INDUSTRIES AT OCTOBER 1949

Industry and Occupation	Men's Rates		Women's Rates		Women's Rates as percentages of Men's Rates
	Weekly				
	s.	d.	s.	d.	
Licensed Residential Establishments					
Clerks and Receptionists ..	113	0	93	0	82·0
Cloakroom Attendants ..	93	0	70	6	75·7
Cooks	123	0	100	6	82·0
Lift-Attendants	93	0	70	6	75·7
Waiters or Waitresses	103	0	83	0	80·5
Unlicensed Places of Refreshment					
Clerks	97	0	74	6	76·7
Waiters	82	0	59	6	72·5
Cooks	99	6	77	0	77·2
Industrial and Staff Canteens					
Assistant Cooks	89	0	60	6	67·8
Cooks	101	0	68	0	67·2
Head Cooks	114	0	83	0	72·8
Domestic Staffs of Hospitals[1]					
Porters	100	0	75	0	75·0
Ward Orderlies	106	0	81	0	76·3
Ambulance Drivers	110	0	85	0	77·2
Cooks	112	0	87	0	77·6
Post Office (Maximum Rates)					
Telegraphists	133	0	103	0	77·4
Telephonists	132	0	101	0	76·5
Agriculture (most areas)	94	0	71	0	75·5

[1] Provincial towns.

Industry and Occupation	Men's Rates		Women's Rates		Women's Rates as percentages of Men's Rates
	Weekly				
Wallpaper Manufacture	108	2	81	5	75·3
Electric Cable Making	92	7	67	10	73·2
Brewing (Sheffield)	104	6	76	1	72·8
Engineering	103	0	75	0	72·8
Bobbin Making	96	6	70	0	72·5
Jute	84	6	61	0	72·2
Shop Assistants (Retail Food)	92	0	66	0	71·8
Drugs and Fine Chemicals	98	0	70	0	71·3
Warehouse Workers (Wholesale Grocery)	97	0	69	0	71·2
Shop Assistants (Drapery)	93	6	67	6	71·1
Iron and Steel Wire	90	0	63	9	70·8
Paper Bag and Box	92	0	65	0	70·5
Clerks (Milk Distribution)	99	6	70	0	70·2
Soap, Candle, etc.	100	0	70	0	70·0
Flax and Hemp Spinning	88	8	61	9	69·6
Flour Milling	100	0	69	6	69·5
Light Castings	95	6	66	0	69·1
Silk	95	0	65	0	68·4
Corn Trade (London)	102	0	68	0	66·7
Carpet Manufacture	92	5	61	2	66·2
Textile Bleaching	92	6	61	0	65·8
Bacon Curing	96	9½	63	3	65·3
Paint	100	0	64	0	64·0
	Hourly				
Jewellery Polishers	2	7½	2	0	76·2
Asbestos	2	1⅞	1	7	73·2
Saw Mill Workers	2	3	1	7¾	72·9
Vehicle Building	2	4	1	8¼	72·5
Road Vehicle Repairing	2	1½	1	6½	72·5
Dressmaking (Wholesale)	1	11½	1	5	72·3
Leather Tanning	2	2	1	6½	71·0
Brewing (West Riding)	2	4½	1	8¼	70·8
Heavy Chemicals	2	3½	1	7½	70·8
Rayon	2	0½	1	5	69·3
Rope Making	2	0¾	1	5	68·7
Glass Container Manufacture	2	1¼	1	5	67·2
Piano Manufacture	2	6½	1	8½	67·1
Shirt Making	2	1½	1	5	66·5
Retail Bespoke Tailoring	2	3¼	1	5½	64·2
Hosiery (Midlands)	2	3⅛	1	5	62·7

Women's wage rates in the preceding table were 71·5 per cent of men's rates, this being the unweighted average of the percentages given in the last column. The highest percentage was 82, and the lowest was 62·7. Some agreements specify the proportion of women's to men's rates; for example, in agreements regulating the wages of workpeople employed in the non-trading services of local government authorities, women are to be paid 75 per cent of the rates paid to men in similar grades, while in the corn trade they are paid two-thirds of the men's rates.

Another comparison is between the minimum rates of adult men and women fixed by Trade Boards and Wage Councils for the lowest grades of workers in the industries covered. Averages of these rates are tabulated below.

AVERAGES OF STATUTORY MINIMUM RATES OF WAGES, 1929 AND 1950[1]

Year	Average of Minimum Weekly Rates		Women's Average as percentage of Men's Average
	Men	Women	
	s. d.	s. d.	
1929	50 0	27 9	55·5
1950	88 11	60 11	68·3

[1] The 1929 figures are averages of the minimum hourly rates (multiplied by 48) fixed by Trade Boards in 43 different branches of industry; the 1950 figures are similar averages for 48 branches of industry. The rates averaged are for adult males 21 years of age and over and for adult females 18 years of age and over.

The narrowing of the difference during the period of twenty-one years is noteworthy, yet it is improbable that the productivity of men in these trades in 1950 was nearly 50 per cent more than that of women, especially as much relatively light work is included. Although these minimum rates are for comparable grades in the sense that they are for similar lowest grades of unskilled work in the trades covered, they are rates for work which in some trades is different in kind, and the higher rates for men are partly a payment for greater physical strength.

In some industries where men and women do the same kind of work, and especially where the work is skilled or semi-skilled, the margin between their rates of pay is narrower. Time rates are sometimes equal; piece-rates are more often equal, and where this is so the biggest pay packets go to those with the biggest output, irrespective of whether they are men or women. In cotton weaving large numbers of men and women do the same kind of work and their wage rates are the same, but men, especially those with dependants, are keener to earn more by taking charge of more looms and they also work on night shifts. In some occupations in the woollen industry men and women are paid at the same rates. These equal pay arrangements in the textile industries are of long standing. In the engineering industries during the war large numbers of women did the same kind of semi-skilled work as men, and were paid at the same rates, and this practice has been continued since the war. Men and women bus conductors in some areas are paid at equal rates.

Civil Service Salaries

Controversy on the question of equal pay for equal work has been greatest in the Civil Service and the teaching profession. In the Civil Service the starting salaries for the lowest grades in the administrative and executive classes, and in other categories, are equal for men and women, but salary increments in these grades are less favourable for women than for men, and at the top of the scales women's salaries are only 80 per cent of men's for Ministry of Labour cadets, 82·8 per cent for executive class junior officers, and 86·6 per cent for assistant principals in the administrative class. In intermediate grades women's salaries are often from 85 per cent to 88 per cent of men's salaries, with smaller differences for the higher paid officers. For a few of the most senior posts the salaries of men and women are equal. These relationships are illustrated in the table on page 302.

For a few professional and technical grades the Government pays the same salaries to men and women, e.g. doctors, physiotherapists, and pharmacists.[1] In recent years the Government has approved the principle of equal pay for general adoption throughout the Civil Service, but has successively postponed its application because of the cost involved until the finances of the Government are more favourable.

For teachers in schools controlled by the public authorities in England and Wales the minimum salaries for women are about 90 per cent of those for men, but the differences widen until at the maximum women's salaries are about 80 per cent of those for men. The scales are illustrated in the table on page 303. They are Burnham salary scales, and similar ratios between the salaries of men and women are established in the Burnham scales for teachers in polytechnics, schools of commerce, and schools of art.

In universities in Britain, the salary scales are equal for men and

[1] For some of these grades, for example pharmacists, employed in the colonies, women's salaries are lower than men's.

BRITISH CIVIL SERVICE
Relative Salaries of Men and Women, 1951–52[1]

Class	Men's Scales	Women's Scales	Ratio of Women's to Men's Salary
Administrative Class	£ £	£ £	Percentage
Assistant Principal ..	400 to 750	400 to 650	100 to 86·6
Principal..	1,000 to 1,375	880 to 1,200	88·0 to 87·3
Assistant Secretary ..	1,500 to 2,000	1,340 to 1,850	89·3 to 92·5
Under Secretary ..	2,500	2,325	95·0
Executive Class			
Junior Executive Officers[2]	300 to 700	300 to 580	100 to 82·8
Higher Executive Officers	715 to 865	600 to 735	83·8 to 84·9
Senior Executive Officers	900 to 1,075	775 to 910	86·1 to 84·6
Chief Executive Officers	1,100 to 1,325	930 to 1,150	84·5 to 86·4
Higher Posts	1,325 to 1,900	1,150 to 1,725	86·4 to 90·8
Inland Revenue			
Inspectors of Taxes ..	390 to 865	390 to 735	100 to 85·0
Inspectors, Higher Grade	900 to 1,160	775 to 1,010	86·1 to 87·1
Senior Inspectors ..	1,200 to 1,475	1,040 to 1,325	86·7 to 89·8
Principal Inspectors ..	1,675	1,675	100
Ministry of Labour and National Service			
Cadets	350 to 700	350 to 560	100 to 80·0
Grade 4 Posts	715 to 915	600 to 760	83·9 to 82·9
Grade 3 Posts	925 to 1,125	775 to 980	83·5 to 87·0
Grade 2 Posts	1,100 to 1,325	930 to 1,150	84·5 to 86·7
Grade 1 Posts	1,325 to 1,475	1,150 to 1,325	86·4 to 89·8
Regional Controllers ..	1,500 to 2,000	1,340 to 1,850	89·3 to 92·5
H.M. Inspector of Schools			
Inspectors	900 to 1,370	800 to 1,200	88·8 to 87·5
Staff Inspectors ..	1,420 to 1,620	1,225 to 1,450	86·2 to 89·5
Divisional Inspectors ..	1,520 to 1,620	1,325 to 1,450	87·0 to 89·5
Chief Inspectors ..	1,800	1,625	90·5
H.M. Inspectors of Factories			
Inspectors, Class 1, B. ..	650 to 900	650 to 800	100 to 88·8
Inspectors, Class 1, A. ..	800 to 1,160	690 to 985	86·1 to 85·0
Superintending Inspectors	1,250 to 1,450	1,075 to 1,275	86·0 to 87·8
Deputy Chief Inspectors	1,800	1,625	90·5
Chief Inspector	2,125	2,125	100
Other Classes[3]			
Assistant Experimental Officers	275 to 586	275 to 489	100 to 83:4
Experimental Officers ..	628 to 786	533 to 655	84·8 to 83·3
Assistant Statisticians ..	400 to 750	400 to 650	100 to 86·7
Main Grade Statisticians	1,000 to 1,375	880 to 1,200	88·0 to 87·3
Welfare Officers (Grade II)	500 to 600	425 to 500	85·0 to 83·3
Research Assistants[2]	390 to 650	390 to 525	100 to 80·6
Scientific Officers ..	440 to 707	440 to 576	100 to 81·5
Senior Scientific Officers[4]	781 to 980	649 to 875	83·1 to 89·3
Principal Scientific Officers[4]	1,033 to 1,377	907 to 1,218	87·8 to 88·4

[1] The salary scales given are for civil servants working in London. In the provinces the scales are somewhat lower. Extra duty allowances are paid to most

women, though in practice the highest posts are largely filled by men, the number of professorships held by women being only 1 or 2 per cent of the number held by men.[5] In some universities abroad, however, the salary scales for the same appointment are lower for women than for men. For example, in South African universities,

BURNHAM ANNUAL SALARY SCALES FOR TEACHERS, APRIL 1951*

Category	Men	Women	Women's Salaries as percentage of Men's Salaries
Qualified Assistants	£	£	
Minimum	375	338	90·1
Maximum	630	504	80·0
Graduates			
Minimum	435	386	88·7
Maximum	690	552	80·0
Head Teachers			
With 101–200† scholars			
Minimum	545	486	89·2
Maximum	800	652	81·5
With 501 to 600 scholars			
Minimum	695	616	88·6
Maximum	950	782	82·3

* Additional payments are made in some schools for "designated" posts and other posts of special responsibility, and for training. In the London area salaries are £36 a year higher, or if 16 years of full-time service has been completed in London or the teacher is 37 years of age the salaries are £48 a year higher.

† Graduates, in charge of primary and secondary schools.

the salaries of women in the lecturer and senior lecturer grades are usually between 80 per cent and 90 per cent of those of men. In the University of Sydney, Australia, the salary scales of lecturers and

of the staff on salaries under £1,350 a year, the allowances in London being 8 per cent of salary. Salaries are raised by annual increments from the minimum to the maximum of the scale.

2 Board of Trade. The starting salary within the scales is determined by age of entry, the minimum being for those who enter at 20 years of age.

3 In various departments.

4 Admiralty; also Ministry of Agriculture and Fisheries (Veterinary Laboratory, Weybridge).

5 Some posts which, though attached to universities, are in effect for Government work, are paid similarly to civil servants, with lower rates for women than for men above minimum salaries; this applies, for example, to bacteriologists and biochemists doing agricultural research.

303

senior lecturers are equal for men and women, but a cost-of-living
addition is somewhat greater for men than for women, but when
the salaries and cost-of-living allowances are combined the difference
in favour of men is only about 3 per cent. In some academic appointments in Dublin, for example at the Veterinary College, the salaries
of women are around 85 per cent of those of men.

WAGE DIFFERENCES BETWEEN LOCALITIES

The differences considered in this section are those between
localities and regions within the same country, though their causes are
similar to those responsible for wage differences from country to
country. They include differences in the efficiency of labour, of
industrial management, organization, and capital equipment, and
also differences in natural resources, in the cost of living, and in
custom and tradition. Theoretically, mobility of labour, capital, and
goods, should remove wage differences resulting from all these
causes except the first, but in practice the various mobilities are so
imperfect and restricted that differences persist. In small countries
the differences are small compared with those in such countries as
the United States, which have several distinct economic and climatic
regions, and some racial localization.

In countries with nation-wide organizations of employers and
workpeople, wages in many industries are regulated by national
agreements. Some of these, in geographically compact countries like
Britain, fix uniform standard wages for an industry throughout the
country, but other national agreements classify towns or districts
into grades (*ortsklasse*) and fix different rates for each grade.[1]
Where towns are graded the trade-union representatives frequently
try in their negotiations to have some towns put into a higher grade,
which would have the effect of increasing the wages of workpeople
in those towns without the wage scales for the various grades of
towns being changed. Many agreements are regional or local, and
wage rates are fixed independently for each region or locality, or, in
many countries, for example, the United States, by agreements with
individual firms. In Britain in some industries wage rates are fixed
independently in separate agreements for England and Wales, for
Scotland, and for Northern Ireland. The Commonwealth Arbitration Court in Australia declares basic rates periodically for the
capital cities of each State, the differences in money wages being
calculated according to differences in the cost of living, so that "real"
basic wages shall be equal.

1 A few agreements classify firms into groups, with different rates for each group.

LOCAL DIFFERENCES IN WAGE RATES OF ADULT MALE WORKPEOPLE, OCTOBER 1, 1949

Occupation	Grade of Towns			Ratio to London (= 100)	
	London	Large Towns	Small Towns and Rural Areas	Large Towns	Small Towns and Rural Areas
	Weekly Rates				
	s. d.	s. d.	s. d.		
Railway Porters.. ..	102 6	99 6	98 6	97·1	96·1
Railway Signalmen ..	123 0	120 0	120 0	97·6	97·6
Hand Compositors[1] ..	140 0	122 6	115 0	87·5	82·1
Shop Assistants (Food)..	96 0	92 0	87 0	95·8	90·6
Shop Assistants (Drapery)	98 0	93 6	89 6	95·4	91·3
Corn Trade Labourers ..	102 0	100 0	94 0	98·0	92·1
Telegraphists[2]	144 0	133 0	123 0	92·4	85·4
Telephonists[2]	140 0	132 0	128 0	94·3	91·4
Postmen[2]	126 0	117 0	109 0	92·9	84·7
Road Haulage Drivers[3]..	107 0	102 0	98 0	95·3	91·6
Road Haulage Porters ..	99 0	96 6	94 0	97·5	94·9
County Council Roadmen	104 0	97 0	94 0	93·3	90·4
Hospital Labourers ..	106 0	100 0	97 0	94·3	91·5
Ward Orderlies	112 0	106 0	103 0	94·6	92·0
Ambulance Drivers ..	116 0	110 0	107 0	94·3	92·2
Hospital Cooks	118 0	112 0	109 0	94·9	92·4
Envelope Making					
Cutters	128 6	122 6	115 0	95·3	89·5
Packers	121 6	104 0	99 0	85·6	81·5
Porters	113 6	99 0	94 0	87·2	82·8
Licensed Residences					
Receptionists	115 0	113 0	110 0	98·3	95·7
Cloakroom Attendants	95 0	93 0	90 0	97·9	94·7
Waiters	105 0	103 0	100 0	98·1	95·2
	Hourly Rates				
Building Craftsmen ..	2 11½	2 10	2 8½	95·8	91·5
Building Labourers ..	2 4½	2 3½	2 2	95·6	91·2
Skilled Cement Workers	2 11	2 10½	2 10	98·6	97·1
Cement Labourers ..	2 3·3	2 2½	2 1·7	97·1	94·1
Land Drainage Labourers	2 4	2 2	2 1½	92·9	91·1
Bakers (1st hands) ..	2 4	2 3½	2 2½	98·2	94·6
Bakers (oven men) ..	2 3½	2 3	2 2	98·2	94·5
Glass Processing					
Skilled	3 0½	2 10½	2 10½	94·5	94·5
Labourers	2 6½	2 4½	2 4½	93·4	93·4

[1] Book and job (men).
[2] The figures are the maximum rates paid to men in the Post Office services.
[3] Drivers of 1-ton to 5-ton vehicles.

In the table on the preceding page, figures are given for a number of occupations in Britain for which wage rates differing by localities are fixed in agreements and wage determinations. In some agreements and determinations only two different scales are fixed, one for London and the second for the rest of the country, but in others there are three, four, or five scales each for a different grade of town. Where there are more than three different scales, the table gives figures only for London, the next grade (which consists entirely or mainly of large towns) and the last grade, consisting mainly of small towns and rural areas.[1] The rates throughout are for men.

The average of the rates tabulated above for large towns is 94·9 per cent of the average rates in London, the range being from less than 2 per cent below the London rates to more than 14 per cent below. Small towns and rural areas averaged 91·5 per cent of the London rates, the range being from less than 3 per cent below the London rates to about 18 per cent below, for hand compositors in the printing industry. It must be emphasized that in many British industries, the rates of wages, unlike those in the table, are uniform throughout the country, with no differences between London and other centres.

---

[1] According to some agreements, London rates apply throughout an area up to a specified number of miles (12 or 15) from Charing Cross. Small towns are defined in some agreements as those with less than 50,000 inhabitants, and in others as those with less than 10,000 inhabitants. In some agreements, large and medium-sized towns are grouped together.

18

Equal Pay for Equal Work[1]

THE PRINCIPLE "equal pay for equal work" together with its converse "unequal pay for unequal work" are part of the problem of relative wages, and are closely related to job evaluation and merit rating which are discussed in another chapter. They can be stated in a more generalized form, that payment should be proportionate to work done. Equal pay for equal work seems so fair that it might be expected to command general agreement and universal application, yet many difficulties are met in putting it into practice. They mainly arise in trying to decide, in the complexities of industrial processes and methods, what is "equal work." Controversy over the adoption of the principle has been most acute on the relation between the pay of men and women, and in many discussions this is the sole problem considered, and the principle is used as a slogan in the campaign against sex discrimination in the fixing of wages. The problem, however, is wider, as many jobs done by men are paid unequally though the work is equal.

Several distinctions must be drawn. A number of workpeople may be doing identical work in the sense that the conditions of the job, the tools, and the material used and the product are the same for all. In other words, the conditions, processes, and products are standardized. Nevertheless, the workpeople cannot be standardized and there may be considerable difference in their experience and efficiency, and therefore in the amount and quality of their output. If the work is suitable for piece rates and the same piece rate is applied to each worker, then the earnings of each worker will depend on his or her output, and the principle of equal pay for equal work will be roughly operative, with, however, inequalities of earnings resulting, and properly so, from differences in efficiency. For reasons given later, the use of equal piece rates may not entirely

[1] *The Report of the Royal Commission on Equal Pay*, 1944–1946 (Cmd. 6937), gives a detailed survey of this subject, which is also reviewed in the *Report of the War Cabinet Committee on Women in Industry*, Cmd. 135, of the year 1919; the latter includes a Minority Report by Mrs. Sidney Webb strongly supporting equal pay for men and women on equal work.

satisfy the principle. If time rates are paid, then the adoption of the principle implies that a different rate should be fixed for each worker according to his or her efficiency. There are, however, many objections to this method, including risks of favouritism, and errors of judgment in determining the efficiency of each worker, resulting in discontent among the workpeople, so that the fixing of "the rate for the job" equally for all workpeople is strongly supported. This can, however, work equitably only if, by careful selection, the workers on the job are approximately equal in efficiency. Such selection also may involve favouritism and errors of judgment, but most classifications are imperfect and "absolute" fairness is scarcely practicable. The aim should be to get as near as possible to it.

In addition to the conditions discussed in the preceding paragraph, consideration must be given to the idea of equal pay for work of equal value to the employer, and to that of equal pay for equal efforts and sacrifices by workpeople. Where overhead costs are big, for example, where workpeople operate costly machines, those workpeople whose output is large are of greater value to the employer than workpeople whose output is small. He may, therefore, either pay them an output bonus in addition to their time wages or piecework earnings, or replace the slower workers and build up a team consisting of workers each of whom has about the same high rate of output.

Work may be equal though done in different industries, for example, the shovelling of coal into furnaces at a textile mill and at a tannery respectively, and, if the conditions are alike, the wages should be equal. In practice, however, imperfect mobility of labour often prevents such wage equality. If the work is done in different localities where the cost of living is unequal, then equal "pay" would involve unequal money wages to yield equal real wages. Where workpeople are on jobs unlike in kind, for example, pattern-makers in engineering, carpenters in building, and cutters in clothing, no exact basis can be found for establishing equality or degrees of inequality. However, if different jobs require similar physical effort, intelligence, training, skill, and experience, are performed under comparable conditions, and have similar prospects, they can be considered as equivalents and there will be a long-term tendency towards wage equality. Because of differences from industry to industry in the demand for and supply of labour, and in capacity to pay, together with low mobility of skilled labour between industries, the tendency will operate only slowly, and often before equality has been reached changes in the relative prosperity and labour market conditions in the industries may cause new divergencies in wages. Any measures which, in the circumstances defined, strengthen the tendency towards equality are advantageous by leading to fairer wage relationships.

Wages in depressed industries usually fall below those paid for work requiring similar skill, energy, and experience in prosperous industries. Thus in Britain in the inter-war years wages in unsheltered industries, i.e. those exposed to foreign competition, fell substantially below those in sheltered, home market industries. As an example, the wages of coal-miners, which, on the basis of the nature of the work should be high relatively to those in most other manual occupations, were considerably below the wages in industries calling for less arduous toil, skill, and experience. Because miners' wages form a large part of the total cost of production of coal, they are closely linked with the "value" or selling price of coal, and in the inter-war years this was low, largely because of the competition of oil and water power. Not until the number of miners was reduced by nearly half a million and until the price of coal rose because of shortage, did the wages of miners rise again to a "fair" relationship with those in other industries. The converse of the above argument is that prosperity and shortage of labour in an industry may cause wages to rise above their "proper" relationship with those in other industries which require similar effort, skill, and experience.

Discrimination in the form of a "colour bar" in some countries excluding coloured workpeople from certain skilled occupations distorts wage relationships both by increasing competition among the coloured workpeople for unskilled work and therefore lowering their wages, and by reducing the number of workpeople in skilled jobs and therefore raising their wages. The colour bar thus artificially widens the wage gap. Not infrequently, coloured workpeople succeed in acquiring skill and in fact do skilled jobs from which they are formally barred, but they are paid at unskilled or semi-skilled rates in violation of the principle of equal pay for equal work.

Women's Wages

A survey of industry shows that many jobs are done exclusively or almost exclusively by men, others by women, and that "overlap" occupations in which men and women are employed together on the same kind of work are relatively few. Occupational segregation of the sexes is based partly on sound reasons and partly on prejudices held by employers or male workers or both. Thus, dock labour, underground mining, iron and steel work, shipping, and locomotive driving, are illustrative of jobs which, because of heavy physical toil and arduous conditions, are done by men.[1] Some textile jobs are done by women, some by men, and some have a mixed labour force. Another example of these differences is the light engineering industry. Some labour laws prohibit the employment of women on work considered unsuitable, e.g. underground mining and night work, while restrictions on overtime are stricter in some industries for women than for men.

It is sometimes argued that because women are not suitable for employment in the heavy industries the supply of women available for the lighter industries is increased relatively to that of men, and this is a cause of their lower wages. But this is more than offset by the fact that the supply of women for paid employment is greatly reduced by the withdrawal of women from the labour market on marriage. Also, wages in the lighter industries in which both men and women are employed are determined by the relation between the demand for and the supply of labour. The supply consists of men and women, and their wages depend on their relative efficiency.

The number of jobs open to women and the size of the overlap area are being increased by the greater use of mechanical aids and power which reduce the amount of physical strength required. The division of hitherto skilled jobs into several semi-skilled processes enables women to become proficient after a few weeks' training and experience, whereas they would not have been willing to undertake an apprenticeship of several years to become skilled artisans as they expect to leave industry on marriage and would not reap the benefit of a long apprenticeship.

The exclusion of women from some occupations is often quite artificial, but the breaking down of prejudices against the employment of women is slowly increasing the number of jobs open to them. A historical example is Florence Nightingale's fight for women to become nurses in military hospitals. Opposition to the opening of the medical and legal professions to women died hard. In many manual trades which now employ only men, the introduction of women is opposed by the workmen, who fear loss of employment or lower wage standards from the competition of women. Employers are concerned with getting work done efficiently, and if they can get it done by women at less cost than by men they will prefer to employ women. However, prejudice and opposition may be so strong that though employers may be satisfied that women could do the work efficiently at less cost, they often decide not to employ them because

[1] In Britain more than four million men, or about 20 per cent of all workpeople, are employed in occupations from which women are excluded because of their lower physical strength.

of objections by the men. If they could replace all the men on the job by women they might do this, but frequently it is impracticable.

The average wage rates and earnings of women are substantially below those of men, as is shown in the section on the relative wages of men and women. In many industries the wages of women are only about two-thirds of men's wages. There are many reasons for the differences, an important one being that the proportion of men who undergo long apprenticeship or other training to become skilled artisans and technicians or to gain professional qualifications is much greater than that of women. This is mainly because most girls expect to marry after a few years, and are unwilling to take a lengthy training for skilled work or professional careers, but prefer to do unskilled or semi-skilled jobs which can be quickly learned. The average wages of men are higher because the proportion of skilled workers is greater than among women. The wages are unequal because the work is unequal. Even, however, if comparisons are made between the wages only of unskilled and semi-skilled men and women, the differences in favour of men are substantial. For some jobs women are more suitable than men, and in these they usually displace men entirely because their greater efficiency combined with lower wages results in appreciably lower labour costs.[1] In many occupations employers are satisfied that women's output is lower than that of men, and they therefore either do not employ them, or, if they do so, it is because they can pay them less than men. It would certainly be unsound to enforce equal pay in occupations in which women on unequal pay can produce only 80 per cent or 90 per cent of men's output. Alternatively, it would be injurious if, in consequence of equal pay, women strained beyond their strength to produce as much as men in order to keep their jobs. On some jobs the lower output of women is because they are not so strong as men.

A much larger proportion of men have dependants to maintain, and they therefore tend to work harder than women and girls to ensure good earnings from piece work, and they are keener to work overtime. Absentee rates, especially from sickness, are somewhat higher among women. Turnover is greater among women, and this results in additional costs. When abnormal conditions arise, or when rapid changes in methods are necessary, women are often less flexible and adaptable than men. Also, though on some jobs there may be little difference in the efficiency of men and women while the

[1] During the Second World War, it was found possible in some munition occupations to replace men by the same number of women instead of in the ratio of three women to two men, as had been expected; this was achieved largely by division of processes.

is going on normally, men are often more able to deal with __rgencies and other unexpected breaks in routine. Where, for any of the reasons given, the output of women is lower than that of men, they cost more in capital overheads, administration, and supervision, and, therefore, even when piece rates are paid, lower rates may be fixed for women to allow for these higher overhead costs. Weaker trade union organization among women is also a cause of their lower wages.

In arguing for payment of higher wages to men than to women, attention is often directed to the fact that large numbers of men maintain a wife and family, whereas the number of dependants maintained by women workers is much less.[1] About 70 per cent of men workers over 21 years of age are married, while more than 70 per cent of women workers are spinsters, and if the principle of payment according to need were applied, then men with families to maintain would receive more than spinsters without dependants and also than bachelors without dependants. This would in effect be a system of family allowances and would result in much inequality of pay for equal work, as a man with a large family who was employed on exactly similar work to a bachelor and a spinster would receive more pay for equal work, or even for less work if he were a less efficient worker. This would lead to difficulties mainly because of departure from the sound wage principle of payment for work done, which is the foundation of the proper financial relation between employers and workpeople. The question of family allowances is examined in the next chapter and the desirability of keeping allowances for dependants separate from the wage system is indicated.

Wage rates, including the relative wages of men and women, are determined mainly by demand and supply, and on the supply side the fact that a large proportion of women workers have only themselves to maintain out of their wages makes them willing to accept lower wages than those of men, who, through their unions, will try to insist on enough to meet family needs. People work mainly to meet their needs, and it is broadly true that the greater the need the greater is the effort made to meet the need. In consequence, women and girls tend in much greater proportions than men to go into lower-paid occupations, and substantial numbers are willing to

[1] If, as is frequent, women receive wages about two-thirds those of men, then a single woman without dependants has a material standard of living higher than that of a married man with a family of average size. Single men would, of course, have standards substantially higher than those of single women, and if needs of dependants were to be taken as the basis for wage differences, then bachelors as well as spinsters would have lower wages than men with families.

accept low wages, as they are not wholly dependent on their pay, but receive help from their parents and work mainly for "pin money." Men are keener to undergo training for higher paid jobs, and those with families will often work harder to get more earnings on piece work and will undertake overtime more readily. These attitudes go far to explain differences between men's and women's wages and earnings where work is unequal, but in no way undermine the justice of equal pay where work is equal.

In some professions men and women are paid equal rates, whether they are in established employment or receive fees from clients, but usually the men greatly outnumber the women, e.g. as doctors and lawyers. Also, although payments are at the same rates, men's earnings are higher and promotions more rapid, except for a few outstandingly able women.

Not only in the professions, but in industry, the Civil Service, and other occupations, application of the principle of equal pay for equal work to men and women alike is economically sound and an expression of elementary social justice. But over a wide field of employment employers believe from their experience that men are more efficient, more resourceful, and more productive, whether because of their greater strength, adaptability, wider experience, or their greater needs for dependants. In occupations where these differences exist or where employers believe they exist, the wages of men will be higher than those of women. If in any such occupations equal rates were fixed for men and women, employers would prefer to employ men, and the employment of women would decline. Specially efficient women would continue to be employed, but there would be danger that some women whose output was not equal to that of men might strain themselves in trying to keep their jobs. In those occupations where women can hold their own with men, the interaction of demand and supply will tend to establish equal pay, that is "the rate for the job," but where their output or value to the employer is less than that of men, these forces will result in wage differentials. The removal of prejudice against employment of women would enable demand and supply to determine those occupations in which the pay of men and women should be equal; demand and supply would also determine the proportions of men and women to be employed with greatest efficiency in different occupations.

19

Family Allowances

PROVISION FOR the dependants of workpeople is closely related to the living wage, and is also linked with equal pay for equal work. In making wage demands workpeople claim that wages must be sufficient to meet their needs and those of their families, and yet these needs vary from workmen who have no dependants to those who have large families, and the question must be faced whether the wage system can suitably cope with such differences. Where, as for example in Australia and New Zealand, wage legislation requires the fixing of living wages, a decision has to be taken on the size of the family for which a man's wage will provide, and in practice the "standard" family for this purpose consists of man, wife, and two or three dependent children. For women workers the wage is based on the needs of women who have to provide for the whole of their requirements, but on the assumption, which is often unwarranted, that they have no dependants.

Such decisions do not meet the problem of differences in the numbers of workers' dependants. For example, a wage which is just adequate for a man with wife and two children, is insufficient for workmen with larger families and leaves a surplus for those with fewer dependants. This unsolved problem was powerfully stated by the late Miss Eleanor Rathbone in her book, *The Disinherited Family*, in which she emphasized the failure of the wage system to provide for large families, and indicated the considerable poverty which resulted. She had a special interest in this problem in her advocacy of "equal citizenship" for men and women alike by removal of the legal, economic, and social disabilities of women. In this connection she argued that one of the main reasons why women were paid less than men was that in fixing wages for men the needs of an average family were influential. She therefore urged the introduction of a system of family allowances to meet the needs of dependants, believing that this would facilitate payment of the same rates of wages to men and women for equal work.

Difficulties arise if family allowances are paid by employers as part of the wage system. The sound principle is for the wage to be payment for work done irrespective of the number of dependants or other needs of workpeople. This enables a proper relationship to be maintained between employers and workpeople and tends to ensure, at least over long periods, that workpeople are paid according to their efficiency. It also implies that women with no dependants would, if their work was equal, be paid the same as women with dependants and also as men without or with dependants. Nevertheless, such a wage system leaves unsolved the problem of provision for dependants.

The cost of maintaining dependants has been greatly increased in recent decades in many countries by the introduction of compulsory elementary education, and the progressive raising of the school-leaving age and the age of entry of young persons into employment. Whereas in former times children began to contribute at an early age towards the cost of their maintenance, nowadays they involve heavy expense up to the age of 14, 15, or 16 years. Indeed, a few generations ago a large family was considered to be an economic asset, with children from nine to fourteen years of age contributing substantially to the family income. The virtual disappearance of these conditions raises an issue to-day which did not exist or was much less significant in earlier times.

The economic burden of family maintenance often involves privation in periods of inflation by the lagging of money wages behind the rise in the cost of living as, for example, during and shortly after the First World War. The wage lag had the effect of lowering the standards of living of workpeople, and the burden was greatest among large families whereas those with no dependants had some margin over their own needs. The rise in prices led to payment of cost-of-living bonuses, and often these consisted of flat-rate additions to the wages of all workpeople, whether skilled or unskilled, or of additions of equal percentages based on the rise in the cost of living. In France, Belgium, and several other European countries, however, some employers adopted the experiment of paying family allowances, on the grounds that these would be of benefit to those workpeople whose need was greatest instead of treating all workpeople alike without consideration of differences in their needs.[1] At first, this system was introduced by individual employers for their own workpeople, and the allowances were paid with the wage. This association of allowances with wages thus arose from attempting to deal with the immediate and urgent problem of hardships

[1] In France the family allowance system was also supported by many in the hope that it would stop the fall in the birth rate, which was causing considerable uneasiness.

caused by the rise in the cost of living to those with large families, and little thought was given to anomalies and difficulties which would result.

Shortly after the end of the war, the system ran into heavy weather because of the onset of depression and unemployment. When considering which of their workers to dismiss, employers who were paying family allowances realized that they could cut their wage bill most by getting rid of workpeople with large families, as these were receiving more in wages together with family allowances than workpeople with few or no dependants. Thus the very people for whose benefit the family allowance system had been introduced were often the ones to suffer unemployment because of it.

In order to meet this difficulty, groups of employers in France and in some other European countries devised a system of equalization funds. Employers in an industry, or in several industries in the same district, would join together to set up a fund to which each employer would contribute, and from which the family allowances would be paid. The essential feature of the employers' contributions was that each employer would regularly pay into the fund an amount based on some criterion independent of the number of children in the families of his workpeople. In many of the funds the criterion used was the number of workpeople, each employer paying into the fund each month a specified number of francs for each of the workpeople on his pay-roll. In some funds the total wage bill of each firm was used as the criterion for the firm's contributions. In the textile industry the number of spindles or the number of looms owned by each firm was sometimes adopted as basis, while in the coal-mining industry the tonnage of coal raised was used in calculating the contributions of each colliery company.

The rate of contribution to any fund depended also on the scale of the family allowances adopted, together with the cost of administering the fund and provision for suitable reserves. The scales of allowances varied considerably. In some funds the allowances were at a flat rate of, say, 20 francs for each dependent child; in other funds the allowances were at a successively higher rate for each additional child, for example, 10 francs for the first child, 20 for the second, 30 for the third, and so on, while in yet others the amount of the allowance was reduced for each additional child, being larger for the first than for the second child, for the second than for the third, and perhaps with no allowances after the fifth or sixth child.

A noteworthy feature of the system was that the allowances were paid from the fund and not by the employer, and were thereby separated from the wage system. Also, in many funds the allowances

316

were paid not to the worker but to his wife, and nurse visitors were employed to visit the homes in order to advise mothers about the health of their children, and to prevent abuses such as claims by workmen for more children than they actually had.

As already indicated, the equalization funds separated the family allowances from the wage system, although the payments by employers to the funds formed part of their total labour costs of production. Following the establishment of equalization funds on the initiative of employers, the main subsequent development in France took the form of legislation in which the State adopted principles and methods to guide and control the evolution of the family allowance system.

Proposals for introducing family allowances in Britain were widely discussed in the inter-war years, and investigations were made into the systems which had been introduced in several of the countries of Continental Europe. Within the trade union movement, although there was considerable support for family allowances, a substantial majority was against any method by which family allowances would be closely associated with the wage system. Nor did trade unionists favour an equalization fund system based on employers' contributions. Fear was expressed that the payment of family allowances might lead to a reduction in the total "real" wage bill. It was thought that, for example, in a time of rising prices, allowances might be paid to workpeople with dependent children, in order to offset the rise in the cost of living, but that the wages of workpeople with no dependent children would not be raised or would be raised in less proportion and therefore the purchasing power of the total amount paid in wages to all workpeople would be reduced.

Throughout the inter-war years no significant development took place in Britain, and only a few undertakings introduced family allowances for their employees. There was, however, growing recognition that if family allowances were to be paid they should be completely separated from the wage system, and after the Second World War legislation was passed introducing a universal system of family allowances financed from the national revenues. The system was one part of the comprehensive social welfare legislation enacted in Britain shortly after the war. It provides for the payment of an allowance for each dependent child after the first, the allowance being at the flat rate of eight shillings a child a week. This rate is not sufficient for the full maintenance of the children in respect of whom it is paid, but is a considerable aid by the State to those with the larger families. The adoption of a flat rate is consistent with the

317

policy generally adopted in British social legislation, which provides the same flat rates of benefit for skilled workpeople and others with high wages or salaries as for unskilled low-paid workers. The family allowance system is universal in its application, and there is no means test.[1]

The family allowance system in Britain must be considered in relation to other measures for the economic benefit of those with dependants. These include free education, tax relief, food subsidies, and also social security benefits which take account of dependants, including the wife as well as children.

[1] In necessitous cases additional aid is provided from National Assistance funds, but payments are subject to a means test.

20

Hours of Work

AFTER WAGES, workpeople show greatest interest in hours of work, and demands for satisfactory hours are increasingly insistent as wage standards improve. People must work to live, and until basic needs are met hours of work are subsidiary. Long hours are closely linked with low standards of living, and both are related to poor natural resources and inefficient methods of production, while rich resources and efficient production permit increased leisure. Regulation of hours of work is, however, simpler than that of wages, and once a major change in normal hours has been made they remain stable over longer periods than wages, as they are much less influenced by changes in the prosperity of industry and in the value of money. Thus, whereas wage rates are often changed at yearly intervals, normal hours tend to remain stable for a decade or even a generation.

The problem of hours of work is wider than the working day or week. It includes the working year, particularly the question of annual holidays, and some people hold the view that in the periods of stable employment a discussion of the practicability of a 2,000-hour year would be preferable to that of a 40-hour week. This might be suitable for some industries, but it has not yet gained much support, and demands tend to concentrate on a guaranteed week rather than a guaranteed year. Other problems include the special conditions of continuous processes involving shift working, and those of occupations which are seasonal and are affected by the weather. In addition to paid annual holidays the granting of a longer vacation with pay after each seven or ten years' service would be appreciated by many workpeople; this is adopted in some professions as "sabbatical" leave. The duration of the working life is another aspect of the problem, and the length of working day and week and the intensity of work should not be a cause of shortening the period of efficient working life. Present discussions are, however, mainly concentrated on the length of working day and week, which will be given special consideration in this chapter.

Two outstanding factors in determining hours of work are the avoidance of undue fatigue and the provision of greater leisure. A third consideration has been prominent in periods of severe unemployment, namely reduction of hours as a means of sharing the available work among a large number of workpeople. In attempting to decide the most satisfactory length of working day and week in different circumstances the productivity of industry and therefore the purchasing power of the wages according as longer or shorter hours are adopted will be dominant. In this connection decisions should be based as far as possible upon information showing for each industry, undertaking or occupation, the optimum hours of work, that is, the hours which, with given methods of production, yield the highest output without undue fatigue. Hitherto, however, only meagre information has been available on optimum hours, and systematic research is needed over an extensive field to provide a basis for future policy. Here it may be noted that optimum hours vary according to intensity of work being less in exacting times and occupations than in more leisurely periods or types of work. They are less in Britain to-day than in the Middle Ages, and less now in Western industrial countries than in India or parts of Africa.

Hours of work should rarely exceed optimum hours, and these occasions should be limited to short emergencies, particularly national emergencies such as war-time, when people may need, as for example in Britain in 1940, to work longer and more intensively than would be reasonable in ordinary times. Such excessive effort can only be maintained for relatively short periods, and it involves strain and drawing upon reserves of energy which, if unduly prolonged, would defeat the purpose of securing higher output. For effort which must be long sustained, hours of work should approximate to the optimum. In ordinary times, normal hours of work should never exceed the optimum, but they may be fixed below the optimum if workpeople prefer more leisure to the higher standard of purchasing power which optimum hours would provide.

Below the optimum workpeople must choose between greater leisure and higher real wages. Social considerations come into the reckoning. Thus, optimum hours may be much longer in some occupations than in others; for example, attendants, or ticket collectors at quiet railway stations may be able to continue on duty for twelve hours a day without undue fatigue. Yet they would be "tied" to their workplace, and if an eight-hour day is worked in most industries and occupations, strong demands for a similar day will be made by workpeople employed in such occupations as attendants so that they may not be at a disadvantage in enjoying the amenities of community life including plays, concerts, evening educational courses and sporting events, the times for which are fixed to be convenient for the main body of workpeople. Also if several members of a family work in occupations with a considerable difference in length of working day, family life tends to be disorganized. Again, within an undertaking the organization of labour often makes it impracticable to have some occupations working half an hour or an hour longer or less than others; thus the passing of legislation limiting the hours of women and juveniles in textile factories had the effect of reducing the hours worked by men also, because of the close interrelation of their work with that of the women and young persons. Hence there is a tendency for hours of work to become fairly standardized within a country over a wide range of industries, and for variations between hours in different occupations to be restricted within narrow limits, the variations being less than if optimum hours were applied to each occupation. If the object of policy is to fix a fairly standardized working day and week throughout industry while approximating to optimum hours, the result will be near to an average of optimum hours in each of the main industries though there may be some differences in hours from industry to industry taking account of the special conditions of each.

With these general principles in mind, the reasons for reducing hours of work will now be examined in more detail. First is the avoiding of undue fatigue. Workpeople have a vital interest in maintaining their health and efficiency year after year and are concerned about their earning capacity throughout their working lives, the duration of which should not be reduced by excessive toil. Many employers also wish to conserve the efficiency of their workpeople, especially those in skilled and responsible jobs, and employers and workpeople have a common interest in reducing hours wherever these are longer than the optimum. Both may gain by the change, the employer by greater output, lower costs, and fewer accidents, and the worker by more leisure, higher wages, and less fatigue and less ill-health. Yet some employers have exploited their workpeople by requiring excessive hours, and then dismissing without compensation those whose health broke down under the strain. Such employers may have gained enhanced profits by this method of casting the burden of broken health upon the worker and his family or upon the community. The cry "Too old at forty," was often a consequence of excessive hours and intensity of toil, although even if hours are reasonable, there are some occupations requiring great physical exertion which older men should relinquish to younger people and themselves turn to lighter tasks.

When in various countries during the nineteenth century hours of work were often ten or more a day and sixty or more a week, some employers could have gained by reducing hours. But as already indicated they were able to avoid the burden resulting from break-downs in health, and could usually replace worn-out workers. Then most of them were convinced that in many processes output was roughly proportionate to hours and that reduced hours would involve increased costs, which they would not risk while their competitors at home or abroad were free to work longer hours. Then there was ignorance, as there still is, of what were optimum hours in each industry, and employers therefore played for safety by putting the brake on demands for reduced hours. As, however, technical processes and mechanization became more exacting in the early years of the present century it became increasingly recognized by employers, as well as workpeople, that a ten-hour day and a fifty-three or fifty-four-hour week were too long for the best results in quality and quantity of output. They might have been appropriate in more leisurely days, but were not suitable for the intensity of modern industrial life. Consequently in British industry and in other countries also, the years 1919 to 1921 saw a widespread adoption of the eight-hour day and the forty-eight-hour week, this change being overdue but had been delayed partly as a result of the war. It was found practicable to reduce weekly hours without reducing weekly wages, and also to expect increased output and increased wages as the processes of industry were progressively improved.

The problem changes when instead of desiring to establish opti-mum hours in each industry or a general average optimum, there is a demand for hours less than the optimum. So long as the purpose is to fix optimum hours, use can be made of objective scientific investigation and standards of measurement, although, as already indicated, the research necessary to establish these standards has rarely been done, and only crude approximations based on inade-quate data have been made. Consequently genuine differences of opinion about optimum hours may arise between employers and workpeople, and these can be overcome only by systematic inquiries. Demand for hours below the optimum is an expression of preference for more leisure instead of more purchasing power, and although demand curves for leisure could be drawn in relation to different standards of living and costs of leisure they would probably be of little value as a practical guide in fixing or reducing hours of work. Decisions would be the result of a complex range of social and psychological as well as economic considerations which could not be measured scientifically.

Once basic needs have been met most people work in order to

enjoy life, particularly by having the material and cultural resources to enjoy leisure. Many of them may enjoy their work, but they want a better proportion between work and leisure, that is, less work and more "play." This desire is perfectly reasonable and natural, but the question must be raised: "What price are workpeople prepared to pay for increased leisure below optimum hours?" The answer is difficult to give and the price to be paid is obscured by the effects upon standards of living of progress in the productive efficiency of industry. There was no price to pay when hours were reduced in 1919 and 1920 from 53 or 54 to 48 a week, because the new hours were nearer the optimum than the old, and with existing equipment it proved practicable by improvements in organization and somewhat greater intensity of work to maintain output and real wages. The problem may be illustrated by current demands for a forty-hour week, which squarely raise the issue whether this is below the optimum for most British industries. Data are not adequate to prove this, but it is improbable that output over the whole of industry would be as high for a forty- as for a forty-eight-hour week, and therefore to make the change while maintaining weekly wages would increase costs of production. The Trades Union Congress, however, propose that a forty-hour five-day week should be established in two stages. If it be assumed that optimum hours for the main British industries under present conditions are within the range of forty-five to forty-eight hours a week, and there are grounds for believing this to be a valid assumption, the general adoption of a forty-four- or forty-five-hour week as a first stage would present little danger to the national economy from increased costs as these hours would still be in the neighbourhood of the optimum. The risks involved in further reductions should not be taken while the international balance of payments remains precarious.

By the time the second stage can reasonably be taken the productivity of industry will have increased by improved organization, techniques, and machinery, so that the forty-hour week could be adopted without lowering standards of living, and might permit of higher standards. This does not, however, mean that the shorter week has been gained without cost. Though the standard of living with the shorter week might be higher than it is to-day or was in 1939, it would be less than if optimum hours were worked, and the difference is the material cost of the increased leisure. It is a concealed cost because of the effects of industrial progress. The cost would not be hidden or obscured if industrial conditions were static. Under dynamic conditions, however, workpeople can benefit from increased productivity either by higher standards of material comfort

323

or by more leisure or by some combination of both, and this last method is reasonable and the one likely to be adopted.

Conditions of production being dynamic the timing of a substantial general reduction in hours of work is important. Such substantial changes could be avoided by making an infinite number of small changes in each factory and industry to correspond with each improvement in productivity. But this would ignore psychological and social aspects of the problem and the fact that the benefits of improved methods in an undertaking or industry tend to be distributed in part to the whole community by lower prices. Although shorter hours than those worked generally throughout industry are first introduced by the more progressive firms and industries, demands for similar reductions become widespread. It would be impracticable for reductions of a few minutes a day to be made every two or three years, and therefore by accumulation or a kind of integration reductions of several hours a week have been made at intervals measured by decades. The more hours are lowered successively below the optimum the greater the concealed cost, and the less also the attraction of more leisure, which is subject to diminishing returns. Therefore, it is likely that demands for reduced hours will become progressively less insistent after hours have been reduced in the future in advanced industrial countries to 30 or 35 a week, though this will be subject to qualification if the pace of industrial productivity is accelerated.

A substantial reduction of weekly hours below the optimum is best timed when industrial progress over a wide field has considerably increased productivity, thus enabling weekly wages to be maintained as hours are reduced. Such progress facilitated the extensive adoption of the eight-hour day in British industry in 1919 and 1920. The rising price level and a tendency for real wages in a number of industries to lag behind the upward price trend enabled hours to be reduced and at the same time money wages to be raised. The problem of wage adjustment is more difficult in periods of stable prices, but provided industrial progress is adequate and demands for wage increases are suspended or restrained, a reduction in hours can be effected without lowering weekly wages. When demands were made for the adoption of a forty-hour five-day week after the Second World War it was widely recognized that because the country had been impoverished by the war, and was no longer a creditor country but heavily in debt, and had an adverse balance of international payments, and was experiencing labour shortage, the time was unfavourable for the immediate adoption in 1946 or 1947 of the whole reduction. In such circumstances the demands could only be met by delaying the reduction in order to permit the national economy and standards of living to be restored. Increase in costs because of reduced hours would have imperilled the success of the drive to expand exports. In timing reduction of hours consideration must be given to the international situation, including not only trade competition but political aspects. Thus, when the Blum Government introduced the forty-hour week in France, even if internal economic and political conditions had been favourable, the international political situation was so adverse with Germany working much longer hours in the Nazi rearmament drive that French security was seriously menaced.

As the working week becomes shorter various questions of distributing the hours have to be considered. In continuous processes two twelve-hour shifts can be replaced by three eight-hour shifts or four six-hour shifts. A forty- to forty-five-hour week can be concentrated in five days without involving an unduly long working day, and workpeople will usually prefer two free days each weekend to going in for a short Saturday shift. In a number of progressive British undertakings it has been found advantageous to concentrate production on five days, using Saturdays for repairs and overhaul of machinery and equipment, and the relatively high costs of operating a short shift on Saturdays are avoided. A five-day week is likely to cause a diminution of absenteeism. In times of labour shortage increased numbers of women workers, particularly married women, would be attracted to industry if systems were organized for them to work half a normal week, one team working the first half of the week and another the second half, or one doing morning shifts and another the afternoon shifts.

In industries which carry high capital costs for machinery and equipment, reductions in working hours below the optimum imply that each unit of output must carry greater overhead costs, and there is also increased risk of plant becoming out of date before it is worn out. These could be avoided and overhead costs reduced if the plant instead of standing idle for approximately three-quarters of the 168 hours in a week were operated by two shifts of workpeople, the first, for example, from 6 a.m. to 2 p.m. and the second from 2 p.m. to 10 p.m., the teams taking the morning shift every second week. This system would involve some adjustments in the organization of social life, but it would have advantages, and the shorter the working week becomes the more practicable and in some industries the more necessary will the system be.

Standard hours below the optimum impose restrictions upon ambitious workers or those who would prefer to work longer and earn more money. Also, optimum hours vary not only with each occupation but with individual workpeople, and in highly organized large-scale undertakings it would be impracticable to meet individual differences by variations in length of working hours. Ambitious workers and those whose optimum hours are longer than the average can usually find an outlet either by greater intensity of work, or by making opportunities for themselves in activities outside the factory.

Hours worked beyond the normal or standard working day, and also work during week-ends, at night, and on public holidays are usually paid at higher rates than those for ordinary hours. Overtime hours are often paid at time-and-a-quarter or time-and-a-half, the additional rate sometimes being increased for overtime beyond two hours, while work on Sundays and public holidays is often paid at double time. It must be noted, however, that in some seasonal occupations, for example building, normal or standard hours are longer in summer than in winter, and overtime rates of pay begin only after these longer standard hours have been worked. The objects of the higher rates of pay for overtime are to compensate the worker for extra fatigue and interference with his leisure-time arrangements, and at the same time to impose the penalty of higher costs on the employer so that he will as far as possible plan to avoid overtime, which would be worked only occasionally at a time of exceptional need. Also, wherever possible workpeople should be warned a day or two ahead that they may be needed for overtime, so that they may be spared the inconvenience of a last-minute call.

However, although workpeople desire to safeguard their leisure, many of them are eager to work overtime because of the higher earnings it brings, and they will manœuvre to gain these higher rates. In 1940, when a seven-day week was worked in some branches of the British engineering industry to meet a desperate shortage of munitions, a tendency developed, as the strain of working day after day without a break began to be felt, for workpeople to take a day off in the middle of the week which was paid at ordinary rates, but to work on Sunday because of the double rates. Sometimes a shorter "normal" working week is demanded, not so much from a desire for increased leisure, but in the expectation that the same hours as before will be worked but that those beyond the new normal will be paid at overtime rates and therefore that earnings will be increased. Thus fairly regular overtime would be worked, and in essence therefore such a demand is really for increased wages and not for reduced hours.

Turning now to the question of reducing hours as a means of

326

sharing the work available in a period of severe unemployment, this method could be applied either in a single industry suffering from a surplus of labour, or to many industries experiencing a trade cyclical depression. In each the situation is temporary, and the reduction of hours would be temporary also. Again, the conditions of unemployment imply reduced output and therefore would not be favourable to maintaining weekly wages, which would involve raising hourly wages for the shorter week. Essentially the method is a sharing of the work and a sharing of the wages instead of concentrating the unemployment on a part of the workers who would be wholly out of work and keeping the others at full-time or nearly full-time work. It is really systematic short-time for all or a large part of the workers. The circumstances, object, and method of such a reduction are therefore quite distinct from those when a long-term increase of leisure is adopted.

During the world depression in the early 1930's when the forty-hour week was discussed at meetings of the International Labour Organization, considerable support came from countries which wanted reduced hours for the purpose of spreading employment and would have agreed to hourly wages remaining unchanged and weekly wages therefore diminished in proportion to the reduction of hours. The representatives of these countries did not, however, make it clear whether or not they wished the reduction of hours to be temporary or permanent, but the main object was a remedy for unemployment, there being fear of serious unrest if large masses of workpeople remained idle. The British trade union representatives took a different line. They considered a shorter working week to be valuable in reducing unemployment, but favoured permanent reduction without any lowering of weekly wages, and argued that technical progress in industry was a cause of unemployment and also provided the means for maintaining or increasing wages for reduced hours. Their policy was opposed by representatives of the British Government and of British employers. For various reasons, including deterioration of international political relations, and particularly the Nazi menace and withdrawal of Germany from the Organization, little progress was made.

Proposals and agreements for establishing a guaranteed week, which became prominent during and after the Second World War, are intended to give security against considerable under-employment rather than against total unemployment. They are, however, more a question of wages than of hours of work and leisure, being concerned with securing to the worker a minimum weekly income. Raising the school-leaving age and earlier compulsory retirement of elderly

327

workers have been supported as remedies for unemployment by reducing the length of working life. The raising of the school-leaving age should, however, be adopted for its own sake as a means of raising the educational standards of the community, and not as a means of holding juvenile workers off the labour market, but in periods of great unemployment among young persons it would be reasonable to require those who reached school-leaving age, but had no jobs, to continue their education for a further period.

Earlier retirement, though advocated as a remedy for unemployment, has often been regarded as a desirable permanent change. This assumes that people would prefer to retire at, say, sixty than at sixty-five or seventy, but this is certainly not valid for large numbers of people so long as they remain fit. From the point of view of the national economy the loss of their services would be a disadvantage, especially in times of labour shortage. Then in Britain and other countries the declining birth rates have been leading towards a growing proportion of old to young people, and to reduce the age of retirement would increase the burden upon the smaller number in the lower age groups of supporting a larger number of aged people. Improvements in health standards are raising the expectation of life, and in consequence older people are likely to be fit to continue working for several years longer than a generation or two ago, and raising the school-leaving age will provide the population with a better educational foundation which will make people more useful throughout their career including their later years. Also machines which older people can easily control are steadily replacing heavy manual toil. For these reasons it would be sound policy to raise and not to lower the age at which people are required to cease work.

This chapter can be suitably concluded by noting that whereas more leisure with rising standards of living is possible only by increased output resulting from greater efficiency of industrial equipment, organization, and labour, the greater amount of leisure facilitates consumption of the increasing output of industry. People who worked twelve hours a day with rarely a holiday had little time for anything but necessaries. Leisure, however, provides opportunities for the use of equipment and facilities for sport, amusement, and hobbies; it creates a demand for better housing and furniture, more clothing, books, travel, and hotel and catering services. This demand, therefore, enables the growing productivity of industry to be more easily absorbed, while the desire for more goods for leisure-time activities will provide a stimulus to labour efficiency and earnings in order that leisure may be more fully enjoyed.

PART IV

State Intervention

21

Purposes and Scope of Intervention

DURING THE heyday of *laisser-faire* in Britain in the nineteenth century there was little intervention by the State in industrial relations. The general policy was to leave the regulation of working conditions for direct negotiation by employers and workpeople. Historically, *laisser-faire* in labour relations as in other fields was quite exceptional, and even in Britain, where this policy was practicable in the nineteenth century because of the special economic and industrial circumstances of the period, it was applied for only a short time, while in other countries where conditions were less clearly favourable it had less application. In the period in Britain when *laisser-faire* was most strongly supported there was some intervention, while in previous centuries intervention had been widespread. The feudal system was a form of intervention, while in times of labour scarcity caused by the Black Death and other pestilences special laws were passed, for example the Statutes of Labourers, requiring the old customary wages to be paid or providing for the fixing of maximum wages. For long periods wages were fixed by the Justices of the Peace in many localities. There were also such measures as the Sumptuary Laws, and the Elizabethan Poor Law and the Statute of Apprentices.

The policy of *laisser-faire* in Britain during the nineteenth century enabled the new industrial system to develop rapidly, and freedom for the workers destroyed the last vestiges of the feudal system. But the stability and security which labourers had enjoyed in rural areas before the Industrial Revolution were also destroyed, and in the factory towns there was often serious distress because of insecurity and unemployment, while harsh conditions of labour were suffered especially by women and children, but also by others who were too weak to protect themselves. It was gradually realized that there were sections of industry which left to themselves could not remedy these hardships, and demands for State intervention became increasingly insistent in the closing decade of the nineteenth century and afterwards.

Apart altogether from humanitarian sympathies, the State has a direct interest in securing standards of living and other conditions necessary for a healthy population and one with good standards of education and industrial efficiency. Removal of hardships and privation can diminish the danger of social unrest. For these purposes therefore the State introduced and progressively raised the standards of industrial safety and welfare by the Factory Acts. It also established systems for fixing minimum wages in industries where sweating existed and where there was lack of organization among employers and workpeople to regulate wages effectively. These forms of intervention, together with social insurance and social security, for the purpose of providing minimum incomes during periods of sickness, accident, unemployment, and old age, allowances for those with large families, and special assistance where the ordinary scales of benefit and other forms of income were insufficient, all these began their first stages of development in Britain and in other European countries during the closing years of the nineteenth century and the early years of the present century.

In many countries laws have been passed to define the functions of trade unions and employers' organizations, to regulate collective agreements, and to impose restrictions on industrial disputes and the conduct of persons taking part in them. The main provisions of such laws have been examined in earlier chapters, including, for example, limiting political action by trade unions and prohibiting intimidation.

The State has a direct interest in preserving industrial peace. Unrest may cause disorder which would be costly to control, and stoppages of work may reduce prosperity and cause the national revenues to fall. Stoppages in some industries may interfere with the success of the Government's armament programme, and this could involve grave risks in periods of international tension. With the object, therefore, of removing or reducing such losses and dangers and of assisting employers and workers towards the settlement of disputes the State has set up machinery for conciliation and arbitration.

Conciliation and arbitration by State machinery may be voluntary or compulsory. Even if arbitration is compulsory but the awards are not binding on the parties and are not legally enforceable, the principle of voluntary agreement is maintained. Such arbitration can help the parties to reach agreement when they had failed to do so by direct negotiation, but there is no interference with the right of the parties to accept or refuse the conditions under which they will work or will offer work. The parties are still in the field of voluntary negotiation with assistance from the State. Even if they bind themselves beforehand to accept the award of an arbitration board they take this decision freely and voluntarily. Only when the State makes binding awards does the responsibility for regulating working conditions pass out of the hands of the parties. Even then they can keep the powers of the State within narrow limits if State arbitration machinery operates only when the parties fail to agree and a dispute occurs, as they can continue to negotiate until they reach agreement instead of giving the State the opportunity to intervene. There is a vast difference between such limited intervention and that exercised in totalitarian countries where the whole economic and social system is controlled by the State. In such countries the interests of employers and workpeople, in peace as in war, are made subservient to those of the State. Thus, the Labour Trustees in Nazi Germany had authority to regulate working conditions throughout industry. Such a system would be entirely out of place in democratic countries.

In the chapters which follow, the problems and methods of intervention by the State in the regulation of wages and in the settlement of industrial disputes by conciliation and arbitration are reviewed, and the main aspects of social security are outlined. The possibilities of a national wages policy, and some problems of industrial relations in nationalized industries are examined.

22

Intervention in Wage Regulation

GOVERNMENT INTERVENTION in the regulation of wages has come later than in the setting up of standards for hours of work, minimum age of employment, and for health and safety in factories. This lateness was due partly to the great difficulties involved in the regulation of wages by the State. It was also because, although *laisser-faire* doctrines were set aside in the nineteenth century in order that the State could restrict such abuses as excessive hours of labour of women and children and the employment of young children in factories and mines, stronger resistance was shown by employers to interference by the State with their freedom to regulate wages. In some periods in the Middle Ages the State even intervened to regulate wages in the interests of employers; for example, in the years of labour shortage after the Black Death the State fixed *maximum* wages, in an attempt to prevent labourers from gaining higher wages.

The State has always been responsible for fixing the wages and salaries of its own employees, but the number of persons employed by the State often was, and in many countries still is, only a small proportion of the total number of employed persons and therefore the wages and salaries fixed by the State for its own personnel were based upon those current in private industry. In recent years, however, the proportion of people employed by the State and by public authorities ultimately responsible to the State has increased substantially in some countries, and this change will inevitably increase the influence of the State on wages and conditions of employment instead of these being dominated by the standards set in private industry.

THE FAIR WAGES CLAUSE

The legislatures of many countries have adopted the general principle of "fair wages" for persons employed by the Government and by contractors undertaking work for the Government, the intention being that the Government should be a "good employer." This was often understood to be that Governments and private employers working on Government contracts should pay to their workpeople rates of wages current among good employers in the locality in which the work for the Government was being done. With the development' of collective bargaining and the fixing of wages by collective agreements or by arbitration, the rates of wages fixed by these means have served as guide to Governments. Thus, in Britain, a Fair Wages Resolution was passed by the House of Commons on October 14, 1946, which required contractors for the Government to pay "rates of wages and observe hours and conditions of labour not less favourable than those established for the trade or industry in the district where the work is carried out by machinery of negotiation or arbitration to which the parties are organizations of employers and trade union representatives respectively of substantial propor- tions of the employers and workers engaged in the trade or industry in the district. In the absence of any rates of wages, hours, or con- ditions of labour so established the contractor shall pay rates of wages and observe hours and conditions of labour which are not less favourable than the general level of wages, hours, and conditions observed by other employers whose general circumstances in the trade or industry in which the contractor is engaged are similar."[1] The provisions of the Fair Wages Resolution are included in the terms of each contract between a Government Department and an employer undertaking work on contract for the department.

INTERVENTION IN PRIVATE INDUSTRY

The main ways by which the State exercises direct control over wages in private industry are by establishing machinery for the continuous regulation of wages throughout defined fields of employ- ment, and by the application of arbitration awards for those em- ployers and workpeople who come before State appointed arbitration tribunals when disagreements have arisen between them. This second method is discussed in the chapter on Conciliation and Arbitration.

Why does the State undertake the regulation of wages in private industry? There is clearly no reason why the State should intervene if wages could be regulated as effectively or more effectively by the employers and workpeople directly concerned. State intervention is not needed in those industries in which employers and workpeople

---

[1] Before a contractor is placed upon a list of firms to be invited to tender for a Government contract he shall give an assurance that to the best of his knowledge and belief he has complied with the general conditions required by the Fair Wages Resolution for at least the previous three months. A contractor shall also recognize the freedom of his workpeople to be members of trade unions.

are sufficiently well organized and have set up effective systems of negotiation for regulating wages. The parties directly concerned, if sufficiently organized, have the advantage of detailed knowledge of the conditions and problems with which they are faced, and can establish and adjust standards of wages which are both practicable and also flexible enough to meet the changing needs of the industry. If, however, there is no satisfactory method of regulating wages in an industry or occupation, and if, in consequence, the wages paid are so low that they involve hardship and privation to the workers, the State has a responsibility for devising methods for remedying such conditions.

In any country with a complex industrial structure certain occupations or branches of industry are likely to be found in which the trade unions are too weak to bargain collectively for the whole or a large part of the industry, and in consequence wages and working conditions are fixed separately by each employer with considerable variation in wages from one firm to another. Some firms may be so inefficient that the wages they can afford to pay are below the "poverty line," while some employers may not hesitate to exploit their workers and keep wages as low as they can. In such circumstances competition between firms may prevent other employers from paying reasonable wages. Here the State can intervene by fixing minimum rates. These rates applicable to all firms, if effectively enforced, would prevent or reduce exploitation, and would compel inefficient firms to improve their efficiency or go out of business.

Investigations conducted in various countries towards the end of the nineteenth century and in the early years of the present century revealed the existence of branches of industry in which organization among workers and employers was not adequate for the effective regulation of wages, and where in consequence the workers suffered severe privation. Some of the worst conditions were found not in factory employment but among home workers and out workers who worked in their own homes or in small workshops on materials supplied to them by persons who distributed work to them on piece-rate or contract terms of payment. Not infrequently the piece rates were so low that even by working long hours a living wage could not be earned. The workers, doing the work in the isolation of their homes or in small groups in workshops, were almost impossible to organize into trade unions. In several European countries (France, Germany, Austria, and Norway), the earliest legislation for the fixing of minimum rates of wages was limited to home workers and out workers. In some other countries State intervention was restricted to the fixing of minimum rates for women and young persons, for example, in Massachusetts and Ontario. This restriction was based on the idea that women and young persons were more liable to exploitation and less able to protect their interests than men, trade union organization being weak or often almost non-existent among women and young persons in some industries.

In Britain, the object of the first legislation on minimum wages (the Trade Boards Act, 1909) was the regulation of wages in branches of industry in which wages were found on investigation to be unduly low, the application of the Act being limited to such industries. There was, however, no restriction within those industries to women and young persons, or to home workers, or out workers, and although the industries selected included considerable numbers of women and home workers, the legislation was applied to all workers including those in factories, and to men as well as to women and young persons. A second Trade Boards Act, passed in 1918, under the influence of the Whitley Committee's recommendations, changed the basis for selecting industries from unduly low wages to lack of organization for the effective regulation of wages. It followed that if an industry in which a Trade Board was set up for the statutory regulation of wages later on developed organizations among employers and workers which could effectively regulate wages by collective bargaining that industry would be withdrawn from statutory control. The number of industries subject to statutory regulation was considerably increased under the 1918 Act. Subsequently, the policy of applying statutory methods of regulating wages in industries in which workers and employers are inadequately organized was extended by special Acts to agriculture, road haulage, and the catering trades.

A further evolution of the British system was made in the Wages Councils Act, 1945, which applied to those industries which had been covered previously by the Trade Boards. This Act brought the system of statutory wage regulation closer to that of collective bargaining by enabling Wages Councils to make proposals not only for fixing minimum rates of wages, but also for requiring employers to allow their workers holidays with pay, for regulating overtime and its remuneration, and for guaranteeing minimum weekly pay, subject to certain conditions, whether the full number of hours have been worked or not.

MACHINERY FOR REGULATION

The kinds of statutory machinery for regulating wages differ considerably, though most of them are based on representation of employers and workpeople, and to that extent resemble collective bargaining. Where statutory wage-fixing bodies include representatives of employers and workpeople, these are chosen as far as possible from such trade unions and employers' organizations as exist, but which are not sufficiently developed to be able by themselves to regulate wages effectively in the industry. They can, however, bring to the deliberations a first-hand knowledge of the conditions and needs of the industry, and in consequence the wage rates finally fixed are likely to be realistically based. An essential part, however, of the membership of statutory wage-fixing boards consists of impartial persons, often three in number, one of whom is chairman. These impartial members guide the discussions, they act as conciliators when sharp divergencies appear between the members representing employers and those representing workpeople, and they endeavour to narrow the differences between these two sides with the object of securing agreement. If they succeed in doing this, the wage rates proposed go forward with the unanimous support of the whole board, and they are brought into force by an order of the responsible minister or other authority. If, however, the two sides fail to agree, the impartial members become virtually arbitrators, and they must decide what is the most suitable solution between the conflicting claims of the employers and workpeople. Usually, they secure the support of one side, and the solution, though not adopted unanimously, becomes the decision or recommendation of the board.

A system of wage fixing in industries inadequately organized would be unworkable without impartial members, and their presence is one of the main features which distinguish statutory from voluntary systems. Another distinguishing feature is that the wages fixed by statutory bodies are legally enforceable, and failure to observe them may result in fines or, in extreme cases, in imprisonment, whereas in some countries wage rates fixed in voluntary collective agreements have no legal force. A further difference is that wages fixed by statutory bodies apply to all employers and workpeople in the trade or industry covered, whereas collective agreements apply only to the parties of the agreement, and, therefore, employers who have not signed the agreement or are not members of an association which has signed the agreement are not bound by it.

A method of statutory wage regulation which avoids the setting up of permanent machinery is for a responsible minister to be given power to apply by the "common rule" the rates of wages fixed by agreement between organizations of employers and workpeople which are considered sufficiently representative for a trade or industry. If he is satisfied after investigation that these rates are suitable he may make an order applying them throughout trade or industry. The rates then have legal force.[1]

In some countries a separate Wages Board or Council is set up for each branch of industry, as in Britain, and these boards work independently of one another.[2] The British Wages Councils do not themselves fix wage rates, but as already indicated recommend rates to the Minister of Labour who issues an order bringing the rates into force if he is satisfied with the recommendations. Any co-ordination which occurs is the result of the advice and assistance available to the different councils from officials of the Ministry of Labour.

An alternative system adopted in some countries is for a Central Board or Commission to be set up with responsibility for fixing wage rates for a number of industries. The members of such a commission consist of an impartial chairman and sometimes two or more impartial members, together with a small number of representatives of employers and trade unions. These members do not have first-hand knowledge of conditions in each of the industries for which they fix rates of wages, and therefore they usually obtain the advice of committees, one for each of the industries covered. Each committee consists of an impartial chairman together with employers' and workers' representatives from the industry concerned, and the recommendations made are based on knowledge of conditions in that industry. The Central Board or Commission may, as far as conditions in the various industries permit, co-ordinate wage-fixing policy for the whole of the industries covered. This method is suitable where the industrial structure of a country is relatively simple, but in countries with more complex industrial conditions a separate board for each industry seems preferable.[3]

In some countries, particularly Australia and New Zealand, compulsory arbitration, which was originally established for the purpose of settling disputes, has developed into a system for the general regulation of wages. The Commonwealth Court of Arbitration

---

[1] This method was adopted in Britain by legislation in 1934 for the cotton manufacturing industry at a time when, owing to severe trade depression, there was danger of a collapse of collective bargaining in this industry because some firms, though members of employers' organizations, paid lower wages than those fixed in the agreements, while other firms withdrew from the organizations in order to be under no obligation to pay the agreed rates.

[2] The Wages Councils Acts provide that central co-ordinating committees may be set up to co-ordinate the work of two or more councils, but little use has been made of this power.

[3] As an example, the central commission system has been used in some Canadian provinces, where statutory wage fixing is limited to women and young persons.

declares basic rates of wages each quarter for skilled, semi-skilled, and unskilled workers, these rates being adjusted to changes in the cost of living, and also at longer intervals to changes in economic prosperity and trends of output. Higher rates than those declared by the Court are fixed by collective bargaining, but employers and trade unionists know that if they fail to reach agreement by negotiation and their dispute comes before the Court, it will make an award in accordance with its basic wage declarations, unless it is satisfied by the evidence submitted that work in the industry or occupation concerned merits an award of higher rates. Factors which lead to higher rates include special skill, and abnormally arduous, unpleasant, or dangerous work.

In some countries a general minimum rate is fixed by the legislature, and this provides a "floor" for the whole wage structure. Thus, in France, in recent years national minimum wages have been fixed in this way, and changes are made periodically, particularly to allow for movements in the cost of living. This method of fixing basic wages brings the problem directly into the political arena with consequent disadvantages; also for other reasons a parliamentary body is not very suitable for fixing wages, and there is the uncertainty of finding parliamentary time to consider wage changes when these seem necessary on economic and social grounds. The method does, however, provide a wide foundation on which the wage superstructure can be built by collective bargaining.

CRITERIA FOR FIXING RATES

Some laws which provide for the setting up of statutory wage-fixing bodies give no indication of the bases or criteria to be used in fixing minimum rates. This is true of the British Trades Board Acts and the Wages Councils Acts, the boards and councils being free to consider all the circumstances which have a bearing on wages. Other laws specifically require the wage-fixing bodies to fix minimum wages at such levels as will provide reasonable standards of living for the workpeople. These, for adult male workers, may be defined as wages sufficient to provide adequately for the needs of a man with a wife and an average number of dependent children, usually two or three. Such indications are, however, too general to be of much use for deciding exactly what wages to fix, and not infrequently the wage-fixing bodies are instructed also to take into consideration the effects of proposed wage levels upon prosperity and employment in the industry.

Inevitably, wage-fixing bodies must give attention to the effects upon employment of any wages they propose to fix. If rates are fixed too high the result may be substantial unemployment, which may be worse for the workpeople than if rates had been lower and unemployment less. However, there must be limits to the lowering of wages in order to maintain employment, for under conditions of severe competition wages might fall so low as to cause quite unacceptable conditions of privation. Small "pockets" of industry unsuited to a country's economic development and standards of living may linger on if their wages are allowed to remain at levels involving hardship and misery to the workpeople. Similarly, within some industries there may be undertakings which are so inefficiently run that they can continue in existence only by paying unduly low wages. Towards such industries and undertakings the right policy seems to be to fix minimum rates of wages at levels which are not unduly low in relation to the wage standards of most other industries in the country, and either their efficiency must be improved in order to be able to pay the rates fixed or the industries and undertakings must cease to exist. This will result in some unemployment, but it is better to have a period of temporary unemployment with transfer of workpeople to more efficient industries and undertakings than to permit the continuation of long-drawn-out misery. This policy has been applied, for example, by the Commonwealth Court of Arbitration in Australia, which has declared that industries or undertakings so unsuited to the Australian economy that they cannot afford to pay minimum wages appropriate according to Australian standards, should go out of business rather than continue in operation by paying wages which involve their workpeople in severe privation. Such a policy would not, however, be applied to an industry of value to a country's economy, but which, because of severe depression, was temporarily unable to maintain its wage standards.

23

Problems of a National Wages Policy

RAPID IMPROVEMENTS in transportation, the growing integration of economic life on a national scale, especially in a country so compact as Great Britain, and the increasing application of national economic policies compel consideration of the need for a national wages policy. A study of the wage structure, with separate scales in scores of different industries and many thousands of occupations indicates the complexity of the problems and might lead to the conclusion that the evolution of a common policy would be quite impracticable. Yet within many industries considerable progress has been made in the establishment of workable wage agreements covering the whole country, but in the past many of the same arguments were used against demands for wages within an industry to be regulated nationally as are now directed against proposals for a national policy to be applied to all industries. The forces now tending towards such a policy are similar to those leading to greater national unification on hours of work, social security, paid holidays, and other working conditions.

During the nineteenth century wages were often fixed independently by each employer or, if regulated collectively, separate agreements independently negotiated were usually concluded for each town or district and were also limited to one craft, or a few related crafts or a single industry. This corresponded closely with the scope of trade unions, which, as has been seen, began as small local organizations and then grew to district size. Next, came contact and co-operation between these separate unions leading ultimately to national federations or amalgamations, nation-wide agreements ollowed, or, if district bargaining was retained because in some federations, e.g. the Miners' Federation, the affiliated district unions retained their independence in wage bargaining, the terms of agreement were more or less influenced or co-ordinated nationally by the federation. The agreements were limited to an industry or craft for which the trade unions and employers' associations retained wage bargaining independence and each fought for the best terms it could get, largely without consideration of the effects upon other industries or crafts or upon the national economy.

To-day, wages are still regulated sectionally by industries and crafts without any overriding national policy, and in the main each industry is "a law unto itself." Most trade unionists are members of unions affiliated to the Trades Union Congress, but, though the Congress through its General Council may promote common action on general questions such as wages and hours, the member-unions have jealously guarded their freedom. Individual unions have sometimes organized joint action including sympathetic strikes, for example, the Triple Alliance formed after the 1914–18 war for mutual support between miners, railwaymen, and dockers, which broke down in 1921 with much mutual recrimination because of failure to agree upon simultaneous action. The General Strike called by the Trades Union Congress in 1926 was a remarkable demonstration of solidarity, but it collapsed owing to the determined attitude of the Government and failed in its object of protecting the coal-miners against wage reductions. In the following year the passing of the Trade Disputes and Trade Unions Act made general and sympathetic strikes illegal until the Act was repealed in 1946. Mutual support between different unions by peaceful means has no doubt achieved some co-ordination, but their practical results in contributing towards a national wages policy have been negligible. Similarly, the Trades Councils formed in many towns are an expression of labour solidarity and have supported the various local unions, especially during disputes, but they have been ineffective in formulating a common policy on wages.

One of the main reasons why collective bargaining has hitherto made so little contribution towards a common wages policy is that economic conditions vary from industry to industry, some being prosperous when others are depressed, and this has made it difficult for trade unions to agree on common demands and act together. The easy course was for each union to do the best for itself, but the result was that strong unions in prosperous industries secured wages much higher than in other industries. Frequently, too, a compact union of key craftsmen would use its bargaining strength to demand high wages which the employers would grant because these men were essential for the running of the industry and because being relatively few in number, their total wages even at high rates represented only a small part of the whole costs of production. Yet, such a union would give no thought or help to unskilled and semi-skilled workers with much lower wages in the same industry. Employers were often even more individualistic towards one another. It is true that many industries are affected together by the booms and depressions of the trade cycle and it might be thought that this would lead to a common

343

policy. But some industries benefit from a boom or are hit by a depression weeks, or even months, earlier than other industries, and in consequence the opportune moment for the union in one industry to demand wage increases or for the employers' organization in an industry to demand wage reductions does not synchronize with that for similar action in other industries. Also, booms and depressions vary in strength in different industries. These factors have caused the failure of attempts by unions to plan common action, and have strengthened the tendency to act independently.

If collective bargaining has not led to the evolution of a national wages policy, Government action has hitherto been only slight and tentative in most countries. This has been largely due to the great complexity of wages in advanced industrial countries, to the influence of *laisser-faire* doctrines and to the preference of Governments to leave the responsibility for wages to employers and workpeople and their organizations. In Great Britain the Government has also been influenced by the strong objection of trade unions and employers' organizations to Government interference with their freedom to negotiate wage agreements. Yet the success of the trade unions in their political support of nationalization and other national economic policies will inevitably involve greater responsibility and participation by the Government in the regulation of wages.

FACTORS TENDING TOWARDS NATIONAL STANDARDS

Differences in wages between industries are limited mainly by mobility of labour which continually acts to reduce inequalities. When owing to unemployment wages in an industry or locality fall, some of the workpeople transfer to more prosperous industries or localities, thereby checking both the fall of wages in the former and rises in the latter. This factor tending towards wage equality for work requiring similar skill in different industries acts, however, only slowly, inequalities often taking a decade or more to smooth out, and during this period workpeople in a depressed industry will receive lower wages than in a prosperous industry for equal work. If a wages policy were applied, it would seem desirable to remove such wage inequalities more rapidly, and this would involve accelerating the transfer of labour.

Another factor tending towards similarity of wages for comparable work in different localities or industries is the practice, frequently adopted in wage bargaining, for workers to support their demands by pointing to the better wages being paid for similar work in other localities or industries. Within an industry, customary relationships tend to become established between wage levels for different grades of skill, so that an increase in the wages in some grades leads to demands for proportionate increases in other grades, unless the type of work has been altered. By these means a rough, long-term relationship is maintained between the standards of living of different categories of workpeople throughout the community. If a national wages policy were applied the operation of such forces would be systematically adjusted.

The economic forces to which reference was made in the two preceding paragraphs tend towards the establishment of national wage standards by reducing disparities between wages in different industries, occupations, and localities. They are not parts of a policy, and operate in a *laisser-faire* economy. During recent years, however, there have been several economic and social developments which are signposts pointing towards a national wages policy. First, distinct progress has been towards a national minimum wage. This movement began around the beginning of the present century when public opinion was shocked by revelations of extremely low wages due to severe competition and bargaining weakness of the workers in certain "sweated" trades, with the result that the Trade Boards Act, 1909, was passed establishing a system for fixing minimum wages in specified branches of industry where wages were unduly low. The scope of the system was considerably extended and modified by the Trade Boards Act, 1918, and again by the Wages Councils Act, 1945, while a somewhat similar method was applied to agriculture and to several other industries by special legislation.[1] Under these acts separate boards were set up for each branch of industry covered, and wages were fixed independently. However, by eliminating exceptionally low wages for unskilled workpeople in these industries and gradually raising their rates towards the level in other industries, there was a tendency towards a national basis.

This tendency has been strengthened in recent years by modifying the old individualistic outlook by a growing social consciousness that "we are all members one of another." An outcome has been the now widely supported policy that, taking into account the productive resources of the country, there is a basic standard of living below which no one, whether at work or not, should fall. Translated into practical action this has resulted in the fixing of social security standards according to the needs of the worker and his family when he is unable to work owing to sickness, unemployment, old age, or

[1] Mention must be made of the Coal Mines (Minimum Wage) Act, 1912, which, however, applied to an industry in which the workers and employers were strongly organized, and the system it established was somewhat outside the main stream of minimum wage legislation.

other causes, and these standards influence and are influenced by the wages of unskilled workpeople. It has also led to the family allowance system, and to the provision of free education, school meals and other benefits, so that millions of families have a standard of living considerably higher than is obtained by wages, and this represents an appreciable levelling-up process. The determination of basic standards has been much influenced by scientific studies into the nutrition required to ensure the health and physical efficiency of the population, and by information obtained in family budget investigations. War-time and post-war rationing, price control, and subsidies supported the conception of a basic standard of living for all.

Once an approximation to a national minimum has been reached, whether by wage boards or other means, a distinct step has been taken in the evolution towards a national wages policy. If the wage of unskilled workers is established then the wages of semi-skilled and skilled workpeople are higher by ratios or "margins" which can be determined largely on the basis of custom, account, however, being taken of changes affecting the relative degrees of skill and conditions of work. Allowance for differences in conditions must, however, be made even in fixing the wages of unskilled workers. Thus, the wage of an unskilled miner working underground should be higher than that of an unskilled worker in a pleasanter and safer industry. Here it may be noted that the living wage principle applied by the New Zealand and Australian courts of arbitration in fixing basic rates for unskilled workers, combined with the "margins" for skill and other principles of wage regulation given in awards for the settlement of disputes, provide the elements of a wages policy which has been evolved during a period of more than forty years.

With the abandonment of *laisser-faire*, the Government has applied economic policies and plans, and has nationalized basic industries. Some of these depend considerably upon wages policy, and can only operate effectively if the course of wages is reasonably steady. The more economic planning by a Government permeates a community the greater becomes the need for a national wages policy. In a nationalized industry the Government as the employer is ultimately responsible for the wages paid, and if several industries are nationalized the Government cannot, in the long run, apply different wage principles to each, and the adoption of a consistent policy becomes inevitable. Where, as in Russia, comprehensive economic plans are applied the control of wages by the State is basic.

Application of a policy of full employment has a special bearing on wages policy. In the past the possibility of unemployment in an industry was a big factor in ensuring that unreasonable wage demands were not pressed. If a trade union insisted on rates of wages beyond the capacity of the industry, unemployment resulted. This might be sound policy during a temporary crisis so as to avoid lowering wages and then raising them again after the crisis, or if the industry was permanently depressed and had a surplus of labour, as the transfer of workpeople to other industries would be accelerated. A general resistance to wage reductions throughout industry could also be justified in certain circumstances, for example, if they would aggravate a depression by causing a further fall in prices by an all-round reduction of purchasing power. But such general resistance would represent a national wages policy in embryo. The essential argument here, however, is that if full employment is maintained a national wages policy seems inevitable.

In periods of economic instability and crisis affecting a whole community the need for a national wages policy is specially great, and Governments may need to apply such policies or give guidance in the public interest. Such action may be illustrated from experience in the United States, Canada, and Great Britain. When President Roosevelt took office in 1933, the United States was in such economic chaos, with collapse of the price and wage structure, that the country was ready to respond to the President's proposal for lifting wages out of the morass. When progress in fixing higher wages under the National Industrial Recovery Act proved too slow he adopted what was known as the President's Re-employment Agreement in which he gave a lead to industry by asking employers throughout the country to agree with him that they would pay their workpeople wherever practicable at a minimum rate of 40 cents an hour or in no case less than 30 cents an hour.

During the Second World War most Governments applied some sort of wages policy, mainly designed to keep inflation within limits. In the United States, for example, a general principle of the Government's policy at one stage of the war was that wage increases should not be granted if they would lead to higher prices. The Canadian Government, in October 1941, issued an order fixing a wage and price ceiling. No increases in basic wage rates were to be granted without permission of the National War-time Labour Board, and it became an offence for any employer to raise his basic wages without such permission. Workers were to receive a cost-of-living bonus but this could not lead to inflation because of the price ceiling controlled by the War-time Prices and Trade Board. In Canada, as elsewhere, the Government desired to prevent inflation and rising costs of production which, without Government control, would have resulted from successive wage increases, shortage of goods, competitive offers of higher wages by employers to tempt workers in acutely short supply to transfer from one undertaking to another with dislocation and injury to the national interests, and from the facility with which employers on war contracts could have passed on to the Government higher costs resulting from wage increases.

In Britain the Government's war-time wages policy, backed by costly food subsidies, savings schemes, taxation, and rationing, was designed to restrain inflationary tendencies, and the Government announced its intention to stabilize the cost of living at about 30 per cent above the 1939 level with the hope that this would keep wages steady. The elements of the Government's war-time wages policy were cautiously outlined in a White Paper on "Price Stabilization and Industrial Policy," published in July 1941. Essentially the object was to maintain wages at a reasonable level and to prevent costs of production from rising rapidly. Attention was directed to the fact that the goods were not there to buy, and increases in wages and other incomes would not raise the general standard of living but merely send up prices, denude shops, and make difficult a fair distribution of the limited supply of goods. It was necessary to bear in mind when dealing with general wage applications that the Government's policy of price stabilization would be made impossible and increases in wage rates would defeat their own object unless such increases were regulated in a manner that would make it practicable to keep prices and inflationary tendencies under control. The Trades Union Congress General Council, fearing increased Government regulation of wages, promptly stated that any attempt to control movements for increases in wages was impracticable and undesirable, but broadly speaking the subsequent action of the trade union movement during the war was restrained so that wage soaring was avoided.

The British Government gave further indications on wages policy in its White Paper on "Employment Policy" published in May 1944.[1] This emphasized that action taken by the Government to maintain expenditure with the object of ensuring a high and stable level of employment would be fruitless "unless wages and prices were kept reasonably stable. This is of vital importance to any employment policy, and must be clearly understood by all sections of the public. If we are to operate with success a policy for maintaining a high and stable level of employment, it will be essential that employers and workers should exercise moderation in wage matters so that increased expenditure provided at the onset of a depression may go to

[1] Cmd. 6527, paragraphs 49–54.

increase the volume of employment." This would not mean inflexible wage rates, as there must, for example, be opportunities for adjusting wages to changes in the form, method or volume of production and for removing anomalies between different grades of workers, both within an industry and in different industries. "The principle of stability does mean, however, that increases in the general level of wage rates must be related to increased productivity due to increased efficiency and effort." Also, "an undue increase in prices due to causes other than increased wages might similarly frustrate action taken by the Government to maintain employment," for example, money made available by the Government to increase employment might be absorbed by a ring of manufacturers formed to maintain prices and result in increased profits instead of more employment.

In this connection it is of interest to give the reply of representatives of the Trades Union Congress when asked by Sir William Beveridge whether under full employment there would inevitably be an inflationary spiral of wages and prices. They said there was no need to fear such a spiral if the Government could convince the trade union movement that "in genuine pursuit of a policy of full employment it is determined to take all other steps that are necessary to control prices and can convince the trade union movement of the need to secure equivalent guarantees that wage movements will not be such as to upset the system of price control."

In the United States shortly after the end of the war, widespread industrial unrest was so greatly hampering the reconversion of the national economy to a peace-time basis that President Truman announced a wages policy which he hoped would provide some guidance to employers and trade unions in their wage negotiations and enable a course to be steered between deflation and inflation. In his statement approval was given to wage increases where the rise in hourly earnings for ordinary time had not equalled war-time increases in the cost of living, where wage rates in a plant were below the competitive level in the industry or locality, or where wages in an industry necessary for reconstruction were too low to attract sufficient manpower. Official pronouncements are especially valuable at times when many industries are faced with uncertainties and need to be advised in general terms on policies that would best serve their own and the country's interests. They are particularly needed in periods when there is danger of inflation or deflation.

SOME ELEMENTS OF A POLICY

If economic policies and plans necessitate the formulation of a national wages policy, much consultation will be required between the Government, employers' organizations, and trade unions to agree upon principles and to devise methods for their application. Flexibility would be necessary to enable adjustments to be made by each industry within the general framework, collective bargaining would be adapted and wages policy would be related to employment and production plans and to price policies.

The main elements of a policy may be summarized as follows:

(1) The provision of minimum standards below which no ordinary unskilled worker would fall.

(2) The provision of appropriate margins for skill and other allowances for the type and conditions of work. These would at first be based upon existing or customary differences, but would be gradually adjusted by removing anomalies. The "rate for the job" would be applied.

(3) Maintenance of reasonable stability between the general level of wages and the cost of living so as to avoid inflation.

(4) Provision for a general rise in the purchasing power of workers' wages as productivity increases. This could be arranged either by raising money wages, by reducing prices, or by a combination of both these methods.

(5) Use of incentives which would give a proper reward for efficiency and output.

(6) The levelling-up of wages in low-paid industries.

An essential purpose of the policy would be to ensure that the benefits of progress would be more rapidly and fairly distributed between different industries than is possible if wages in each industry are left to the free play of economic forces. Thus, in the 1920's and 1930's coal-mining and agriculture were essential for the national prosperity, but their wages were unduly low. In such circumstances a co-ordination of production, employment, and wages policies on a national scale is needed to reduce wage disparities between depressed and prosperous industries.

POSSIBILITIES AND LIMITATIONS

In theory it would be possible for a national authority to fix a minimum wage rate for unskilled workpeople throughout industry, and then to fix higher rates for semi-skilled and skilled workers on the basis of detailed job evaluation studies into the degree of skill, training, and other requirements of each occupation. Additions could also be made to compensate workpeople in unpleasant or dangerous occupations. The differentials would be altered periodically as the requirements of occupations changed, the rate for any occupation being reduced if the work was simplified by some invention or division of the process, or increased if the job became more exacting. Then, the whole of the rates could be raised or lowered in proportion to changes in the cost of living so as to maintain the purchasing power of the wages. An index of national production per head could be used to raise or lower all wage rates, thus enabling all workpeople to benefit from increased output resulting from the progress of inventions and the use of improved methods. Direction of labour would be necessary to secure rapid transfer of workpeople from declining to expanding industries, and subsidies might be required to help an industry during a period of difficulty.

In practice, however, such a system would not provide the flexibility needed in advanced industrial countries to enable the different industries to adjust themselves to changes in economic conditions including the effects of foreign competition. Also, it implies a submissiveness by employers and workpeople in accepting the decisions of a central authority which contrasts sharply with the independence and love of freedom shown in many countries by trade unions and employers' organizations.

A national wages authority set up by the Government can be a suitable instrument in a country where workers and employers are insufficiently organized to regulate wages effectively by collective bargaining, and where the industrial structure is simple. It can also be effective in dictatorship countries. However, in countries where trade unions and employers' organizations are strong and independent and where collective bargaining is well established an authority appointed by the Government to fix wages throughout industry would be impracticable. All that the trade unions and employers' organizations would be able to do would be to submit facts and arguments to the authority, which would then give its decisions. Whenever these decisions were unacceptable to the employers or trade unions their enforcement would be impossible, and the status of the authority would be weakened. In the circumstances defined the responsibility for regulating wages must rest with the organizations of employers and of workpeople. The industrial organizations could not, without losing their freedom, see the power of decision taken from them and vested in a State authority, while a system which attempted to divide responsibility between such an authority and the industrial organizations would be unworkable.

These arguments must not be taken to imply that little or nothing can be done to devise and apply a national wages policy and to secure improvements in the wage structure by bringing relative wages more into harmony with the skills and other qualities required in each occupation and industry. Solutions can be devised which are intermediate between the rigidity of centralized control and the chaos of independent negotiations. There will be many loose ends, uncertainties and deviations, but this approach is much more realistic than that of attempting to apply a national policy by a Government body with over-riding powers.

Consultation and co-operation at the national level between Governments, trade unions, and employers' organizations are usually closer in times of national economic crisis, when common factors affecting all industries are prominent, than in more stable periods. Thus, in the post-war years of reconstruction, 1946–50, with shortages of goods and dangers of inflation, various countries applied a national wages policy in some form. In the Scandinavian countries, for example, a considerable measure of agreement was reached between the central organizations of employers and trade unions, in co-operation with the Governments, on regulating wages uniformly throughout industry. In Sweden, a wage stop was applied during 1949 and 1950 on the basis of such consultations. A wage stop was adopted in Norway in 1947 by agreement between the Government and the two central organizations, while in Norway and Denmark uniform cost-of-living increases were accepted by the central organizations.[1] Early in 1950 a general wage increase in Denmark resulted from central negotiations.

In Britain, the British Employers' Confederation and the Trades Union Congress have less authority over their affiliated bodies, and no negotiations for the regulation of wages have been attempted between them, partly no doubt because in a bigger country the trade unions and employers' organizations in the main industries are more powerful and their problems more complex than in the Scandinavian countries. Yet for more than two years from early 1948 the Government's policy that only in exceptional circumstances were wage claims for increased wages justified, was accepted with some reservations by the Trades Union Congress, though it was not approved by some of the affiliated unions.[2] A great measure of restraint was,

[1] War-time wage stops or wage ceilings were applied by Governments in many countries, and this method has been used also in other periods of grave national emergency.

[2] Immediately after the devaluation of sterling in September 1949, the British Government favoured an intensification of wage restraint which approximated closely to a wage stop policy in order that the harvest of benefits from devaluation to the export trade might be reaped. This policy was successful, and eight months later, in May 1950, the Chancellor of the Exchequer indicated that "a limited degree of relaxation of the very rigid standards laid down after devaluation" might be afforded, and he expressed the desire that such relaxation should be

however, shown by most of the individual unions, which are free from any control by the T.U.C. in the negotiation of wages and working conditions within their own industries, and during this period increases in rates of wages were small. Even unions which disagreed with the policy did not go on strike when they failed to secure their demands by negotiation, but acquiesced in slight increases awarded by arbitration courts.

The restraint shown in all these countries was based on a recognition of grave economic difficulties not only by the Governments and employers but also by most trade union leaders and members. In such a period of full employment the trade unions could have forced increases in money rates of wages, but, unless accompanied by corresponding increases in output, these higher money wages would have resulted in higher costs of production, causing inflation at home and reduced sales abroad, to the detriment of the whole economy. The British trade union leaders recognized the dangers from increasing costs at a time when Britain had an adverse balance in her international payments and needed to increase her exports in order to stabilize the economy. However, a policy of freezing wages can be applied only during short periods of special difficulty, and when these come to an end must be replaced by a more positive policy.

Although the main responsibility for devising and applying a national wages policy should rest with the great industrial organizations, Governments can exercise a powerful influence both directly and by publishing those facts which indicate the practicable limits within which general adjustments of wages could be made. Because the Government is a big employer of labour, it is a principal party in determining the wages and salaries of its employees, including civil servants and workpeople in Government armament and other factories. It is also able to influence the wages paid by private employers for work on Government contracts, though it has hitherto limited its influence to the inclusion of the "fair wages clause" as one of the terms of the contract. Then there are the large numbers of teachers, local government employees, and members of the medical and dental professions in Britain and some other countries, whose remuneration is determined or influenced by the Government through financial grants or subsidies in support of their work. The scales of pay of this multitude of people reacts upon rates of remuneration of

"brought about by some orderly method which paid full regard to the continuing effects of inflation." Actually he was advocating maintenance of the original policy of wage restraint of 1948, while withdrawing the additional limitations urged after devaluation.

persons in private employment just as these rates react upon those in the public services.

Governments can also exert a big influence on wages by their taxation policy, and by social services which in Britain have been estimated to cost an average of about fifty-seven shillings a week for a family consisting of man, wife, and two dependent children. They can also cause variations from year to year in the part of the national income used for capital investment, and these variations affect the proportion of the national income available for wages.

Publication by the Government of statistics bearing on wages, and the use of these data as basis for statements of the Government's views on the wage policy best suited to the country's economic needs must exert a profound influence on the industrial organizations in formulating their own policies, on arbitration tribunals to which disputes between the industrial organizations are referred for settlement, and on wages councils and other statutory bodies empowered to regulate wages in specified trades or industries. Disagreements might arise between the Government and the industrial organizations on the validity of the statistics and on the conclusions and interpretations placed upon them by the Government. These could be narrowed down if the industrial organizations gave increased attention to statistical and economic research and employed more trained statisticians and economists. This would reduce the risks of misunderstanding or misinterpretation of the statistics, and might lead to improvement in the data compiled by the Government. There would also be value in setting up a National Consultative Council on Wages, consisting of representatives of the Government and of the central industrial organizations. This Council would enable the Government to be fully aware of the views of the industrial organizations before issuing its statements on wages policy, and would ensure that the industrial organizations were well informed about the relationship between wages and the needs of the national economy. It would not give detailed consideration to the relative levels of wages from industry to industry nor to the differentials between occupations within each industry. It would, however, examine the problem of undermanned industries with a view to determining the extent to which wage increases in those industries would be effective in attracting workpeople to them.

A National Consultative Council, in countries with well-developed systems of collective bargaining, would take as its starting point that the main responsibility for regulating wages should rest upon the industrial organizations. To the extent to which these organizations approved, any disputes which they failed to settle by negotiation should be referred to arbitration, and such reference would be encouraged by the Government.[1] For trades and industries in which collective bargaining is not sufficiently developed for the effective regulation of wages, statutory methods would be applied along the lines of the British Wages Councils.

A main task of the Consultative Council would be to consider how in conditions of full employment to avoid the generation of an inflationary spiral due to increases in wages being made too rapidly instead of keeping in step with growth of production. In relation to this objective it should discuss the total amount by which the national wages bill could reasonably be altered each year, taking into account changes both in production and in the cost of living. In periods of normal expansion of production resulting from inventions and improved methods, with a stable cost of living, the wages bill might be increased by 2 or 3 per cent each year, or in present circumstances in Britain between £90 million and £140 million a year. In more favourable conditions the increase could be greater, while in times of economic crisis or depression the movement would be halted or some reductions might be necessary. The industrial organizations might disagree between themselves and with the Government about the amount, or might not be willing to commit themselves to any figure. Nevertheless, the Government should publish its estimate as part of its statement on wages policy, and the amount would serve as a guide to the industrial organizations. It would be the amount which could be afforded without dislocating the economy of the country.

If in any year the cost of living had changed, this would be taken into consideration in estimating the amount by which the wages bill could reasonably be altered. Thus, in Britain, if the total wages bill is taken to be £4,470 million, i.e. the amount estimated for 1950, and the cost of living rose 3 per cent, which is about the average of its annual increase between 1947 and 1950 as measured by the Interim Index of Retail Prices, the expansion of the wages bill in a year in order to maintain the purchasing power of the general level of wages unchanged would be about £130 million. Assuming an additional increase made practicable by a 3 per cent growth in output per head, the total annual increase in the wages bill in the conditions defined would be in the order of £270 million.

It is practicable to make such estimates based on forecasts of the probable trends of productivity and prices, and the estimates would be a guide to negotiating bodies. Generally each industry should secure a fair share of the practicable total increase. Special circumstances affecting any industry would be taken into consideration, but

[1] The subject of arbitration is discussed in Chapter 24.

exaggerated claims by the trade unions in an industry or undue caution or restraint by an employers' organization would encounter criticism and opposition. A trade union which tried to get too big a share of the practicable increase would not be viewed favourably by unions in other industries.

In this connection it is of interest to review for recent years the part represented by wages and salaries in the British national income. Official estimates published by the Government are given on page 357.[1] These statistics show that during the seven years 1946 to 1952, the average annual increase in wages was £315 million, or about 10 per cent each year. During the six years 1934 to 1939, the average annual increase was £82·5 million, or about 5·4 per cent yearly.[2] The much greater increases in post-war years compared with those during the war were the result partly of the return to civilian life of millions of men from the armed forces whose service pay and allowances were not included in wages. Among reasons for the larger increases after than before the war are the effect of the rise in the cost of living on wage rates, and the greater level of employment with more opportunities for piecework and overtime earnings. The movement from civilian work to the fighting services and back again partly explains the fall in the wage proportion of the national income to less than 34 per cent towards the end of the war, and its subsequent rise to over 43 per cent. In comparing this last figure with the pre-war percentage (38·4) account must be taken of the higher value of the social services to wage earners since the war, and also of the greater numbers in the armed forces.[3] Whatever the wage changes due to increases in production and in the cost of living, the wage proportion of the national income will change only slowly and within narrow limits in normal times.

In the preceding paragraphs, attention has been directed to guidance which the Government and central organizations of employers and of workpeople might usefully give towards the adoption of a flexible wages policy. The application of that policy would be the task mainly of the employers' organizations and trade unions in each separate industry. Acceptance of central influence and advice would

[1] For the years 1938 to 1945 they are taken from Cmd. 7099 and for the years 1946 to 1952 from *National Income and Expenditure*, published by H.M. Stationery Office. Some differences in compilation render the statistics from 1946 onwards not strictly comparable with the earlier figures.

[2] These are calculated from Professor Bowley's estimates, which also show hat in the years 1934 to 1937, wages averaged 38·4 per cent of the national ncome.

[3] Salaries after the war, unlike wages, formed a smaller proportion of the ational income than before the war.

Wages and Salaries in Relation to the National Income 1938–52

Year	National Income (Personal)	Wages				Salaries			
		Amount	Percentage of National Income	Amount of Increase Over Preceding Year	Percentage Increase Over Preceding Year	Amount	Percentage of National Income	Amount of Increase Over Preceding Year	Percentage Increase Over Preceding Year
	£ million	£ million		£ million		£ million		£ million	
1938	4,671	1,735	37·1	—	—	1,110	23·8	—	—
1939	5,037	1,835	36·4	100	5·8	1,150	22·8	40	3·6
1940	5,980	2,108	35·3	273	15·0	1,215	20·3	65	5·7
1941	6,941	2,404	34·6	296	14·0	1,340	19·3	125	10·3
1942	7,664	2,660	34·7	256	10·6	1,370	17·9	30	2·2
1943	8,171	2,805	34·3	145	5·4	1,420	17·4	50	3·7
1944	8,366	2,840	33·9	35	1·2	1,465	17·5	45	3·2
1945	8,340	2,780	33·3	−60	−2·1	1,530	18·3	65	4·4
1946	8,615	3,250	37·7	470	16·9	1,620	18·8	90	5·9
1947	9,234	3,690	39·9	440	13·5	1,760	19·0	140	8·6
1948	9,828	4,140	41·1	450	12·2	1,975	20·1	215	12·2
1949	10,416	4,365	41·9	225	5·4	2,120	20·3	145	7·3
1950	10,900	4,585	42·1	220	5·0	2,275	20·9	155	7·3
1951	11,855	5,090	42·9	505	11·0	2,550	21·6	275	12·1
1952	12,628	5,460	43·2	370	7·2	2,755	21·8	205	8·0

357

leave decisions on the proper degree of flexibility to be decided by negotiation within each industry, and the parties to these negotiations would also have to settle many important problems internal to each industry. Each industry would have to decide what proportion it would try to secure of the total likely to be available for the whole of industry. Among other wage problems which would call for settlement within each industry are the appropriate differentials to be paid for skill, dangerous work, work under unpleasant conditions, and other special features of each occupation, and such differentials would need to be altered as processes change. Anomalies in relative wages between different occupations are frequent in many industries, some occupations being underpaid and others overpaid in relation to the skills and other qualities required, and their removal involves difficult negotiation.

In some industries highly complicated scales of wages have been evolved in negotiations extending over many years, and they require to be simplified and brought up-to-date. In particular, incentive methods of payment based on the processes and products of the past have been revised so often that they no longer provide a proper stimulus to production; further tinkering with them is of little use, and they should be replaced by systems suited to present-day needs.[1] There is also the problem of introducing or extending the use of incentive wage methods in industries where they have hitherto had little application. The detailed devising of incentive wage rates must be undertaken at workshop level, but general principles can be established by negotiation on an industry-wide basis and the application of the detailed schemes at workplaces can be subjected to general supervision by district joint committees.[2]

Some wage problems within industries are referred to arbitration tribunals, which usefully supplement the processes of direct negotiation. One of the fears, especially of trade unions, is that they would lose freedom of action from compulsory arbitration and that, when disputes arose, wages and conditions of work would be regulated by awards of the Courts. A more flexible system could, however, be evolved along the lines of awards and recommendations made during 1950 for the settlement of disputes in British coal-mining and engineering industries. In the coal-mining industry the National Reference Tribunal awarded a lump sum of £3,500,000 a year for wage increases,

---

[1] Several British industries have considered such changes in recent years, for example the cotton industry recommendations of the Evershed Committee.

[2] On December 15, 1950, an agreement along these lines was reached in Britain between the National Federation of Building Trades Employers and the National Federation of Building Trades Operatives.

leaving the National Union of Mineworkers to negotiate with the National Coal Board about the distribution of this sum among the workers; the tribunal did, however, suggest the advisability of using part of the sum to increase by five shillings a week the minimum rates of the lowest-paid workers, and the remainder for the purpose of smaller increases to maintain differentials for some of the categories above the minimum rates. In the engineering dispute the National Arbitration Tribunal made no award but recommended a basis on which the parties might be able to reach agreement, but indicating that if agreement was not reached the tribunal would make an award. The basis was broader than the offer previously made by the employers, which had been rejected by the unions, and the fact that it led to an agreement between the parties illustrates the value of general recommendations made by an impartial authority, while leaving the details to be worked out by negotiation.

In addition to arbitration, another way in which the parties to collective agreements within an industry can be assisted is for the Government to make agreements binding on all employers and workers throughout the industry, provided the parties ask the Government to do so and the Government is satisfied after investigation that the agreements are sufficiently representative and that extension of their application would be in the interests of the industry.

These examples are enough to show that if the trade unions and employers within separate industries act voluntarily in close conformity with a national wages policy, they would have so many vital wage problems to regulate that they would be able to retain the interest of their members. In particular, the trade unions could continue to show to workpeople the need for maintaining and increasing their bargaining strength in order to take part effectively in the regulation of wages and in other measures for the protection and welfare of their members.

It is recognized that a national wages policy could not be applied if powerful individual trade unions insist on forcing their demands, in conditions of full employment, without regard for the interests of the community and of other groups of workpeople. There is, however, a reasonable expectation that responsible trade union leaders and rank and file members will face economic facts and recognize that a flexible system of co-ordination is in their own interests. No doubt one union or another will occasionally wander away from the path, but in the main the movement will realize that the method of working in watertight compartments, each union acting independently in wage policy, is becoming out of date. Each union and each employers' organization will continue to negotiate collective agreements for their members, but in doing so will be influenced by a broader policy based on guidance given by the Government and by the central organizations of employers and of workpeople. The task is difficult and calls for high qualities of leadership.

24

Conciliation and Arbitration

STATE INTERVENTION in industrial disputes which is now widely applied throughout the world, usually begins after a period of severe industrial unrest. The losses of the disputants themselves, those suffered by employers and workpeople in other undertakings and industries, and the inconvenience to the public, lead to strong demands for the State to intervene by providing a system for conciliation and arbitration. Members of the community are injured and yet their voice is not heard in disputes unless the State acts for them. In addition to responsibilities of the State to prevent or reduce these losses and inconveniences, the State has direct interests in maintaining industrial peace. For example, its rearmament programme may be delayed by stoppages in the engineering, transport, or coal-mining industries, and this may be dangerous in periods of international tension. Also, prolonged stoppages in big industries may cause loss of revenue to the State.

In Britain, widespread industrial conflicts, resulting from the growth of militant trade unionism especially among semi-skilled and unskilled workpeople, led to the passing of the Conciliation Act, 1896, and in the same period outbursts of industrial unrest in Australia and New Zealand were responsible for the passing of legislation introducing systems of conciliation and compulsory arbitration in those countries. In time of war the dangers from stoppages in essential industries are so great that strikes and lockouts are prohibited and compulsory arbitration introduced on pressure from the whole community, including workpeople and employers.

It is generally agreed that in industries in which employers and workpeople are well organized the responsibility for regulation of wages and working conditions should as far as possible be theirs. But however comprehensive is the negotiating machinery in industry it sometimes breaks down, and there are big advantages in having some final tribunal to which the dispute can be submitted.[1] This must be impartial, of high standing, free from politics, and free to

[1] Disputes, other than unofficial ones, usually occur over the interpretation of existing agreements or from failure to reach new ones.

make awards or recommendations without being controlled by the Government.

Whether its awards are binding or not, there is a strong case for the compulsory consideration by tribunals presided over by impartial chairmen, of all important disputes, especially those involving large numbers of workpeople, if the parties fail to agree. If negotiations have reached a point when no progress seems possible and a stoppage is imminent, neither party may be willing voluntarily to propose arbitration, as each may fear that the other would consider this to be a sign of weakness in the proposers. Yet both parties are anxious to avoid a stoppage and would welcome impartial investigation and award, and if this is compulsory the psychological difficulty of reticence to suggest arbitration would not arise.

Once investigation has been made into the facts and circumstances of the dispute, the information made public, and an award or recommendations for a settlement are widely known, the chances of acceptance are very great, as is shown by experience. Rank and file members will be better informed about the matters in dispute, including the difficulties of the other side, and the negotiators whose tempers had become heated in the later stages of the controversy have time to cool down and be more ready to support a new approach. At the height of the struggle they may have committed themselves to final, irreconcilable demands which they would refuse in negotiation to moderate for fear of "loss of face," and yet they may accept terms awarded by an impartial authority.[1] The leaders could go to their members saying that they had made every effort both in negotiation and before the arbitration tribunal to secure the conditions demanded, that they had not agreed to less, that the decision, which fails to meet their claims, is not theirs but the tribunal's, but that, in the circumstances, they advise acceptance of the award. Members of the public, well informed by the investigation, will not view with sympathy the rejection of an award by an impartial tribunal which seems to be fair and reasonable. The public is an interested and informed party, and public opinion is a powerful factor in industrial disputes. An arbitration tribunal as a "court of final appeal" gives good prospects of enabling reason to replace force. It must be emphasized, too, that success depends largely upon well-developed disciplined organization of employers and workpeople, and a sense of responsibility not only to their members but to the community.

[1] Often the terms of an award are similar to those which the parties could have arranged by negotiation among themselves if they had not committed themselves to irreconcilable demands.

Arbitration tribunals may play a much bigger part in the determination of working conditions than merely by making awards when disputes come before them. Awards may have a direct effect only infrequently on an industry or branch of industry, as several years may elapse before another dispute brings the same industry before the tribunal again, and industries with good records of industrial peace may rarely if ever appear before it. However, the terms of awards and the principles upon which they are based may become widely known throughout industry, and by gradually building up a body of "case law," may influence collective agreements. During collective bargaining the parties know that if they disagree on matters which have already been the subject of awards for some other locality or industry, the tribunal will be likely, if they go before it with similar issues, to reach a decision for them along the same lines. Instead, therefore, of going to the tribunal they may increasingly agree between themselves on terms similar to those of awards already made. If one side is reluctant to agree, it knows that, under a compulsory arbitration system, if the negotiations break down, the other side will probably get what it wants from the tribunal. The development of such principles and precedents takes a considerable time owing to the many differences in conditions of the disputes submitted to arbitration.

In addition to these indirect influences the arbitration systems in some countries play a direct part in the general regulation of wages and working conditions. Thus, the arbitration courts in the Commonwealth of Australia and in New Zealand declare basic wages for unskilled workpeople and adjust them at regular intervals to changes in the cost of living and also when necessary to economic conditions. These basic rates have a big effect on the wages of all grades of workpeople throughout the industries of these countries. In Australia, New Zealand, and some other countries employers' organizations and trade unions can apply to arbitration courts to have collective agreements registered so that they may have the force of awards. The courts, therefore, have a much wider role than the settlement of disputes.

Although precedents are applied in suitable conditions and certain legal forms are observed, arbitration in labour disputes differs in various ways from ordinary legal processes. The basis for reaching decisions is usually less clearly defined, and instead of applying laws or dealing with existing contracts the awards often define working conditions for the future and involve adaptations to changing conditions for which there may be no precedent. The attitude adopted resembles the flexibility of courts of equity, while the gradual development of agreed principles is somewhat akin to the evolution of common law, being based upon those customs which become widely accepted as fair and reasonable.

A criticism directed against arbitration, whether compulsory or voluntary, is that tribunals can do very little more than to "split the difference" between the two sides. It cannot, however, be assumed that an arbitration award which splits the difference is valueless, as it may keep the peace. Another objection to arbitration is that employers and trade unions will be more perfunctory in their direct negotiations and also during conciliation proceedings, as they know they can throw responsibility on the tribunal. They may agree on lesser matters but leave the main issues unsettled, knowing that they can safely disagree at this stage as arbitration is there as a last resort. They can then go back to their respective members and say, as already indicated, that throughout the proceedings they insisted on maintaining their demands, and that the decision, which fails to meet their claims, is not theirs but the tribunal's. Whenever this happens, the advantages in industrial relations resulting from agreement by mutual concessions and direct responsibility of the parties are lost. In the absence of compulsory arbitration, the leaders on both sides know that a breakdown in negotiations will result in a stoppage and they therefore often go to great lengths in making concessions. Criticism has been directed against the Australian and New Zealand systems of compulsory arbitration on the ground that the parties to disputes do not sufficiently try to effect settlements before going to the arbitration court. It is essential to retain the fullest sense of responsibility of the parties for finding a solution, and the processes of direct negotiation must not be weakened. The danger may be avoided by deferring reference of a dispute to an arbitration tribunal until little if any further progress could be made by direct negotiation towards settling more of the points at issue and narrowing the margin of difference between the disputants. Such power to defer reference is given by legislation in various countries; it is exercised in Britain, for example, by the Minister of Labour.

In the chapter on collective bargaining, mention was made of the practice of many employers' organizations and trade unions to agree to refer to conciliation and, if necessary, to arbitration any differences which they are not able to settle by negotiation. They do this voluntarily in order to reduce or prevent stoppages of work. It was also indicated that such agreements may be *ad hoc* when a stoppage seems imminent, or there may be standing agreements that if at any time direct negotiations fail, the processes of conciliation and arbitration will be used. The parties may, and often do, set up their own conciliation and arbitration procedures, including the selection of an impartial chairman to preside over a joint conciliation conference or committee and the choice of an arbitrator. If the State has established voluntary conciliation and arbitration systems the parties may ask for these facilities to be used to help them, or they may make their own arrangements without using the resources of the State. Or the State may apply systems of compulsory conciliation and arbitration.

The following are the main kinds of State intervention in industrial disputes: (1) voluntary conciliation which leaves the parties free to use the facilities or not as they wish; (2) voluntary arbitration which leaves the parties similarly free; (3) compulsory conciliation which requires parties in dispute to comply with a specific conciliation procedure; (4) compulsory arbitration without making awards binding and without prohibiting strikes and lock-outs after the arbitration procedure is completed, and (5) compulsory arbitration with binding awards, with prohibition of strikes and lock-outs, and with penalties for failure to observe these conditions. Several of these systems can be maintained side by side, and it is an advantage for the State to have a range of alternatives so that it can use the method most likely to be successful in the special circumstances of each dispute.

CONCILIATION

In most countries conciliation is tried before disputes are referred to arbitration. Two main kinds of conciliation system must be distinguished, one consisting of conciliators or industrial relations officers who give their whole time to keeping in touch with both sides in industry, trying to adjust differences before they become acute, and if possible bringing the parties together if more serious clashes develop. Usually regional officers are appointed to keep in touch with local industries, and they make regular reports to headquarters. The system includes a chief conciliation officer or commissioner and several other senior officers to deal with disputes which extend over a number of regions and involve large numbers of workpeople. Much informal work is done to secure agreements, and, where desirable, formal meetings are held consisting of representatives in equal numbers of employers and workers from the industry concerned, with a conciliation officer as chairman. Conciliation committees with such membership are widely used in Australia and New Zealand.

The second system, which is often used, as in Britain, alongside the first, is for the responsible Government department to prepare a list of persons suitable to be independent chairmen of conciliation committees, another list consisting of persons with experience and understanding and reflecting the views of the employers' side of industry, and a third list similarly for the workers' side. When a dispute occurs the parties may agree to set up a joint conciliation committee of their own representatives in equal numbers under a chairman chosen by them or appointed by the responsible minister. If the parties wish, the chairman may be assisted by one or two persons from the list on the employers' side and a similar number from the list on the workers' side, but they are persons not connected with the industry involved in the dispute.

Joint conciliation committees, unlike arbitration tribunals, have the advantage of being directly representative of each separate industry or occupation. In some countries, e.g. Australia and New Zealand, matters on which agreement is reached by conciliation are usually taken formally before the arbitration court, not for re-examination or modification, but for incorporation in an award of the court so as to give the agreements legal force and the scope of an award. In Britain, by contrast, agreements reached by conciliation processes are the same as any other agreements and have no legal force.

The responsible minister is usually empowered, whenever a dispute has occurred or is feared, to inquire into the causes and to take steps to bring the parties together under a chairman mutually agreed upon or appointed by the minister. The British Minister of Labour has this power under the Conciliation Act, 1896, by which also he may appoint a conciliator on the request of either party, but he can refer a dispute to arbitration only on the request of both parties. In some countries the responsible minister has power to make conciliation compulsory, but whether it is voluntary or compulsory the independent chairmen or conciliators are limited to trying to get agreed solutions, and they have no powers of decision if the parties fail to agree. Conciliation systems vary greatly in detail from country to country, but their main features are those outlined above.

VOLUNTARY ARBITRATION

Arbitration is voluntary if the parties, having failed to settle their differences by negotiation, agree to submit them to arbitration. It is equally voluntary whether the parties agree beforehand to accept the award of the tribunal or reserve the right to reject it. If one of the parties refuses to take part then there can be no voluntary arbitration. This is recognized in the British Conciliation Act, 1896, and the Industrial Courts Act, 1919, each of which gives the Minister of Labour authority to refer a dispute to arbitration only if both parties agree. A dispute may be referred to a tribunal set up *ad hoc* to deal only with it, or reference may be made to a permanent or standing tribunal. The British Act of 1896 provides for *ad hoc* tribunals, but the Industrial Court set up under the 1919 Act is a permanent body with full-time members and deals in succession with disputes in a wide range of industries and occupations. In *ad hoc* tribunals the arbitrators have other occupations and can give only a small part of their time to the work of the tribunals, and, being often changed and acting only infrequently, they have little contact with one another and cannot evolve a body of consistent principles.

Where arbitration is voluntary the use made of facilities provided by the State depends entirely on the disputing parties, and in Britain, for example, many big industries have never taken a dispute to a State tribunal for voluntary arbitration. This is because some industries have made their own standing arrangements for arbitration which they consider better suited to their needs than a tribunal set up by the State, while other industries prefer to deal in their own way with each dispute as it arises. Permanently established tribunals include the National Reference Tribunal for Coalmining, the Railway Staffs National Tribunal, and the Civil Service Arbitration Tribunal.

COMPULSORY ARBITRATION

When a system of compulsory arbitration is applied, the State requires the parties to a dispute to submit their differences to an arbitration tribunal, which, after considering the facts and arguments submitted to it, makes an award giving the terms of settlement. Usually compulsory arbitration laws provide that awards shall be binding upon the parties to disputes, but this is not essential, as by some laws it is obligatory to submit disputes to arbitration but the parties are free to accept or reject awards. Compulsory arbitration must be distinguished from all forms of voluntary agreements between disputants to submit their differences to arbitration, even though they may undertake beforehand that the award shall be binding. Arbitration arranged by such agreements is voluntary. To protect its own interests or to safeguard the community, the State may apply compulsory arbitration to disputes in all industries or may limit it to disputes in a few specified industries, for example, water, gas and electricity supply, and transport, whose interruption would cause special inconvenience and loss to the community. Compulsory arbitration with prohibition of strikes and lock-outs is often adopted in time of war by countries which prefer voluntary methods in peace-time. This is because stoppages of work would weaken the war effort of the nation and they are therefore made illegal with the support of public opinion, including that of employers and trade unions.

The compulsion of despotism differs greatly from compulsion in a democracy. In a totalitarian State where the Government dominates the life of the people, including their industrial relations, the trade unions and employers' organizations if they exist are controlled by and subservient to the Government, and the adoption of compulsory arbitration with prohibition of strikes and lock-outs presents little difficulty. In democratic countries, however, where employers and workpeople are strongly organized and have wide scope for freedom of action, compulsory arbitration can be successful only if it is supported by employers' organizations and trade unions. The basis is consent, not coercion. This support was forthcoming, for example, in Great Britain under war-time conditions, while in Australia and New Zealand compulsory arbitration, introduced after a period of severe conflict, was supported by public opinion, including that of employers and workers, most of whom were tired of costly trials of strength and were ready to try a more rational method of settling disputes.

The adoption of compulsory arbitration involves no departure from democratic principles. It would be just as false to argue that compulsory arbitration takes away democratic freedom as that compulsory education or taxation are inconsistent with democracy. No countries are more democratic than Australia and New Zealand, both of which have had compulsory arbitration since the early years of the present century. In those countries the organizations of employers and workpeople state their case freely as independent bodies before the courts, and if they were not generally satisfied with the system and were prepared to give up the advantages they gain from it, they could make it unworkable. The fact that it operates so fully is evidence that in most industries it has secured the support and effective co-operation of employers and workpeople.

Although strikes and lock-outs are widely recognized to be crude and primitive instruments of policy, with losses usually outweighing gains and rarely leading to fair results, employers' organizations and trade unions in many countries have hitherto been unwilling in peace-time to give up these trials of strength as a last resort. For example,

British trade unions, though conducting negotiations with a high sense of responsibility in most industries, have attached great importance to the right to strike, regarding it as essential that they should be free to refuse to work whenever wages or other conditions are unacceptable to them and they could not secure improvements by agreement. Various reasons are given for this hostility to prohibition of strikes and lock-outs. Both sides, while normally ready to go to great lengths in making concessions and agreeing to compromise solutions, believe that questions of vital principle may arise on which neither side is prepared to compromise and a conflict becomes inevitable. Also in some circumstances a stoppage may be the most effective means of focusing attention on a serious grievance and of securing redress. Some believe that employers would be less willing to agree to improved conditions if risk of strikes was removed, but this is not a strong argument, as dissatisfied workpeople can always "go slow" though remaining at work, and reduce output while pressing their claims. Employers and trade unions alike prefer to settle their own affairs without intervention by outsiders, even the State, and they fear that arbitration procedures may involve delays.

Related to some of these objections is unwillingness to have the functions of the State increased. The State has often been unfavourable to trade unionists, who therefore feared its intervention, and there is much evidence to show that in the past the law was biased against them. Thus in Great Britain in the nineteenth century the law itself was often unfavourable to the trade unions, while magistrates frequently adopted a hostile attitude when dealing with cases involving workers' rights and trade union activities, and harsh sentences were imposed, the transportation of the Tolpuddle martyrs being an outstanding example.[1] Such being the workers' experience of the ordinary courts, it is not surprising that they opposed the setting up of courts of arbitration with powers to fix wages and working conditions. They were convinced that these courts would be unsympathetic and make awards against their interests and in favour of the employers, and that, being bound to observe these awards, their position would be weakened. They were therefore suspicious of and showed opposition to any proposals which would take away the right to strike.

Many trade union leaders have believed that members of arbitration courts because of their education, status, and social relations, including closer and more frequent contacts with employers, would view the case presented by employers more sympathetically than

[1] Much more ruthless was the treatment of trade unions in Nazi Germany, and of the "free" trade unions in Fascist countries.

that of the workers, and in consequence arbitration awards would be biased consciously or unconsciously against the workers. Though this fear is still sometimes expressed, there is no evidence that it is well founded, and most workers would agree that tribunals show a high standard of impartiality. Conversely, complaints are occasionally made by employers that, owing to political considerations, persons who are biased in favour of the workers have sometimes been appointed to arbitration tribunals, for example, in Australian States where Labour Governments have had considerable tenure of office. Evidently in making appointments to a court or tribunal, a Government will wish to select persons who are in sympathy with the general trend of opinion on social questions, as is well illustrated by the history of the Supreme Court of the United States. No substantial evidence has, however, been put forward to show any continuous or appreciable bias. In particular, the success of compulsory arbitration in Australia and New Zealand throughout half a century is due to the reputation for impartiality which the courts have gained. Clearly the necessary support from both employers and trade unions for a system of compulsory arbitration can be secured only if there is confidence that the arbitration authorities will be strictly impartial. This does not imply that both sides will be satisfied with every award, but it does imply that they accept the awards as practicable and reasonable taking all the circumstances into consideration, and that, though some awards may appear to lean to one side, a review of a series of awards will show no noticeable bias. Where there is sufficient assurance of such impartiality, both employers and workpeople can avoid the losses which are often severe from strikes and lock-outs, by accepting and supporting the orderly and constitutional methods of compulsory arbitration in place of primitive trials of strength. Under present conditions in Great Britain the impartiality of tribunals set up to arbitrate on labour disputes is generally accepted, and this is true also in many other countries.

From the above review it is clear that in democratic countries the success of any arbitration system depends upon the support of employers' organizations and trade unions. This is well illustrated by British experience in the decade beginning in 1940. In that year, at the height of the perils of the Second World War, compulsory arbitration, prohibition of strikes and lock-outs, and penalties for such stoppages were introduced by governmental Order in agreement with the British Employers' Confederation and the Trades Union Congress, the National Arbitration Tribunal being set up to issue binding awards for the settlement of disputes. This was intended to be a war-time measure, but it was continued for five years after the end of the war by an agreement between the Government, the Confederation, and the Congress, which provided that it would be terminated at any time on the request of either of those bodies.

In 1951 this request was made by the Trades Union Congress because of growing uneasiness when criminal proceedings were taken against workpeople who had gone on strike in violation of the terms of the Order and were liable to fine or imprisonment. However, both Congress and the Confederation wished to retain many features of the system, and after discussions with the Government the Order of 1940 was replaced by one which provided for compulsory arbitration without binding awards or prohibition of strikes and lock-outs. The National Arbitration Tribunal was replaced by the Industrial Disputes Tribunal, consisting of independent and "partisan" members, to which disputes are referred by the Minister of Labour. No action can be taken against people for not observing the Tribunal's awards, and the application of awards depends on their acceptance by the parties concerned.[1]

COURTS OF INQUIRY

Courts of inquiry which the British Minister of Labour can set up under the Industrial Courts Act, 1919, have features which somewhat resemble compulsory arbitration tribunals whose awards are not binding on the parties. The Minister may, whether or not the parties have referred a dispute to him, appoint a court of inquiry consisting of one or several persons to make an investigation and report on the dispute. A court may require persons who appear to have relevant information to furnish such information and, if necessary, to give evidence on oath, though there is no penalty for failure to do so. Reports, which are laid before both Houses of Parliament, give impartial statements of the facts, and also recommendations or conclusions which closely resemble awards. The recommendations have no binding force, although they are usually accepted by the parties as basis for a settlement. The power to set up courts of inquiry has been sparingly used, having been reserved for important disputes for which other methods were less suitable.

MEMBERSHIP OF ARBITRATION TRIBUNALS

Arbitration tribunals whether voluntary or compulsory show one main difference in their composition. Some consist of impartial

[1] Usually cases are heard by three independent and two "partisan" members, though some cases are heard by only one impartial and two "partisan" members. Disputes over recognition of trade unions by employers, or over reinstatement of workpeople who have been dismissed are outside the scope of the Tribunal.

persons only. Thus the Australian Commonwealth Court is of this type, consisting of a chief judge and several other judges. For ordinary cases each judge sits separately, usually specializing on a group of industries, but on general questions, for example, the determination of the basic wage, they sit together.

Other tribunals, sometimes known as "partisan" tribunals, consist of one or more impartial arbitrators with whom sit assessors representing employers and workpeople respectively. An impartial member presides. Usually there are two or four assessors who are not drawn from the particular industry appearing before the tribunal, but take part in hearings and decisions affecting all other industries that come before it. An advantage claimed for this kind of tribunal is that it ensures that the point of view of each side is more fully appreciated than by tribunals which are composed solely of impartial members. The two sides may be more satisfied with an award if they know that there has been within the tribunal itself someone fully aware of their attitudes. Assessors can sometimes assist the impartial member or members considerably by agreeing on many matters of detail, either with or without informal conversations with the representatives of the industry concerned, leaving only a few matters of main importance for decision by the impartial member or members. They may also be able readily and informally to obtain from the parties to the dispute information which elucidates points raised in formal statements made to the tribunal.

The chairmen of tribunals are often experienced members of the legal profession, some of whom especially when newly appointed find themselves on strange ground in dealing with wages, hours, and other economic and social questions brought before them. Except when they are interpreting disputed terms of existing agreements, most of their work is not judicial but is more akin to legislation under delegated powers. Members with legal training are certainly well trained in sifting evidence and in giving judgments. After hearing a number of cases they become familiar with the underlying economic, industrial, and social problems, while in choosing lawyers for membership of tribunals it is frequently possible to find some who are interested in and well informed about such affairs. Alternatively, experienced economists with some knowledge of law often make effective chairmen or members.

The view is sometimes expressed that frequent changes in the membership of permanent tribunals are desirable so that there would be less danger of weakening the reputation for impartiality which would follow if either workers or employers believed that certain members were biased against them. Also, it is argued that, without frequent changes, the attitude and decisions of tribunals would tend to become stereotyped, rigid, and official, and that assessors would tend to lose touch with the interests respectively of employers and workpeople whom they have been chosen to represent. These arguments do not apply to *ad hoc* tribunals, and the experience of permanent tribunals shows that they are heavily outweighed by the advantages of stability and continuity. The presidents and members of tribunals often serve for many years without difficulties arising. It is specially important that tribunals should be independent of Government, and, to ensure this, the presidents and other full-time members are given security of tenure similar to that of law court judges.

Spokesmen for the Parties

In submitting facts and arguments to arbitration tribunals each side has a leading spokesman, who, in highly organized industries in many advanced countries, is from the industry concerned. He is supported by other representatives from the industry, some of whom may supplement the data he presents. In some arbitrations, written statements are prepared by each side for the tribunal, and may also be exchanged between the sides before the hearings begin. In less well-organized industries, the workers' side especially may not be able to find a spokesman from among themselves who can effectively present their case, and may ask someone from outside the industry or occupation to do this for them, Thus, experienced trade union officials who have acquired knowledge of arbitration procedure may act for the workers in a succession of hearings involving different industries, being, however, supported in each case by trade union officials from the industry concerned.

An alternative is for each party to employ counsel to present their case. This is often done in Australia and New Zealand. It ensures that the arguments are put by persons fully conversant with court procedure, and tends to facilitate the work of the tribunal. Some lawyers specialize in industrial arbitration cases. Employment of counsel involves the danger that the proceedings may become too juridicial, and there is the disadvantage that the parties directly concerned may be unduly passive in the hearings.

THE "COMMON RULE"

The primary purpose of arbitration is to preserve industrial peace by impartial hearings and awards which are fair and reasonable settlements of the disputes. A question which must be considered is whether awards should apply only to the disputants or should have a wider application. A dispute may arise at a single factory or locality, but the terms of the award may be suitable for application to all employers and workpeople in the same industry or occupation. Such extension from particular cases to others in similar conditions is known as the "common rule."

Originally awards of arbitration tribunals in settlement of a dispute were limited to the parties involved in the dispute. This, however, raised two difficulties. Employers who are bound to pay rates of wages fixed in an award may find themselves in competition with firms not so bound. Also, if an employer is legally bound to apply award conditions to his workpeople who are trade union members he will find it awkward to treat them better than his non-unionist workpeople, and to avoid discrimination he is likely to apply the same conditions to both groups. This problem does not arise if the award is extended to cover such non-disputants.

The practice varies in different countries. In Australia and New Zealand the tendency is towards the application of awards to all workpeople, whether union members or not, employed by any undertaking subject to an award, and also for extension of an award to all firms in an industry, including new firms starting during the currency of an award. In some Australian States an award applies only to firms cited or named at the time the case is heard by the arbitration court, but usually the unions make certain that all employers in the industry are cited, thereby ensuring the general application of the award. In Britain the awards made in the compulsory arbitration system of the Second World War were applicable whenever appropriate to all firms in the industry concerned and not merely to those involved in the disputes.[1]

ENFORCEMENT OF BINDING AWARDS

Enforcement of awards and prohibition of strikes and lock-outs both raise the question whether penalties can be imposed effectively

[1] The principle is the same as that in a British Act of Parliament passed in 1934 which gave the Minister of Labour power to extend rates of wages agreed between representative organizations in the cotton manufacturing industry to employers not members of the appropriate organization. The Minister was empowered to issue such an order only if organizations representing the majority of employers and workpeople jointly apply for an order to be issued. Also he would issue such an order only if a board consisting of three impartial members together with six assessors from each side was satisfied that the organizations which were parties to the agreement were representative and were unanimous that extension of the agreement was expedient. The purpose of the Act was to prevent a minority of employers and workers in a period of depression from offering or accepting employment at wages lower than those in collective agreements and thereby threatening to undermine the whole structure of agreements.

upon an organization or its members for failing to observe the terms of an award or for causing a stoppage. It may be impracticable to prosecute and penalize the individual members, whose numbers on the workers' side would often be large, and who would, except in unofficial strikes, have been acting on instructions from their leaders. The organization could be fined, but this may be undesirable. There is the difficulty that if stoppages are illegal and yet there are no satisfactory or effective means of enforcement, contempt for the law might develop. It seems preferable therefore from these considerations, that compulsory arbitration should be applied as a last stage in the attempt to find acceptable terms, but if the trade unions or the employers are not willing to work under the conditions of the award, they should have the right to call a strike or lock-out. Such stoppages would, however, be infrequent if organizations are well disciplined and have responsible leadership.

During the Second World War and in the early years of reconstruction after the war, although strikes were illegal in Great Britain and trade union leaders consistently supported peaceful methods of settling disputes, a number of unofficial strikes took place and it was often impracticable to apply penalties. Peace-time experience in Australia and New Zealand shows that strikes are not prevented by making them illegal. When workpeople go on strike they are collectively refusing to work under conditions laid down in an award, and, notwithstanding the illegality of striking, have no feeling of guilt, of doing something criminal, or of meriting penalties of fine or imprisonment. Public opinion may disapprove of the use of the strike weapon and support compulsory arbitration and yet not be in favour of penalties for striking being imposed upon workpeople for refusing to work under specified conditions. There is also the practical difficulty of collecting fines from large numbers of individuals or of putting them in prison.

Under most of the compulsory arbitration systems of Australia and New Zealand the laws originally provided that fines could be imposed for strikes against the provisions of awards. This penalty is not now widely used, although in some States, e.g. Western Australia and New Zealand, it has been retained and fines are sometimes imposed either on the individual workers or on the unions. Sometimes fines are imposed by the magistrates but are not collected, the view being held that attempts to collect the fines would cause bitterness and a deterioration of industrial relations. Yet the law is not amended, as the liability to prosecution is considered of some value as a deterrent. In New Zealand the penalty of a fine has been more widely supported, and fines have been more frequently imposed than in Australia, though they are not always collected.

Formerly strikes against awards of the Australian Commonwealth Court were punishable by fine, but in recent years the penalty has been withdrawn, without, however, making any noticeable difference in the extent to which the Court's awards are observed in practice. This is largely because the awards are usually accepted, sometimes with reluctance, by the two sides and because public opinion strongly supports observance of the Court's awards. The Court can, however, use the penalty of de-registering a union for striking against an award, though this is rarely done. Only registered unions are recognized by the Court, and registration is usually granted only to one union for a given branch of industry or category of workpeople. A de-registered union has no means of ensuring to its members the conditions of work fixed in an award of the Court, and also incurs the risk that a rival union may be formed, secure registration and consequently be able to present its case before the Court and obtain the benefit of binding awards. In these circumstances the de-registered union is likely to suffer loss of membership, and the penalty is rightly feared by many unions. Therefore, though not fully satisfied with some awards, they will observe them so as to maintain their standing with the Court. They also value other advantages of registration, which include the application of the "common rule" to some awards so that, instead of being effective only for the parties to the dispute, they are made binding upon the whole of the industry or occupation. A few strongly organized unions have believed that, when circumstances were favourable, they could gain more by direct action than from the Court, and have sometimes withdrawn their registration in order to pursue militant tactics. As such unions are strong enough to have no fear of rival unions, de-registration by the Court would not undermine their authority and would not be an effective sanction.

A less drastic penalty is suspension of an award. The members of a union may be inclined to resist a new award because they dislike one or two of its terms. Yet the award may contain many provisions which they desire, some having been in force for years under previous awards, and they may, therefore, refrain from strike action so as not to ruin the risk of losing the protection of the whole award.

Mention may be made of two other penalties which have been tried in Australia. Under the Transport Workers' Act, 1929, after prolonged unrest among dock-workers, a system was introduced at specified ports by which only licensed dock-workers could obtain employment, and licences could be withdrawn from workers who refused to work under the terms of an award of the Commonwealth Court, or who failed to comply with any lawful order. The system acted as a powerful deterrent at the ports where it was applied, while at other ports stoppages became rare as the workers wished to avoid extension of the system.

In Western Australia in 1938, the State Arbitration Court made awards providing for paid annual holidays in certain industries, but by the terms of the awards the period fixed for the holidays would be reduced by the number of days during which the workers had been on strike during the year. The provision of paid holidays is, however, a reasonable condition of employment, which should not be reduced as a penalty for stoppages of work because of industrial disputes.

Compulsory arbitration depends little for its success on fear of penalties, but mainly on the influence of impartial hearings and awards on the parties in dispute. Criticism is sometimes directed against compulsory arbitration because it fails to prevent all stoppages, but no law is observed 100 per cent. The test of success is whether the system is effective in reducing substantially the losses from disputes. Also, if the penalties of fine or imprisonment arouse strong opposition as they did in Britain in 1949 and 1950, it seems desirable to replace compulsory arbitration with binding awards and penalties by compulsory arbitration without binding awards, and to rely on the fairness of the awards to win acceptance. Some strikes are directed against the terms of an award, but many are sudden outbursts by workpeople, who, having some grievance about which they feel strongly, take immediate action instead of using the regular but, to them, leisurely procedure of conciliation and arbitration. When such spontaneous outbreaks occur, the union leaders usually urge the men to return to work and adopt constitutional methods for the consideration of their grievance. Workpeople who are not organized or are members of unregistered unions can, under some laws, go on strike without running the risk of penalties. Sporadic strikes by unorganized workpeople are not, however, of great importance, while many unions are registered in order to secure the benefits of registration. In Australia and New Zealand, however, there are militant trade unions in strong strategic positions, for example in coal-mining and dock labour, which as already noted use the arbitration courts when this suits them, but at other times, when they consider it will better serve their interests, they become de-registered and use the weapon of the strike or threats of strike. They try to get the best of both worlds, their militancy and the difficulty of imposing effective penalties enabling them to continue to use these tactics, and they have been responsible for the heaviest losses from strikes.

EFFECTS ON TRADE UNIONS AND EMPLOYERS' ORGANIZATIONS

State systems of conciliation and arbitration have facilitated the formation and growth of trade unions and employers' organizations, their influence having been particularly marked in industries in which difficulties of organization are great. Organizations which are admitted before tribunals gain a recognized status. The fact that the courts in Australia and New Zealand deal only with registered organizations encourages the formation of permanent and properly constituted bodies. Compulsory arbitration provides trade unions with a constitutional procedure for remedying injustices, while employers gain protection against extreme demands. The courts in Australia and New Zealand have also given protection when employers have discriminated against union members, and they have from time to time acted in ways which have secured preference in employment for union members. The New Zealand Industrial Conciliation and Arbitration Act, 1936, went so far as to introduce compulsory unionism by providing that all workers subject to any award or industrial agreement registered under the Act must become members of a union. An argument advanced in favour of preference for unionists and also for compulsory unionism is that the members of the union by their organization and subscriptions and by the work of putting their case before the court have secured improved conditions for their members and that it is unfair that other workpeople should enjoy these benefits on equal terms without having made contributions to the union.

Certain trade unions, usually the weaker ones, favour limiting the operation of awards to members of unions, fearing that some workers may not join the union if they can enjoy the benefits without becoming members. Some trade unionists in Australia and New Zealand complain about the apathy shown by their members towards the movement, and attribute this to compulsory arbitration. In countries, however, in which compulsory arbitration has not been introduced or has played a much smaller part, complaints are also made about the apathy and lack of interest of large numbers of trade unionists. There seems no doubt that, once the fight for recognition by employers has been won and machinery for regulating working conditions and settling disputes has been established, including voluntary methods or compulsory arbitration, the interest and excitement of

378

militancy are largely replaced by the calmer processes of negotiation. These processes must inevitably be conducted by a small number of leaders, either in voluntary collective bargaining with the employers or before arbitration tribunals. In these circumstances the rank and file members are only occasionally likely to be roused to a high level of activity and enthusiasm by some special grievance or urgent demand.

Arbitration tribunals which are permanent and have years of experience develop a body of general principles on which their awards are based, and these principles may have a powerful influence on collective bargaining. Also, systems of conciliation and arbitration in effect represent the public in industrial relations, and public opinion usually welcomes them as reasonable means of settling disputes. Where this constitutional procedure is available for industry, public opinion exerts its influence for the preservation of industrial peace by supporting awards as fair adjustments of contending claims.

25

Relations in Nationalized Industries

THE MOST comprehensive intervention of the State in industrial relations is where the State becomes the employer and is responsible for the operation of an undertaking or industry. Thus in a nationalized industry, whether controlled by a Government department or by a public corporation or board responsible to a minister under conditions defined by legislation, the Government is in effect the employer of labour. In the event of a dispute or clash of interests it can no longer "hold the ring," it is in the ring as one of the contestants. It cannot stand aside while the combatants fight to a finish, as it may do in a conflict in private industry, or intervene as an independent and impartial party to try to effect a settlement by conciliation or arbitration. It cannot be judge in its own cause. It must therefore be specially vigilant to prevent serious clashes, and where they arise it must make every effort to secure a fair and reasonable settlement by negotiation. It has, however, a responsibility to other nationalized industries and to private industries, and would be open to criticism if it used its resources to accede to demands which involved favouring one industry in ways which would be unfair to others.

From the ordinary workers' point of view, however, the similarities between working conditions and industrial relations in a nationalized industry and those in private undertakings are greater than the differences. They must do their work in accordance with instructions given by their foreman, with whom they are likely to find the same causes of disagreement and clashes of personality as in private industry. Their hours of work and wages will in the long run keep approximately in line with those in private industry. They will encounter the same stresses and strains from changes in processes and methods of work, including those which arise from the greater use of labour-saving machines. They will experience the effects of changes in demand for their products and services, whether due to competition of other goods and services, to foreign competition, or to variations in the general level of prosperity. In consequence they will have to negotiate wage changes, with all the possibilities of disagreement, and will experience unemployment.

The difference from private industry which is mainly emphasized by supporters of nationalization is that the profit motive is eliminated, and therefore workpeople will be more satisfied with their conditions and status. Yet in practice in their daily work they experience almost all the same irritations and frictions. Nor is it true that the profit motive is eliminated. If an industry made a profit before nationalization it should be expected to do so afterwards, the main difference being that the profits would accrue to the whole community and not to private shareholders; but in gaining this benefit the community is also called upon to bear the risks of loss. Nationalized industries cannot escape economic risks and must pay current rates of interest on capital which they need for expanding or improving their equipment. Their cash profits over a period of years would normally go to the Exchequer and would benefit taxpayers. Instead, however, of attempting to secure substantial money profits the alternative policy could be adopted of reducing prices to consumers. Clearly the "profits" of a nationalized industry must be widely shared by the community and not used to confer special benefits upon the workpeople of the industry. As already indicated, their wages and conditions should, as far as practicable, be kept in line with those of workpeople in other industries, whether nationalized or not. They have no claim to preferential treatment. This is indicated by the use of the "fair wages" clause in Government contracts. The State as employer should be a "good" employer, but its standards will correspond closely with those of good employers in private industry.

Another difference between nationalized and private industry is that the first has only one employer, whereas in a private industry there may be many independent firms. This implies that there is no competition within a nationalized industry, though it may be in competition with other industries, for example, railway with road transport, or coal with oil. However, in the administration of a nationalized industry, the controlling authority will make comparisons between the different units with the object of determining their relative efficiencies. For this purpose it will adopt standards or tests of efficiency, whether in terms of physical output, quality of services, or costs, and will put pressure on those units which fall without good reasons substantially below standard. Such pressure will, according to circumstances, be put on management or on labour at the units concerned with a view to securing improvements. Thus in Britain, the National Coal Board has issued warnings to the workpeople at certain collieries that their output was unduly low owing to restrictive practices and that penalties would be imposed unless productivity increased. Evidence of poor work was given by comparisons with previous production at the same pits and with other pits working under comparable conditions. Such inefficiency must be sharply distinguished from low output at uneconomic units, for example coal pits with poor seams or where the seams are nearing exhaustion, these representing conditions for which neither management nor workpeople are responsible.

The fact that a nationalized industry is controlled by a single authority implies that wages and working conditions will tend to become more standardized throughout the industry, and that an industry-wide system of industrial relations must be established. The industry is a unified undertaking, and unlike the separate firms in private industry which differ from one another in their capacity to pay, the controlling authority of a nationalized industry must treat all its workpeople in accordance with the same general principles. Even in private industry there are limits to variations in wages and conditions; the operation of collective agreements and the effects of mobility of labour from firm to firm both tend to reduce inequalities. Indeed, in some industries where collective agreements are highly developed the variation from firm to firm in wages and hours of work is slight, while in a highly integrated giant undertaking in private industry which has developed into a monopoly by absorption or amalgamation of formerly competing firms the conditions of labour are usually standardized in ways closely resembling those in a nationalized industry.

Because the controlling authority of a nationalized industry must apply the same general principles to all its workpeople, it will try progressively to devise and apply a so-called "scientific" wage structure. If recently nationalized many wage anomalies will be found which are the result of historical factors, including wage differences due to no other cause than that they had been paid by the separate firms, and a long time will be needed and many difficulties must be overcome before a suitable structure can be approved and applied. The objective should be the establishment of scales of wages so that a worker wherever employed shall be paid a wage equal to that paid to other workers of equal skill, training, and experience working under similar conditions. In other words, the principle must be "equal pay for equal work," and its application will include wage differentials for differences of skill, and additional payments for work under unpleasant or dangerous conditions. Allowances should be made for differences in the cost of living between districts, so the "equality" would be of real wages and not of money wages. Also, some differences in wages between districts may be maintained if workers in lower-paid districts are, because of inertia or for social reasons, unwilling to move to districts where pay is higher. Where appropriate, piece rates or other output methods of payment should be applied, and this would permit of differences in earnings between workers of different efficiency in the same wage grade. It follows that, once a sound wage structure is in operation, a worker employed, for example, at a thin coal seam which is difficult to work will earn amounts equal to those received by workers of the same grade and equal efficiency in another part of the country, who, because they are getting coal at a rich, easily worked seam, are producing two or three times as much. The same principle should be applied also to hours of work, paid holidays, and other conditions.

In private industry each company is independent of others, and whereas some may be making big profits others may be near bankruptcy. Under nationalization, absence of competition within the industry and the fact that the industry is financially a single unit enable surpluses from the better producing units to be used to assist the poorer ones, including some running at a loss. Thus in the British coal-mining industry the reports of the National Coal Board show big losses in some districts carried by surpluses in others. This facilitates the adoption of greater uniformity of labour conditions throughout the industry.

Methods of negotiation and consultation for dealing with the problems reviewed above and with the many other questions requiring discussion between management and representatives of the workpeople are likely to be comprehensive and highly integrated in a nationalized industry. They will include arrangements for joint consultation at factory, workshop, or colliery level on working conditions, methods of improving productive efficiency, and disputes. Systematic arrangements will be made for joint consultation and negotiations at district and regional levels, and also nationally. Throughout the whole system there will usually be advantages in having, at each level, one set of joint committees or conferences on constructive co-operation and another for collective bargaining for the regulation of wages, working conditions, and settlement of disputes.

In these committees and conferences, management will be represented by those mainly responsible for administration of the subjects to be discussed, and consequently there will be different representation of management according as questions, for example, of mechanization, safety, or wages are under consideration, although some of managements' representatives may be interested in many different problems and may provide a common element over a wide range of subjects. In principle, the representatives of management at all levels are responsible for applying a general or unified policy throughout the whole of the nationalized industry. This involves the danger that decisions may be delayed at lower levels in order that authority may be obtained at the highest level, especially where the problem raises new questions of principle. Such delays are likely to cause irritation among the workpeople which may result in stoppages of work. In private industry the workers' representatives at factory or colliery levels are usually dealing with principals who can reach agreements and final decisions, whereas in a nationalized industry management may be unwilling to commit itself until its recommendations are approved by higher authority. Such delays can be reduced by decentralization of control so that, at each level, the representatives of management can reach binding decisions over a reasonably wide field. Such decentralization is difficult, and on many questions impracticable, in a newly nationalized industry. Decentralization depends upon the adoption at the highest level of clearly defined general principles and policies which can, with suitable allowance for differences in local and regional conditions, be applied throughout the industry. Considerable time and experience of unified control are necessary for devising such an integrated policy and body of principles.

Representation of the workpeople is largely undertaken by the trade unions, and is likely to be more complex than representation of the administration; it is dependent upon the structure, organization, and policy of the unions. Where a powerful trade union organized on industrial lines aims to include all sections of workers in the industry in its ranks, it may claim to be the sole representative of the workers. Whether this claim will be recognized by the controlling authority of the industry will depend upon the strength of the union in relation to that of other unions, including those whose members are employed in particular crafts or processes. The authority will decide to recognize one union or more unions according to which will ensure the most effective representation of all the main categories of workpeople and at the same time provide the best bases for negotiation for the regulation of working conditions and the best prospect of preserving industrial peace. This problem of representation is illustrated by the refusal of the British National Coal Board to recognize certain district associations of winding enginemen, who, in the opinion of the Board, could be effectively represented by the National Union of Mineworkers. Conversely, in the nationalized British Railways the National Association of Locomotive Drivers and Firemen, and the Transport Salaried Staffs' Association are recognized by the Railway Executive for separate representation from the National Union of Railwaymen, on the grounds that drivers and firemen and clerks are powerfully organized by their own union and could not be properly represented by the National Union of Railwaymen.

Consideration must be given to the question of strikes in nationalized industries. The nationalization of an industry provides no reason why the right to strike should be denied or modified, though, as is indicated below, the problem is not the same as in private industry. In a nationalized industry a complete system of negotiation and for dealing with disputes from the lowest to the highest levels is likely to be established. This system may be cumbersome, and will often seem slow to a local group of workers with a grievance, and they may go on strike to force immediate attention to their demands. However, such strikes are almost always unofficial, as the union is likely to be taking part in negotiations at the stage officially reached by the dispute. Official strikes led by the trade unions cannot be ruled out in nationalized industries, though they are likely to be rare. They might occur on some major industry-wide issue on which the controlling authority and the unions come into severe and bitter conflict. With statesmanlike leadership on both sides such a conflict could scarcely arise, and the whole structure of negotiation, conciliation, inquiry, and arbitration would provide means for reaching a settlement. In the event, however, of failure to do so, it would become more difficult than in private industry to draw the line between an industrial dispute and action designed to coerce the Government, and the Government might decide to use all its force and authority to secure an early resumption of work.

In circumstances involving the risk of a major stoppage the Government is in a more favourable position than private employers to secure a settlement, at least temporarily, by granting a subsidy or providing protection of some kind to assist the industry. This method should rarely be used, and certainly not to "buy" industrial peace by conceding unreasonable demands by a section of labour. The Government is responsible for keeping a fair balance between the industry concerned, other nationalized industries, and private industries.

What part, if any, should the workers of a nationalized industry play in the appointment of managerial officials? In considering this question it must be recognized that these officials are responsible to the community for the operation of the industry, and that formally members of the controlling board should be appointed by the Government, and the board will then appoint the heirarchy of officials. These are in no way responsible to the workers of the industry, who are themselves in effect appointed in like manner and are also responsible to the community. Informally, however, the workers are likely to influence the appointment of some of the managerial staff. Thus, in the appointment of foremen and junior managers, some of the more reliable workpeople or representatives of the trade union may be consulted and their opinions taken into consideration in making the final selection. For higher level appointments of officials who will deal with labour problems, including members specializing in labour affairs on the controlling authority, the trade unions may exercise great influence, and many of these officials may have had long experience in the trade union movement. They will have sympathy with and understanding of the workers' point of view, but once they become officials of a nationalized industry it is their job to serve not sectional interests but the interests of the whole community. At the same time, the trade unions, by having no formal responsibility for the administration and its officials, preserve their own independence and freedom of action.

26

Social Security

SOCIAL SECURITY is a subject big enough to require a volume or even several volumes to itself, and some of its problems, for example, actuarial questions, are outside the field of industrial relations. Other parts of social security are, however, so closely connected with industrial relations that they claim a place in this volume. Security is one of the main aspirations of the workers, and its attainment strengthens the foundations of industrial peace. From the middle of the nineteenth century many trade unions included sickness, unemployment, and other social security benefits among their main activities, while nowadays they not infrequently demand old age pensions or other forms of social security in collective bargaining with employers instead of trying to gain wage increases. This was done, for example, by powerful unions in the United States a few years after the end of the Second World War, and somewhat similar demands have been made in British industries. In France family allowances provided from employers' contributions have been associated with the wage system for several decades. In many State systems of social security the revenues are largely built up from contributions of workers and employers, and the employers' payments are a labour cost or a tax on employment which inevitably affects wages. Contributions made by the State are financed in a large part from taxes paid by employers and workers, and under present conditions of less inequalities of incomes in Britain, the part paid in this way by the workers is substantial.

Social security cash benefits are closely linked with the wage system, being in effect a continuation of income during periods when, for such reasons as sickness, unemployment, and old age, the workers' wages cease. Also, the necessary funds are formed by a pooling of contributions by or on behalf of all workers, and these funds are then distributed to those who experience cessation of earnings. In Britain, many of the cash benefits of social security represent mainly a transfer of incomes not from rich and poor, but among the wage earners themselves, e.g. from the healthy to the sick, from the employed to the unemployed, and from those who run the gauntlet of industrial accidents without a scratch to those who have the misfortune to be victims. These are redistributions of incomes within the same social class. However, in Britain the costs of childrens' allowances (after the first child),[1] and the National Health Service, are borne mainly by the taxpayer and are therefore distributed over the whole community, with the rich paying heavily as a result of the progressive system of taxation in force.

An important question of social security policy is the proportion of the workers' earnings which should be left to him for his own independent use and the proportion which should be compulsorily deducted for use in ways dictated by the State outside the control of the individual. This question is difficult to answer. Some risks can only be covered effectively by common action, and some needs can be met much more economically by comprehensive organization than by individual efforts, including voluntary co-operation. The principle should be adopted of making deductions from wages only where the gains from compulsory social organization can be shown to be substantial, and where the freedom, initiative, and sense of responsibility of the individual would not be seriously undermined. Otherwise there is a danger of keeping people in tutelage and treating them as children when they should be free to work out their own destiny. The application of doctrinaire principles and the momentum of State machinery should be continually challenged and greater freedom should be restored wherever this is likely to strengthen the moral fibre of individual character and personality. Already in Britain the combined direct contribution in respect of male workers is 11s. 2d. a week, or more than 10 per cent of an unskilled worker's wage, and if to this is added the workers' payments through taxation to the cost of the National Health Service, family allowances, education, the State's part of the cost of old age pensions, and National Assistance, the potential resources withdrawn from a worker reaches the substantial total of more than £1 a week, or 15 to 20 per cent of his wage according as he is skilled or unskilled.

In 1911 the pill of the workers' contribution was sugared by the slogan "ninepence for fourpence," but, whatever may have been the realities then, it must be recognized that a high proportion of the total cost is now borne directly or indirectly by the beneficiaries themselves. Increased social security benefits involve, under present British conditions, increased contributions from the beneficiaries and their employers, sufficient to cover a large part of the increased costs. Nor can the beneficiaries as a whole evade such higher costs by

---

1 Allowances are paid for the first child also if the worker is in receipt of sickness, accident, or unemployment benefit.

increases in wages, though there may be some shifting of the burden from workers who are strongly organized and in industries where economic conditions are favourable to those in a weaker position. Although in many systems of social security both employers and workpeople contribute substantially, the combined amount is a labour cost, and from the economic point of view the amount might equally well be paid wholly by the employers or wholly by the workers, though there are psychological advantages in each paying a similar share.

The connection between wages and unemployment insurance is particularly close, as, if wages are fixed too high unemployment with its drain on social security funds will be increased. On the other hand, the existence of substantial unemployment benefits tends to reduce the pressure of the unemployed to get jobs, and this strengthens the bargaining power of the trade unions. A system of children's allowances has a similar effect especially if these allowances are continued when workers are on strike.

Social security is provided in other ways than by State systems, and some of them are even more directly linked with industrial relations. Many trade unions have their own sickness, unemployment, and old age schemes. Also large numbers of firms have established savings funds, sickness benefits, and old age pensions for their workpeople. The provisions of these schemes are usually discussed with the workers before being introduced, the workers are often represented in the committees which administer them, and sometimes the general provisions of these schemes are the outcome of collective negotiation. Sometimes in collective bargaining an agreement is reached on the adoption of some form of social protection or welfare as an alternative to, or in modification of, a wage claim.

The effects of social security on the worker's will to produce must not be overlooked. What truth is there in the statement that "security is mankind's chiefest enemy"? Does security weaken initiative and breed slackness? Does it undermine enterprise and the willingness to take risks? Does it sap the pioneering spirit on which progress so largely depends? These are serious questions, and before they can be answered much more experience is needed of the effects of comprehensive systems of social security. In effect, payments are made by the productive to the unproductive, that is, by those who are fit and employed to the aged, the sick, and the unemployed. Most sick and unemployed of working age will become producers again, and the help they get from social security will usually enable them to work better when they return to their jobs than if they had deteriorated because of severe privation. The problem is mainly one of the effects of the system on initiative, independence, and efficiency. Properly devised and administered, social security, though it will be abused by some, is likely to facilitate increased production by reducing the harm done to the main body of workpeople by the fears, anxieties, and privations of insecurity. It must never be forgotten, however, that the resources to provide social security benefits are largely due to the energy, ability, and initiative of the relatively small group of really enterprising people from all classes, and there should be more joy in Westminster and Whitehall over one who blazes a new trail and is willing to take its risks than over ninety and nine who stagnate in the sheepfold of social security.[1]

ORIGIN AND DEVELOPMENT

The germ of social security is in the provision made by the family, village, tribe, or clan for its sick, infirm, and aged members. Among nomadic peoples their way of life made it difficult to give this care, and often the infirm and aged were left behind as stragglers to fend for themselves, which frequently meant death from starvation or from hostile tribes. In more settled communities, however, the fit usually aided the unfit, and in the large centres of population individual charity was supplemented by organized assistance, by guilds, by monasteries, and other religious foundations, and by the whole community as under the Elizabethan Poor Law.

Social security began, therefore, on a voluntary and local basis. With the rapid development of industry and transport in the nineteenth century and mobility of labour, the sense of personal and local responsibility was weakened, and the need arose for more extensive and comprehensive schemes. Yet in that period, action remained largely voluntary, except in the public relief of destitution, as the State was dominated by *laissez-faire* doctrine in economic and social affairs. Haphazard and indiscriminate private charity was supplemented and in part replaced by the work of charitable organizations. The plausible beggar still plied his "trade" by playing, often successfully, on the feelings of warm-hearted people, but organizations were more able to help those in greatest need. Charity,

---

[1] In his Report on Social Insurance and Allied Services (Cmd. 6404) Sir William Beveridge said (pp. 6 and 7): "The State in organizing social security should not stifle incentive, opportunity, responsibility; in establishing a national minimum it should leave room and encouragement for voluntary action by each individual to provide more than that minimum for himself and for his family." He also expresses his opinion (p. 167) that: "Properly devised, controlled, and financed it, i.e. unified social insurance, need have no depressing effect on incentive."

however, is essentially help provided by one group of people for the benefit of another distinct group; it is in no way a form of mutual aid, and it contains no germ of the insurance principle or of forethought in the accumulation of funds "before the event."

Mutual aid was attractive to people who, in the main, were not of the type to be recipients of charity, and they joined together partly to protect themselves against the need for charity. This method developed greatly during the nineteenth century among people living in the same locality or working in the same occupation. In an *ad hoc* way the spirit of mutual aid is shown at its best in the splendid spontaneous practical support given to victims of a disaster, for example, in a mining village. Such aid is given with a warmth of sympathy and understanding which more organized assistance rarely shows, but while it meets the immediate need it is rarely sustained sufficiently when the impact of the disaster weakens. Hence more stable forms of mutual aid were organized, including many local sickness and burial funds. The trade unions on a wider geographical basis made such activities, including pensions and unemployment schemes, an important part of their work, while friendly societies were formed in growing numbers to meet similar needs. By 1939 in Britain the registered friendly societies, including trade unions, had an approved society membership of 5½ million persons. Also an increasing number of firms introduced schemes for their own workpeople. Alongside these non-profit-making societies there developed life insurance companies, some of which were on a mutual basis, distributing profits among the persons insured, but others paid dividends to shareholders. These companies usually maintained a fairly close relation, determined actuarially, between the contributions or premiums paid and the risks involved.

Towards the end of the nineteenth century the decline of *laissez-faire* opened the way for State schemes of social insurance to supplement voluntary provision and State relief of destitution. Intervention by the State was at first tentative and cautious, so much so that the earliest measures dealt not with the greatest needs but with those involving the least responsibility of the State. This was one of the reasons why workmen's compensation was one of the first State measures of social security to be adopted, with the main responsibility resting on the employers through the application of the policy of employers' liability. Schemes involving direct State responsibility and an elaborate administrative system were usually left till later, and were then introduced piecemeal, each problem—sickness, unemployment, old age, and the rest—being dealt with at different times, as determined by the force of political and social pressures, and each had its own independent legislation and administration. Many anomalies resulted, including payment of different rates of benefit according as to whether people were sick, unemployed, or victims of accidents though their needs were the same; also the administration was complex and sometimes confusing. Demands were therefore made for co-ordination and unification, and also for comprehensiveness to fill gaps left by the piecemeal evolution. Unification and comprehensiveness have gone furthest in Britain, where as was aptly said at the time of extension of social security to all citizens, whatever their income or occupation, "The British people joined together in a single national friendly society for mutual support during the common misfortunes of life. The new system is essentially the culmination of half a century of piecemeal social reform now carried to a logical conclusion."[1]

THE PROBLEM OF RISK

The "ideal" risk for insurance is where each of a number of individuals has an equal chance of experiencing some loss or misfortune involving a known monetary outlay, there is no foreknowledge of who will incur this expense, those who will suffer the loss are a small proportion of the total number of individuals who run the risk, and this proportion is known exactly or with a high degree of probability. The total outlay can be calculated, and the risk can be covered by collecting equally from each individual an amount which aggregated will equal the total required.

No social security risk comes near to this ideal. In some industries and occupations the risks of accidents or unemployment are greater than in others. Such differences have often led to special insurance schemes for different industries, with higher rates of contribution where the risks are great than where they are small. Thus there might be one to cover risks of accidents in coal-mining with high contributions, and another for clerical workers with low contributions, and so on. Alternatively all may be included in one scheme but with contributions varied according to the risk of each industry or occupation. Civil servants and teachers would not need to contribute as much as dockers or shipbuilders to cover their own risk of unemployment. In some unemployment insurance schemes covering most industries, specified industries are excluded because their workpeople enjoy stability of employment; it was for this reason that railway workers in Britain were for many years excluded from unemployment insurance. Within an industry some workers are so reliable and

1 *The Times*, July 6, 1948.

efficient that they rarely lose their jobs, whereas others who are less competent and dependable are the first to be dismissed when trade becomes slack. The former, therefore, run less risk of unemployment than the latter, and theoretically their risk could be covered for lower contributions; in practice, however, it would be difficult to make this distinction, except by the method of reducing the future rates of contribution of those workpeople who had drawn no unemployment benefit or not more than a small amount of benefit during a specified period.[1]

In considering sickness risk, any workman is liable to have periods of illness, but some occupations have higher sickness rates than others, and some individuals are fitter and have much less sickness than others. In making provision for old age, private insurance companies fix lower rates of premium for some occupations than for others, and also for individuals according to their medical history.

Some opponents of social insurance argue that people should cover their risks by private savings, including voluntary insurance, but large numbers of workpeople would not exercise the necessary foresight. Also a workman may have a serious accident, illness, or prolonged unemployment while so young that he would not have had time to save more than a small part of the money necessary to cover his needs and those of his family. Nor would he be able to meet these risks fully, if at all, by private insurance. Old age can be covered better by insurance than by savings, as no one in early life can know whether he will die "in harness" or after a short illness without dependants at 64 years of age just before retiring and therefore will need no provision for old age, or whether he must save to cover the "risk" of living to a hundred years of age. Voluntary insurance enables these individual variations to be spread on the basis of actuarial calculations, but for various reasons many people will not make adequate provision or even any provision by this method of saving.

Trends of thought in social security are quite different. Not only is individual action recognized as inadequate, but there is growing support for merging the different risks of the various occupational groups into a larger unity. Emphasis is placed, not on the differentiation, but on the integration of society, on social solidarity with uniformity of contributions and benefits. All members of the community are regarded as being knit together in a closely woven fabric. The most individualistic members of a community are much more

---

[1] In the British system a workman who has had a good record of employment over a period of years has the right subsequently to draw unemployment benefit for a longer period than those who have fallen below the required standard.

dependent upon the services of others than they would be willing to admit even if they gave thought to the extent to which their own ways of living are based on the efforts of multitudes of others, past as well as present. This mutual interdependence is the foundation of social responsibility. It has received its widest recognition in the British scheme of national insurance with its uniform rates of contributions and of benefits applicable without distinction to all industries. The new conception of mutual responsibility is well illustrated by the British system for covering the risks of industrial accidents. The former method of employers' liability, involving insurance premiums at different rates determined by the risks of each industry, has been largely replaced by a system of uniform contributions by all employers and workpeople, the basic principle being that employers and workpeople in industries with only low accident risks depend on those employed in industries with high rates of risk. The safe industries depend on the products of risky industries; bank clerks, domestic servants and their employers need the services of coal-miners, seamen, and railway workers. With this community of interests, it is fair that risks throughout industry should be pooled and that all industries should share equally in covering the costs. The general effect is that the risky industries draw out more from the pool than they pay in, and the safe industries contribute more than they receive in benefits.

In so far as the heavier risks of some industries are fully covered by a comprehensive uniform scheme of insurance to which all industries contribute, their workpeople have no case for demanding higher wages because of the greater risks they run. They can, however, do so to the extent that the benefits received are insufficient for full compensation.

FINANCIAL ASPECTS, CONTRIBUTIONS, AND BENEFITS

The money necessary to provide social security benefits may be provided either by the contributory or the non-contributory method. Where the latter is adopted the funds are drawn from the revenues of the State, and this method can be supported on grounds of simplicity and because the tax system which provides these revenues can be adjusted so that the whole burden of taxation is distributed fairly between different sections of the community. In the contributory system, either the workers or the employers or more usually both contribute, and often the State also participates by paying a specified amount per head or a lump sum and frequently also bears the cost of administration. Every variety and combination of these methods is in operation in one country or another, and many countries have mixed systems. Thus, in Britain, children's allowances, National Assistance, and some old age pensions are non-contributory, while most other social security benefits are based on a tripartite system of contributions by the workers or other beneficiaries, by the employers, and by the State out of its general revenues. In the United States the costs of unemployment benefits and old age pensions are based on contributions by employers in the form of percentages of the wages they pay, and in most countries the cost of industrial accident compensation is borne by employers.

Joint contributions by employers and workpeople tend to make insurance schemes more acceptable than if the burden, apart from State participation, were borne either by the employers alone or by the workpeople alone. It is reasonable that workpeople who are the beneficiaries, should contribute. In effect, their contributions are a form of taxation and can be supported on the "benefit" principle of taxation. If substantial, they serve as a check on irresponsible or exaggerated demands for increased benefits, it being realized that such increases will involve higher contributions. Also where beneficiaries make substantial contributions they are in a stronger position to claim benefits as a right without having to submit to a means test.

Employers' contributions are, in effect, a tax on employment, or they may be regarded as part of the labour costs of production. From the economic point of view the results would be mainly the same whether an amount equal to the total of the joint contributions is paid wholly by the employers, wholly by the workpeople, or divided equally or in other proportions between them. The combined contribution is essentially a part of wages; if paid wholly by the employers, wage rates would be correspondingly lower, and if paid wholly by the workers their wage rates would be correspondingly higher. Amounts which are paid in contributions could otherwise have been paid in wages. The problem is complicated by some shiftings of the burden or incidence of the contributions, a part of which may be passed on to consumers by a rise in prices, and the extent to which this can be done will vary according to the conditions of market demand for different commodities. Also workers in a strong bargaining position may gain increases in wages which in effect pay part of their insurance contributions, but other workers are less favourably placed. However, such price and wage changes would have taken place as a result of the forces of demand for and supply of the commodities and labour, and are largely independent of the contributions. Also, formally workpeople cannot put forward demands for wage increases to cover their insurance contributions any more than taxpayers can demand increases in income to enable them to pay their taxes.

Mainly, therefore, the combined contributions of employers and workpeople are borne by the workpeople and the formal distribution of the amount in defined proportions between employers and workpeople is arranged largely because of its psychological value. As already noted, when in 1911 the Lloyd George scheme based on contributions of 4d. by workers, 3d. by employers, and 2d. by the State was launched, the propaganda slogan "ninepence for fourpence" was widely used to win support. This was psychologically effective and politically expedient, but economically unsound. Forty years later the corresponding proportions based on the relation of total benefits, including the National Health Services and Children's Allowances, to the nominal contributions of the workers were around "tenpence for twopence," but actually the workers carried a much higher part of the cost, especially as, with wealth more evenly distributed, they pay largely by individual taxation on commodities and directly by income tax to the revenues of the State and therefore to the State's contributions to social insurance and to its non-contributory social security benefits. Under present conditions in Britain the workers pay for a large part of what they get, and to a considerable extent the effect of social insurance and social security schemes is to collect from all and to redistribute the funds to those in need.[1]

In devising or revising a social insurance scheme one of the main considerations is the amount which workpeople can afford to contribute. This will depend in part on the extent to which the scheme will relieve them of expenditure which they had hitherto met in other ways. It will largely be determined, however, by levels of wages, and in particular unskilled workers will not be able to afford as much as skilled workers. For this reason the rates of contribution in most countries vary with the rates of wages, often the contribution being a specified percentage of the wage, and usually benefits vary in proportion to contributions.[2] In Britain, however, contributions and also benefits are at a flat rate, being the same amounts in money for highly paid skilled craftsmen as for the lowest paid unskilled labourers. The contributions are therefore based on what low-paid

[1] In some years before the Second World War, dock-workers in Britain because of heavy unemployment draw an average of four shillings a week from the unemployment insurance fund, while contributing only ninepence a week, the difference being largely made up from industries with little unemployment.

[2] In New Zealand, contributions are graduated according to income, but benefits are at a flat rate.

workers can afford, and this leaves highly paid people opportunity, if they wish, to make voluntary savings and insurance as additional provision in relation to their higher standards of living. The effect of this flat-rate system is that most unskilled workers directly contribute between 4½ and 5½ per cent of their wages, semi-skilled workers between 4 and 4½ per cent, and skilled workers between 2½ and 4 per cent.

Flat-rate contributions are more practicable where the range between the wages of most unskilled workers and most skilled workers is fairly narrow, than where there is wide dispersion. Where the wages in some occupations are very low the insurance benefits based on the small contributions which would be all that such workers could afford would be quite inappropriate for well-paid workers. In such circumstances the alternatives would be either heavy subsidies by the State for the benefit of workers in the low-paid occupations, or the adoption of a system of contributions and of benefits at rates varying with the wages of each of the main grades of workers. In Britain, flat-rate contributions have been levied from the beginning of State social insurance in 1911, but the results of minimum wage legislation and of extension of collective bargaining among unskilled workers in eliminating sweated wages and generally raising the relative wage levels of unskilled workers, together with the big rise in agricultural wages, have facilitated the retention of the flat-rate system when social insurance became much more comprehensive and costly than in its initial stages.

Most systems are restricted to people with incomes below a specified level, it being assumed that these are the people who need social insurance and that others can provide for themselves. Some categories whose wages are low, for example, domestic servants, agricultural workers, and people scattered in sparsely populated rural regions, are often excluded because of administrative difficulties in collecting contributions, providing benefits and exercising effective supervision. In Britain these categories were left outside the system in the early stages of its evolution, as were also at one period those with incomes over £250 a year and at a later period over £420 a year. From July 1948, however, everyone was brought in, whatever their income or occupation. This was largely because many manual and clerical people with incomes over £420 a year needed the benefits of social insurance, but also for reasons of social solidarity.

The liabilities of some risks are difficult to forecast, and rates of contribution have not infrequently been insufficient to cover benefits. Numbers of old age pension schemes have proved actuarially unsound and contributions have had to be increased, while risks of unemployment have often been underestimated. For example, in 1931, the British unemployment insurance fund paid out nearly £1 million a week more than its income from contributions, owing to exceptionally severe depression of industry and trade. This resulted in the fund running heavily into debt, and in order to ensure future financial soundness, the responsibility for maintaining workpeople whose unemployment lasted longer than a specified period was transferred from the contributory insurance fund to a system of unemployment assistance financed from the general revenues of the State. Financial soundness in an unemployment insurance scheme can be secured only if it is designed to cover unemployment caused by declining industries, moving to new jobs, seasonal unemployment, and slumps of moderate intensity, but not prolonged deep depressions. Here it may be noted that a contributory unemployment insurance system is of some value as a stabilizer, the excess of benefits over contributions helping to sustain consumption in depressions, while the excess of contributions in a period of boom is anti-inflationary.

A question of special financial interest is whether social insurance schemes should use the regular contributions to build up large funds earmarked for the provision of specified benefits or whether in return for the payment of appropriate contributions by or on behalf of the beneficiaries the State should become responsible for the benefits and should pay them year by year out of its current revenues as required. This is mainly important for old age pensions for which beneficiaries may contribute for forty years or more before drawing benefits. For several decades after the inauguration of such a scheme the revenue from contributions will greatly exceed the expenditure in benefits, and if the contributions were set aside in a fund the amount would become enormous. The investment of such a fund would involve complex financial problems, and there would be the danger also that the fund might be raided by an unscrupulous or needy Government.

The setting aside of contributions in a fund to-day will not feed, clothe, and house the contributants forty years hence. People of working age in the next generation, i.e. those who are children to-day, will provide the goods and services needed by those who have then retired from work. Provision for the aged must be made in succession by each generation of workers. However, by contributing now for old age pensions a person consumes less than he would otherwise do, and if this saving is invested in capital goods the production of the next generation will be increased and will facilitate provision of his pension. The present generation thus makes provision for its needs when it has retired from work by passing on to the next generation of workers adequate material capital and also human capital in the form of better health and education. These resources and not a nominal fund are the means of providing for benefits in the future.

In fixing the amounts of benefits, attention is properly directed to the needs of the insured person and his family rather than to the causes such as sickness, unemployment, and old age which are responsible for his being in need. Thus, apart from provision of medical treatment, the financial needs of an insured person and his family are approximately the same whatever the cause of his not being at work and receiving earnings. Yet this is often overlooked when provisions for the various risks are made piecemeal, by legislation passed at different times and under the influence of different political conditions. Thus, in Britain in the 1930's, the unemployment insurance scheme provided benefits for dependants, whereas the sickness insurance scheme did not, and the effect of this was if a man with wife and two children was unemployed he received 32s. a week, but if he was off work owing to sickness he received only 15s.[1] Such anomalies were removed when the unified scheme came into force in 1948.

In deciding upon standards of social security benefits, whether by insurance or assistance, two principles are in conflict: (1) that each individual or family should receive at least the minimum for maintenance; (2) that a person should receive more when he is employed than when he is not working. The main causes of conflict between these two principles are low wages in some occupations, and wide differences in number of dependants, which assistance takes into consideration but the wage system usually does not. Formerly, under the poor law in Britain and similarly in other countries the second principle, generally known as that of "less eligibility," was widely approved, it being believed that the incentive to honest work would be undermined and the moral fibre of the people weakened unless the standard of relief was below the earnings of the lowest wage classes, which in the days of sweated labour were very low indeed, and it is doubtful whether the principle was fully applied even in the harsh days of the nineteenth century. Less eligibility in maintenance standards was, however, reinforced by the workhouse test, the stigma of pauperism, and loss of the franchise. The general assumption was that the poor were responsible for their poverty, and little

[1] The rates of benefit during unemployment were 17s. a week for an unemployed man, 9s. for his wife, and 3s. for each dependent child; the rate of sickness benefit was 15s. for the man, but with no addition for dependants.

if any allowance was made for misfortune resulting from the chances and changes of economic circumstances.

As already indicated, the present century has seen a great change in attitudes towards poverty, and social insurance benefits are generally paid as a right without rigorous investigation or the imposition of harsh conditions. Yet rates of social insurance benefits still usually remain substantially below the rates of wages earned by insured persons. They are, therefore, to be regarded more as an aid than as fully covering need; they are rarely sufficient for subsistence, but though requiring to be supplemented by other resources they do provide a steady and reliable means of mitigating hardship during periods when income from work is not available. Also, insured persons who have no savings or other resources of their own can in many countries apply for aid to supplement their social insurance benefits, but such aid is granted only if inquiry into their means shows that their resources are insufficient.[1] Such social assistance out of public revenues can similarly be obtained by persons who have exhausted their right to social insurance benefits and can prove that they are in need.

A study of social insurance rates of benefit in many countries shows a wide variety of standards and, in particular, a wide range in the proportions which benefits form of the wage standards of the beneficiaries. Rates of benefit are sometimes as low as a fifth or a quarter of the rates of wages, and they rarely exceed three-quarters of the wage. In the United States, for example, unemployment benefits are 50 per cent of wages; in Venezuela, sickness cash benefits are two-thirds of the wages of each of several wage grades. In Britain, where rates of benefit are at a uniform or flat rate irrespective of the industry, occupation, or earnings of the insured worker the percentages vary considerably, being substantially higher for low-paid, unskilled workers than for skilled workers, as is shown by illustrative examples in the following table.[2] In calculating the percentages, allowance is made for the social insurance contributions deducted from wages when the man is at work but which he does not pay when in receipt of benefit. Childrens' allowances are also taken into account both for those at work and for those in receipt of benefits.

Thus skilled men without dependants get cash benefits equal to

[1] In Britain, as is indicated later, National Assistance rates are higher than insurance rates of benefit, and this demonstrates that insurance benefits are not regarded as providing full maintenance.
[2] The benefit rates are 32s. 6d. a week for a man, 21s. 6d. for his wife, 10s. 6d. for his first child, and for other children the addition is 2s. 6d. for each child.

little more than 20 per cent of their wages, and skilled men with families get about 42 to 45 per cent. On the other hand, the benefits received by unskilled workers with families amount to 55 to 60 per cent of their wages. In this connection it may be noted that the proportion of unskilled workers with large families is greater than among skilled workers.

The British system of a uniform rate of benefits for all insured persons irrespective of their wages differs from those in almost all

Number of Dependants	Proportion of Benefits to Wage	
	Of Unskilled Worker earning £5 10s. a Week	Of Skilled Worker earning £7 10s. a Week
	Percentage	Percentage
Man without dependants.. ..	31	22
Man with wife and one child ..	61	45
Man with wife and three children	57	43
Man with wife and five children..	55	42

other countries, where the method of paying benefits proportionate to wages is widely adopted. For example, in Britain the insurance benefits for a man with wife and one child is 64s. 6d. a week, whether his wage is £5 or £10 a week, whereas under the proportionate system with benefits at the rate of 50 per cent of wages, as for unemployment in the United States, a man earning the equivalent of £5 a week would receive £2 10s. in benefits, but if his wage equalled £10 a week his benefit rate would be £5 a week. In many proportionate schemes, however, instead of applying the same percentage to all levels of wages, somewhat higher percentages are applied to lower-paid grades of workers.

The proportionate method has the advantage over the flat-rate system of relating benefits when not at work more closely to the worker's earnings and standard of living when he is working. The flat-rate system is, however, easier to administer. It leaves somewhat greater necessity and responsibility for the better paid workers to supplement by their own savings, including voluntary insurance, the compulsory insurance benefits they are entitled to receive, which being inevitably related to the wage standards of low-paid workers are much below their own customary way of living. This also leads to demands for supplementary pensions, such as those introduced for British coal-miners.

A similar but special problem arises in fixing benefits for victims of industrial accidents and diseases. In most schemes, which are based on employers' liability, compensation is calculated on estimates of loss of earnings, and well-paid skilled workers receive more than low-paid workers. This is a reasonable principle to apply, but it often involves complex litigation, especially as estimates are made of the prospects of future earnings by disabled workmen, on which wide differences of opinion may arise. Also the claims are made by workmen with the support of their trade union against the employers, who are thus in hostile camps with consequent injury to industrial relations. In Britain, workmen's compensation determined by earnings was based on employer's liability until the new Industrial Injuries Insurance scheme came into force after the end of the Second World War. This provides rates of benefit for permanent injury on the basis of loss of faculty, the maximum rate being for total disablement, and proportions of this rate are paid for loss of a leg, or an arm, or an eye, and so on. These rates are paid equally to skilled and unskilled workers alike, no account being taken of their earnings before injury.[1] Also, once the degree of injury and corresponding rate of benefit have been fixed this benefit is continued however much the worker may subsequently earn.

As already noted, the great majority of contributory schemes provide benefits as a right without any means test. For all benefits other than contributory pensions New Zealand is an exception but the means limit is high, benefits being reduced or withheld only for those whose private resources are substantial, and in practice all manual workers and others with modest means receive full benefits; middle-class people receive reduced benefits and the rich "are sent empty away." In some non-contributory schemes benefits are paid without any means test, for example children's allowances in Britain, but a means test is usual in non-contributory schemes. Without a means test benefits are received by some people who do not need them, and to this extent the resources available are not distributed in the best way; with a means test a specified scale of benefits could be provided by lower rates of contribution. However, a means test is greatly disliked in contributory schemes, it involves irritating inquiries into individual resources and somewhat discourages thrift and voluntary savings, but in most non-contributory schemes a means test is considered essential.

Contributory insurance schemes with their standard rates of benefit go a long way in helping large numbers of people over periods

[1] Outside the Industrial Injuries Insurance scheme, disabled workers may claim compensation from their employers by court action.

of difficulty. The very fact, however, that benefits are at standard rates implies that no allowance is made for the special circumstances of people who require additional aid. As was mentioned above, insurance benefits are usually substantially below subsistence level, and people who are entirely without other resources need more help. Also, in order to keep insurance schemes from running heavily into debt some benefits are paid only for limited periods of so many weeks, and most people who have thus exhausted their right to benefits are likely also to have drained their other resources and find themselves penniless. These, and other circumstances not covered by social insurance become the responsibility of public assistance schemes which deal with the residual problems of poverty. They are financed out of the general revenues, and grants are made only where need is proved.

The practice in Britain may be given as an illustration of insurance benefits below subsistence level and the higher grants made under National Assistance. Insurance benefits, together with children's allowances, for example, during sickness or unemployment, for a man with wife and three dependent children total 68s. 6d. a week. Under National Assistance, a married couple with three children aged thirteen, nine, and four, could expect to have a minimum income, after paying rent, of 99s. 6d. a week.[1] As rents range from a few shillings to £1 or more a week, and average about 10s. 10d. a week,[2] the monetary value of assistance grants for families of the size mentioned averages around £5 10s. 6d. a week, which is almost as high as the minimum rates of wages and childrens' allowances paid to adult male workers with families of similar size in some low-paid industries.

This chapter has dealt with social security methods for meeting various risks, but alongside the provision of benefits and grants in cash and in kind, measures are being increasingly applied for the rehabilitation of those who have become victims of the risks. Also, progress is being made in devising preventive measures to diminish the risks themselves.

[1] Cmd. 7767, pp. 11 and 12.
[2] For householders with dependants only. See Cmd. 7767, pp. 44, 54, and 55.

PART V

International Aspects

27

International Aspects

IN MANY ways, industrial relations in their international aspects closely resemble those within countries, but there are also marked contrasts for which national frontiers are responsible. It is necessary, therefore, to review both the similarities and the differences. To those who envisage with Tennyson a "parliament of man" and a "federation of the world" in their most complete forms, capital, labour, and commodities would move freely throughout the world without the present obstructions and hindrances at national boundaries. Certainly Tennyson had no thought of a planned world economy in which mankind would break free from national bondage only to find itself in the chains of a supra-national despotism. Business men would establish their factories wherever they could get the best results, workpeople would move to the places where they could secure the best working conditions and standards of living, and, allowing for costs of transportation, goods would sell in those markets where they were in greatest demand.

In such circumstances, if, for example, steel workers in South Wales found it desirable to combine with steel workers in Yorkshire, the same reasons would lead them to enter into association with steel workers of the Ruhr, Stalingrad and Pittsburgh. Similarly, employers in an industry would join together for consultation and protection of common interests. Even in the world as it is to-day, with strongly entrenched national sovereignties, considerable progress has been made in the formation of such associations which cut across the lines of national frontiers and establish interests which transcend those of nation States. Their main objects, as within countries, are to try to work out a common policy for improving standards of working conditions and to organize mutual support for attempts within each country to give effect to the policy, as well as to resist any lowering of standards. The main methods of co-operation are exchange of information and the holding of conferences for the formulation of principles and policies. Mutual assistance may be given to workers in any country who are involved in a strike on some vital question, this support sometimes taking the form of financial aid, or boycott of goods: workers involved in a strike or lock-out in one country are rarely supported by a strike of workers in another country, though an exception must be made of North America where "international" unions with members both in the United States and in Canada not infrequently organize sympathetic strikes in both countries.

Although the reasons for forming international organizations of employers and of workpeople are similar to those which have led to the establishment of national organizations, in practice the former organizations have been much weaker and less effective than the latter. The interests that bring them together are not so strong, while the rivalries, differences and grounds for misunderstandings are greater. One big difficulty is due to the wide differences in wages and standards of working conditions from country to country. These are results of many causes, including greater natural resources and capital equipment in relation to population in some countries than in others, higher standards of health and education which increase the efficiency of management and labour, and fortune or misfortune in escaping or being involved in long, costly, and devastating wars. The resulting differences in working conditions impose limits upon the adoption of common standards, and rule out entirely a programme to secure wage equality, except possibly between two or three geographically adjacent countries in which economic conditions and standards of living are approximately the same.

Internally, especially within countries which are compact and well integrated economically and socially, conditions are much more favourable for the application of common standards, including wage standards, industry by industry. There are also powerful influences tending towards the adoption between industries of equal or closely similar standards for hours of work, paid holidays, and other working conditions, although wages may differ appreciably from industry to industry according to variations in their prosperity. Within a country, mobility of labour is a much more potent factor in reducing inequalities than it is internationally where cost of movement is greater, less information is available about conditions and prospects, differences of language, habits and traditions are deterrents, and where these obstacles to movement are often reinforced by prohibitions, quotas and other barriers, sometimes to emigration and more frequently to immigration. Also the tendencies for movements of capital and trade in goods to reduce inequalities between countries are much slower in action and are more hampered by restrictions than within countries.

Thus, internally, competition between firms for labour and between workpeople for jobs acts much more quickly than it does externally to smooth out differences. Workpeople in an industry are largely interchangeable, and the younger people especially move readily from factory to factory and from district to district. For every one who would seriously contemplate emigrating, hundreds are willing to change their jobs between firms at home. They are, therefore, greatly interested in striving to establish basic standards so that as they move about they will be protected from worse conditions than in their previous job. Similarly, many employers see advantages in securing protection against those firms which would undercut reasonable labour standards, and they therefore form associations and conclude collective agreements which often establish industry-wide standards. It is true that, just as some countries are more prosperous and enjoy higher standards of living than others, so some firms within a country are more efficient and more prosperous than others and their workpeople benefit therefrom, but the benefits tend to be more in the form of greater security of employment, and in the amenities of employment than in higher wage rates and shorter hours. If they pay somewhat higher wages, this policy, together with amenities and greater security of employment, enable them, through the competition of workpeople for these advantages, to secure a working force more efficient than the average.

Workpeople and employers in countries with high wages and advanced standards of working conditions have a common interest in the raising of standards in backward countries. They frequently complain of unfair competition based on low labour standards, and support action by their Governments to protect them by tariffs and in other ways against such competition. Yet the mere fact that labour standards are low in a country does not imply unfair competition, for the low labour standards are often associated with such poor productive efficiency that the advanced countries can undersell them in world markets. In such conditions a raising of labour standards in backward countries, unless accompanied by at least proportionate increases in productive efficiency, would do harm to their economy and cause unemployment among their workpeople. It is not denied, however, that exploitation of labour in some countries results in unfair international competition, and that the ending of such exploitation would reduce unfair competition or bring it to an end to the benefit both of industry and labour in other countries and of the workers who had previously suffered from exploitation.

One of the most effective means of raising standards of working conditions in backward countries is by introducing up-to-date capital equipment, scientific methods and organization, and this was given recognition shortly after the end of the Second World War by President Truman's plan for organizing technical assistance for such countries with the aid of American dollars and funds from other countries to be administered by the United Nations. It had been recognized even earlier by the British Government in establishing the Colonial Development and Welfare Fund, and there has also been, since the war, the Colonial Development Corporation. All these schemes are intended to promote the economic and social well-being of the native populations as well as the better utilization of resources for the benefit of the whole world, and they may be contrasted with some earlier enterprises in backward areas where the main object was to benefit the promoters and investors, any improvement in the lot of the native populations being incidental.

The introduction of up-to-date machinery and methods in hitherto backward countries is not, however, without its difficulties. A too rapid transformation of methods of production among native peoples causes dislocations in their ways of living which may be harmful, and safeguards are needed to ensure that the transitions are made with due regard to social and moral standards and are not dictated solely by material considerations. The modernization of production in backward countries can also give rise to serious international misunderstandings and frictions. This is illustrated by some of the consequences of the rapid industrialization of Japan during the present century. Previously, Japan had isolated herself from the world, and, with a large population and primitive methods of production, the standard of living of the workers was very low. Then she quickly equipped several of her industries with modern machines and methods as efficient, or even more efficient, than those in use in countries which had been industrialized earlier. The industries thus developed included textiles, iron and steel, shipbuilding, and some branches of engineering, and the efficiency of these industries was in marked contrast with the old-fashioned methods still in use in agriculture and many domestic handicraft industries. In consequence of the existence of a large and growing supply of labour and of the generally low labour standards, the few modernized industries were able to attract all the labour they needed at wages little above the low levels paid in the old-fashioned industries. Their products could be sold in world markets at prices often considerably below those of their competitors because efficiency in these few industries on which capital developments had been concentrated was high and wages low, and this gave rise abroad to complaints of unfair competition based on unduly low labour standards. There was some evidence of unfair trade practices and of labour exploitation, but the main cause of low Japanese prices in world markets was the existence in Japan of large reserves of labour willing to work for low wages.

So long as the general level of wages in Japan was only one-half or one-third of that in the more industrially developed countries the Japanese employers in the few industries they had modernized could not be expected to pay the same wages as their foreign competitors. Only when a large part of Japanese production had been modernized would the general level of wages approach those in other advanced countries, and this process is slow because of shortage of capital. It may be noted that when business men in industrialized countries have set up modern factories in places where wages are low, whether in their own countries or abroad, the effects on prices and competition are similar to those outlined for Japan.

Much evidence could be produced to prove that the present wage standards in different countries measured in terms of the goods and services which the money wages will buy show a much wider range than that of the efficiencies of the workpeople. Whereas "real" wages in countries with the highest standards are three, four, or fivefold those in countries with the lowest standards, the relative efficiencies of physically fit workpeople supplied with similar machinery, power, resources, organization, and management, are within much narrower limits, especially on mass production processes with semi-automatic machines; most differences would be within a range of 50 per cent, and few would show differences between the lowest productive efficiency and the highest of more than double. The experience of numbers of international companies which have established factories with similar machinery, management, and methods in different countries gives support to this conclusion. Also the high wages paid in the United States in the steel, automobile, and other mass-production industries are earned by workpeople, large numbers of whom are emigrants from Italy, Poland, the Ukraine, and other countries of Southern and Eastern Europe where wages are much lower, or they are the children in the first or second generation of such emigrants. It is true that those who emigrated may have been the more vigorous and enterprising, and they may have had the stimulus of greater freedom and opportunity, but the differences between the efficiencies of those who emigrated and those who remained behind is much less than the differences in their wages. Working with similar management and machinery the differences in their relative productivity would become negligible. The wider international distribution of up-to-date machinery is dependent partly on the rate at which it can be produced by the advanced industrial countries in quantities surplus to their own needs, but is greatly hampered by political factors and especially risks of war.

Enough has been said to show the complexities of trying to secure any effective international regulation of labour standards. The difficulties are so great that decisions of any practical significance are meagre by contrast with the effectiveness of laws and agreements on labour conditions which operate within many countries, and scarcely any progress has been made towards collective bargaining and the reaching of collective agreements internationally. One consequence of the difficulties is that the international trade union movement has tended to divert its attention from industrial questions to the more exciting but often extremely nebulous discussion of political affairs. Trade unionists from many of the countries of continental Europe have been more inclined than those of Britain and North America to favour political objectives, some of which have proved impracticable or so remote as to cause disillusionment and disruption.

Two political aspirations which have been much discussed at international trade union meetings are prevention of war and the overthrow of capitalism. At times considerable support seemed forthcoming for concerted action by workers in different countries to "down tools" in periods of international crisis and outbreak of war to prevent production of munitions and transport of troops and supplies, thereby bringing hostilities to a standstill. Yet in practice, in such periods of tension, the vows of international solidarity have been broken and the organized workpeople of each country have supported their own Governments. National loyalties and international rivalries proved much stronger than aspirations for world brotherhood of working men. This is not surprising in view of long-standing animosities between States, including misunderstandings due to differences in ideologies, and the effects upon employment and standards of living of the clash of international trade competition, which can throw men out of work. Trade unionism has, therefore, been ineffective in preventing wars, and although occasionally seamen and dock-workers have refused to move munitions and supplies consigned to some country at war because their sympathies were with the other side, such action, though causing temporary embarrassment, has rarely had any considerable influence on the course of events. It must also be noted that there is danger to the security of countries whose trade union movements keenly and successfully support policies of peace and disarmament, if other countries are more strongly armed because trade unionism, owing to weakness, ineffectiveness, or indifference, has not exerted a similar influence.

Many trade unionists have linked together abolition of war with abolition of capitalism, arguing that wars are caused by the greed of capitalists and especially the manœuvres of armament firms to

412

maintain international tension in order to expand the demand for their products. In fact, clashes between States have much deeper origins than the current economic system, as is proved by the age-long history of wars involving communities with economic and social systems very different from those of to-day. It might be thought that the trade unionists of the various countries would find less difficulty in agreeing on programmes and methods for the over-throw of capitalism than for the abolition of war, but actually these have given rise to bitter controversies and dissensions. This is because of wide differences in ideologies and in the stages of economic and social development in the various countries. Even in the short span of the second quarter of the present century there has existed simul-taneously several kinds of capitalism and various forms of socialism and communism, including Fascism, National Socialism, and Soviet Communism, each supported to a greater or less extent by the work-people of the respective countries. Many trade unionists do not agree that the capitalist system should be overthrown, preferring instead to use their bargaining power to get the best terms from their employers. Some favour nationalization of basic industries only, some regard the abolition of private capitalism as a long-term objective but favour moving towards it by stages while others support measures for its early complete realization; some urge plans for the overthrow of capitalism by revolution but others favour evolutionary methods. Some again want to replace private capitalism by national ownership and control as a form of State socialism, but others demand syndicalism, with workpeople controlling the industries in which they work.

Where freedom of trade union organization is denied and the movement is driven underground by a despotic Government the only hope of progress may be through revolution. The position is very different in countries where Governments are chosen by democratic methods, and where trade unionism is recognized by employers for the purposes of collective bargaining and is brought into consultation by the Government. So great are the differences in attitudes that the representatives of the workers from some countries support policies in international conferences which are quite unrelated to the needs of workers in others.

In view of these differences it is not surprising to find divisions and irreconcilable conflicts within the international trade union move-ments. Nor has there yet emerged any common trend to provide a basis for greater unity. If, in some countries opinion moves to-day to the left, in others it moves to the right, and these changes are determined largely by the distinctive internal needs and political and social evolution of each country. A world organization bringing together the trade union movements of all countries has hitherto proved unworkable, and the most that has been practicable is to bring together those national movements which have sufficiently similar objectives and methods to enable them to "talk the same language" and work together with reasonable understanding. On the employers' side the attempt has not even been made to establish an organization to include all countries.

These difficulties and divisions in international aspects of industrial relations reflect the complexities and chaos which exist throughout the whole field of international relations. Because of national rivalries and the clash of sovereignties, Governments have hitherto failed to prevent war and to secure effective economic co-operation. Their failure to do so was shown by the collapse of the League of Nations as an instrument for peace, and so long as these rivalries persist the rate of progress in promoting improvements in labour standards by international action will be slow and setbacks frequent.

KINDS AND FUNCTIONS OF INTERNATIONAL ORGANIZATIONS

International organizations in the field of industrial relations are of two types, those which are representative separately of each trade or industry, and those which cover many industries. On the workers' side the former are known as International Trade Secretariats, and about thirty have been set up, the biggest being the International Transport Workers' Federation, the Miners' International Federation, the International Metal Workers' Federation, and the International Federation of Building and Woodworkers. Each federation is made up of national unions with membership in the industry, but several unions from one country may usually affiliate in a federation if they have members in the industry; for example, in the International Transport Workers' Federation several British Unions are affiliated including three railway unions, the National Union of Seamen, and the Transport and General Workers' Union. Also a national union with membership in several industries may be a member of more than one International Trade Secretariat.

Within each country, unions in the various industries have found it necessary to join together in a national central organization, and a similar need has arisen internationally. This could be met by two main alternative methods. Either the International Trade Secretariats, in addition to the work done by each in its own industry, could combine together for general purposes, or an international organization for such purposes could be formed of representatives from the central trade union organization of each country. Each method has advantages, and considerable contention has arisen between the supporters of each. In practice those who have favoured the second alternative have been successful, and in 1913, following earlier attempts, the International Federation of Trade Unions, consisting of only one central organization from each country, was formed on a permanent basis. In order, however, to promote co-operation between the International Trade Secretariats and the International Federation of Trade Unions an arrangement was made for representatives of the Secretariats to attend congresses of the Federation, with the right to speak but not to vote.

Joint conferences were also held and agreement was reached that the Secretariats would not take final decisions on questions outside their own industries without first consulting the Federation. In order further to avoid conflict of membership and authority the Federation decided to affiliate only national trade union centres, but not trade unions in individual industries. It was desired that the individual unions in a country would affiliate both to the national centre and to the appropriate international secretariat. Also, if workers in one industry in any country were in difficulties and desired strike funds or other help its union would appeal to the International Trade Secretariat with which it was affiliated, but if the need was wider, involving several or all industries, the national centre would appeal to the Federation. This agreement was reached after proposals had been made to form an international strike fund, but it was thought preferable to deal with each problem as it arose and to raise funds as needed.

The Federation also co-operated closely with the Labour and Socialist International, which consisted of Labour or Socialist political parties from the various countries. In principle, the scope of the Federation's work was industrial, and that of the Labour and Socialist International was political, but in practice this demarkation was not observed, and much overlapping resulted, though on some questions joint committees were set up to avoid duplication of effort, and especially to prevent these two organizations, which had much in common, from pursuing inconsistent or even conflicting policies.

These organizations collapsed during the First World War, but were soon formed again after hostilities ended. In the inter-war years, in addition to considering industrial, social and economic questions affecting labour standards including systems of social security and methods to combat unemployment, the international trade union movement was faced with difficult problems of constitution and membership, and these problems have continued since the end of the Second World War. The greatest problem of all resulted from the formation of communist trade unions in various countries and the Moscow controlled Red International of Labour Unions. Others were due to the difficulty of securing close contacts and co-operation between trade unions in widely separated parts of the world, and to the policy of the International Federation of Trade Unions of restricting membership to only one national centre from each country.

The belief that workers everywhere are faced with similar basic problems has created an aspiration for a world-wide organization of trade unionists to work for the emancipation of the workers in all countries, to secure improvements in their working conditions and to promote international friendship and understanding so as to bring wars to an end and establish the brotherhood of man. After the Soviet revolution, much sympathy was felt by workers in other countries for the Russian workers, this being shown both by opposition to military measures taken by some Governments to overthrow the Soviet Government, and by their efforts to bring the Soviet trade union movement into active association with those of other countries. However, notwithstanding this sympathy and desire for unity, all efforts to bring the Russian trade unions into the International Federation of Trade Unions and the International Trade Secretariats resulted in failure.

The reasons for this failure were fundamental differences in the purposes and methods of the Russian movement from those in most other countries, together with its distrust of and hostility towards trade unionism in capitalist countries. One chasm which could not be bridged was the difference between the Federation and the Red International of Labour Unions on the autonomy of the national centres. The Federation was formed on the understanding that, although it was hoped that national centres would give effect to decisions of the Federation, they were not bound to do so; similarly, the autonomy of the national unions affiliated with the Secretariats was safeguarded. The Red International would not agree to recognize the autonomy of national centres or unions. It also became evident that the main purpose of the Red International was to undermine and destroy the Federation, and during the 1930's efforts to secure co-operation ceased.

During the Second World War the international trade union movement again collapsed largely because of the occupation of most European countries by Germany, but contacts were maintained in London between exiled leaders, and plans were discussed for rebuilding it on broader foundations as soon as Nazi power was broken. Russia having been in partnership with Britain, the United States and other countries in "The Grand Alliance" which defeated Hitler's Germany, the time seemed opportune for uniting the Russian trade union movement with those of other countries in a single organization representative of communist and non-communist workers. This was indeed achieved when the World Federation of Trade Unions was formed, but the old conflicts, suspicions, and distrusts immediately emerged, and after a brief existence in a continuous state of high tension the ill-assorted marriage ended in divorce. The non-communist movements took steps to form an International Confederation of Free Trade Unions, while the communist movements maintained an international organization which includes the Russian unions, those of the satellite countries behind the Iron Curtain, and also communist unions in other countries, including, for example, France and Italy, where numerically strong communist unions had been formed in rivalry with non-communist unions.

This was not the only cleavage preventing world unity. In some countries there has long been division into socialist trade unions, and Christian or Catholic trade unions which do not believe in class warfare and the overthrow of capitalism, and support conciliatory relations with employers. Some workers in the same trade or industry join a socialist union and others a Christian union, and these unions have formed separate national centres. In most countries the membership of Christian unions is much less than that of the socialist unions, though in Holland they are about equal in strength. In Germany before Hitler destroyed all trade unions the Christian unions had a large membership though much less than that of the socialist unions, but when trade unionism was revived after the Nazi collapse the leaders succeeded in establishing a united movement instead of restoring the former divisions. The Christian unions have set up their own international, called the International Federation of Christian Trade Unions, consisting of national centres of Christian unions from a number of Western European countries. Before the Second World War it included several countries of Central Europe, but communist control behind the Iron Curtain has since prevented their participation in its work.

Ideological differences between unions within countries, as illustrated by the divisions into communist and non-communist, socialist and Christian unions are not the only causes of difficulties in international organization. Industrial and historical factors, and rivalries between leaders sometimes cause divisions within countries,

417

as, for example, the organization of workpeople in the United States into the rival camps of the American Federation of Labour and the Congress of Industrial Organizations. Such divisions often involve conflicts, and an international organization is unwilling to have its meetings disturbed by the clash of dissensions within countries. To avoid these dangers was one of the main reasons why the International Federation of Trade Unions adopted the policy of affiliating only one national centre from each country, but this policy also had its difficulties. Thus, when the American Federation of Labour became affiliated in 1937, the many American members of the Congress of Industrial Organizations were unrepresented.

Time and expense involved in sending delegates from distant countries have been obstacles to international co-operation between trade union movements widely separated geographically. This was the main reason why the predominant influences in the International Trade Secretariats and in the International Federation of Trade Unions were European; each had its headquarters and most of its members in Europe. It was also one of the reasons facilitating the formation of the Pan-American Federation of Labour, although the trade union movements of some American countries were affiliated also to the International Federation. With the development of air transport the time factor has ceased to be significant, though expense of travel and also differences in the labour problems which arise in the main geographical areas of the world remain important.

The work of the Secretariats, being mainly concerned with single industries, is more specialized and detailed, more industrial and less political than that of broader-based organizations such as the International Confederation of Free Trade Unions. The essential purpose of each secretariat is to promote the interests of the workers of its own industry by common action in all the associated countries, by encouraging organization among the workers, by providing material help, and by protecting members of affiliated unions who go to work outside their own country. As far as possible a common programme or policy is established on wages, hours of work, paid holidays, age of entry into industry, and other conditions of labour. The pooling and exchange of information on developments in the industry in each country are arranged. When workers in an industry in any country are involved in a dispute the Secretariat may organize financial and other assistance, including boycotts and refusal to take part in the transport of goods of the employers concerned. The possibilities of effective action are greatest in industries which are by nature international, particularly transport (seamen, dockers, and personnel of airways), and are least in industries sheltered from foreign competition.

The functions of the International Confederation of Free Trade Unions are based on recognition that the industrial and social problems of workpeople in all industries and countries have many common elements. The Confederation is interested in securing and maintaining freedom of association, the right to collective bargaining, and the right to strike, and in using these freedoms to win improvements in working conditions, status, and social security. Many demands for international minimum standards are expressed in general terms, but others are more specific, for example that for an eight-hour day. Among other subjects discussed, mention may be made of economic planning, unemployment, industrial accidents and diseases, joint consultation, migration of labour, workers' education, and representation of trade unions on public bodies dealing with economic affairs. Many proposals are submitted to the International Labour Organization, and the Confederation convenes the workers' group of delegates to International Labour Conferences with the object of securing agreement between them on the policy they should adopt in the work of the conferences. Encouragement and assistance is given to the growth of trade unionism in the colonies. The staff of the Confederation arrange for exchange of information and documents, translation of national labour legislation, and compilation of trade union statistics. Support is sometimes provided for trade union movements involved in extensive industrial disputes. For example, funds were raised to assist British unions during the general strike and coal industry stoppage of 1926. Relief work was undertaken for the benefit of workers in countries suffering from severe economic distress, help being given, for example, to Russian and Austrian workers during the chaotic conditions in those countries after the end of the First World War, and to German trade unions many of whose members experienced great privation as a result of the catastrophic inflation of the currency in 1923.

The pre-war Federation was much concerned about the menace of Fascist and other Governments hostile to trade unionism, its liberties and aspirations, and it assisted trade union victims of the tyranny of such Governments, particularly in Italy, Germany, and Spain. In this struggle against Fascism and reaction it worked in close association with the Labour and Socialist International, with which it also co-operated in support of anti-militarist policies and disarmament, including abolition of national air forces. In times of international tension, attempts were sometimes made to ban the transport of war cargoes to certain countries, and the general strike was favoured as a weapon which the workers could use to prevent war, but sufficient recognition was not always given to the dangers to peace-loving countries if they used such methods effectively and so became the prey of aggressors whose workpeople were unable to take similar action or supported their Government's aggressive policy. The movement is inspired by conceptions of an international workers' commonwealth, but problems within each country have claimed so large a part of the energies and resources of the affiliated national trade union organizations that many of the grandiose international policies have hitherto lacked effective backing. Success has, however, been achieved where objectives have been more realistic and practicable.

Employers also have formed international organizations to enable them to co-operate on labour questions. The International Organization of Employers was set up in 1919 with headquarters in Brussels. Its membership is restricted to the central employers' organizations dealing with labour affairs in the various countries which maintain a free enterprise system, and in 1950 the number of countries represented was twenty-five, including the leading industrial countries of the world. Britain is represented by the British Employers' Confederation, a central body which specializes on general labour questions, but some countries are represented by national central organizations which deal not only with labour matters but also with industrial, commercial, and other economic affairs; for example, the United States of America is represented by its National Association of Manufacturers and its Chamber of Commerce. The International Organization of Employers provides the means by which these national organizations can co-operate closely on those international aspects of general labour questions which arise at meetings of the International Labour Organization and the Economic and Social Council of the United Nations. Like the international trade union movement, it has been granted the highest grade of consultative status by the Economic and Social Council.

International employers' organizations have also been set up for a number of individual industries, but they differ widely in functions, degree of activity and representative capacity. Many of them have other activities in addition to labour questions. Like International Trade Secretariats, some collapsed during the war, but have since been reconstituted.

THE INTERNATIONAL LABOUR ORGANIZATION

The focus of industrial relations in the international field is the International Labour Organization which brings together representatives of Governments, employers, and workpeople from the various countries on an official basis. This organization was formed in 1919 in accordance with provisions of the Treaties of Peace which ended the First World War, provisions as remarkable and as unexpected as any which have ever appeared in treaties between States. Usually such agreements deal only with frontiers, reparations, military affairs, and other aspects of power politics, but the treaties of 1919 also envisaged the need for continuous international investigation into and agreements for improving standards of living and working conditions throughout the world, and provided for the setting up of a permanent organization for the achievement of these objects.

The inclusion of these provisions in the Treaties of Peace was partly to implement war-time pledges by Governments in various countries that measures would be taken after the war to improve working conditions and meet as far as practicable the aspirations of workpeople for a raising of their status, and it was recognized that progress along these lines would be facilitated by international co-operation. Also, the promotion of improved international relations was seen to depend in part on the establishment of fair and reasonable conditions of labour, since hardship and misery resulting from unduly low wages, excessive hours, and other harsh treatment of labour is a cause of social unrest which in its turn is a danger to the peace of the world. Thus, there was a close link between the International Labour Organization in its work of strengthening the foundations of industrial peace by promoting social justice, and the League of Nations designed to promote international peace by securing better political relations and economic co-operation between States. This connection between industrial peace and international peace has been continued since the Second World War by the association of the International Labour Organization with the United Nations.

Two decades or more before 1919 Governments had already given tentative recognition of the need for international co-operation in the regulation of labour standards, and one or two *ad hoc* conferences had been held at the beginning of the century. These conferences were convened and organized by diplomatic procedures, and dealt with such subjects as prohibition of the use of white phosphorus in the manufacture of matches because of its serious menace to the health of workpeople, and the prohibition or restriction of night work by women and young persons. Agreements by a conference were put in

the form of draft treaties, which were then submitted to each participating Government for consideration, and if the agreements were
ratified became binding obligations between Governments. These
conferences lacked permanence and had no secretariat to give continuity to their work, but they contained the germ from which the
International Labour Organization grew, and some of their methods
were incorporated in its constitution.

A detailed study of the constitution, methods, and results of the
International Labour Organization is beyond the scope of this
volume, but an outline of some of its most noteworthy features must
be given. One is the functional representation which its constitution
provides. Each member country is entitled to send four delegates to
meetings of the International Labour Conference, two being representatives of the Government and the others being a representative
of organized employers and of organized workers respectively. The
participation of these functional representatives is a recognition of
the status of organizations of employers and of workers in the regulation of labour conditions, it gives opportunity for their points of
view to be fully expressed, and ensures their active interest in the
work of the Organization.

This tripartite system assumes a capitalist society, with Governments, free or independent employers' organizations and free trade
unions as the parties directly concerned in the regulation of labour
conditions. The emergence of Fascism, which tampered with the
independence of trade unions and employers' organizations, the
destruction of these bodies by the Nazis, and the liquidation of
private capitalism in Russia raised delicate problems of representation, while difficulties arise from the spreading of nationalization in
some countries. For years the workers' delegates from other countries challenged the credentials of the Italian workers' delegate on
the grounds that he was not a genuine representative of the Italian
workers, and although he was admitted to meetings of the conference
the workers' group refused to appoint him as a workers' representative on any of the committees. The German problem was solved by
the early resignation of Germany from the Organization. If Russia
were to take an active part in the work of the Organization her
"employers" would, no doubt, be represented by persons drawn
from the management side of factories and from the great industrial
trusts or national undertakings, but the distinction between "Government" and "employer" which was envisaged by the constitution
would be substantially altered. Russia has, however, taken very
little part in the work of the Organization, and while retaining
membership has shown hostility to it. Indeed, when the structure of

the United Nations and its specialized agencies was being planned at the San Francisco Conference, Russia attempted to destroy the Organization. Also when the communist delegates from Poland and Czechoslovakia at the 1950 session of the International Labour Conference failed in certain political manœuvres they withdrew from the Conference and took no further part in its work.

The original tripartite system is inevitably modified by increase in the number of nationalized industries in Britain and other countries, and the question must be raised whether, for example, the British Employers' Confederation can properly represent the National Coal Board and the controlling authorities of other nationalized industries. These bodies are not affiliated to the Confederation, and whatever autonomy their constitutions may give to them they are creatures of the Government, and, being subject to its authority, their representatives are in a position quite distinct from that of employers in private industry. All this implies that the structure of the International Labour Organization cannot remain static but must be flexible enough to adapt itself to changes in the patterns of industrial organization in member States.

The Organization is in no way a super-State; its agreements on labour standards have no force in any country unless that country decides to put them into effect, and therefore national sovereignty is fully safeguarded. Yet the constitution goes about as far as is possible in an organization with the functional representation described towards securing wide application of its agreements, without surrender of national sovereignty. This is because a draft convention requires for its adoption a two-thirds majority of votes cast at the conference, and in practice a draft convention has little chance of adoption unless a substantial majority of Government delegates vote for it. If a draft convention is supported by many workers' delegates and also by many employers' delegates it is likely to secure the votes of many Government delegates. Where many workers oppose a draft convention or abstain from voting for it because they consider it too weak to safeguard their interests, it cannot gain the requisite two-thirds majority unless it is widely supported by Governments. The same is true if many employers fail to vote for a draft convention because they consider it impracticable.

A further article of the Constitution requires each member State to submit without delay each draft convention adopted by the Conference to its Parliament or other competent authority, so that its ratification and application within the country may be considered. They cannot be pigeon-holed and forgotten, and each Government which voted for a convention at the conference is generally under a moral obligation to ratify it.[1] Yet unfortunately, notwithstanding these provisions devised by the authors of the Constitution, their hopes have not been fully realized, and many Governments vote for draft conventions and fail to ratify them. This irresponsibility not only reduces the range of application of agreements, thereby diminishing the effectiveness of international co-operation, but is unfair to those countries which meet their moral obligations by ratifying.

A country which ratifies a convention undertakes a binding mutual undertaking which is in the nature of a treaty with other ratifying countries to observe the terms of the convention, and to report regularly to the International Labour Organization on the application of the convention. But in so far as the application of a convention imposes a burden on industry the ratifying countries are placed at a disadvantage in trade competition with those countries which have not ratified it. Also the ratifying countries are exposed to criticism at International Labour Conferences if their reports on the application of conventions, which are examined by an international committee of experts, reveal any failure to give full effect to the terms of a convention, but such criticisms are open to objection if they come from countries which have not ratified the convention. Some countries have protected themselves against possible disadvantages in trade competition by adopting the device of conditional ratification, which means that they will apply a convention only when specified countries, i.e. their principal competitors, have also ratified it.

Since the establishment of the International Labour Organization in 1919, it had in its long succession of conferences, up to 1950, adopted 98 draft conventions which go some way towards providing the framework of a code of fair international competition.[2] Inevitably, however, in view of the wide range in wages and working conditions in different countries most of the conventions and recommendations lay down general principles and methods, but each country determines, where appropriate, the actual standards. For example, on minimum wages a draft convention lays down the principle that Governments should be responsible for setting up statutory systems

[1] This obligation does not, of course, apply to a Government which voted against or abstained from voting for a draft convention; also, if the country has had a change of Government, the new one is not bound by the votes of its predecessor, and a change in conditions making a convention no longer acceptable in the country would justify non-ratification.

[2] Many recommendations have also been adopted.

to fix minimum wages in industries where wages are unduly low and where no voluntary system has evolved; but the Government of each country is independently responsible for deciding which these industries are and what rates of wages shall be fixed. Similarly, in the many conventions on social insurance, valuable principles and methods based on systematic study of the practical experience of many countries are defined but each country applying a convention is free to fix independently its own money rates of contribution and scales of benefit without taking into account the rates and scales of other countries. All this is very far from the establishment of international minimum standards, and in considering the work and potentialities of the International Labour Organization it must be remembered how impracticable is the fixing of such standards.

Attempts to fix real international minima would break down because if they were based on conditions in countries with the lowest standards they would be of no interest to countries with much higher standards, while conventions based on conditions in countries with high standards would be much beyond the reach of countries with medium or low conditions. This difficulty has led to proposals for holding regional conferences attended by countries with similar conditions and problems, for example, Asiatic countries, African countries, or South American countries, which would adopt draft conventions suitable for application in the region. However, although regional conferences have been held for other purposes they have not attempted to adopt conventions for regional application, partly, no doubt, because of the difficulty of defining satisfactorily a geographical region in which the countries have reasonably similar conditions.

An alternative is the preparation of a convention which defines more than one standard, a low or minimum standard considered suitable for application in countries with low levels of working conditions, an intermediate standard and an advanced standard. Countries ratifying such a convention would indicate which standard it considered appropriate to its own conditions. Already in 1919 in the draft convention on the 8-hour day this standard was adopted for application in most countries, but a longer working day was specified for India, China, and certain other oriental countries pending the early adoption by them of the 8-hour day. This method has been used in several more recent conventions.

Special problems arise in the application of conventions in colonial areas, which are not self-governing and are known as non-metropolitan territories by contrast with the responsible metropolitan country. Some conventions appropriate to the conditions only of colonies have been adopted, and create no special difficulty. Other conventions are more general and are intended for application in metropolitan and non-metropolitan countries, but, as conditions in the latter are usually relatively backward, provision is made that in non-metropolitan countries the convention shall be applied with such modifications as are warranted by the circumstances of those countries. These modifications are made by each metropolitan country concerned, and therefore different standards may be applied by different metropolitan countries in colonies in which similar conditions exist. However, such discrepancies can be pointed out in international discussions on the application of conventions and pressure applied to ensure reasonable uniformity of application in territories where conditions are similar. In this connection one further point must be noted, i.e. there are sovereign or metropolitan countries which have within their own boundaries regions in which conditions closely resemble those in the colonies of other countries: yet if such a country ratifies a convention it must apply it throughout the country, without making any modifications appropriate to the special conditions in its backward regions along the lines of the modifications permissible in colonies.

Federal Governments have a special problem if the subject of a convention is one which falls within the competence of the separate States or other components of the federation. The Federal Government is responsible for foreign relations on behalf of the whole federation, but it cannot ratify such a convention and assume responsibility for its application throughout the federation unless each separate part undertakes to apply the convention. This is highly unlikely if the federation is made up of many parts, for example, the United States with forty-eight States. A somewhat similar problem arises if labour conditions in a country are equal to or in advance of those defined in a convention but are fixed and enforced not by the Government but by voluntary collective agreements. In these circumstances the Government cannot bind itself internationally by ratifying a convention if employers' organizations and trade unions in any industry are free at any time to conclude new collective agreements fixing conditions below the standards set in the convention. Practically, however, where collective agreements have reached stability and conform with conditions defined in a convention, *de facto* application of a convention could be recognized even though *de jure* ratification would not strictly be possible.

The International Labour Organization has many other activities in addition to the preparing of draft conventions and recommendations. It is particularly valuable in providing a centre for exchange of information and experience on labour conditions throughout the world, and it makes available translations of the texts of labour legislation in various countries. Its conferences facilitate direct contacts between representatives of Governments, employers, and workers from many countries, and provide a platform on which exploitation and unfair treatment of workers in any country can be brought to the notice of the world. Experts on the permanent staff of the Organization are available to advise the less advanced countries in preparing and applying labour legislation, using for this purpose their knowledge of methods found successful in advanced countries. Technical assistance is also arranged not only on such subjects as social security, minimum wage regulation, and labour inspection, but also on time and motion study, training workpeople and supervisors, incentive wages, and other ways of increasing output.

Labour standards are closely linked with productive efficiency, and both must advance at a similar pace. If a country tries to move forward too rapidly in raising its labour standards without making corresponding improvements in productive efficiency, it will soon feel the strain of international competition. There are even greater dangers. A country's security may be put in peril if in a time of international tension it raises its labour standards at the expense of its productivity and thereby places itself at a disadvantage in relation to a potential enemy. This is well illustrated by the introduction of a 40-hour week in France by the Blum Government in the late 1930's at a time when Hitler's Germany was working a much longer week and was thereby increasing its output of armaments and making other preparations for war.

28

Conclusions

THE FUNDAMENTAL purpose of industrial relations is to facilitate production by securing harmonious working associations between labour, management, and capital. The main problems are not strikes and lock-outs but the regulation of working conditions, and the promotion of better understanding between management and workpeople at the place of work. Technical efficiency, with up-to-date machinery, lay-out, and organization, are not enough alone to make a business profitable. Good human relations are at least as important for success.

A business is a social world in miniature. Its members form a hierarchy each with special qualities of ability, skill, and experience, with different functions, and with distinctive personalities, temperaments, and loyalties. By competent leadership these individuals must be formed into a team working together for the prosperity of the undertaking on which they depend for their standards of living. Attempts at coercion or the use of cajolery will fail to secure the best relations and high standards of efficiency from workpeople. Only by fair and friendly dealing, and above all by convincing workpeople that it is in their interests to work well, can good relations and prosperity be gained. If a business succeeds, all will benefit who are associated with it, but if, because of friction, strains, inefficiency, or any other reason it fails or just manages to keep alive, all will be losers.[1]

The British workpeople have a passion for freedom which is one of the qualities of their greatness, yet in industry they often bind themselves with restrictive practices. They have a genius for kindliness and toleration, and yet many have allowed themselves to be deluded into class antagonisms by bitter and often malicious and unfounded criticisms of the economic system. They stand out for justice and fair dealing and yet they will often acquiesce in slackness at work

---

[1] The first secretary of the Production Department of the British Trades Union Congress has said: "In my own experience I know of no case in which, over a period, wages have dropped while profits have risen. In fact, as every trade union official knows, there is a definite correlation between the two."

and make no protest against those who injure their fellow-men by failing to do a fair day's work.

In many countries doctrinaire ideas of the class struggle have for many years unnecessarily disturbed industrial relations and have led many workpeople to worship false gods. Support is given to the teachings of Marx on the exploitation of labour, the inevitability of conflict, and the overthrow of capitalism; yet his labour theory of value and his forecast of historical evolution predicting the decline and fall of capitalism have no foundation.

Industry is indeed a joint enterprise, and, to quote from a book published as long ago as 1831, "Capital and labour are destined to journey together to the end of time."[1] This is true, and it is of mutual advantage that they should travel amicably together. Capital and management without labour would be sterile, and labour without capital and management would be disorganized, ill-equipped, and ineffective. Each needs the other, and those who preach class war are either fools or knaves or are ignorant of the factors which provide prosperity, welfare, and better standards of living. Yet evolution will bring changes in the status both of capital and labour, and one road to greater harmony in industry would be for workpeople to become part owners of the capital they use and to have a more direct interest in the profits of industry.

The distinction between the two "sides" in industry is much overstressed. This has resulted from the organization of workpeople and employers into separate camps and from the trials of strength between them. Yet within any business as in any organism there are many components, each with a functional specialization but each necessary and complementary to the others. Some of the more enlightened of the trade union leaders recognize that the "two sides" attitude should be broken down and more attention given to matters of common interest to workers and management alike. This implies abandonment of doctrines of class conflict which only serve to divert attention from the main issues. Employers cannot be expected to welcome joint consultation at any level if they are convinced that the purpose of labour is to displace them. Nor can industrial relations be cordial and constructive if workers believe that employers desire to keep standards of living low and wish for depressions so as to reduce their wages and bring them again into a state of subservience. Yet those workpeople who take advantage of prosperity to do less than a fair day's work have only themselves to blame if employers retaliate when the opportunity comes. Unfor-

[1] *Capital and Labour*, 1831, published by the Society for the Diffusion of Useful Knowledge.

tunately the guilty do not suffer alone but do harm to the delicate fabric of mutual confidence and understanding, and trade unions could render valuable service by taking measures against that minority of workers who thus poison industrial relations.

Labour, capital, and management associate together to satisfy the needs of consumers. Consumers do not demand capital and labour separately but want the goods they produce. Capital and labour are therefore jointly demanded by consumers and both have a common interest in producing goods of the quality, quantity, and price which will provide consumers with what they want. Only in the division of the revenues of industry between the producers are there conflicting interests, and these are not only between capital and labour but between all the different categories of people who work together in production. Skilled workers' interests are different from those of unskilled, clerical from manual, managerial from operatives, suppliers of capital and entrepreneurs from others in a complexity of competing claims. Yet when these claims, difficult as they are to reconcile, have been regulated by collective negotiation, the day-to-day problems of relations at the workplace should rarely lead to conflicts. At the workplace the common interest of all is in efficient production.

Industrial relations differ greatly in different countries. Britain with longer experience and traditions has evolved a smoother working system of collective bargaining than the United States, but in the United States there is less class consciousness. Also, as is indicated in the Anglo-American Productivity Reports, operatives in the United States are more "productivity-minded," are dissatisfied with existing ways of doing things, do not impose restrictive practices so widely, but welcome new methods and new machines provided these give opportunities for bigger earnings.

Notwithstanding many bitter struggles, trade unions in the United States do not base their policy in class divisions and doctrinaire policies. They recognize the value of the profit motive, and that the prosperity of workers depends on that of the firm which employs them. They consider that their job is not merely to safeguard the workers, but to assist in improving efficiency. These attitudes have been given robust expression in posters issued by the Wisconsin State Federation of Labour, one of which reads: "If you take a man's pay, work for him," and another says: "The greatest crime a company can commit against its employees is not to make a profit." A third headed "Loyalty" urges workers to speak well of their employer, to work well for him, "stand by him and stand by the institution he represents. If put to a pinch, an ounce of loyalty is worth a pound of cleverness. If you must vilify, condemn, and eternally disparage—resign your position, and when you are outside damn to your heart's content—but as long as you are a part of an institution do not condemn it. If you do that, you are loosening the tendrils that are holding you to the institution, and at the first high wind that comes along you will be uprooted and blown away and probably will never know the reason why."[1]

Britain is one of that small minority of nations whose people are better fed, better housed, better educated, have more leisure, and a broader basis of social security than nine-tenths of the rest of the world. These advantages are largely a heritage from the past. As *The Times* indicated in a leading article on the problems which Britain had to face after the ceremony and rejoicings of the Coronation of Queen Elizabeth II were over, these standards have been extended throughout the population by a crusade to abolish want. It is not in the nature of crusaders to count the cost, but those who believe in the Welfare State and desire to see it firmly established must consider ways and means. Yet not only are there many who put rights before duties and efficient service, but "one of the seeming paradoxes of recent British history is that deliberate efforts to evolve a so-called classless society have caused there to be a livelier class-consciousness than before."[2] This carries with it grave dangers to welfare and prosperity.

In a highly competitive world the standards of the Welfare State can be maintained and improved only by the exercise of the virtues of honest work, thrift, and fair dealing between man and man. These are basic elements for genuine unity in industry, and are vital for that larger unity which is essential for the continued prosperity and greatness of any people. Peace and goodwill are linked with plenty and prosperity, and they imply not only freedom from severe strikes and lock-outs, which are only a small part of the problem, but constructive co-operation in day-to-day relations at the place of work. A "quiet realm" is a necessary prelude for "fruitful fields and a prosperous industry."

[1] Quoted in Paper G.I., prepared by the Ministry of Labour and National Service for the Conference on Human Relations in Industry, London, March 1953. This paper, giving some conclusions drawn from reports of the Anglo-American Productivity teams, called attention to the direct, personal, and informal relations between management and workpeople in American industry, and among the examples reference was made to the president of a United States company employing 450 workers who makes a practice of touring the whole factory three times a day, and makes a point of speaking to a number of different operatives on each visit. [2] *The Times*, June 3, 1953

SHORT BIBLIOGRAPHY OF RECENT PUBLICATIONS[1]

GENERAL

Industrial Relations Handbook, Ministry of Labour and National Service, 1951.

Industrial Relations in Great Britain, J. H. Richardson, Geneva, 1938.

The Social Problems of an Industrial Civilisation, Elton Mayo, Cambridge, Mass., 1945.

The Human Factor in Business, B. S. Rowntree, 1938.

Industrial Relations, International Labour Office, Geneva, 1948.

Leadership in a Free Society, T. N. Whitehead, Oxford, 1937.

The Industrial Worker, T. N. Whitehead, Oxford, 1938.

Men at Work, C. A. Oakley, 1945.

Christianity and Human Relations in Industry, Sir George Schuster, 1951.

Human Relations in Modern Industry, R. F. Tregold, 1949.

Labour, P. Sargant Florence, 1949.

Industrial Relations in New Zealand, A. E. C. Hare, Wellington, 1946.

Industrial Relations in Sweden, C. A. Myers, Cambridge, Mass., 1951.

The International Labour Code, International Labour Office, Geneva, 1951.

The Handbook of Industrial Relations, J. C. Aspley and E. Whitmore, Chicago, 1948.

The Future of Industrial Man, P. F. Drucker, 1943.

The Managerial Revolution, J. Burnham, 1941.

Teamwork in Industry, F. J. Burns-Morton, 1948.

Economics of Labour and Industrial Relations, G. F. Bloom and H. R. Northrup, Philadelphia, 1950.

Unions, Management and the Public, E. W. Bakke and C. Kerr, New York, 1948.

Industrial Relations and the Social Order, W. E. Moore, New York, 1951.

Labor Relations and Human Relations, B. M. Selekman, New York, 1947.

The Challenge of Industrial Relations, S. H. Slichter, Ithaca.

Ministry of Labour Gazette, monthly.

Annual Reports, Ministry of Labour and National Service.

Human Relations, Tavistock Institute, quarterly.

International Labour Review, International Labour Office, Geneva, monthly.

PERSONNEL MANAGEMENT

Personnel Management, C. H. Northcott, 1950.

Management and Labour, K. G. Fenelon, 1939.

Problems in Personnel Administration, Richard P. Calhoon, New York, 1950.

The Management of Personnel and Labour Relations, G. S. Watkins, New York, 1950.

[1] Unless otherwise indicated the works mentioned were published in London.

BIBLIOGRAPHY

The Changing Culture of a Factory, Elliot Jaques, 1951.
The Foreman, National Institute of Industrial Psychology, 1951.
Introduction to Foremanship, edited by H. McFarland Davies, 1950.
The New Foremanship, F. J. Burns, Vol. I, 1948, Vol. II, 1949.
Personnel Management and Industrial Relations, D. Yoder, New York, 1949.
Dynamic Administration, Mary Parker Follett, 1943.
Report of Conference on Joint Consultation, Training within Industry, Works Information and Personnel Management, Ministry of Labour and National Service, 1948.
Report of Conference on Human Relations in Industry, Ministry of Labour and National Service, 1952.
Roads to Agreement, Stuart Chase, 1952.
The Hawthorne Investigations, L. Urwick and E. F. L. Brech, 1949.
Motion and Time Study, R. M. Barnes, New York, 1952.
The Purpose and Practice of Motion Study, Anne G. Shaw. Manchester, 1952.
Administering Changes: A Case Study of Human Relations in a Factory, Harriet O. Ronken and Paul R. Lawrence, Boston, Mass., 1952.
Personnel Management, Journal of the Institute of Personnel Management, bi-monthly.
Industrial Welfare and Personnel Management, Industrial Welfare Society, bi-monthly.
Journal of the Institute of Industrial Administration, monthly.
Personnel, American Management Association, New York, monthly.

INDUSTRIAL PSYCHOLOGY AND INDUSTRIAL HEALTH

What is Industrial Psychology? Sir F. C. Bartlett, 1949.
Psychology in Industry, N. R. F. Maier, 1947.
An Introduction to Industrial Psychology, May Smith, 1952.
Industrial Psychology, J. Tiffin, 1951.
Psychology—General, Industrial and Social, J. M. Fraser, 1951.
The Psychology of Selecting Employees, D. A. Laird, 1937.
The Psychology of the Interview, R. C. Oldfield, 1941.
Aptitudes and Aptitude Testing, W. Bingham, 1937.
The Measurement of Abilities, P. E. Vernon, 1940.
The Worker's Point of View, Acton Society Trust, 1952.
Skill and Age, A. T. Welford and others, 1951.
Health in Relation to Occupation, H. M. Vernon, 1939.
Fatigue and Impairment in Man, S. H. Bartley and E. Chute, New York, 1947.
Reports of the Industrial Health Research Board.
Occupational Psychology, Journal of the National Institute of Industrial Psychology, quarterly.
Welfare and Safety Pamphlets, Ministry of Labour.
Annual Reports of the Chief Inspector of Factories, Ministry of Labour.

433

JOINT CONSULTATION

Joint Consultation over Thirty Years, Sir Charles Renold, 1951.
Joint Consultation in British Industry, National Institute of Industrial Psychology, 1952.
Cooperation in Industry, International Labour Office, Geneva, 1951.
The Framework of Joint Consultation, Acton Society Trust, 1952.
Joint Consultation in Industry—A Sociological Approach, W. H. Scott, 1952.
Management and Men, G. S. Walpole, 1944.

WAGES AND INCENTIVES

Wages, International Labour Office, Geneva, 1948.
Wage Incentives, J. K. Louden, New York, 1944.
Payment by Results, International Labour Office, Geneva, 1951.
Incentives and Contentment, P. Hall and H. W. Locke, 1938.
Incentives and Management in British Industry, R. P. Lynton, 1949.
Compensating Industrial Effort, Z. C. Dickinson, 1937.
Wage Incentive Methods, C. W. Lytle, 1942.

PROFIT-SHARING AND CO-PARTNERSHIP

Profit-Sharing and Stock Ownership for Wage-Earners and Executives, Bryce M. Stewart and W. J. Couper, New York, 1945.
Partnership in Industry, F. W. Raffety, 1928.
Profit-Sharing and Copartnership, Annual articles in Ministry of Labour Gazette.
Co-partnership, Journal of the Industrial Co-partnership Association, quarterly.

TRADE UNIONISM

The History of Trade Unionism, Sydney and Beatrice Webb, reprinted 1950.
British Trade Unionism, Political and Economic Planning, 1949.
The Right to Organise and its Limits, K. Braun, Washington, 1950.
Comparative Labor Movements, W. Galenson, New York, 1952.
British Trade Unionism To-day, G. D. H. Cole, 1939.
British Trade Unions, N. Barou, 1947.
Trade Unions in the New Society, Harold Laski, 1949.
Labor in America: A History, Foster Rhea Dulles, New York, 1949.
Organised Labour in Four Continents, H. A. Marquand, 1939.
Soviet Trade Unions, J. Deutscher, 1950.
The International Labour Movement, John Price, Oxford, 1945.
Are Trade Unions Obstructive? John Hilton and others, 1935.
The Miners, R. P. Arnot, 1949.
The Story of the Engineers, J. P. Jeffery, 1946.
From Tolpuddle to T.U.C., G. E. Fussell, 1948.
Labour, Trades Union Congress, monthly.
Annual Reports, Trades Union Congress.

BIBLIOGRAPHY

COLLECTIVE RELATIONS

Report on Collective Agreements between Employers and Workpeople in Great Britain and Northern Ireland (Volume I), Ministry of Labour, 1934.

Collective Bargaining Provisions, U.S. Bureau of Labor Statistics, Washington, 1947–50.

Joint Committee on Labor-Management Relations, U.S. Congress, Washington, 1948.

Government and Collective Bargaining, F. Witney, Philadelphia, 1951.

Cooperation in Industry, International Labour Office, Geneva, 1951.

Industrial Negotiation and Arbitration, M. Turner-Samuels, Q.C., M.P., assisted by D. J. Turner-Samuels. 1951.

Labour Relations in London Transport, H. A. Clegg, 1950.

Strikes, K. G. J. Knowles, Oxford, 1951.

British Methods of Industrial Peace, D. Chang, New York, 1936.

Industrial Peace in Our Time, H. Somervell, 1950.

The Settlement of Industrial Disputes, K. Braun, Philadelphia, 1944.

STATE INTERVENTION

Industrial Conciliation and Arbitration in Great Britain, Ian Sharp, 1951.

Industrial Arbitration in Great Britain, W. W. M. Amulree, Oxford, 1929.

Arbitration Principles and the Industrial Court, M. T. Rankin, London, 1931.

Government Regulation of Industrial Relations, G. W. Taylor, New York, 1948.

British Wage Boards, D. Sells, 1939.

Minimum Wage-Fixing Machinery in Agriculture, International Labour Office, Geneva, 1950.

Studies in Australian Labour Law and Relations, O. de R. Foenander, Melbourne, 1952.

The Law Governing Labor Disputes and Collective Bargaining, L. Teller, New York, 1950.

The Law of Labor Relations, B. Werne, New York, 1951.

American Labor and the Government, G. W. Miller, New York, 1948.

Labour Courts: An International Survey of Judicial Systems for the Settlement of Disputes, International Labour Office, Geneva, 1938.

Trade Unions and the State, W. Milne-Bailey, 1934.

Trade Unions and the Law, H. G. Strauss, 1946.

Early Factory Legislation, M. W. Thomas, 1948.

The Factories Act, 1937, H. Samuels, 1943.

Factory Inspection in Great Britain, T. K. Djang, 1942.

Social Security, W. A. Robson, 1943.

Social Insurance and Allied Services, Sir William Beveridge, 1942.

INDEX

439

GEORGE ALLEN & UNWIN LTD

Head Office:
40 Museum Street, London, W.C.1
Telephone: 01-405 8577

Sales, Distribution and Accounts Departments
Park Lane, Hemel Hempstead, Herts.
Telephone: 0442 3244

Athens: 7 Stadiou Street, Athens 125
Auckland: P.O. Box 36013, Northcote Central, N.4
Barbados: P.O. Box 222, Bridgetown
Beirut: Deeb Building, Jeanne d'Arc Street
Bombay: 103/5 Fort Street, Bombay 1
Calcutta: 285J Bepin Behari Ganguli Street, Calcutta 12
Cape Town: 68 Shortmarket Street
Dacca: Alico Building, 18 Motijheel, Dacca 2
Delhi: 1/18D Asaf Ali Road, New Delhi 1
Hong Kong: 105 Wing on Mansion, 26 Hankow Road, Kowloon
Ibadan: P.O. Box 62
Karachi: Karachi Chambers, McLeod Road
Lahore: 22 Falettis' Hotel, Egerston Road
Madras: 2/18 Mount Road, Madras 6
Manila: P.O. Box 157, Quezon City D-505
Mexico: Villalongin 32, Mexico 5, D.F.
Nairobi: P.O. Box 30583
Rio de Janeiro: Caixa Postal 2537-Zc-00
Singapore: 36c Prinsep Street, Singapore 7
Sydney: N.S.W.: Bradbury House, 55 York Street
Tokyo: C.P.O. Box 1728, Tokyo 100-91
Toronto: 145 Adelaide Street West, Toronto 1

WELFARE AND COMPETITION

TIBOR SCITOVSKY

One of the most brilliant in this field, Professor Scitovsky is already in the forefront of the younger generation of economists. This is his first major publication, the fruit of several years' work and fully up to the high standard the Editors have endeavoured to maintain in the Library of Economics. It is a work which has been eagerly expected by all American economists who were aware of its preparation, for it may well prove of considerable importance not only for economic theory but also for applied economics.

The work deals with general economic theory, other than employment theory. It contains the theory of pure and monopolistic competition, with special emphasis upon welfare aspects—that is, on the efficiency of the different forms of competition. Beginning with an analysis of the consumer and of the individual firm, the main stress is nevertheless laid on the analysis of the economic system as a whole.

Professor Scitovsky's purpose is to explain the working of the market economy and the pricing system, to appraise their efficiency, and to compare their efficiency under different competitive conditions. Pure competition is presented as a frankly unrealistic model to be used only as a yardstick for appraising the efficiency of the real economy. But most of the book is concerned with the firm's behaviour and the efficiency of the economic system under varying forms of monopolistic competition.

Unwin University Book.　　　　　*Seventh Impression*　　　　　*Demy 8vo.*

GEORGE ALLEN & UNWIN LTD